Wood frame house
construction

$19.95

WOOD FRAME HOUSE CONSTRUCTION

Edited by Gerald E. Sherwood, P.E.
and Robert C. Stroh, Ph.D.

ARMONK PRESS
a division of M. E. Sharpe, Inc.
Armonk, NY and London, England

Published by Armonk Press, a division of M. E. Sharpe, Inc.
                80 Business Park Drive, Armonk, New York 10504
in association with The National Association of Home Builders
                15th & M Streets, Washington, DC 20005

Library of Congress Cataloging in Publication Data

National Association of Home Builders (U.S.)
    Woodframe house construction.

    Bibliography: p.
    Includes index.
    1. Wooden-frame houses—Design and construction. I. Title.

TH4818.W6N37   1988   690'.837   87-35153
ISBN 0-87332-466-8
ISBN 0-87332-467-6 (pbk.)

Typeset by Owl Graphics
Cover design by Steinbrenner Associates
Printed in the United States of America

Table of Contents

Introduction

This book presents sound principles for wood frame house construction and suggestions for selecting materials that will assist in the construction of a good house. It can be used as a working guide to modern construction practice and techniques, as a textbook, and as a standard to judge the quality of house construction.

The book's organization reflects the general progression of activity, from conception to completed structure, in building a wood frame house. Certain steps inevitably cut across categories or fail to fit neatly into any scheme, but the book's sections reflect the broad sequence of procedure.

The first chapter describes matters that should be considered or dealt with before the beginning of construction. The next three chapters — *"Laying the Groundwork," "Framing and Closing In,"* and *"Completing the Shell"* — describe steps that are usually taken in that order. Chapters 5 through 7 —*"Specialty Items," "Working Inside,"* and *"Finishing Touches"* — describe tasks that branch increasingly out from the sequential requirements of basic construction; they can often be done in some order other than that presented here, or in parallel

with each other. Chapter 8, *"Special Topics,"* describes some additional questions and considerations that are often associated with wood frame construction.

An annotated list of suggestions for additional readings on specific subjects, and a glossary, appear at the end of the book. Many of the terms in the glossary appear in the text.

The first edition of this work appeared in 1955 and was based on a series of pamphlets that had been produced, since 1910, by the Forest Products Laboratory (FPL). This first edition was written entirely by FPL scientists O.C. Heyer and L.O. Anderson and was published as U.S. Department of Agriculture Handbook No. 73. The handbook quickly became popular both with building professionals and the public. Educational institutions adopted it as a text and this has continued to be the major use of the book.

As new technology became available and construction practices changed, the handbook became dated. It was revised by FPL scientist L.O. Anderson and published again in 1970. Slight revisions were made in 1975. By the early 1980s, the need for a full revision had become evident. More and more, the text failed to reflect advances in home building brought about by the availability of new materials, the use of more manufactured components, and changes in construction techniques. Accordingly, the National Research Center of the National Association of Home Builders (NAHB), under a cooperative agreement with the Forest Service's Forest Products Laboratory, prepared this new edition, incorporating up-to-date technology.

The authors gratefully acknowledge the technical assistance of the following key contributors: *NAHB National Research Center*: Hugh D. Angleton, E. Lee Fisher, Ralph J. Johnson, Carey F. Lively, Donald F. Luebs, R. Christopher Mathis, Richard A. Morris, and Ralph Lee Smith; *U.S. Department of Agriculture, Forest Service, Forest Products Laboratory*: Rodney C. DeGroot, and William C. Feist; and *National Association of Home Builders*: Michael J. Shibley.

The authors also acknowledge the support and cooperation of the organizations that made up the steering committee that guided the work: *Canadian Wood Council, National Association of Home Builders, National Forest Products Association, National Lumber and Building Material Dealers Association, U.S. Department of Agriculture, Forest Service*, and *U.S. Department of Housing and Urban Development*.

CHAPTER 1

Before Construction Starts

The construction of a home is a complex process that requires detailed planning. It is often advisable to engage the services of an architect or experienced builder to assist in the process.

LOCAL REGULATIONS

Site selection may be the first step taken, or the house plan may be developed first and a site then chosen. Whichever is done first, both steps must conform to local requirements for house construction and land use. In addition, periodic inspections by local officials will be required as the house is built. Building code regulations generally include structural, plumbing, electrical, and mechanical design criteria, as well as light and ventilation, egress, fire safety, sanitary equipment, and security. Local jurisdictions sometimes modify model codes to reflect particular requirements for such things as snow loads, strong winds, and seismic activity. In many communities, zoning and subdivision ordinances and regulations govern the type, density, and uses of permitted buildings, and such matters as setback from the property line.

Administration and enforcement of building codes and ordinances is coordinated through the local building inspection department, while land-use matters are handled by the zoning department. In many or most cases, it will be necessary to submit the house plan to the building inspection department and a site plan to the zoning department for official approval before the start of construction. However, the staffs of these offices are available to confer with and assist the home builder before such formal submissions. It is good practice to meet with them at an early stage of the planning process to assure that the formal submission, when it is made, conforms to local requirements.

Model Codes

Local codes, standards, and ordinances are generally derived from model documents. Most local building codes are based on or adapted from codes developed by one or more of four major code organizations. The organizations and the types of codes they have developed are as follows:

BOCA *Building Officials and Code Administrators International, Inc.*

4051 W. Flossmoor Road
Country Club Hills, IL 60477-5795
(312) 799-2300

National Code Series: building, plumbing, mechanical, fire prevention, energy conservation, existing structures, and other specialty codes.

SBCCI   *Southern Building Code Congress International, Inc.*

900 Montclair Road
Birmingham, AL 35213
(205) 591-1853

Standard Code Series: building, plumbing, mechanical, fire prevention, and other specialty codes.

ICBO   *International Conference of Building Officials*

5360 South Workman Mill Road
Whittier, CA 90601
(213) 699-0451

Uniform Code Series: building, plumbing, mechanical, fire, and other specialty codes.

CABO   *Council of American Building Officials*

5203 Leesburg Pike
Falls Church, VA 22041
(703) 931-4533

One- and Two-Family Dwelling Code and the Model Energy Code.

The National Fire Protection Association (NFPA), Batterymarch Park, Quincy, MA 02269, also issues codes and standards vital to the housing industry. The NFPA publishes and maintains the National Electric Code (NFPA 70) and the One-and Two-Family Dwelling Electrical Code (NFPA). Both are recognized and referenced by the model code organizations in their own code documents.

Inspections

After the building permit has been issued and construction begins, inspections are required at various stages of completion. They are usually required at the completion of footings, framing, electrical work, plumbing, and mechanical features, with a final inspection upon completion of construction.

Footing inspections are conducted on the open trenches and/or formwork before concrete is poured. If steel reinforcement is required, it is inspected at the same time. The depth of the footing below grade is checked to ensure proper level and footing size, and soil conditions are checked to insure that the footing provides proper bearing.

Framing must be inspected for grade, size, and placement before being covered with finish materials. While the framing is open, rough electrical wiring and plumbing are installed. Insulation and vapor retarders, as required, are placed in the walls and ceiling and coordinated with the electrical, plumbing, and mechanical installations. Before any ductwork or mechanical equipment is enclosed, it must receive inspections and approvals for compliance with building, electrical, plumbing, and mechanical codes.

Once these inspections are completed and approvals obtained, the house is ready to receive finish materials on the interior. A final inspection is required after all necessary electrical and plumbing fixtures, duct registers and/or baseboard units, roofing materials, and doors and windows are installed.

The final inspection includes approvals on numerous other finishing details necessary to complete the house. In many jurisdictions, a certificate of occupancy is issued after all final approvals are secured.

SITE SELECTION

Selecting a lot on which to build a home requires an investigation of the legal history of the land, the plans for the land and surrounding areas, and the characteristics of the soils and underlying geology. In some cases, the investigation is best performed by a qualified land planner or engineer. In other situations, the staff of local government offices can be of assistance.

The investigation of the property's legal history, commonly called a title search, is usually performed by an attorney or title-search company. Title searchers check to see if there are outstanding liens against the property and to confirm the correctness of previous transfers.

Another consideration is the zoning status of the property and surrounding areas, and the status of the area in the municipality's master plan. Important factors here would include plans to expand the transportation network and how these plans might affect the location of the home.

The physical characteristics of the lot include a boundary description or survey, which will likely be required in the land-recording procedures. The official survey must be performed by a licensed surveyor.

Local offices of the U.S. Department of Agriculture (USDA) Soil Conservation Service are an excellent source of data describing an area's soil conditions and geology. This information is important if a well is to be drilled or a septic system is to be installed. The information may also affect the choice of the foundation system, particularly in areas where unstable soils occur.

The government or private organizations that provide electricity, natural gas, water, storm sewers, sanitary sewers, and telephone service should be contacted regarding the availability of these services.

HOUSE DESIGN

A good way to begin designing a home is to visit model homes and collect ideas. Professional and trade magazines frequently offer floor-plan files, which also contain many ideas. It may be desirable to hire a professional architect to develop the final plans.

In general, a simple plan (and selection of an uncomplicated roof) offer important construction advantages. Construction will be more rapid and there will be less waste, when more complex designs are avoided.

Two other factors to consider in choosing a design are the relative ease of possible future expansion of the house and its ultimate resalability. For example, an "expandable" house may have a more steeply pitched roof, thus providing space for future rooms in the attic area. It might also be desirable to include second-floor dormers in the original design. Additional rooms can thus be provided at a much lower cost than by adding to the side or rear of the house at a future date. Expandability and resale value are among the matters on which professional advice may be useful.

Other features of the design can affect costs.

• The size of the house, its width and length, determines whether standard-length joists and rafters and standard spacings can be used without wasting material. An architect or builder will have this information. The dimensions chosen can also allow standard-width sheets of sheathing materials to be used on both interior and exterior. Other dimensions that require waste or ripping add to labor and material costs.

• Rooms can be arranged so that plumbing and heating lines are short, and risers can serve more than one room. Roughing in plumbing and heating lines to the second floor will also reduce costs when the second floor is completed, but will not add appreciably to original construction costs.

• While a rectangular plan is the most economical from many standpoints, it should not always govern the final design. A rectangular plan for the house proper, with a full basement, can be made more desirable by a garage or porch wing of a different size or alignment. Such attachments require only shallow footings, without the excavation necessary for basement areas.

• The choice of foundation type, such as slab, crawl space, or basement, also affects costs. This selection should be based on climate and the family's need for storage, hobby, or recreation space. While space in the basement is not as desirable as space in areas above grade, its cost per cubic foot is a great deal lower. The design of a slab-type house usually includes some additional space for heating, laundry, and storage; this extra area may often cost as much as a full basement. Many multilevel houses include habitable rooms over concrete slabs as well as a full basement.

• Many contemporary house designs include a flat or low-pitched roof that allows a light truss to serve as both ceiling joists and rafters. This procedure generally reduces the cost of materials and labor compared to that of a pitched roof. However, not all house styles are adaptable to such a roof. Savings can often be realized by using preassembled roof trusses for pitched roofs. Dealers who handle large quantities of lumber are usually equipped to furnish trusses of this type.

• Pitched roofs are of gable or hip design, with the gambrel roof a variation of each. The hip roof is somewhat more difficult to frame than the gable roof, but usually requires less trim and siding. Painting is much simpler in the hip roof because of reduced wall area from elimination of the gable, and because of accessibility. In the gambrel roof, which is adapted to two-story houses, roof shingles also serve as siding over the steep-pitched portions. A roof of this type provides a greater amount of headroom than the more common type gable.

MATERIALS SELECTION

The grade and type of materials used in a house can vary greatly, and the choices involved can affect the cost. It is poor practice to use a low-grade or inferior material that could result in excessive maintenance costs. It is equally uneconomical to use materials of a higher grade than is required for strength or appearance.

Concrete blocks can be used for foundation walls rather than poured concrete. While it is less costly to provide a good water-resistant surface on a poured wall than on a block wall, a common hollow concrete block has better insulating properties than a poured concrete wall of equal thickness. Costs often vary by area. A third alternative is the pressure-treated wood foundation, which may offer even greater cost reductions.

If precast blocks are available, they can be considered for chimneys. These blocks are made to take flue linings of varied sizes and are laid up more rapidly than brick. Concrete block units can also be used in laying up the base for a first-floor fireplace, rather than bricks. Prefabricated, lightweight chimneys that require no masonry may also save money.

Dimension lumber for framing varies somewhat in cost by species, grade, and size. Use the better grades for joists and rafters and the lower grades for studs. Do not use better grades of lumber than are needed. Proper moisture content is an important factor; this is discussed later.

Conventional items such as cabinets, moldings, windows, and other millwork, which are carried as stock or can be easily obtained, also reduce costs. There are numerous choices of millwork components from many manufacturers. Any special non-standard materials that require extra machine set-ups will be much more expensive.

The use of a single material for wall covering and for floor covering can provide substantial savings. A combination subfloor/underlayment of ⅝-inch or ¾-inch tongue-and-groove plywood will serve both as subfloor and as a base for resilient tile or similar material, as well as for carpeting. Panel siding consisting of 4-foot-wide full-height sheets of plywood or similar material may serve both as sheathing and as a finish siding. For example, exterior particle-board with a painted finish can be used as corner bracing on the stud wall and may also qualify as a panel siding. Plywood may be obtained with a paper overlay, as well as rough sawn, striated, reverse board and batten, brushed, and other finishes.

The costs of exterior siding or other finish materials often vary substantially. Many factory-primed sidings are available that require only finish coats after they are applied. A rough-sawn, low-grade cedar or similar species in board-and-batten pattern

with a stained finish will often reduce the overall cost of exterior coverings. Many species and textures of plywood are available for the exterior.

Corrosion-resistant nails will add slightly to the initial cost but will save many dollars in reduced maintenance costs. In applying exterior siding and trim, galvanized or other rust-resistant nails reduce the need for frequent treatment or refinishing. Stainless steel or aluminum nails are a must on siding that has a natural finish.

There are many cost-related considerations in the choice of flooring, trim, and other interior finish. Areas that will be fully carpeted do not require a finish floor, but the replacement cost of the carpeting may be substantially greater than the cost of the original finish floor.

Species of woods used for trim, jambs, and other interior moldings vary from relatively low-cost softwoods to more expensive hardwoods such as oak or birch. Softwoods are usually painted, while hardwoods are given a natural finish or are lightly stained. The softwoods, though lower in cost, are less resistant to damage from blows and other impacts.

Cost considerations are also involved in the selection of panel and flush doors. Hollow-core flush doors cost less and are satisfactory for interior use, but exterior flush doors should have a solid core to resist warping. Flush doors can be obtained in a number of wood species and grades. Unselected gum, for example, might be given a paint finish, while the more costly woods are best finished with a varnish or sealer. The standard exterior panel door harmonizes with many styles of architecture.

On-site labor time has a substantial impact on construction costs. The size of the operation generally governs the method of construction. A contractor might use two carpenter crews — one for framing and one for interior finishing. Close cooperation with subcontractors such as plumbers, plasterers, and electricians avoids wasted time. Delivery of items when needed, so that storage is not a problem, also reduces on-site erection time.

Power equipment, such as a radial-arm saw, skill saw, or automatic nailer, helps reduce the time required for framing, and most progressive contractors use it. Such equipment not only reduces assembly time for floor, wall, and roof framing and sheathing, but is helpful in applying siding and exterior and interior trim. For example, a radial-arm saw facilitates square cuts and equal lengths, which result in better nailing and more rigid joints.

When gypsum wallboard finish is used, many contractors employ the horizontal method of application. This method brings the taped joint below eye level, and large room-size sheets may be used. Vertical joints may be made at window or door openings. This reduces the number of joints to be treated and results in a better looking wall.

It may be possible to reduce the costs of staining and painting of the exterior and interior surfaces and trim. One cost study of interior painting indicated that prestaining jambs, stops, casing, and other trim before application would result in substantial savings. These are normally stained or sealed after they have been fitted and nailed.

FINANCIAL PLANNING

Financial planning should be done early in the preconstruction process. It is good procedure to visit the loan officer of a lending institution to discuss your plans. Be prepared to discuss preliminary house plans, the approximate size and location of the building lot, your income and other financial resources, and a general description of how the construction will be accomplished. If some of the construction will be performed on a do-it-yourself basis, be prepared to describe your experience and training in order to assure the loan officer that you are capable of doing the job.

An experienced loan officer will be able to estimate the costs you will incur, based on his or her knowledge of the local building industry. The loan officer will also be able to estimate the size of the loan for which you can expect to qualify.

It is recommended that more than one lending institution be contacted. There is often considerable variation from lender to lender as to the types of loans, loan amounts, interest rates, and down payments.

Once a lender has been selected, the loan office will likely offer guidance on the professional assistance you should seek. They may recommend that a professional architect or builder assist in such matters as the final house design, plan preparation, detailed estimating of labor and materials, and selection of contractor.

Table 1
Typical Draw Schedule

Draw	Amount	Requirements
1	15%	Land survey completed Building permit issued Foundation walls or slab completed First joists and subfloor in place Insurance policy in place
2	15%	All exterior walls framed and sheathed Roof complete Well dug, if applicable
3	10%	All interior framing in place Heating, plumbing, and electrical roughed in Bathtub set
4	20%	All exterior walls complete All windows set All exterior door hung Interior wall covering complete
5	15%	All trim work complete Basement floor poured, if applicable Heating plant in space and connected Septic system completed, if applicable
6	15%	Interior and exterior painting complete Cabinets installed All tile work complete Plumbing, heating, and electrical fixtures operating
7	10%	All appliances operating Air conditioning operating, if applicable Driveways, walkways, and walls complete Finish grading complete Sodding/seeding and shrubbery planted

Some lenders require two loan agreements. One loan is a short-term construction loan, and the other is the long-term mortgage. The construction loan is designed to provide the builder with the financial resources necessary to pay for the construction of the home as it progresses. A typical schedule for disbursing the construction loan money, commonly referred to as a "draw schedule," is shown in Table 1.

The interest rate on the construction loan may be higher than on the mortgage. This higher rate, however, is paid only on the money disbursed and only during the term of the construction. Once the house is complete and ready for occupancy, the construction loan amount may be transferred to the lower interest, longer term mortgage.

MATERIAL DELIVERY

Care of materials after they arrive at the site and the conditions to which they are exposed, are generally important. On-site storage problems are reduced if loads of material are delivered when they are needed. The first load, delivered after the foundation has been completed, might include all the materials required for the wood-floor system. A second load, at a later date, could provide the materials for framing and sheathing the walls. A third load could be for roof and ceiling framing and roof sheathing.

Materials for factory-built or preassembled houses can be delivered in one large truckload, because a crew erects the house in a matter of hours. This technique virtually eliminates the need for protection of materials on the site.

The builder of a single house may not be able to arrange staged delivery to coincide with construction needs, and some type of on-site protection may therefore be required. This is true for such millwork items as window and door frames, doors, and moldings. Finished cabinets, floor underlayment, flooring, and other more critical items should be delivered only after the house is enclosed, to give them complete protection from the weather. During the fall, winter, and spring months, the house should be heated so that finished wood materials will not be affected by weather. Exposure to moisture and cold will change the dimensions of materials such as flooring, causing problems.

EFFICIENT USE OF MATERIALS

Materials used in wood frame house construction are produced in a limited number of standard dimensions. Framing lumber is produced in lengths ranging from 8 to 18 feet in 2-foot increments. Wood, metal, and plastic siding as well as wood trim materials are produced in lengths ranging from 8 to 16 feet in 2-foot increments. Panel products such as plywood, fiberboard, and gypsum wallboard are produced in 4-foot widths, which may range in length from 8 to 16 feet in 2-foot increments.

As already noted, a house laid out with a view toward maximum use of materials in their standard dimensions, will cost less per square foot than a house designed without such consideration. Since most building materials are produced in some multiple of 2 feet, it follows that a house plan laid out in multiples of 2 feet will provide for efficient material usage in floor construction, exterior walls, and roof. It is good practice to determine the dimensions of building materials stocked by local suppliers before designing the house.

Comparing alternative materials and methods to determine the least costly combination that will result in an acceptable product is called value engineering. *Reducing Home Building Costs with Optimum Value Engineered Design and Construction* (NAHB Research Foundation, 1977), cited in the **Additional Readings**, discusses value engineering as it applies to home building. The discussion covers the entire sequence of planning, engineering, and construction techniques that work together to produce a house with efficient use of material and labor. Value engineering concepts and practices have been incorporated at many places in this book.

ENERGY CONSERVATION

Numerous house design and construction features save energy. Some, such as reduced glass area, may actually lower the cost of the house. Others, such as added insulation, increase the cost in one respect but allow cost savings in other respects such as smaller air conditioners and heating systems, smaller flues, and lower service entrance wiring costs.

Calculating the saving associated with energy-conserving features is complex and will vary with climate, house type, type and cost of fuel or energy, cost of labor and materials, and type and efficiency of the heating and cooling systems. An expert should be consulted to perform the calculation. The decision to incorporate specific energy-conserving features in the design and construction of the house should be based on a comparison of their cost to their savings.

Presented below are brief discussions of a variety of energy-conserving design and construction features that are likely to be cost-effective as long as the prices of energy remain high. Many of these features are discussed in more detail in *Insulation Manual: Homes and Apartments* (NAHB Research Foundation, 1979) cited in the **Additional Readings** section.

Reducing Conduction

Conduction is the movement of heat directly through materials. Every material has a resistance to heat flow, referred to as R-value. A vacuum stops conduction entirely; materials containing air layers, pockets, or bubbles have substantial resistance. Dense materials like metal, glass, and concrete have little resistance and are poor insulators.

- Insulation in walls makes a large difference in heat loss. Installing R-11 insulation, rather than none, in the wall cavities of a typical 1600-square-foot, one-story, single-family detached home in an area where the indoor-outdoor temperature difference is 70° F will reduce total heat loss and gain by nearly 20 percent.

- Installing R-13 insulation rather than R-11 in the wall cavities of this house will result in another 2 percent savings.

- An additional 5 percent savings is possible by replacing the typical ½-inch insulating board sheathing with 1-inch-thick polystyrene rigid-foam sheathing.

- If the walls of the house had been constructed with 2x6 studs placed 24 inches on center, there would have been space in the wall cavity for R-19 insulation. Installation of R-19 insulation rather than R-11 insulation increases the savings by 6 percent.

- Assuming that the roof of the house was constructed with engineered roof trusses spaced 24 inches on center, the heat loss through the ceiling will be reduced by 8 percent if R-19 ceiling insulation is installed rather than R-11. Using R-30 ceiling insulation rather than R-19 saves an additional 4 percent.

- Properly installed insulation will reduce heat loss and heat gain. Cover all insulated areas completely; extend ceiling insulation over the top of the top plate; insulate behind the band joist; insulate soffits of cantilevered floor construction; cut insulation batts to fit narrow stud spaces and leave enough surplus to staple the flanges; butt the ends of insulation batts tightly against one another; shove batts tightly against the top and bottom plates in the wall cavities; put insulation behind pipes, wires, and electrical outlet boxes in exterior walls; and stuff insulation into all cracks around door and window frames and into all other odd-shaped areas, and staple polyethylene over these areas to form a vapor retarder.

- Reducing the ratio of exterior wall area to floor area will reduce energy demand. Theoretically, a two-story square house (approximately a cube) has the least heat loss. However, with R-11 and R-19 insulation used in walls and ceilings, a one-story home relatively deep from front to back has essentially the same heat loss as a two-story home, all other factors being equal.

- A one-story home, 32 feet deep by 50 feet long, could have 2 percent less heat loss than a home having the same area but whose dimensions are 24x66½ feet (assuming R-11 wall insulation). The savings results from the difference in the ratio of exterior wall area to floor area between the two homes.

- Avoiding the L-, T-, and H-shaped house designs conserves energy. A 24x50 foot house with a 20x20 foot "L" has the same area as the 32x50 foot rectangular house, but could have about 3 percent greater heat loss.

- Reducing the wall height in the 1600-square-foot one-story home described above from 8 feet to 7 feet 6 inches, even with full-thick wall insulation, could save another 1 percent of the total energy consumption.

- Glass is a poor insulator. Reducing window area can substantially reduce heating and cooling costs. The window area of the typical home is probably equal to about 15 percent of the wall area. This area can be reduced under most codes to 10 percent. In the 1600-square-foot house, this could mean a reduction of from 9 to 18 percent in energy consumption if single-glass storm sash are used or from 5 to 10 percent with double window glass or storm sash (conductive heat loss only). But this strategy must be tempered depending on window orientation, shading, and climate.

- When reducing window area, it is preferable to do so by raising the sill height rather than lowering the top of the window opening. This has two advantages. First, it retains the height of the upper portion of the window which provides better natural illumination. Second, it helps to reduce heat gain in the summer because the upper portion of the window is more easily shaded by the roof overhang.

- In a house with 200 square feet of window area equally distributed on all four sides, heat gain may be reduced 2000 Btuh with double glazing or storm windows as compared with single glazing.

• Assuming that the 1600-square-foot house has two standard size exterior doors, the addition of two wood storm doors may save 2 percent of the heating energy in winter, and two metal storm doors may save 1 percent.

• The use of 24-inch on-center wall framing and the adoption of the wall framing techniques set forth in the *Manual of Lumber and Plywood Saving Techniques for Residential Light-Frame Construction* (NAHB Research Foundation, 1971) can reduce heat loss by about 2 percent over traditional framing techniques. This loss occurs because heat loss through the wood section is greater than through the fully insulated cavity. This calculation assumes that ½-inch insulating board is used for sheathing and that the siding is ⅝-inch wood or plywood.

• Assuming that the 1600-square-foot house has a full basement and that the average basement wall exposure above grade is 2 feet, the heat loss through the typical 8-inch block wall and basement floor may be more than 20 percent of the total for the building. Adding furring strips and R-3 or masonry wall insulation covered with either gypsumboard or ⅜-inch plywood reduces heat loss by about 10 percent. If 2x3s, 24 inches on center, are placed 1 inch inside the wall and R-11 insulation is used with ⅜-inch gypsumboard or ¼-inch plywood, about another 6 percent can be saved.

• For a slab-on-grade house, the use of 1x12-inch wide R-4 slab-edge insulation can reduce the heating load by 14 percent compared to using no edge insulation. The use of 2x24-inch wide R-8 slab-edge insulation can save an additional 8 percent.

• Grading the ground so that it slopes away from the house will allow the surface water to drain away from the dwelling. This grading will help to keep the earth next to the foundation wall drier (and thus warmer), which will reduce heat loss through that wall.

• If the house is built on an unheated crawl space, vents that can be closed in winter and a vapor-retarding ground cover will reduce heat loss even when the floors are insulated.

• A preferable and more economic design than the unheated crawl space is a heated crawl-space plenum. Use a vapor retarder on the ground and insulation on the perimeter walls rather than in the floor.

Although earth is a poor insulator, in great enough thicknesses it can save energy. Earth-bermed or "basement" houses with subgrade living space are inexpensive to heat and cool.

Reducing Convection (Air Infiltration)

Convection is the movement of warm air. In a house, pressure differentials force warm air out of cracks in the ceiling and cracks on one side of the house while drawing cold drafts into the house through cracks on the other side. In an old house, the air can be completely replaced in half an hour, or 48 times a day. In a reasonably tight new house, the air may change once every two hours. Convection heat losses and summer heat gains can be reduced by installing caulking, weatherstripping, and other physical barriers to seal up the cracks.

• Use sill sealer between the top of the foundation wall and the band joist or sill plate in frame construction, to reduce air infiltration. Use sill sealer or flexible caulking between the bottom exterior wall plate and the floor sheathing in western or platform framing.

• Use a 1x4 for the bottom wall plate (rather than a 2x4) because a 1x4 is flexible enough in most cases to conform to irregularities in the floor surface. This procedure reduces air infiltration and also cuts heat loss through the framing material.

• Caulk outside cracks at doors, windows, around other openings or penetrations of the wall, and at corners.

• Pay special attention to avoiding, eliminating, or sealing cracks that can allow air to enter the house, including areas around pipe or wire penetrations of the exterior walls.

• Nail sheathing tightly to the framing to minimize air infiltration into the stud space. Even if the stud space is filled with insulation, air leakage will increase convection and conduction losses that will reduce the wall's thermal efficiency.

• For the same reasons, replace wall sheathing damaged during construction.

• The quality of windows greatly influences the amount of air infiltration. A poorly fitting window without weatherstripping will allow about 5½ times more air infiltration than will an average window with weatherstripping.

• Storm windows not only reduce heat loss, they also reduce air infiltration. For best results, they must be tightly fitted.

• Exterior doors are a major source of air infiltration. Even a well-fitted door allows as much air infiltration as a poorly fitted double-hung window. This loss may be doubled for wood doors, since they tend to warp. Storm doors cut this air infiltration in half.

• Weatherstrip attic access doors, and apply one or more pieces of rigid insulation cut to the size to the attic side of the door. This insulation can improve the thermal characteristics of either panel or hollow-core doors.

• Weatherstrip the attic scuttle hole, and insulate the back of the scuttle closure panel.

• Stuff mineral wool insulation around pipes, flues, or chimneys penetrating into the attic space, especially when building houses in cold climates.

• Even when the ceiling insulation has a vapor retarder, good practice calls for 1 square foot of attic ventilation area for each 300 square feet of ceiling area. Increased ventilation of the attic space can reduce air temperatures during the summer and thereby decrease air-conditioning loads. Sufficient data are not available to pinpoint the effect of ventilation on the heating load. The actual reduction is also affected to a great extent by the amount of attic insulation used. At the R-19 level of insulation use, attic temperature reduction due to increased ventilation reduces heat gain only to a minor extent. Climate is also an important factor affecting heat gain. Except in the most severe cooling-load climates, mechanical attic ventilation (fans) may well use more energy than it saves. This situation is due to flow of conditioned air from the home into the attic space, which has a slightly lower air pressure when the exhaust fan is running. The lower air pressure induces air flow into the attic from the living space of the house.

• If a range hood is installed, use the recirculating type in cold climates and the exhaust-to-outside-air type in warm climates where the air-conditioning load is more important than the heating load. Local regulations may require a window in the kitchen in order to use the recirculating type of hood.

• In cold climates, minimize the use of exhaust fans. Research has shown that these fans can be the source of very large amounts of infiltration air. When they are necessary, a model with a positive damper closure is recommended.

• If a fireplace is installed, it should be equipped with a damper to cut heat loss when the fireplace is not in use. A removable sheet metal closure or glass doors for the opening will cut heat loss even more when the fireplace is not in use.

• Garages and carports can help reduce the heating load. In cold climates, attached garages or carports should be placed on the north, northeast, or northwest sides of the house to block the wind and to permit full access to the low winter sun.

Reducing Radiation

Radiation is the movement of heat through space and air. It can be stopped by reflectance or by shading with solid objects. Short-wavelength ultraviolet light rays from the sun, which can penetrate glass, change to long-wavelength infrared heat waves when they strike a dark color. These infrared rays are trapped inside the structure since they do not readily pass through glass. In passive solar heating, ultraviolet rays from the sun pass through windows, are absorbed by a dark surface, and are re-emitted as infrared heat rays that are trapped inside the house. This is the "greenhouse effect."

• If appropriate, use more glass on the south wall of the house and provide shading with the right amount of roof overhang to reduce heat gain in summer.

• Shading southern-exposure glass with a roof overhang reduces heat gain in the summer without impairing heat gain in the winter. At the 35° latitude (North Carolina, Oklahoma, Las Vegas), a 28-inch overhang will provide complete shading in the summer for floor-to-ceiling glass having a southern exposure. This shading will reduce summer heat gain through the glass by 50 percent.

• If there is a choice, solar gain can be maximized by aligning the ridge of the house on an approximately east-west axis. Perpendiculars to the house ridge may have an azimuth angle 25° east or 25° west of south without greatly reducing the potential solar gain.

• The area, location, and shading of windows and the use of double glazing or storm sash have an important effect on reducing heat gain loads for air conditioning.

• Occasionally, it is possible to locate the dwelling or windows to take advantage of the shadow cast by trees to reduce solar heat gain in the summer.

• In hot climates, garages or carports attached to the east or west side of the dwelling shade glazing on the east or west walls, thereby reducing solar heat gain.

• Even with a well-insulated ceiling, the color of the roof makes a difference in heat gain. A light-colored roof surface lowers the design load requirement for cooling.

Efficiency of HVAC and Appliances

The use of efficient heating, ventilating, and air conditioning (HVAC) equipment and appliances, as well as efficient installation techniques, can save energy.

• Avoid oversized heating and cooling equipment. One of the most important energy conservation measures that can be taken is to determine the heat-loss and heat-gain requirements of the dwelling and install equipment no larger than that required. Oversized equipment results in short periods of operation, higher first cost, higher operating costs, poor comfort conditions, and lower seasonal efficiency. Specify air conditioners having high Seasonal Energy Efficiency Ratios (SEER). In areas of high humidity, consider SEERs ranging from 8.0 to 10.0.

• If electricity is to be the source of energy for heating and the house is to be air-conditioned, consider using a heat pump. Heat pumps use about one-third to one-half the energy of electric resistance heating. In extremely hot and cold climates, check with the local power supplier on the applicability of heat pumps.

• Sizing of heat pumps by a professional engineer should be based on analysis of both the heating load and the cooling load. Somewhat more weight should be given to the dominant load, but with careful attention to the heating load output of the heat pump at average outdoor temperatures for the local climate.

• The HVAC subcontractor should install warm-air furnaces so that they will be relatively simple for the homeowner to change the filters. Clogged filters reduce fuel efficiency for both heating and cooling.

• Consider installing a clock thermostat so that the thermostat can be set back at night and the furnace started automatically in the morning. Reducing the temperature for 8 hours at night by 5°F in Chicago will save 7 percent of the annual heating bill; setting the thermostat back 7½°F will save 9 percent; and setting it back 10°F will save 11 percent. In warm climates like Los Angeles, the percentage savings are greater, (12, 14 and 16 percent, respectively) but the total dollar savings will be

smaller than in cold climates. This may not be applicable when using heat pumps.

• Avoid placing heating and cooling ducts in nonconditioned space such as attics. If this is not possible, insulate the ducts. Wrap metal duct joints in nonconditioned spaces with duct tape to minimize leakage, even when they are to be wrapped with insulation. Heat loss through poorly fit, unwrapped duct joints located in nonconditioned spaces can be as high as 25 percent of the total demand.

• Place air-conditioning condensers where they will receive afternoon shade from the house, trees, garage, or carport; this will increase condenser efficiency and reduce energy use slightly.

• Locate the water heater as close as possible to the area of greatest demand for hot water. This is usually the kitchen-laundry area. Avoid placing hot water pipes in unheated areas such as attics or crawl spaces. If this is not possible, use pipe insulation.

• Set the water heater temperature at 120° to 125°. If the temperature settings are not marked on the thermostat, 120°F may be estimated by assuming that the middle setting is equal to a temperature of about 140° to 150°F. A setting of 120°F is hot enough for bathing, washing, clothes washing, and dishwashing. (The 150°F setting is not high enough to sanitize dishes or clothes, that requires 180°F for at least two minutes.) This step can save as much as half the energy required for water heating — a very important item because water heating is frequently the second largest energy user in the home.

• Install a low-water-consumption shower head. Studies show that bathing accounts for about 40 percent of the hot water used in the typical household.

• Some appliances and mechanical electrical equipment are more energy efficient than others. When selecting these items, consider their comparative energy usage.

• A side-by-side refrigerator-freezer may use up to 45 percent more energy than the over-under refrigerator-freezer.

• Some frostless refrigerators use up to 50 percent more energy than the regular defrost type. This is an average of perhaps 350 Btu more energy every hour all year long.

• Microwave ovens use less energy than conventional gas or electric ovens. Self-cleaning ovens reportedly require less energy for cooking but have a high energy consumption for cleaning.

Reducing Lighting

• Lighting is the fourth largest energy user in the typical home, accounting for about 3.4 percent of the total energy bill. During the winter, heat loss from lighting is gained in the structure, so it is not lost. In the summer, however, it is estimated that lighting adds about 600 to 700 Btuh to the average cooling requirement in a typical dwelling. Not much can be done about this in terms of installed capacity, although the use of less general purpose lighting and more task lighting will tend to cut the total energy used for lighting.

• Use fluorescent lights when possible because they produce nearly four times as much light per watt as does the typical incandescent bulb.

• Fixtures that use one large bulb are substantially more efficient than those that use several smaller bulbs because the lumens/watt are greater for larger bulbs.

• Light-color finishes for walls, ceilings, and floors enhance the level of natural light. Paints that have a high light-reflectance value are available, even in colors.

• Do not use recessed or "bullet" lamps that penetrate into nonconditioned space such as an attic. All heat from such lamps is lost. Also, the fixture can be a major source of air infiltration and an opening for the entry of outdoor noise.

Passive Solar Heating

The use of passive solar heating and natural cooling provide the opportunity to reduce energy costs even further. In a completely passive solar home that is carefully designed and thermally protected, heating costs may be reduced by as much as one-half to two-thirds depending on the climate, location, and other factors. This is accomplished with proper design, the appropriate use of south glazing, and heat storage materials.

Passive solar heating requires careful attention to design. It is easy to provide an excessive amount of glass with improper orientation; this can not only cause wintertime overheating, but can increase air-conditioning loads. Also, improper designs can add to cost without yielding appropriate benefits. Professional assistance should be obtained when considering passive solar designs. The three most common passive solar systems are called direct gain, sunspace, and Trombe wall.

There are two kinds of direct-gain systems, one sometimes called sun tempering and the other called direct gain. In sun tempering, additional south-facing glazing is added along with a proper overhang or shading system to prevent excessive heat gain in the summertime. In this system, the amount of additional south-facing glazing is limited to the amount that will not cause overheating without the addition of concrete, brick, block, slate, tile or other heat absorbent/storage material. In the direct gain system, south-facing glazing, properly shaded against heat gain in the summer, is added along with additional thermal storage, mass, water, or phase-change materials to store the extra heat and release it slowly when the sun is not shining.

In the sunspace or sunroom design, substantial amounts of glazing and heat-storage material are provided along with a system for transferring excessive heat from the sunroom to the adjacent room or rooms. In most instances, it has been found that overhead glazing or sloped glazing admit too much unwanted heat.

The Trombe wall system typically consists of a masonry wall, sometimes vented and sometimes not, inside the dwelling close to a large span of exterior glazing. The sun warms the wall in the daytime, which gradually loses the excess heat to the dwelling during the night. Shading is essential to prevent this from occurring in the summer.

All these systems have advantages and disadvantages, but the sun-tempering, direct-gain and sunroom designs are the most popular.

Natural cooling is another method of conserving energy in the summertime using architectural and mechanical techniques. Shading, dehumidification, the use of natural and mechanical ventilation, and increasing air motion (for example, with overhead fans) are techniques that help reduce summertime energy consumption.

PROTECTION OF MATERIALS

In normal construction procedures, after the excavation is complete, some dimension lumber and sheathing materials are delivered to the job. After delivery, it is the builder's responsibility to protect these materials against wetting and other damage. Rapid use of structural and framing materials minimizes storage problems. Structural and framing materials in place in a house before it is enclosed may become wet during a storm, but exposed surfaces can dry out quickly in subsequent dry weather without causing damage, as compared with materials stacked for storage.

Lumber should not be stored in tightly stacked piles without some type of protection. If lumber is not to be used for several days or a week, it should be unloaded onto skids with a 6-inch clearance above the soil. The pile should then be covered with waterproof paper, canvas, or polyethylene so that it sheds water. However, the cover should allow air to circulate and not enclose the pile to the groundline. In a tight enclosure, moisture from the ground may affect the moisture content of lumber. The use of a polyethylene cover over the ground before lumber is piled will reduce moisture rise. The same type of protection should be given to sheathing-grade plywood.

After the framing and the application of wall and roof sheathing have been completed, the exterior roof trim, such as the cornice and rake finish, is installed. During this period, the shingles may have been delivered. Asphalt shingles should be stored so that bundles lie flat without bending; curved or buckled shingles often result in an unsightly roof. Wood shingles can be stored with only moderate protection from rain.

Window and exterior door frames should not be delivered until they can be installed. In normal construction procedures, these frames are installed after the roof is completed and the roofing installed. Generally, window units are ready for installation with sash and weatherstrip in place, and all wood is protected by a dip treatment with a water-repellent preservative. Such units, even though so treated, should be protected against moisture or mechanical damage. If it is not possible to install frames when they arrive, place them upright on a dry base and cover them.

Siding materials can be protected by storing them temporarily in the house or garage. Place them so they will not be stepped on and split. Wood bevel siding is usually bundled with the pieces face to face, to protect the surfaces from mechanical damage and soiling. Some manufacturers treat their siding with a water-repellent material and pack it in bundles with an outer protective wrap. All siding materials that cannot be installed immediately should be pro-

tected against exposure to conditions that could appreciably change their moisture content.

Insulation should be stored inside the house. These materials are generally not installed until the electrical, heating, and plumbing trades have completed the roughing-in phases of their work.

Millwork, floor underlayment, flooring, and interior trim manufactured by reputable companies are normally shipped at a moisture content satisfactory for immediate use. However, if storage conditions at the lumber company or in an unheated house during the inclement seasons are not satisfactory, the wood parts will pick up moisture. The results may not be apparent immediately. If material with too high a moisture content is installed, openings will appear during the following heating season between flooring strips and at poorly matched joints in the trim because members have dried out and shrunk.

In flooring, for instance, the recommended moisture content at installation varies from 10 percent in the damp southern states to 6 or 7 percent elsewhere. In examining wood floors with cracks between the boards, it has been found that in most cases the material picked up moisture after manufacture and before it was installed. As such material redries during the heating season, it shrinks and the boards separate. Some of the moisture pickup may occur before the flooring is delivered to the building, but such pickup often occurs after delivery and before installation.

In an unheated building under construction, the relative humidity will average much higher than that in an occupied house. Thus, the flooring and finish tend to absorb moisture. To prevent moisture pickup at the building and to dry out any excess moisture picked up between manufacture and delivery, the humidity must be reduced below what is considered normal in an unheated house. This reduction may be accomplished by maintaining a temperature above the outdoor temperature even during the warmer seasons.

Before any floor underlayment, flooring, or interior finish is delivered, the outside doors and windows should be hung and the heating plant installed to supply heat. For warm-weather control, when the workers leave at night, the thermostat should be set to maintain a temperature of 15° F above the average outdoor temperature. In the morning when the workers return, the thermostat can be set back so that the burner will not operate. During the fall, winter, and spring, the temperature should be kept at about 60° F.

Several days before flooring is to be laid, bundles should be opened and the boards spread about so that their surfaces can dry out evenly. This will permit the drying of moisture picked up before delivery. Wood wall paneling and floor underlayment should also be exposed to the heated conditions of the house so the material will approach the moisture content it reaches in service. Actually, it is good practice to expose all interior finish to this period of moisture adjustment. Supplying some heat to the house in damp weather, even during the summer months, will be justified by improved appearance and owner satisfaction.

SUBCONTRACTING

Nearly all home construction requires the use of subcontractors to perform particular tasks. Subcontractors possess special knowledge and skills and have access to special equipment. It is not uncommon for professional home builders to function as general contractors, hiring subcontractors for the entire construction process.

Subcontractors fall into two general categories: those supplying only labor and those supplying both labor and materials. Subcontractors providing only labor will expect their materials to be available at the building site. This type of subcontractor would include those for masonry, framing, and roofing. Subcontractors supplying both labor and materials would include those for excavation, plumbing, electrical, heating, and air conditioning.

Agreements with subcontractors should take the form of written contracts. The first step is to prepare a detailed written list of the work to be performed and then to obtain bids from at least three potential subcontractors. Local professional builders can tell you about the performance history of subcontractors from whom you receive bids.

The specifications that form the basis for the subcontractor's bid should include a clear statement of local licensing and bonding requirements, responsibility for obtaining permits and inspections, and responsibility for liability insurance. When the work is completed, the subcontractor should sign a release indicating that he has received full payment for his services.

WORK SCHEDULE

A work schedule should be prepared, including each major task to be performed and an estimate of how long each task will take. This schedule can be used for such purposes as arranging for material deliveries, scheduling the work of subcontractors, and coordinating the timing of inspections of the work in process.

Developing a work schedule requires a thorough knowledge of the sequence of tasks to be performed and the time that it ordinarily takes to accomplish each task. Local architects or builders can assist in the preparation of such a schedule. Figure 1 shows a typical work schedule: it calls for the completion of construction approximately 75 days after the start. It must be understood that construction can start only after financing has been arranged and appropriate permits have been obtained. Such preconstruction activities can take as long as, or longer than, the actual construction.

In this schedule, the first week is devoted to preparing the site, excavating the foundation, and installing temporary utility service. During the second week, foundation footings are prepared and water and sewer lines are installed below ground. A footing inspection takes place, and the footings and foundations are completed during this week.

The third week is devoted to erecting the framing of the floors, walls, and roof, applying the cornice trim to the roof line, and installing windows and exterior doors. Rough plumbing is also installed, sheathing and decking are applied, and the rough electrical wiring can be installed.

The cornice trim work will probably extend from the fourth into the fifth week. When it is complete, the roof-covering material can be installed and the exterior paint applied. During exterior painting, the rough heating, ventilating, and air-conditioning (HVAC) equipment can be installed. At this point, a series of open framing inspections normally occur. In addition to an inspection of the structural integrity of the framing, the rough plumbing, electrical, and HVAC work are usually inspected at this time.

During the sixth week, insulation and vapor retarders may be installed, followed by the application of interior wall finish such as gypsum wallboard. If the exterior covering is to be brick, the brick is installed during the sixth week. Interior wall finish, and exterior brick work if applicable, will probably extend into the seventh week. During the

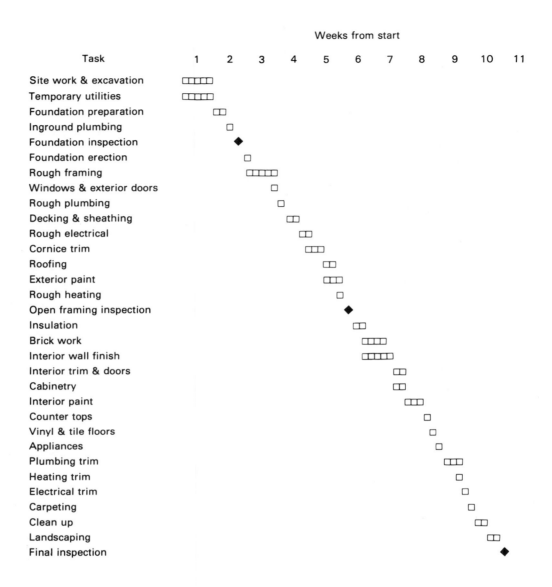

Figure 1. Typical work schedule

latter part of the seventh week the interior trim, interior doors, and cabinetry can be installed.

Interior work continues during the eighth week including painting, counter top installation, and laying of vinyl or tile floors. During the ninth week, major appliances are installed and the finish plumbing, electrical and heating work is performed. Carpeting is installed and the house cleaned to prepare for occupancy during the tenth week. The final landscaping is also done.

Final inspection of the completed home takes place during the eleventh week. When this inspection is completed and the work is certified and acceptable, the house is ready for occupancy.

CHAPTER 2

Laying The Groundwork

This chapter discusses the tasks related to site preparation, construction of footings and foundations, and construction of retaining walls.

SITE PREPARATION

Before excavating for the new home, the subsoil conditions must be determined by test borings and/or by checking existing houses near the site. It is good practice to examine the type of foundations used in neighboring houses — this might influence the design of the new house. A rock ledge may be encountered at the chosen site, necessitating costly removal. A high water table may require design changes from a full basement to crawl space or concrete slab construction. If the area has been filled, the footings should always extend through to undisturbed soil. Any variation from standard construction practices will increase the cost of the foundation and footings.

Placement of the House

Most local building codes require that a plot plan be a part of the house plan that is submitted for approval. Zoning regulations usually specify such matters as minimum setback and side-yard require-ments. The placement of the house on the lot must conform to these requirements. When the plot of land is surveyed, the corners will be marked by the surveyor. The surveyor should also mark the corners of the area within the lot in which the house may be built to be in compliance with local regulations.

In preparation for establishing the exact corners of the house, stakes should be driven in the ground to mark the approximate location of the driveway and house. This approximate positioning should take into account the terrain, avoiding rock out-croppings and preserving trees that are to remain. Space should be reserved for a septic field and/or a water well, if applicable. The positioning of the water well with respect to the septic field is fre-quently controlled by health department regula-tions. The location of the water well should also take into account the need to provide access for a drilling rig. For energy efficiency, the side of the house with the most windows should face to the south.

All trees should be removed from the driveway area, from within the house's foundation area, and from within 15 to 20 feet of the house foundation. This clearing provides space for excavation and for a bulldozer to backfill around the house without getting too close to the foundation wall. It may be desirable to retain other trees on the lot: deciduous trees that would shade the south side of the house in the summer while admitting the winter sun may be left standing, and evergreen trees may be retained on the north side of the house to serve as a windbreak. On the east and west sides of the house, evergreen trees serve to shade low-angle morning and evening sun in the summer and should be retained.

The next step is to locate the exact corners of the house. This must be done accurately and squareness must be established, since all subsequent construction will be based on this outline. To facilitate this process, the exact length of the diagonal of each rectangular section of the house outline should be calculated. (Refer to Chapter 8, section on "Square Corners.") Use three steel tape measures to lay out two adjoining sides of the house and the associated diagonal. The measuring tapes should be held level and plumb bobs used to establish the corner points on the ground. Stakes should be driven at each of the three corners, and a nail driven in the top of each stake should be used to mark the exact location of the plumb bob. The fourth corner should be established by using two of the steel tape measures to measure the exact lengths of the two remaining sides. The fourth corner stake should be driven into the ground and a nail driven into the top of the stake under the tip of the plumb bob to indicate the exact corner location.

An alternative approach to establishing the exact corners is to measure and stake the two corners for one side. Starting from one end, measure the length of an adjoining side. Using the "3-4-5" rule for a perfect 90° corner, measure along one of the sides some number of 3-foot units (such as 3, 6, 9, or 12 feet). Measure along the other side a like number of 4-foot units (such as 4, 8, 12, or 16 feet). The hypotenuse of the triangle formed by the distances measured along the two sides will be an equal number of 5-foot units (such as 5, 10, 15, or 20 feet) if the corner is exactly 90°. Adjust the position of the added side and stake the third corner. Proceed around the outline of the house measuring the lengths of the sides and adjusting for 90° corners.

When the location of the house has been precisely established, the next step is to set the batter boards (Figure 2) to retain the exact outline of the house during construction of the foundation. The height of these boards is sometimes used to establish the height of the footings and foundation wall.

Drive three 2x4-inch or larger stakes of suitable length at each corner location a minimum of 4 feet beyond the lines of the foundation. Use a surveyor's level to establish level marks on the stakes. Nail 1x6-inch or 1x8-inch boards horizontally so the tops are all at the same level at all corners. A string (pulled taut) is then held across the top of opposite boards at two corners and adjusted so that it will be exactly over the nails in the tops of the corner stakes at either end; a plumb bob is handy for setting the lines. A saw kerf or nail is placed at the outside edge of the board where the lines cross, so that the string may be replaced if broken or disturbed. After similar cuts or nails are located in all eight batter boards, the lines of the house will be established. Check the diagonals again to make sure that the corners are square, and adjust as necessary.

The plot plan may be prepared after the exact house location has been established. The plot plan should show the lot outline as established by the surveyor and the outline of the house foundation and driveway. If applicable, it should also show the location of the septic system and water well.

Site Access and Services

Before construction begins, provision must be made for access to the site for equipment and delivery trucks; for basic power, telephone, and water during construction; and for storing large quantities of a variety of materials throughout construction. Access to the building lot will probably be required for heavy vehicles such as cement trucks and loaded delivery trucks. The season, the soil conditions, and slope of the building site are major factors to be considered. It may be necessary to excavate an access road and to provide some form of temporary road surface, such as crushed stone.

Electric power and water are needed for many construction tasks. Providing electric power may require that the utility company install a temporary electric service entrance. The need for water may require that a well be drilled or temporary water service be installed at a nearby fire hydrant. Other support services that may be considered for the building site include telephones and toilets.

Plans must be made for storage of materials at the site. This storage should not interfere with other activities. Considerations for the location of building materials delivered to the site include easy access for delivery trucks and convenience to the construction activity. Trees and other vegetation removed during site clearing should be piled away from the

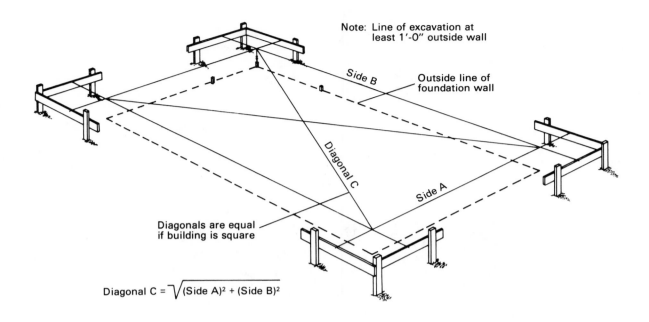

Note: Line of excavation at
least 1'-0" outside wall

Side B

Outside line of
foundation wall

Diagonal C

Side A

Diagonals are equal
if building is square

Diagonal C = $\sqrt{(\text{Side A})^2 + (\text{Side B})^2}$

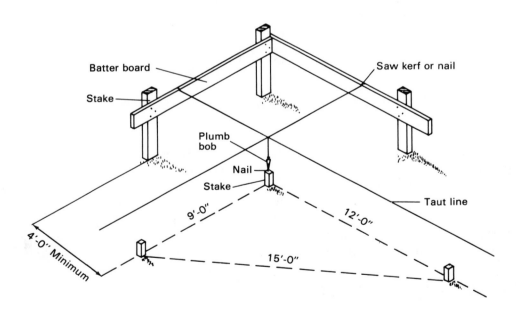

Batter board

Saw kerf or nail

Stake

Plumb
bob

Nail

Stake

Taut line

9'-0"

12'-0"

4'-0" Minimum

15'-0"

Figure 2. Staking and laying out the house

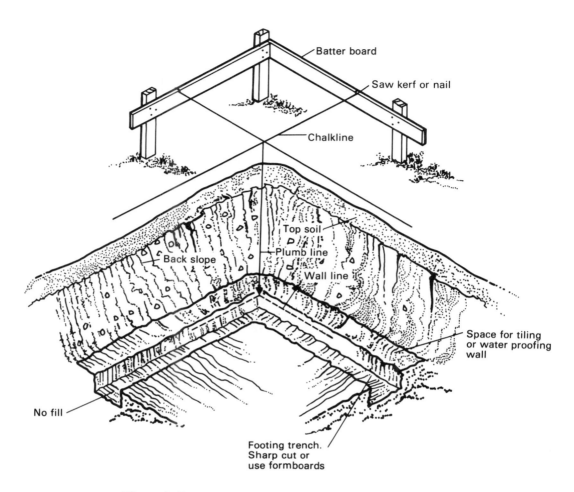

Figure 3. Establishing corners for excavation and footing

construction area and out of the path of trenches, wells, or septic tanks. Topsoil that has been removed can be saved for landscaping. Subsoil removed during the excavation for a basement foundation can be saved and used for backfill. Erosion control may also be important. Well-placed straw bales frequently provide an adequate temporary solution.

EXCAVATION AND FOOTINGS

Various types of earth-moving equipment are used for basement excavation. Topsoil is often stripped and stockpiled for future use by bulldozer or front-end loader. The excavation can be done with a front-end loader, power shovel, or similar equipment. Backhoes are used to excavate for the walls of houses built on slabs or for a crawl space, if the soil is stable enough to prevent caving. This

method eliminates the need for forming below grade when footings are not required.

Excavation is preferably carried only down to the level of the top of the footings or the bottom of the basement floor, because some soils become soft upon exposure to air or water. Unless formboards are to be used, it is not advisable to make the final excavation for footings until it is nearly time to pour the concrete.

The excavation must be wide enough to provide space to work when constructing and waterproofing the foundation wall, and for laying draintile if it is necessary (Figure 3). The steepness of the back slope of the excavation is determined by the subsoil encountered. With clay or other stable soil, the back slope can be nearly vertical. When sand is encountered, an inclined slope is required to prevent caving.

Some contractors only rough stake the perimeter of the building for the removal of the soil. When the proper floor elevation has been reached, the footing layout is made and the soil removed to form the footing. After the concrete for the footings is poured and has set, the foundation wall's outline is established on the footings and marked for the placement of the formwork or concrete block wall.

Footings

Footings act as the base of the foundation wall and transmit the superimposed load to the soil. The type and size of footings should be suitable for the soil condition, and in cold climates the footings should be far enough below finished grade level to be protected from frost. Local codes usually establish this depth, which is often four feet or more in northern sections of the United States and in Canada.

Poured concrete is generally used for footings, although developments in treated wood foundation systems permit all-weather construction and provide reliable foundations for crawlspace houses. For pressure-treated wood foundation walls (refer to section on "Foundation Walls"), gravel is recommended as a less expensive alternative.

Where fill has been used to raise the level of the house, the footings must extend below the fill to undisturbed earth. In areas having fine clay soil which expands when it becomes wet and shrinks when it dries, irregular settlement of the foundation system and building may occur. A professional engineer should be consulted when building a house on this expansive clay soil.

Wall Footings. Well-designed foundation wall footings are important in preventing settling or cracks in foundation walls. One method of determining the size, often used with most normal soils, is based on the proposed wall thickness. As a general rule, the footing depth should be equal to the wall thickness (Figure 4A) and the footings should project beyond each side of the wall one-half the wall thickness. The footing bearing area, however, should be designed on the basis of the load of the structure and the bearing capacity of the soil (Table 2). If the soil is of low load-bearing capacity, wider footings with steel reinforcement may be required. Local regulations often specify footing dimensions. This also applies to column and fireplace footings.

Table 2

Foundation-wall footing widths for typical single-family dwelling loads

Total design load per linear foot of footings (in pounds)	Allowable soil-bearing capacity in pounds per square foot			
	1500	*2000*	*2500*	*3000*
1000	8″	6″	4.8″	4″
1500	12″	9″	7.2″	6″
2000	16″	12″	9.6″	8″
2500	20″	15″	12″	10″

Source: NAHB Research Foundation. *Reducing Home Building Costs with OVE Design and Construction,* 1977.

The following are a few rules for footing design and construction:
1. Footings should be at least 6 inches thick.
2. If footing excavation is too deep, fill with concrete — never replace soil.
3. Use formboards for footings where soil conditions prevent sharply cut trenches.
4. Place the bottom of footings below the frostline.
5. Reinforce footings with steel rods where they cross pipe trenches.
6. In freezing weather, cover with straw or supply with heat.

Pier, Post, and Column Footings. Footings for piers, posts, or columns (Figure 4B) should be square and should include a pedestal on which the member will bear. A 4-inch or 6-inch solid concrete cap block laid flat on the footing can serve as a pedestal. More aesthetically pleasing pedestals may be installed, but these require the construction of a form and pouring concrete. The finished pedestal height must be at least equal to the thickness of the concrete floor slab; its sides can be vertical or sloped outward; and its top dimensions must equal or exceed the dimensions of the base of the pier, post, or column it will support. Bolts for the bottom bearing plate of steel posts and for the metal post bases for wood posts are usually set when the pedestal is poured. At other times, steel posts are set directly on the footing and the concrete floor is

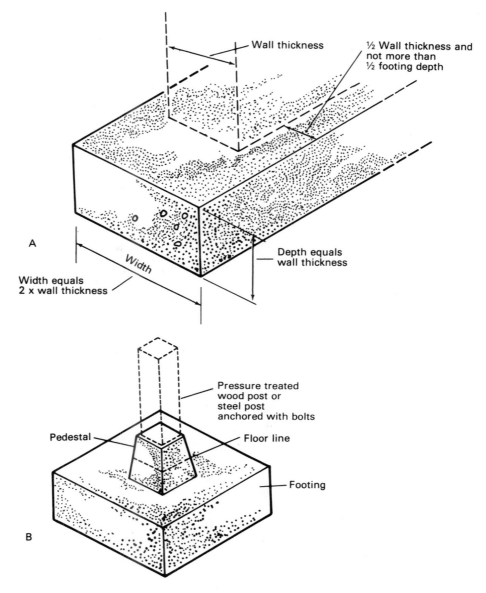

Figure 4. Concrete footing: (A) wall footing; (B) post footing

poured around them. Concrete is never poured around wooden posts. Concrete blocks are sometimes used as pedestals, especially in crawl-space construction.

Footings vary in size depending on the superimposed load, the allowable soil bearing capacity, and the spacing of the piers, posts, or columns. Common sizes are 24x24x12 inches and 30x30x12 inches (Table 3). Footings for fireplaces, furnaces, and chimneys should ordinarily be poured at the same time as other footings.

Stepped Footings. Stepped footings are often used where the lot slopes to the front or rear and the garage or living areas are at basement level. The vertical part of the step is poured as part of the footing. The bottom of the footing is always placed on undisturbed soil and located below the frostline. Each run of the footing should be horizontal.

The vertical step between footings should be at least 6 inches thick and the same width as the footings (Figure 5). The height of the step should not be more than three-fourths of the adjacent horizontal

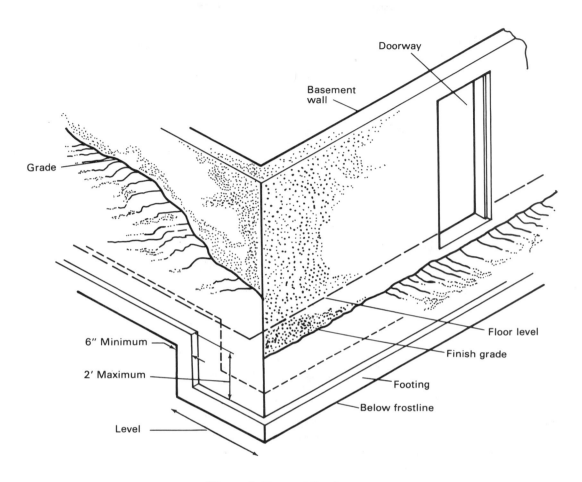

Figure 5. Stepped footing

footing width, not exceeding 2 feet. On steep slopes, more than one step may be required. On very steep slopes, special footings may be needed. For example, two separate footings may be required. The lower footing is poured and the lower wall is constructed up to the level of the upper footing. Forms for the upper footing are then built to extend the upper footing over the top of the lower wall. The extended portion of the upper footing is reinforced and tied to the lower wall with steel reinforcing rods. Alternatively, reinforced concrete lintels can be used to bridge from the upper footing to the lower wall. Because of the complexity of these designs, an engineer should be consulted.

Ordering Concrete

Concrete and masonry units such as concrete block serve various purposes in most house designs, including concrete-slab and crawl-space houses with poured concrete or concrete block foundation walls.

For small jobs, instructions for do-it-yourself mixing are usually available on the bag of portland cement. The mixture generally includes one part air-entrained portland cement, two parts sand, and four parts 1½-inch crushed rock (referred to as "aggregate"). These are mixed together and water is then added, little by little, until the mixture is completely wet but can still be piled. Too much water will weaken the concrete.

Table 3

Column-footing sizes for typical single-family dwelling loads

Total design load (in pounds)	Allowable soil-bearing capacity in pounds per square foot			
	1500	2000	2500	3000
5000	22"x22"	19"x19"	17"x17"	16"x16"
10000	31"x31"	27"x27"	24"x24"	22"x22"
15000		33"x33"	30"x30"	27"x27"
20000			34"x34"	31"x31"

Source: NAHB Research Foundation. *Reducing Home Building Costs with OVE Design and Construction*, 1977.

A great amount of concrete is supplied by ready-mix plants, even in rural areas. Concrete in this form is normally ordered by the number of bags per cubic yard, in addition to aggregate size and water content requirements. A five-bag mix is considered adequate for most residential work. Where high strength or reinforcing is required, a six-bag mix is commonly specified.

The size of gravel or crushed rock ("aggregate") that can be obtained varies in different locations, and it may be necessary to change the cement ratio from that normally recommended. Generally speaking, if the aggregate is smaller than the normal 1½-inch, it is good practice to use a higher cement/aggregate ratio. For example, when gravel size is a maximum of 1 inch, add one-quarter bag of cement to the five-bag mix; when gravel size is a maximum of ¾-inch, add one-half bag; and for ⅜-inch size add one full bag.

Pouring Concrete

Concrete should be poured (or placed) continuously and kept practically level throughout the area being poured. The concrete should be rodded or vibrated to remove air pockets and force the concrete into all parts of the forms. In hot weather, protect concrete from rapid drying. It should be kept moist for several days after pouring. Rapid drying significantly lowers its strength and may injure the exposed surfaces of sidewalks and drives.

In very cold weather, keep the temperature of the concrete above freezing until it has set. The rate at which concrete sets is affected by temperature, being much slower at 40° F and below than at higher temperatures. In cold weather, the use of heated water and aggregate during mixing is good practice. In severely cold weather, insulation or heat should be used until the concrete has set. Further discussion of working with concrete under various weather conditions is presented in Chapter 8 under "All-weather Construction." Also refer to the section titled "Concrete" in Chapter 8 for a discussion of various characteristics of concrete that can be altered with various additives to meet specific needs.

FOUNDATION WALLS

Foundation walls form an enclosure for basements or crawl spaces and carry wall, floor, roof, and other building loads. The two types of walls most commonly used are cast-in-place (poured) concrete and concrete block. Pressure-treated wood foundation walls offer an alternative and are accepted by most codes. Preservative-treated posts and poles offer many possibilities for low-cost foundation systems and can also serve as a structural framework for the walls and roof.

Height of Foundation Walls

It is common practice to establish the depth of the excavation, and consequently the height of the foundation, by using the highest elevation of the excavation's perimeter as the control point (Figure 6). This method will ensure good drainage if sufficient foundation height is allowed for the sloping of the final grade (Figure 7). Foundation walls at least 7 feet 4 inches high are desirable for full basements; 8-foot walls are commonly used.

Foundation walls should be extended at least 8 inches above the finished grade around the outside of the house. This will help protect the wood finish and framing members from soil moisture. Also, in termite-infested areas, wooden building materials should start well above the grass level, so that there will be an opportunity to observe any termite tubes between the soil and the wood and to take protective measures before damage develops. Enough height should be provided in crawl spaces to permit perio-

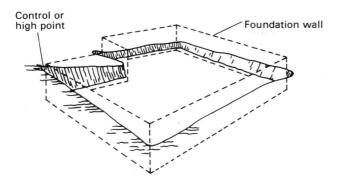

Figure 6. Establishing depth of excavation

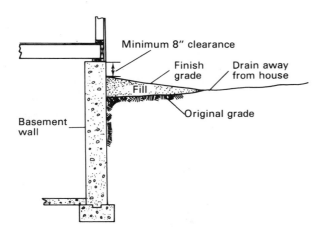

Figure 7. Finished grade (sloped for drainage)

dic inspection for termites and to install soil covers to minimize the effects of ground moisture on framing members.

The finish grade at the building line might be 4 to 12 inches or more above the original ground level. In sloping lots (Figure 7), this distance may amount to 12 inches or more. In very steeply sloped lots, a retaining wall is often necessary.

For houses having a crawl space, the distance between the ground level and underside of the joists should be at least 18 inches. Where the interior ground level is excavated or otherwise below the outside finish grade, 4-inch foundation drains covered with draining gravel and 15-pound roofing felt should be installed around the interior base of the wall and extended to the natural grade outside the foundation.

Treated Wood Basement Foundation Walls

Basements constructed of pressure-treated lumber and plywood have met with considerable acceptance in many areas of the United States and Canada. Thousands of homes have been built with this method, which offers some unique advantages: electrical wiring is readily installed; insulation may be installed between the studs; and standard interior wall finish materials are easily nailed over the studs. Other advantages include suitability for construction in cold weather and the potential for prefabrication. Typical wall panels can be fabricated from pressure-treated wood, including footing plates (Figure 8). The panels may be erected rapidly on site, reducing construction time and avoiding delays due to weather. Since carpenters erect the panels, there are fewer tradesmen to coordinate. Where basement walls extend above grade, they are easily painted or covered with the same siding materials as the house walls.

Preservative treatment for residential all-weather wood foundations is prescribed in American Wood Preservers Bureau (AWPB) Standard FDN. Each piece of lumber that has been treated in accordance with this standard bears the AWPB stamp. Lumber and plywood treated in accordance with this standard is extremely durable. (Refer to Chapter 8, section on "Pressure-Treated Wood.")

Construction of a pressure-treated wood basement begins with excavation to the required level in the usual manner. Plumbing lines to be located below the basement floor area are installed as necessary. The entire basement area is then covered with a minimum 4-inch-thick layer of crushed stone or gravel extending approximately 6 inches beyond the footing line. The stone or gravel bed is carefully leveled. The gravel or crushed stone serves to distribute footing loads 4 inches or more on each side of the footing plate. Wall panels are then installed on top of the footing plate, fastened together, and braced in place. Joints are caulked, and the entire exterior of the foundation wall that is below grade is draped with a continuous sheet of 6-mil polyethylene.

The stone or gravel bed is covered with 6-mil polyethylene, over which a standard concrete slab floor is poured. A sump and pump may be desirable to assure a dry basement. The first-story floor must be securely fastened to the top of the wood basement walls to resist the inward force of backfill. Where

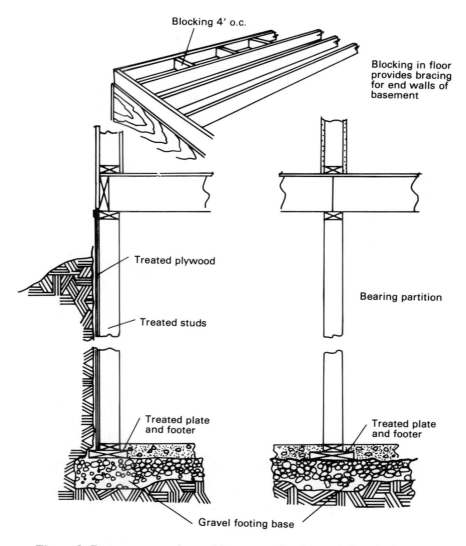

Figure 8. Pressure-treated wood basement footing and foundation wall

soil pressure is substantial, it may be necessary to use framing angles at this point. Solid blocking should be installed 48 inches on center in the joist space at end walls to transmit foundation wall loads to the floor. The wood foundation wall should not be backfilled until the basement floor and the first-story floor are in place.

Standard engineering procedures can be used in designing treated wood basement walls. As with other basement wall designs, the controlling factors are the height of backfill and soil conditions. Table 4 summarizes typical framing requirements for different heights of fill, and typical footing plate sizes required for one- and two-story houses up to 28 feet wide. Pressure-treated ½-inch thick standard C-D

grade (exterior glue) plywood should be installed with the face grain across studs. Blocking at horizontal plywood joints is not required if joints are at least 4 feet above the bottom plate. These specifications are based on a soil condition with 30 pounds per cubic foot equivalent fluid weight.

Poured-Concrete Basement Foundation Walls

Wall thicknesses and types of construction are ordinarily controlled by local building regulations. Thicknesses of poured or cast-in-place concrete basement walls may vary from 8 to 10 inches and concrete block walls from 8 to 12 inches, depending on story heights and length of unsupported walls.

Table 4

Framing requirements for pressure-treated wood basement walls.

Number of stories	Height of fill	Nominal stud size[1]	Minimum required "f"-value[2]	Minimum required "E"-value[2]	Nominal footing plate size
1	24″	2x4	1130	1,400,000	2x8
	48″	2x4	1435	1,600,000	2x8
	72″	2x6	1260	1,600,000	2x8
	86″	2x6	1520	1,800,000	2x8
2	24″	2x4	1435	1,600,000	2x10
	48″	2x6	1000	1,400,000	2x10
	72″	2x6	1260	1,600,000	2x10
	86″	2x6	1520	1,800,000	2x10

Source: NAHB Research Foundation. *Reducing Home Building Costs with OVE Design and Construction,* 1977.

[1] Assumes stud spacing of 12 inches and 30 pounds-per-cubic-foot equivalent fluid weight of soil.

[2] See Appendix A for strength properties of common species and grades of lumber.

Clear wall height should be no less than 7 feet from the top of the finished basement floor to the bottom of the joists; greater clearance is usually desirable to provide adequate headroom under girders, pipes, and ducts. Many contractors pour 8-foot-high concrete walls above the footings, which provide a clearance of 7 feet 8 inches from the top of the finished concrete floor to the bottom of the joists. Concrete block walls, 11 courses above the footings with 4-inch-solid cap-block, will provide a height of about 7 feet 4 inches to the joists from the basement floor.

Crawl-space foundation wall heights are determined by frost depths and by maintaining adequate underfloor access, usually 18 to 24 inches from the ground to the bottom of the floor framing members.

Poured-concrete walls (Figure 9) require forming that must be tight, well-braced, and tied, to withstand the forces of the pouring operation and the fluid concrete. The walls should be double-formed (formwork constructed for each wall face). Reusable forms are used in the majority of poured walls. Panels can consist of wood framing with plywood facings and are fastened together with clips or other ties. Wood sheathing boards and studs with horizontal members and braces are sometimes used in the construction of forms. As in reusable forms, formwork should be plumb, straight, and sufficiently braced to withstand pouring. Frames for basement windows, doors, and other openings are set in place as the forming is erected, along with forms for the beam pockets which are located to support the ends of the floor beam.

Reusable forms usually require little bracing other than horizontal members and sufficient blocking and bracing to keep them in place during pouring. Forms constructed with vertical studs and waterproof plywood or lumber sheathing require horizontal whalers and bracing.

Level marks of some type, such as nails along the form, should be used to assure a level foundation top, thus providing a level sill plate and floor framing.

As with footings, concrete should be poured continuously and rodded or vibrated constantly to remove air pockets and to work the material under window frames and other blocking. Care should be taken to avoid excessive vibrating since this may cause the large aggregates in the concrete to settle to the bottom and weaken the wall. If wood spacer blocks are used, they should be removed and not permitted to become buried in the concrete. Anchor bolts, spaced 8 feet on center, for the sill plate should be placed while the concrete is still plastic. Concrete should always be protected when outside temperatures are below freezing.

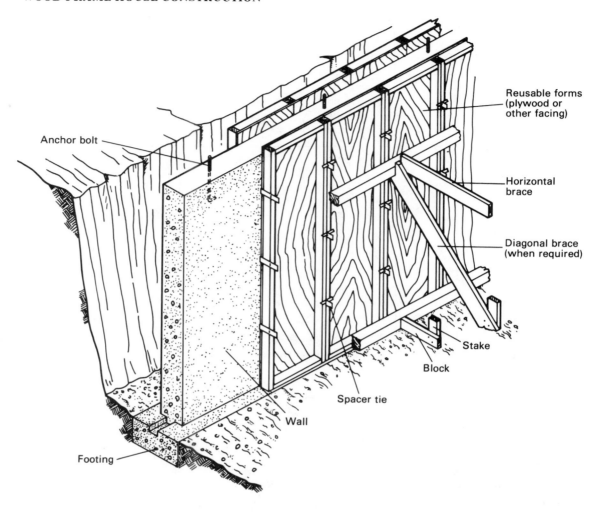

Figure 9. Forming for cast-in-place concrete foundation walls

Forms should not be removed until the concrete has hardened and acquired sufficient strength to support loads imposed during the early stages of construction. At least two days, and preferably longer, are required when temperatures are well above freezing, and perhaps a week when outside temperatures are below freezing. Never backfill until the floor framing and basement slab are in place.

Poured-concrete walls can be dampproofed with one heavy coat, cold or hot, of tar or asphalt. The coat should be applied to the outside from the footings to the finish gradeline, when the surface of the concrete has dried enough to assure good adhesion. Such coatings are usually sufficient to make a wall watertight against ordinary seepage such as may occur after a rainstorm. In addition, the backfill

around the outside of the wall may consist of gravel. The objective of a gravel backfill is to prevent soil from holding water against the foundation wall and to allow the water to flow quickly down to the draintile at the base of the wall. Instead of gravel backfill, a drainboard composed of plastic fibers or polystyrene beads can be installed against the foundation wall. This material serves the same function as the gravel backfill. In poorly drained soils, a membrane may be necessary as described in the following paragraphs.

Masonry Basement Foundations

Concrete blocks are available in various sizes and forms, but the blocks most commonly used are 8, 10, or 12 inches wide. Modular blocks that allow for the

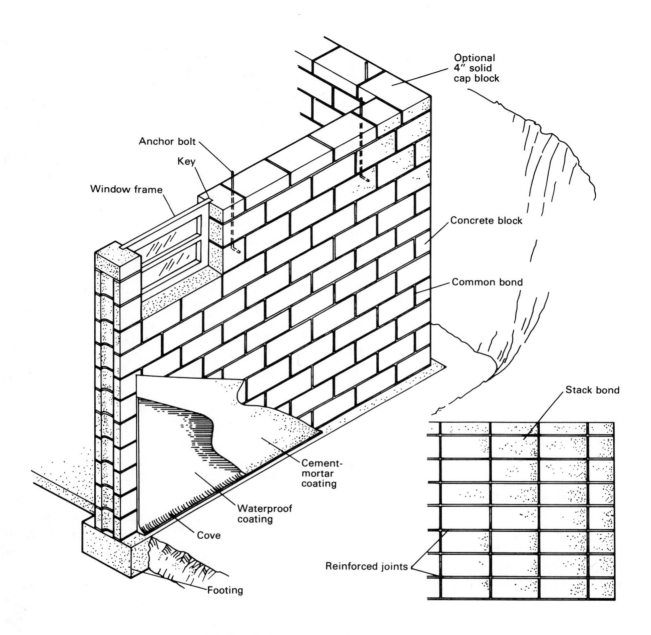

Figure 10. Concrete-block foundation wall

thickness and width of the mortar joint are usually about 7⅝ inches high and 15⅝ inches long. Such blocks form a wall with mortar joints spaced 8 inches from centerline to centerline vertically and 16 inches from centerline to centerline horizontally.

Block courses start at the footing and are laid up with mortar joints of about ⅜ inch, usually in a common bond (staggered vertical joints). Joints should be tooled smooth to resist water seepage. Full bedding of mortar should be used on all contact surfaces of the block. When pilasters (columnlike projections) are used to carry the concentrated loads at the ends of a beam or girder, they are placed on the interior side of the wall and terminated at the bottom of the beam or girder supported. Pilasters can be formed by laying up wider blocks than are used in the rest of the wall, from the footing to the bottom of the supported beam.

Basement door and window frames should be set with keys for rigidity and to prevent air leakage, and anchor bolts for sills are usually placed through the top two rows of blocks (Figure 10). The bent bottom

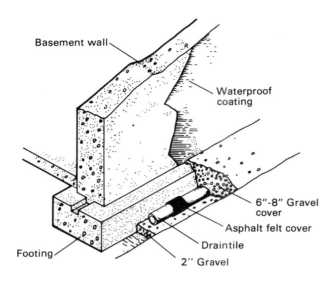

Figure 11. Draintile for soil drainage at outer foundation walls

end of the anchor bolt should be positioned under the lower block and the block openings should be filled solidly with mortar or concrete.

When an exposed block foundation is used as a finished wall for basement rooms, the stack bond pattern may be used for a pleasing effect. This pattern is achieved by placing blocks one above the other, resulting in continuous vertical mortar joints. However, when this system is used, it is necessary to incorporate joint reinforcing every second course. This reinforcing usually consists of small diameter steel trusses 6, 8, or 10 inches wide and 16 feet long, which are laid flat on the bed of mortar between block courses. To gain additional strength, reinforcing rods can be installed vertically in some of the block cores and the cores filled with concrete.

Freshly laid block walls should be protected when temperatures are below freezing. Freezing of the mortar before it has set will often result in low adhesion, low strength, and joint failure. The wall may be waterproofed by applying a coating of cement-mortar over the block with a cove formed at the juncture with the footing (Figure 10). When the mortar is dry, a coating of asphalt or other waterproofing will normally assure a dry basement. Other methods include the application of a 6-mil polyethylene film over the asphalt to provide a water barrier or the installation of a drainboard, described previously, against the asphalt coating before backfilling.

Draintile

Foundation or footing drains must often be used around foundations enclosing basements, or habitable spaces below the outside finish grade (Figure 11), in sloping or low areas or any location where it is necessary to drain away subsurface water. This precaution can help prevent damp basements and wet floors. Drainage is often necessary where habitable rooms are developed in the basement or where houses are located near the bottom of a long slope that is subjected to heavy runoff.

Drains are installed at or below the area to be protected. They should drain toward a ditch or into a sump where the water can be pumped to a storm sewer. Perforated plastic drainpipe, 4 inches in diameter, is ordinarily placed at the bottom of the footing level on top of a 2-inch gravel bed (Figure 11). Another 6 to 8 inches of gravel is used over the pipe. In some cases, 12-inch-long clay tile is used to form the drain. Tiles are spaced about ⅛ inch apart and joints are covered with a strip of asphalt felt. Drainage is toward the outfall or ditch. Dry wells for drainage water are used only when the soil conditions are favorable for this method of disposal. Local building regulations vary and should be consulted before construction of the drainage system.

Basement Floors

Basements are normally finished with a concrete floor whether or not the area is to contain habitable rooms. Structurally, the floor keeps the soil pressure from pushing in the bottom of the foundation wall. These floors are cast in place after all improvements such as sewer and waterlines have been connected. Concrete slabs should not be poured on recently filled areas unless such areas have been thoroughly compacted.

At least one floor drain should be installed in a basement floor, usually near the laundry area. Large basements may require two or more floor drains. Positioning and installation of the drain and piping should precede the pouring of the concrete floor.

A base for the concrete consisting of 4 inches of compacted gravel should be installed. This gravel base breaks the capillary action between the soil and the concrete, and helps to maintain a drier floor. The gravel also serves to store temporarily any groundwater that may seep beneath the slab. Rather than being forced to the floor surface through cracks in the slab, the water is able to migrate to floor drains beneath the slab. A 6-mil polyethylene film may also be used on top of the gravel base to keep moisture from migrating through the slab into the basement.

Basement floor slabs should be either level or sloped toward floor drains. Before the concrete is poured, 2x4s (which are actually 3½ inches wide) are installed on edge on the basement floor at 8-foot intervals. The top edges of these 2x4s are used to set the depth of the concrete for the floor slab and to determine the level or sloped nature of the surface. Setting the elevation of the tops of these 2x4s should be done with a surveyor's level. A less precise alternative is to measure down from the bottom edge of the floor joists installed overhead.

The concrete is then poured. A straight 10-foot 2x4 is used as a screed spanning the 2x4 forms installed on the floor at 8-foot intervals. The screed is worked back and forth to bring the concrete to the level of the top edges of the 2x4 forms. Concrete should be added to low spots beneath the screed. The 2x4 forms should be removed as soon as the screeding process is completed. The disturbed concrete should then be leveled, adding concrete as needed.

Crawl Spaces

In some areas of the country, crawl-space houses are often built in preference to houses constructed over a basement or on a concrete slab. It is possible to construct a satisfactory house of this type by using a good soil cover, a small amount of ventilation, and enough insulation to reduce heat loss.

Crawl-space houses offer cost reductions over full-basement houses. Little or no excavation or grading is required except for footings and walls. In mild climates, footings are located only slightly below the finish grade. However, in the northern states and in Canada, where frost penetrates deeply, the footing is often located 4 or more feet below the finish grade. In this case, full-basement or raised-entry construction may offer much more space with little additional cost. The footings should always be poured over undisturbed soil and never over fill, unless special piers and grade beams are used.

Treated-Wood Crawl Spaces. Crawl-space foundation walls can be constructed of pressure-treated lumber and plywood, described previously in the section on treated-wood basement foundations. This method offers opportunities for prefabrication not possible with concrete or masonry foundations.

Panels are assembled in the same manner as pressure-treated wood basement foundation walls using pressure-treated studs, plates, and plywood facing. However, since a crawl space requires no more than 24 inches of headroom, the ½-inch-thick plywood facing need extend only 2 feet down from the top plate to the level of the crawl-space floor, while the unfaced studs continue down to the frost-line (Figure 12). Pressure-treated 2x4 studs may be spaced at 24 inches on center for single-story construction. For two stories, a spacing of 12 inches on center is necessary.

Construction begins with excavation to the level of the crawl-space floor. If local frost conditions require greater depth, a trench of appropriate width is dug around the perimeter, allowing the wall to extend down to the required depth. The bottom of the trench is covered with a layer of crushed stone or gravel with a minimum depth of 4 inches, which is carefully leveled. Wall panels are installed over footers placed on the gravel and braced in place, plywood joints are caulked, and the wall is covered with 6-mil polyethylene below grade on the exterior.

A wood-frame center bearing wall may also be used. This wall should be assembled from 2x4 studs spaced at 24 inches on center. A plywood facing is not required. The walls may be supported on a stone or gravel bed in a shallow trench (Figure 12). As an alternative, center support may be provided by a conventional beam supported on columns or piers.

Masonry for Crawl Spaces. Construction of a masonry wall for a crawl space is much the same as required for a full basement except that no excavation is required within the walls. Waterproofing and draintile are normally not required for this type of construction. Masonry piers replace the wood or steel posts used to support the center beam of the basement house. Footing size and wall thicknesses vary by location and soil conditions. A common minimum thickness for walls in single-story frame houses is 8 inches for hollow concrete block and 6 inches for poured concrete. Minimum footing thickness is 6 inches; width is 12 inches for concrete block and 10 inches for poured concrete.

Poured-concrete or concrete-block piers are often used to support floor beams in crawl-space houses.

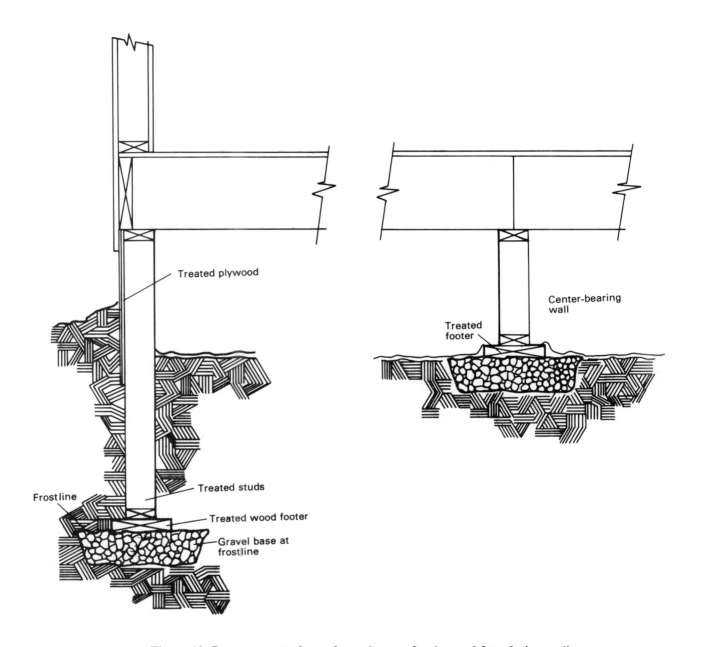

Figure 12. Pressure-treated wood crawl-space footing and foundation wall

They should extend at least 12 inches above the groundline. The minimum size for a concrete block pier should be 8x16 inches with a 16x24-inch concrete footing that is 8 inches thick. A solid cap block is used as a top course. Poured-concrete piers should be at least 10x10 inches in size with a 20x20-inch footing that is 8 inches thick.

Unreinforced concrete piers should be no greater in height than 10 times their least cross-sectional dimension. Concrete block piers should be no higher than four times the least cross-sectional dimension. Spacing of piers should not exceed 8 feet on center under exterior wall beams and interior girders set at right angles to the floor joists, and should not exceed 12 feet on center under exterior wall beams set parallel to the floor joists. Exterior wall piers should not extend above grade more than four times their least dimension unless supported laterally by masonry or concrete walls. For wall footing sizes, the size of the pier footing should be

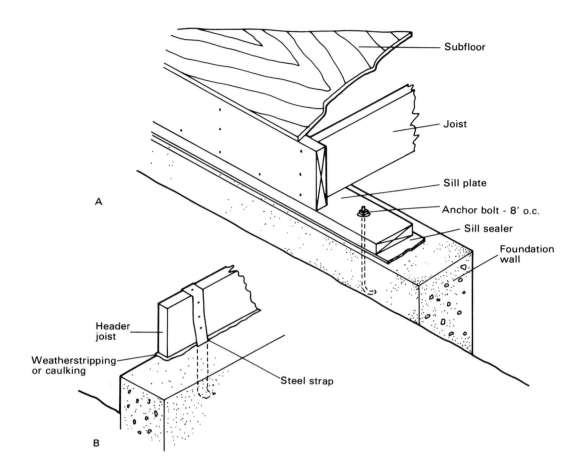

Figure 13. Anchoring floor system to foundation wall:
(A) anchor bolts; (B) steel strap

based on the load and the bearing capacity of the soil.

Sill Plate Anchors

In wood frame construction, the sill plate should be anchored to the foundation wall with ½-inch bolts spaced about 8 feet apart (Figure 13A). In some areas, sill plates are fastened with masonry nails or power-actuated nails, but such nails do not have the uplift resistance of bolts. In high-wind and storm areas, well-anchored plates are very important.

A sill sealer is often used under the sill plate on cast-in-place walls to fill any irregularities between the plate and the wall. Anchor bolts should be embedded 8 inches or more in poured-concrete walls and 16 inches or more in block walls with concrete-filled cores. The bent end of the anchor bolt should be hooked under a block and the core filled with concrete. If termite shields are used, they should be installed under the plate and sill sealer.

Some contractors construct wood-frame houses without using a sill plate. The floor system must then be anchored with steel strapping, which is placed during the pour or between block joints. The strap is bent over and nailed to the floor joist or header joist (Figure 13B). The use of concrete or mortar beam fill provides resistance to air and insect entry.

Reinforcing in Poured Walls

Poured-concrete walls normally do not require steel reinforcing except over window or door openings located below the top of the wall. This type of construction requires that a properly designed steel or reinforced concrete lintel be built over the frame

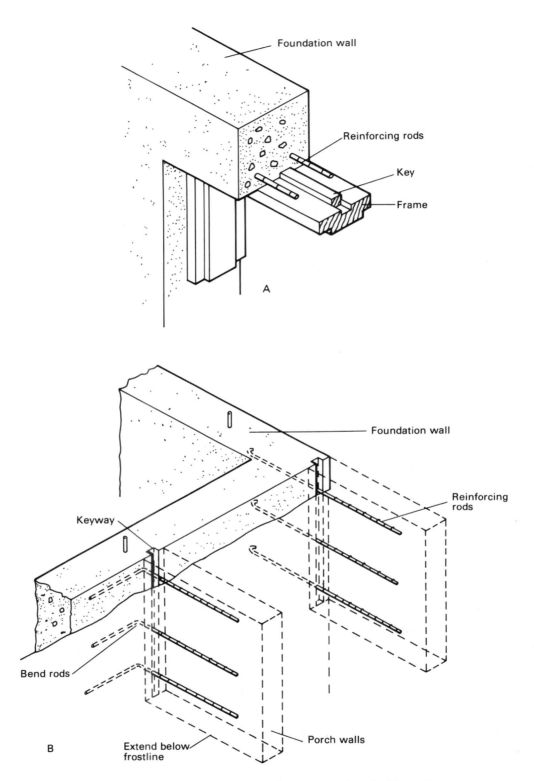

**Figure 14. Steel reinforcing rods in concrete foundation walls:
(A) over window and door openings; (B) for porch or garage walls**

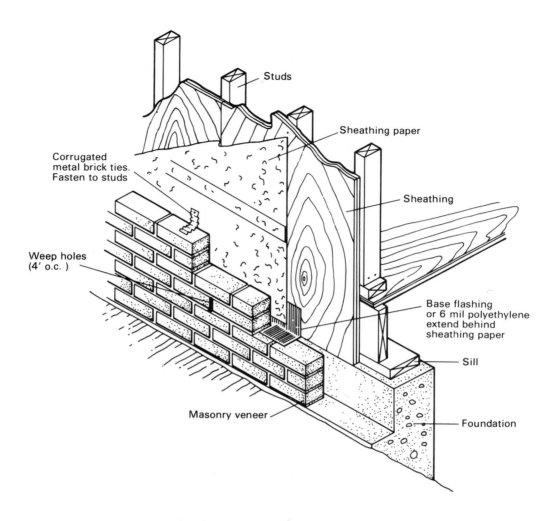

Studs

Sheathing paper

Corrugated
metal brick ties.
Fasten to studs

Sheathing

Weep holes
(4' o.c.)

Base flashing
or 6 mil polyethylene
extend behind
sheathing paper

Sill

Masonry veneer

Foundation

Figure 15. Foundation ledge for masonry veneer

(Figure 14A). Rods are set in place about 1½ inches above the opening while the concrete is being poured. Frames should be prime painted or treated before installation. For concrete-block walls, a similar reinforced poured-concrete or precast lintel is commonly used.

Where concrete work includes a connecting porch or garage wall not poured with the main basement wall, reinforcing rod ties must be provided (Figure 14B). These rods are placed during pouring of the main wall. Depending on the size and depth, at least three ½-inch deformed rods should be used at the intersection of each wall. Keyways may also be used to resist lateral movement. Such connecting walls should extend below normal frostline and be supported by undisturbed ground. Porch walls require footings if they extend more than 3 feet from the main wall or if the porch walls will carry a roof load.

Wall extensions in concrete-block walls are also built of block and are constructed at the same time as the main walls over a footing placed below frostline.

Masonry Veneer Over Frame Walls

If brick or masonry veneer is used for the outside finish over wood-frame walls, the foundation must include a supporting ledge or offset about 5 inches wide (Figure 15). This results in a "finger space" of about 1 inch between the veneer and the sheathing for ease in laying the brick.

When a block foundation is constructed, the supporting ledge for the brick veneer can be provided by using two different block sizes. For example, 12-inch block can be installed from the footing to the level where the brick veneer would begin; 8-inch block can be used from that point upward to support the house framing. A combination of 10-inch and 6-inch block can also be used. The resulting 4-inch ledge requires that the brick veneer be installed with a ½-inch overhang to provide "finger space" for laying the brick.

To provide a brick veneer ledge for a pressure-treated wood foundation house, a pressure-treated 2x4 wall must be built outside the primary foundation wall. This method requires that the primary wall have a 2x12 bottom plate which also supports the outer 2x4 wall. No sheathing is applied to the outer wall.

A base flashing or 6-mil polyethylene film is used at the brick course below the bottom of the sheathing and framing to collect condensation that may run down the wall behind the brick. The vertical leg of the flashing should be behind the sheathing paper. Weep holes, to provide drainage, are located on 4-foot centers at this course. They are formed by omitting the mortar in a vertical joint between bricks. Galvanized steel brick ties, spaced about 32 inches apart horizontally and 16 inches vertically, should be used to bond the brick veneer to the framework. Where sheathing other than wood is used, the ties should be secured to the studs.

Brick should be laid in a full bed of mortar. Mortar should not be dropped into the space between the brick veneer and the sheathing. Outside joints should be tooled to a smooth finish to achieve maximum resistance to water penetration. Masonry laid during the cold weather should be protected from freezing until after the mortar has set.

Notch for Wood Beams

When basement beams or girders are wood, the wall notch or pocket for such members should be large enough to allow at least a ½-inch clearance at the sides and ends of the beam for ventilation (Figure 16). Unless pressure-treated wood is used, there is a decay hazard where beams and girders are so tightly set in wall notches that moisture cannot readily escape.

Protection Against Termites

Certain areas of the country, particularly the Atlantic Coast, Gulf States, Mississippi and Ohio Valleys, and southern California, are infested with

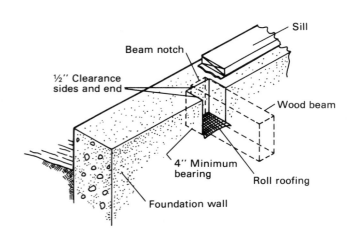

Figure 16. Foundation wall notch for wood beams

wood-destroying termites. In such areas, wood construction over a masonry foundation should be protected by one or more of the following methods:

1. Poured or precast concrete foundation walls.
2. Masonry unit foundation walls capped with reinforced concrete.
3. Metal shields made of rust-resistant material. Metal shields are effective only if they extend beyond the masonry walls and are continuous, with no gaps or loose joints.
4. Wood-preservative treatment. This method protects only the members treated.
5. Treatment of soil with insecticide. This is one of the most common and most effective protective measures.

Additional information on termite protection appears in Chapter 8.

Crawl-Space Ventilation and Soil Cover

Crawl spaces below the floor of basementless houses and under porches should be ventilated and protected from ground moisture by the use of a soil or ground cover (Figure 17). The use of a soil cover, preferably 6-mil polyethylene, is normally recommended under all conditions. It protects wood framing members from ground moisture and permits the use of small, inconspicuous vents.

Such protection will minimize the effect of ground moisture on wood framing members. High humid-

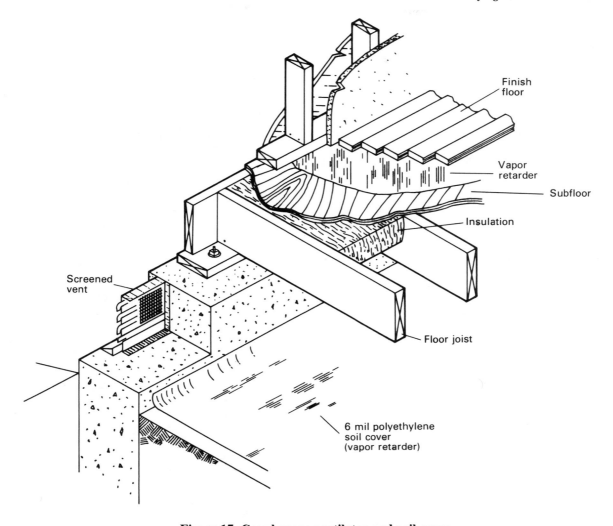

Finish floor

Vapor retarder

Subfloor

Insulation

Screened vent

Floor joist

6 mil polyethylene soil cover (vapor retarder)

Figure 17. Crawl-space ventilator and soil cover

ity and soil moisture may cause the moisture content in the wood to rise high enough to cause staining and decay of untreated members.

Where there is a partial basement open to the crawl-space area, no wall vents are required if there is an operable window. The use of a soil cover in the crawl-space area is nevertheless recommended.

For crawl spaces with no adjoining basement, the net ventilating area required with a soil cover is 1/1600 of the ground area. For a ground area of 1200 square feet, the required ventilating area is 0.75 square feet. This area should be divided between two small vents located on opposite sides of the crawl space. Vents should be covered with a corrosion resistant screen of No. 8 mesh (Figure 17). It should be noted that the total free (net) area of the vents is somewhat less than the total area of the opening, due to the presence of the vent frames, and the screening and louvers. The net free area will be indicated on the vent purchased from a building supplier.

Where the choice is made not to use a ground cover, the total free (net) area of the vents should be equal to 1/160 of the ground area. For a ground area of 1200 square feet a total net ventilating area of about 8 square feet is required. This area can be provided by installing four vents, each with 2 square feet of free ventilating area. A larger number of vents of smaller size, providing the same net ratio, can be used. The vents should be the type that can be closed during cold weather to reduce heat loss and the possibility of frozen pipes.

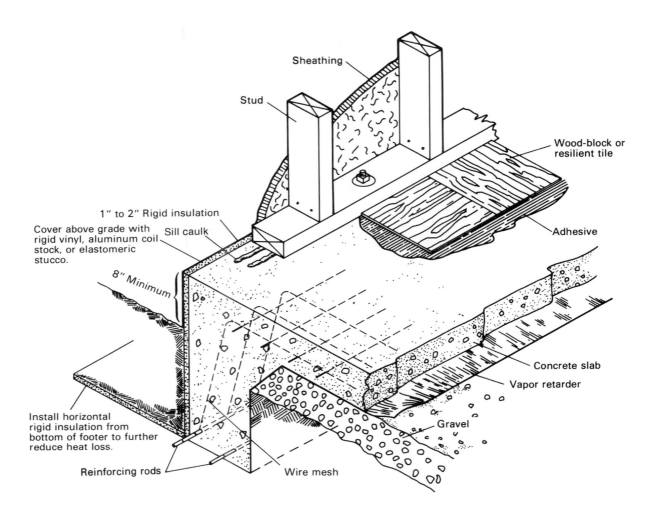

Figure 18. Combined floor slab and footing foundation system

Concrete Floor Slabs on Ground

The number of new one-story houses with full basements has declined in recent years, particularly in the warmer parts of the United States. As previously noted, this is due in part to lower construction costs of houses without basements. It also reflects an apparent decrease in need for basement space.

Traditionally, basements provided space for a central heating plant, for storage and handling of bulk fuel and ashes, and for laundry and utility equipment. The increased use of electricity, oil, and natural gas for heating has virtually eliminated the need for large coal furnaces and for storage of coal and ashes. Space can be compactly provided on the ground floor level for a modern heating plant,

laundry, and utilities, and the need for a basement often disappears.

A common type of floor construction for houses without basements is a concrete slab. Sloping ground or low areas are usually not ideal for slab-on-grade construction because structural and drainage problems can add to costs. However, split-level houses often have a portion of the foundation designed for a grade slab. In such instances, the slope of the lot is taken into account and can become an advantage.

Basic requirements for construction of concrete floor slabs include the following:

1. Finish floor level should be high enough above the natural ground level so that finish grade around the house can be sloped away

for good drainage. The top of the slab should
be no less than 8 inches above ground.

2. Topsoil should be removed and sewer and
water lines installed, then covered with 4 to 6
inches of gravel, crushed rock, or clean sand,
well tamped in place.

3. A vapor retarder consisting of a heavy plastic
film, such as 6-mil polyethylene, should be
used under the concrete slab. Joints should be
lapped at least 4 inches. The vapor retarder
should not be punctured during placing of the
concrete. Certain types of rigid foam insulation such as extruded polystyrene can serve as
a vapor retarder beneath the slab if the joints
are taped.

4. A permanent, waterproof, nonabsorbent type
of rigid insulation should be installed around
the perimeter of the slab. Insulation may
extend down on the inside or outside of the
slab vertically and under the slab edge horizontally a total distance of 24 inches.

5. Concrete slabs should be at least 3½ inches
thick.

6. After leveling and screeding, the surface
should be floated with wood or metal floats
while the concrete is still plastic. If a smooth,
dense surface is needed for the installation of
wood or resilient tile with adhesives, the surface should be steel troweled.

Combined Slab and Foundation

A combined slab and foundation, sometimes
referred to as a thickened-edge or monolithic slab, is
a viable choice in warm climates where frost penetration is not a problem and where soil conditions
are especially favorable. It consists of a shallow
perimeter reinforced footing poured with the slab
over a vapor retarder (Figure 18). The bottom of the
footing should be at least 1 foot below the natural
gradeline and should be supported on solid, unfilled,
well-drained ground.

Independent Concrete Slab and Foundation Walls

In climates where the ground freezes to any
appreciable depth during the winter, the walls of the
house must be supported by foundations or piers
that extend below the frostline to solid bearing on
unfilled soil. In such construction, the concrete slab
and the foundation wall are usually separate. Two
typical systems are suitable for such conditions
(Figures 19 and 20).

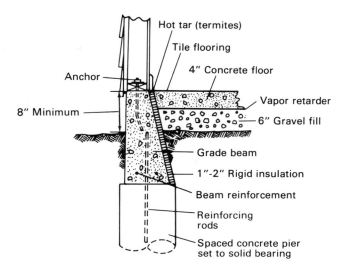

Figure 19. Reinforced grade beam for concrete slab giving moderate resistance to frost heave when piers are used

Reinforced grade beams separate from the concrete slab are used in many parts of the country
(Figure 19). When the soil has inadequate bearing
capacity, reinforced concrete piers can be installed
beneath the grade beam. These piers carry the load
of the house down to rock or stronger soil. The piers
are also effective in counteracting frost heave under
the grade beam in moderately cold climates. In more
severe climates the foundation wall is typically built
as shown in Figure 20 using concrete block or
poured concrete resting on spread footings. The
depth of the footings must be below the frostline;
their width is determined by the bearing capacity of
the soil and the load of the structure.

Insulation Requirements for Concrete Floor Slabs on Ground

Except in warm climates, perimeter insulation for
slabs is necessary to reduce heat loss and to provide
warmer floors during the heating season. Proper
locations for this insulation under several conditions are shown in Figures 18, 19, and 20. The
thickness of the insulation will depend on the climate and on the materials used. Some insulations
have more than twice the insulating value of others.
The resistance (R) per inch of thickness, as well as
the heating design temperature, should govern the
amount required. Two general rules are:

1. For average winter low temperatures of 0°F
and higher (moderate climates), the total R

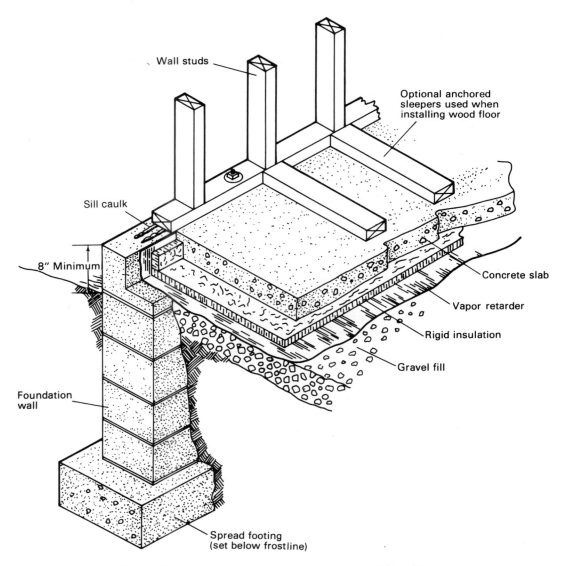

Figure 20. Independent concrete slab and foundation wall system for deep frostline climates

should be about 10.0 and the insulation should extend vertically along the side of the slab (Figure 18) or horizontally under the slab (Figure 20) for not less than 2 feet.

2. For average winter low temperatures of -20° F and lower (cold climates), the total R should be about 10.0 without floor heating and the insulation should extend vertically along the side of the slab (Figure 18) or horizontally under the slab (Figure 20) for not less than 4 feet.

Table 5 shows these factors in more detail. The values shown are minimum; an increase in insulation will result in lower heat losses.

Protection Against Termites

In areas where termites are a problem, soil should be chemically treated around the perimeter of the slab and around pipe or other penetrations through the slab.

Floor Slab Insulation

The properties desired in insulation for floor slabs include:

1. Resistance to heat transmission.
2. Resistance to absorption or retention of moisture.

3. Durability when exposed to dampness and frost.
4. Resistance to crushing due to floor loads, weight of slab, and/or expansion forces.
5. Resistance to fungus or insect attack.

Moisture that might affect insulating materials can come from vapor inside the house and dampness in the soil. Vapor retarders and coatings may retard but not entirely prevent the penetration of moisture into the insulation. Dampness may reduce the crushing strength of insulation, which in turn may permit the edge of the slab to settle. Compression of the insulation reduces its efficiency. Four inches of drained gravel placed between the soil and the insulation will break the capillary movement of water into the insulation, and a 6-mil polyethylene film over the insulation will block the movement of vapor. Commonly used insulation materials are extruded polystyrene or expanded polystyrene with a density of 2 pounds per cubic foot.

Table 5

Resistance values used in determining minimum amount of edge insulation for concrete floor slabs on ground for various design temperatures

Low temperatures	Depth insulation extends below grade	Resistance (R) factor	
		No floor heating	Floor heating
-20° F	4'	10.0	10.0
-10° F	4'	10.0	10.0
0° F	4'	10.0	10.0
+10° F	2'	7.5	10.0
+20° F	2'	5.0	7.5

RETAINING WALLS

Retaining walls are used to alter topography or to improve storm water management. In some local jurisdictions, a special permit is required to erect a retaining wall in excess of a given height, such as 36 inches. Materials used in retaining wall construction include pressure-treated wood, masonry, and poured concrete.

Pressure-treated rectangular wood timbers or railroad ties may be used to construct retaining walls (Figure 21). The timbers are stacked so that the butted ends of the members in one course are offset from the butted ends of the members in the courses above and below. The bottom course should be placed at the base of a level trench. In well-drained sandy soil, there is no need for special footing preparation and materials. In less well-drained soils, 12 to 24 inches of gravel backfill behind the wall and a 6-inch-deep gravel footing are desirable. Each course of timbers should be nailed to the course below, using galvanized spikes whose length is 1½ times the thickness of the timbers. Every other course of timbers should include members inserted perpendicularly to the face of the wall and nailed with spikes to the lower course. These perpendicular tieback members should extend horizontally into the soil behind the wall for a distance equal to their distance above the base of the wall. The end of the tieback member should be nailed to a deadman timber 24 inches in length that has been buried horizontally in the soil and aligned parallel to the timbers in the wall. These tiebacks and deadmen should be installed every 4 to 6 feet along the retaining wall. The tiebacks and deadmen in a course should be located midway between those in the second course below. The objective of the deadmen and tiebacks is to prevent the finished wall from tipping over under the pressure from the soil retained by the wall.

Figure 22 shows an alternative retaining-wall design. Pressure-treated rectangular timbers or railroad ties are set in holes spaced 4 feet apart. Rough-sawn pressure-treated 2-inch lumber is then placed behind vertical members. The 2-inch crosspieces are held in place by back filling as they are placed. In poorly drained soils, the backfill should consist of 12 to 24 inches of gravel. In this design, the vertical members should be set in postholes to a depth of 4 feet or to frostline depth, whichever is greater, to resist tipping from the pressure of the retained soil.

The third retaining-wall design involves the use of pressure-treated plywood and pressure-treated 4-inch round or rectangular posts (Figure 23). The pressure-treated posts are set in holes to the depth of the frostline at 24-inch intervals. Pressure-treated

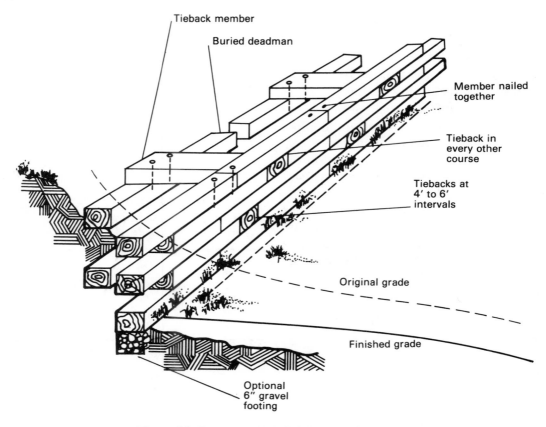

Figure 21. Pressure-treated timber retaining wall

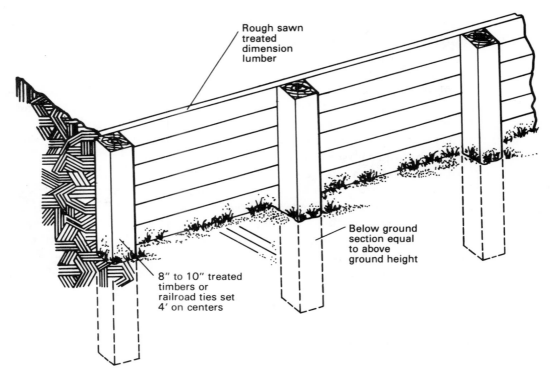

Figure 22. Pressure-treated timber-and-lumber retaining wall

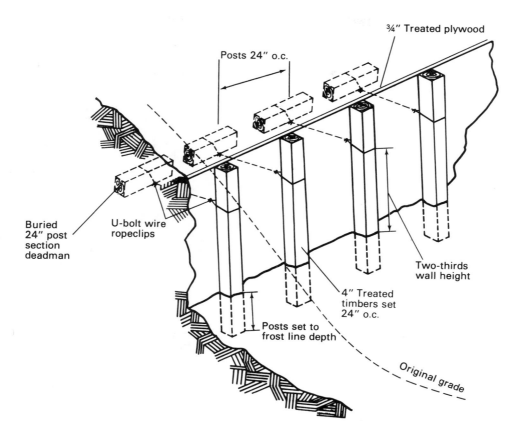

Figure 23. Pressure-treated post-and-plywood retaining wall

¾-inch plywood is then placed behind the posts and held in place by the backfill. Holes are drilled through the plywood on each side of the posts at two-thirds the height of the wall. Plastic-coated galvanized wire rope is then installed through the holes and around each of the posts and fixed in place by a U-bolt wire rope clip behind the plywood. A 24-inch section of the treated post material is buried in the soil to the depth of the wire rope that is attached to the vertical posts. These deadmen should be buried behind the wall a distance not less than their height above the base of the wall. The free end of each of the wire ropes is then wrapped around the buried post sections and fixed in place by a U-bolt wire rope clip. The wire rope in this design serves to tie the vertical posts to the buried deadmen and therefore carries the load of the soil retained by the wall. To carry this load, the wire rope should have a breaking strength of not less than 1000 pounds. All cut ends and drilled holes in the pressure-treated wood and plywood should be brushed with a liberal treatment of preservative chemical. As with other

retaining-wall designs, 12 to 24 inches of gravel backfill behind the wall are recommended in poorly drained soils.

Figure 24 shows a retaining wall of reinforced-concrete blocks. An extra-wide footing is dug to a depth below the frostline. Before concrete is poured, ⅝-inch diameter steel reinforcing rods with a 90° bend are installed. These rods, placed on 16-inch centers, extend from the back to the front of the footing and then turn upward to the height of the wall. After the footing concrete has hardened, 2-core, 12-inch concrete blocks are laid so that the upturned reinforcing rods pass through the open cores of the block. After the block mortar has set, a wooden form is constructed on top of the blocks to form the mold for a 4-inch reinforced-concrete beam. Two straight ⅝-inch steel reinforcing rods spaced 4 inches apart are laid on the beam form and wired to the vertical reinforcing rods. Concrete is then poured into the beam form and rodded into the open block cores. After the concrete has set, 12 to 24 inches of gravel should be used as backfill behind

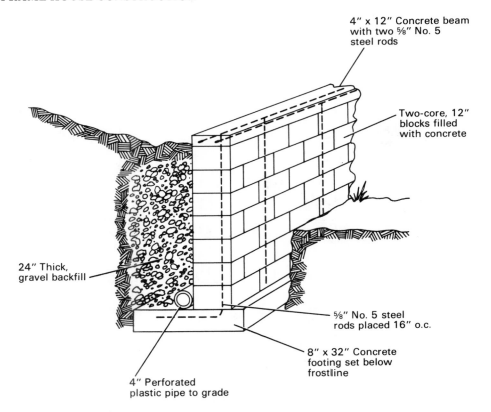

4" x 12" Concrete beam with two ⅝" No. 5 steel rods

Two-core, 12" blocks filled with concrete

24" Thick, gravel backfill

⅝" No. 5 steel rods placed 16" o.c.

8" x 32" Concrete footing set below frostline

4" Perforated plastic pipe to grade

Figure 24. Reinforced concrete-block retaining wall (maximum 4-feet high above grade)

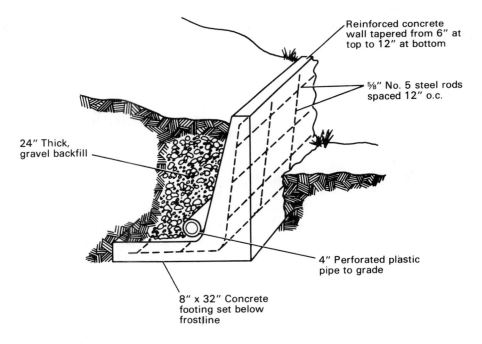

Reinforced concrete wall tapered from 6" at top to 12" at bottom

⅝" No. 5 steel rods spaced 12" o.c.

24" Thick, gravel backfill

4" Perforated plastic pipe to grade

8" x 32" Concrete footing set below frostline

Figure 25. Reinforced concrete retaining wall (maximum 4-feet high above grade)

the wall to provide drainage and to minimize the pressure from behind the wall caused by freezing.

As an alternative to concrete block, the retaining wall can be constructed solely of poured concrete (Figure 25). The footing for the wall is dug to a depth below the frostline. A form is then built in which to pour the concrete for the footing and wall as a single unit. The form for the face of the wall should be vertical, but the back of the wall should be built at an angle to provide a wall that is thicker at the base. Reinforcing rods (⅝-inch) should be placed in the form and wired together to form a lattice with the rods spaced on 12-inch centers. Concrete is poured in the form to the depth of the footing and allowed to set partially before the concrete is poured for the vertical portion of the wall. Backfilling the wall with 12 to 24 inches of gravel is recommended.

CHAPTER 3

Framing And Closing In

This chapter addresses the tasks related to erecting the structural framing and creating an enclosure that provides some degree of protection from the elements.

FLOOR FRAMING

Floor framing consists of columns or posts, beams, sill plates, joists, and subfloor. Assembled on a foundation, they form a level, anchored platform for the rest of the house and a strong diaphragm to keep the lateral earth pressure from pushing in the top of the foundation wall. The columns or posts and beams of wood or steel, which support the joists over a basement, are sometimes replaced with frame or masonry walls when the basement area is divided into rooms. Second-story floors are generally supported on load-bearing walls on the first story. Wood-frame houses may also be constructed over a crawl space with floor framing similar to that used over a basement, or on a concrete slab as shown in the section on "Foundation Walls."

Factors in Design

An important consideration in the design of a wood floor system is wood shrinkage. When wood with a high moisture content is used, subsequent shrinkage can result in cracks, sticking doors, and other problems. This problem is particularly important where wood beams are used because of potential shrinkage relative to foundation walls. The moisture content of beams and joists used in floor framing should not exceed 19 percent; a maximum moisture content of about 15 percent is much more desirable. Dimension material can be obtained at these moisture contents when specified.

Grades of dimension lumber vary considerably by species. For the specific uses described in this book, material is divided into five categories. The first category is the highest quality, the second better than average, the third average, and the fourth and fifth for more economical construction. Joists and beams are usually made from the second category material of a species, while sills and posts are usually of the third or fourth category.

Stairways and other openings that penetrate the floor structure should be located so as to interrupt as few members as possible. Straight-run stairs are the most cost effective. Stairs should be oriented parallel to floor joists so that only one joist need be interrupted with 24-inch on-center joist spacing. Wherever possible, the stair opening should be coordinated with a normal joist location on at least

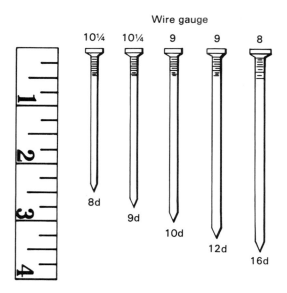

Figure 26. Common nails

one side. Stairways should never interrupt a structural beam or bearing wall when it can be avoided. Other openings, such as those for clothes chutes and flue holes, should also be located to avoid interrupting framing members. Ample clearance for such openings will generally be provided by 24-inch on-center spacing of the joists.

Recommended Nailing Practices

Wood members are most commonly joined together with nails, but on occasion metal straps, lag screws, bolts, staples, and adhesives can be used. Proper fastening of frame members and covering materials provides rigidity and strength. For example, proper fastening of intersecting walls usually reduces plaster cracking at the inside corners.

The recommendations in the section on "Nailing Schedule" (Chapter 8) are based on good nailing practices for the framing and sheathing of a well-constructed wood-frame house. Sizes of common wire nails are shown in Figure 26.

When houses are in hurricane areas, they should be provided with supplemental fasteners called hurricane straps or tiedowns to anchor the floor, walls, and roof to the foundation. This procedure is discussed in Chapter 8 under "Wind, Snow, and Seismic Loads."

Sill Plate

A wood-frame floor system should be anchored to the foundation to resist wind forces acting on the structure. This anchorage is usually done with a 2x6-inch sill plate attached to the foundation by ½-inch anchor bolts at 8-foot intervals. Floor joists are toe-nailed to the sill plate (Figure 27A). The sill plate may also be attached with anchor straps that are embedded in the foundation in the same manner and at the same spacing as anchor bolts. These devices do not require holes in the sill plate; metal straps are simply bent up around the plate and nailed. Anchor straps are less exacting and do not interfere with other framing, as conventional bolts often do.

Sill plates may be eliminated where the top of a poured-concrete (Figure 27B) or concrete-block (Figure 28B) foundation is sufficiently level and accurate. Joists may bear directly on a solid concrete wall or on a top course of solid concrete block. They may also bear directly on cross webs of hollow-core block or on cores that have been filled with mortar. Where the sill plate is omitted, anchorage of the floor system may be provided by anchor strap devices, as described above. The straps should be spaced to coincide with joist locations so that each may be nailed directly to the side of a joist (Figure 28).

As noted previously, a pressure-treated wood foundation does not require a sill plate or special anchor devices. Floor joists bear directly on the top foundation wall plate and are toe-nailed to provide anchorage.

Posts and Girders

Wood posts or steel columns are generally used in the basement to support wood or steel beams. Masonry piers or wood posts are commonly employed in crawl-space houses.

Steel pipe columns can be used to support either wood or steel beams. They are normally supplied with a steel-bearing plate at each end. Secure anchoring to the beam is important (Figure 29).

Wood posts should be solid, pressure-treated, and not less than 6x6 inches in size for free-standing use in a basement. When combined with a framed wall, they may be 4x6 inches to conform to the width of the studs. Wood posts should be squared at both ends and securely fastened to the beam (Figure 30).

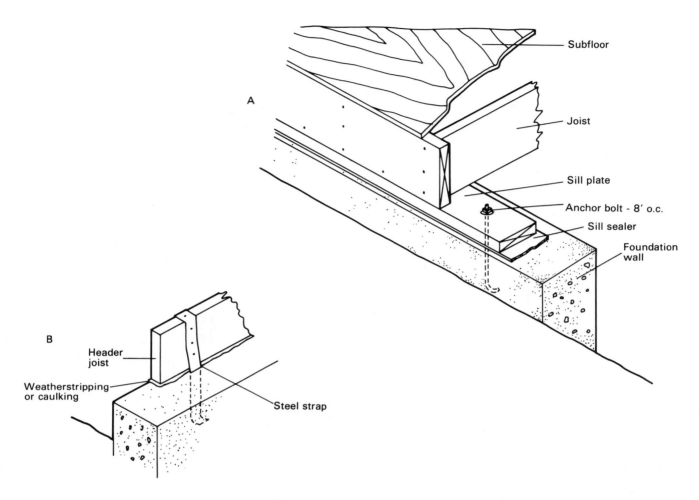

Figure 27. Anchoring floor system to poured-concrete foundation wall: (A) with sill plates; (B) without sill plates

The bottom of the post should rest on and be pinned to a masonry pedestal 2 to 3 inches above the finish floor.

Center Beam

Wood-frame floor construction typically employs a beam or girder to provide intermediate support for the first floor. In two-story construction, the beam generally supports the second floor as well by use of a load-bearing wall extending along the center of the first story.

For maximum benefit in reducing joist spans, beams and bearing walls should be located along the centerline of the structure. In some cases it may be desirable to offset the center support 1 foot from the centerline to provide for even-length joists, as with 26- or 30-foot-deep floor systems. However, as discussed later, this is not necessary if off-center spliced joists are used.

The center beam usually bears on the foundation at each end and is supported along its length by columns or piers. The spacing of columns or piers is adjusted to the spanning capability of the beam for a particular design load. Two basic types of center beams, wood and steel, are commonly used. The decision should be based on a comparison of the total installed cost of each, including intermediate support columns or piers, and footings. Other considerations include delivery, scheduling, and ease of construction.

Wood center beams are of two types—solid and built-up. The built-up beam is preferable because it

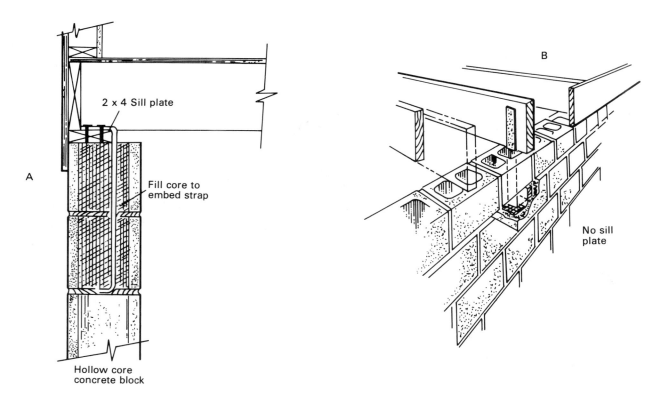

Figure 28. Anchoring floor system to poured-concrete foundation wall: (A) with sill plates; (B) without sill plates

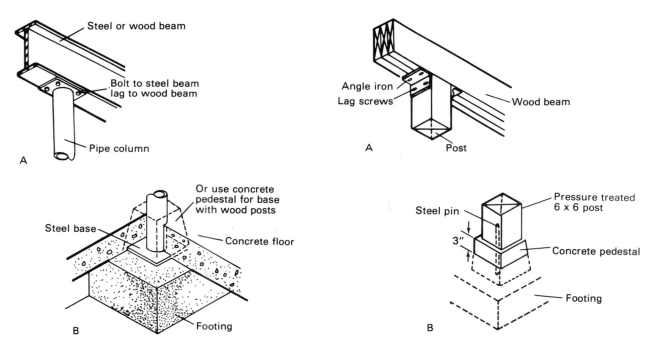

Figure 29. Steel post support for wood or steel beam: (A) connection to beam; (B) base support

Figure 30. Wood post support for wood beam: (A) connection to beam; (B) base support

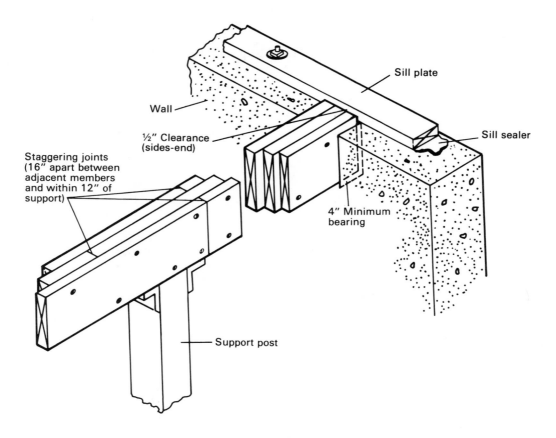

Figure 31. Typical built-up wood beam installation

can be made up from drier dimension material and is more stable. For equal widths, the built-up beam is stronger than the solid beam.

Built-Up Wood Beams

Built-up beams are constructed by nailing three or four layers of dimension lumber together. The built-up beam may be made longer than any of the individual members by butting the ends of the members together. These butt joints must be staggered between adjacent layers so that they are separated by 16 inches. In addition, the built-up beam must be supported by a column or pier positioned within 12 inches of the butt joints (Figure 31).

Table 6 shows typical allowable spans for built-up wood beams. Dry lumber should always be used to avoid settlement problems caused by shrinkage of the built-up beam and the joists it supports. It is not necessary to use a wood plate over wood beams, since floor joists may be nailed directly to the beam.

Ends of wood beams should bear at least 4 inches on the masonry walls or pilasters. When wood is untreated, a ½-inch air space should be provided at each end and side of wood beams framing into masonry (Figure 31). The top of the beam should be level with the top of the sill plates on the foundation walls.

Steel I-Beams

Steel I-beams are often used because of their greater strength and stiffness which enable them to carry a given load over a given span with a beam of lesser depth, thus providing greater headroom or reducing the requirement for additional supporting posts. Allowable spans for steel I-beams are shown in Table 7. However, steel beams require an additional supplier, which can complicate delivery schedules. They are also heavier and more difficult to handle in the field. The total cost of a steel beam, including columns or piers, is generally greater than that of a wood beam.

Where steel beams are used, a 2x4- or 2x6-inch wood plate is usually attached to the top surface by bolting, or by driving nails part way into the sides of

TABLE 6

Allowable spans for built-up wood center beams[1]

Beam Composition	Width of Structure (in feet)	Minimum required Bending stress (f) of 1000 psi[2]		Minimum required Bending stress (f) of 1500 psi[2]	
		One-story	Two-story	One-story	Two-story
3 — 2x8s	24	6'7"	—	8'1"	4'7"
	26	6'4"	—	7'9"	4'3"
	28	6'2"	—	7'5"	—
	32	5'5"	—	6'6"	—
4 — 2x8s	24	7'8"	5'2"	9'4"	6'2"
	26	7'4"	4'9"	9'0"	5'8"
	28	7'1"	4'5"	8'8"	5'4"
	32	6'7"	—	8'1"	4'8"
3 — 2x10s	24	8'5"	4'11"	10'4"	7'6"
	26	8'1"	4'7"	9'11"	5'6"
	28	7'10"	4'3"	9'6"	5'1"
	32	6'11"	—	8'4"	4'6"
4 — 2x10s	24	9'9"	5'7"	11'11"	7'10"
	26	9'4"	6'1"	11'6"	7'3"
	28	9'0"	5'8"	11'1"	6'9"
	32	8'5"	5'0"	10'4"	6'0"
3 — 2x12s	24	10'3"	6'0"	12'7"	7'2"
	26	9'10"	5'6"	12'1"	6'8"
	28	9'6"	5'2"	11'7"	6'2"
	32	8'5"	4'6"	10'2"	5'2"
4 — 2x12s	24	11'10"	8'0"	14'6"	9'7"
	26	11'5"	7'5"	13'11"	8'10"
	28	11'0"	6'10"	13'5"	8'3"
	32	10'3"	6'0"	12'7"	7'3"

Source: NAHB Research Foundation. *Manual of Lumber- and Plywood-Saving Techniques for Residential Light-Frame Construction*, 1971.

[1] The allowable spans shown assume a clear-span trussed roof construction. In two-story construction, a load-bearing center partition has been assumed. The built-up wood center beam and/or the load-bearing partition in two-story construction may be offset from the centerline of the house by up to 1 foot.

[2] The Bending Stress (f) measures the strength and varies with the species and grade of lumber as shown in Appendix A.

the plate and bending the protruding nail shanks over the edges of the beam flange. Floor joists are then toe-nailed to the beam plate to anchor the floor and to provide lateral bracing for the beam. A beam plate is not required if the floor joists are secured by other means.

Beam-Joist Installation

In the simplest method of floor framing, the joists bear directly on top of the wood or steel beam. The top of the beam coincides with the top of the foundation or anchored sill (Figure 31). This method assumes that basement wall heights provide adequate headroom below the girder. When a forced-air heating sytem is to be installed, this arrangement of beam and joists provides space for the main duct to be run parallel to the beam and for the laterals to be run between the joists above the level of the beam.

As previously noted, beams and joists should be constructed of dry lumber to reduce problems caused by settlement due to shrinkage. This settlement is of particular concern when wood joists bear

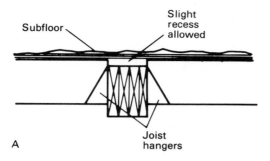

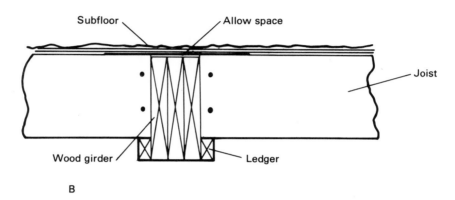

**Figure 32. Joists butted to side of wood beam:
(A) supported by joist hangers; (B) supported by ledger**

directly on top of the wood beam at the center of the house while bearing on the concrete foundation wall at the outer ends. To equalize the depth of wood at the beam and at the outer wall — and thereby equalize shrinkage potential — joists should be attached to the side of the wood beam using joist hangers or supporting ledger strips (Figure 32). The simplest method is to use steel joist hangers (Figure 32A). Where ledgers are used, joists must always bear on the ledgers (Figure 32B). It is important that a small space be allowed above the beam to provide for shrinkage of the joists.

Joists may be butted to a steel beam in the same general way as is illustrated for a wood beam, with joists resting on a wood ledger that is bolted to the web (Figure 33).

Floor Joists

Floor joists are selected primarily to meet strength and stiffness requirements. Strength requirements depend on the loads to be carried. Stiffness requirements place an arbitrary control on deflection under load. Stiffness is also important in limiting vibra-

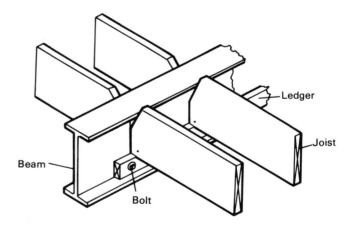

Figure 33. Steel beam with joists bearing on ledger

tions from moving loads — often a cause of annoyance to occupants.

Wood floor joists are generally of 2-inch nominal thickness and of 8-, 10-, or 12-inch nominal depth. The size required depends upon the loading, length of span, spacing between joists, and species and grade of lumber used. After the sill plates have been

Table 7

Allowable spans between columns or piers supporting steel center beams[1]

Steel-beam designation[2]	Total width of house	Maximum clear span	
		For 1-story house	For 2-story house
8B10.0	24	13'9"	10'0"
	26	13'3"	9'8"
	28	12'9"	9'4"
	32	11'11"	8'9"
10B11.5	24	16'0"	11'8"
	26	15'5"	11'3"
	28	14'10"	10'10"
	32	13'10"	10'2"
8W17.0	24	19'4"	14'1"
	26	18'7"	13'7"
	28	17'11"	13'1"
	32	16'9"	12'4"
10B17.0	24	20'9"	15'2"
	26	20'0"	14'7"
	28	19'3"	14'1"
	32	18'0"	13'2"
10W21.0	24	23'2"	17'5"
	26	22'8"	16'9"
	28	22'2"	16'2"
	32	20'9"	15'2"

Source: United States Steel Corporation (USX). *Steel Beam Stress & Deflection Estimator for use in calculating sizes of laterally supported beams for residential and light construction.*

[1] Based on a continuous beam over two equal spans with a maximum of ½-inch deflection at design load and assuming a clear span trussed roof.

[2] The steel beam designations presented are those most commonly available at building-material suppliers. The designation gives the height of the beam in inches, a letter designating the type of I-beam, and the weight of the beam in pounds per linear foot. (An "8B10.0" I-beam is an 8 inches high, type B I-beam that weighs 10.0 pounds per linear foot.)

anchored to the foundation walls and the center beam installed, the joists are laid out according to the house design. The center-to-center spacings most commonly used are 24 inches or 16 inches.

Span tables for floor joists, provided by the National Forest Products Association or local building codes, can be used as guidelines. Table 8 is a simplified version for joists spaced 24 inches on center. The sizes shown in the table are minimums; it is sometimes desirable to use the next larger lumber size than that listed in the table.

Joists should be inspected visually for straightness when they are being placed. Any joists having a slight crook edgewise should be placed with the crown on top. A crowned joist will tend to straighten out when subfloor and normal floor loads are applied. Joists that are not crowned should be inspected for the presence of knots along the edge. The largest edge knots should be placed on top, because knots on the upper side of a joist are placed in compression and will have less effect on strength.

The header joist is fastened by nailing through it into the end of each joist with three 12d or 16d nails. In addition, the header joist and the stringer joists parallel to the exterior wall in platform construction (Figure 34) are toe-nailed to the sill with 10d or 12d nails spaced 16 inches on center. Each joist should be toe-nailed to the sill and center beam with two 10d or three 8d nails, then nailed to each other with three 12d nails where they lap over the center beam. If joists are butted over the center beam, they should be joined with a nominal 2-inch scab nailed to each joist with three 12d nails.

An "off center" splice may be used in framing floor joists. This system often allows the use of one smaller joist size when center supports are present. In off-center splicing, long joists are cantilevered over the center support and spliced to short joists (Figure 35). The locations of the splices over the center beam are alternated. Depending on the span, species, and joist size, the overhang varies between about 2 and 3 feet. Metal splice plates are used on each side of the joints. Selecting the proper plate size and installing the plate must be done by a truss fabricator.

Joists should be at least doubled under parallel load-bearing partition walls. Solid blocking should be used in place of doubled joists when access from below is needed for installing heating ducts in the load-bearing partition (Figure 34). It is not necessary, however, to double joists under nonload-bearing parallel partitions. In fact, it is not necessary to locate a nonload-bearing partition over a floor joist; the floor sheathing is normally adequate to support the partition between joists (Figure 36).

Header Joist

The header joist, or band joist, used across the ends of floor joists has traditionally been the same size as floor joists. One function of a header joist is to brace floor joists temporarily in position prior to

Table 8

Allowable spans for simple floor joists spaced 24 inches on center[1]

Allowable spans for living areas (40 lbs. per sq. ft. live load assumed)

Modulus of elasticity in 1,000,000 psi (E)[2]	1.0	1.1	1.2	1.3	1.4	1.5	1.6	1.7	1.8	1.9	2.0
Minimum required bending stress(f)[3]	1050	1120	1190	1250	1310	1380	1440	1500	1550	1610	1670
Joist size: 2x6	7'3"	7'6"	7'9"	7'11"	8'2"	8'4"	8'6"	8'8"	8'10"	9'0"	9'2"
2x8	9'7"	9'11"	10'2"	10'6"	10'9"	11'0"	11'3"	11'5"	11'8"	11'11"	12'1"
2x10	12'3"	12'8"	13'0"	13'4"	13'8"	14'0"	14'4"	14'7"	14'11"	15'2"	15'5"
2x12	14'11"	15'4"	15'10"	16'3"	16'8"	17'0"	17'5"	17'9"	18'1"	18'5"	18'9"

Allowable spans for sleeping areas (30 lbs. per sq. ft. live load assumed)

Modulus of elasticity in 1,000,000 psi (E)[2]	1.1	1.2	1.3	1.4	1.5	1.6	1.7	1.8	1.9	2.0	
Minimum required bending stress(f)[3]	1020	1080	1150	1210	1270	1330	1390	1450	1510	1560	1620
Joist size: 2x6	8'0"	8'3"	8'6"	8'9"	8'11"	9'2"	9'4"	9'7"	9'9"	9'11"	10'1"
2x8	10'7"	10'11"	11'3"	11'6"	11'10"	12'1"	12'4"	12'7"	12'10"	13'1"	13'4"
2x10	13'6"	13'11"	14'4"	14'8"	15'1"	15'5"	15'9"	16'1"	16'5"	16'8"	17'0"
2x12	16'5"	16'11"	17'5"	17'11"	18'4"	18'9"	19'2"	19'7"	19'11"	20'3"	20'8"

Source: National Forest Products Association. *Span Tables for Joists and Rafters,* 1977.

Note: Other tables should be used for other joist spacings (e.g., 16 inches on center).

[1] For allowable spans for simple floor joists spaced 16 inches on center, refer to Appendix B.

[2] The modulus of elasticity measures stiffness and varies with the species and grade of lumber, as shown in Appendix A.

[3] The bending stress (f) measures strength and varies with the species and grade of lumber, as shown in Appendix A.

application of the subfloor. The header joist also helps to support stud loads in conventional construction, where wall studs do not necessarily align with floor joists.

With modular planning, however, each wall stud should bear directly over a floor joist. A nominal 1-inch-thick header joist may therefore be used in place of the traditional 2-inch-thick header. A header joist of nominal 1-inch-thick lumber uses less material and is easier to install using 8d nails.

Glued Floor Design

When a plywood subfloor is properly glued to floor joists with a construction adhesive, the subfloor and floor joists tend to act together as a single structural member. The composite T-beam thus formed will span a greater distance than can be spanned if the floor is fastened only with nails.

Glue-nailing of the plywood subfloor is recommended as a cost-effective method of increasing the stiffness and/or allowable span of a floor as shown in Table 9. Glue-nailing is also highly effective in reducing floor squeaks and loose nails which may otherwise be encountered at a later time due to shrinkage of joists.

Bridging

Bridging between wood joists is no longer required by any of the model building codes in normal house construction, i.e., spans not exceeding 15 feet and

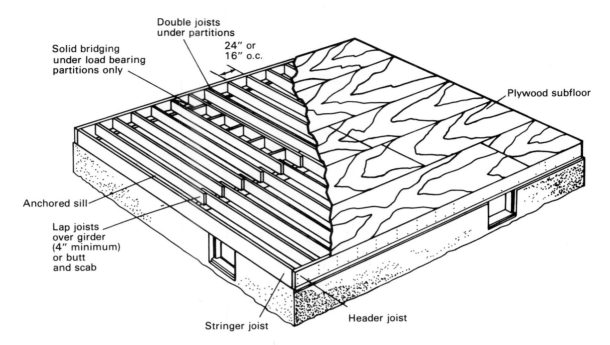

Figure 34. Typical platform construction

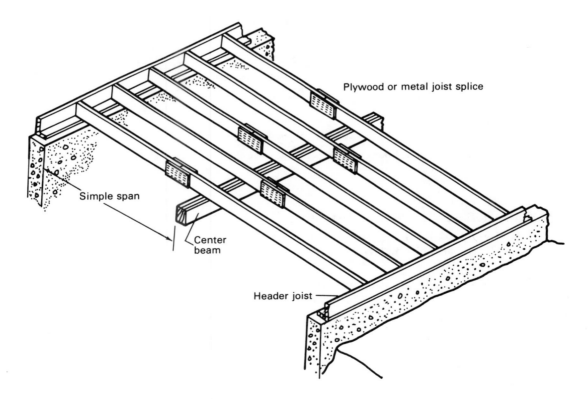

**Figure 35. Off-center spliced joist system allowing use of
one short joist in every pair of joists**

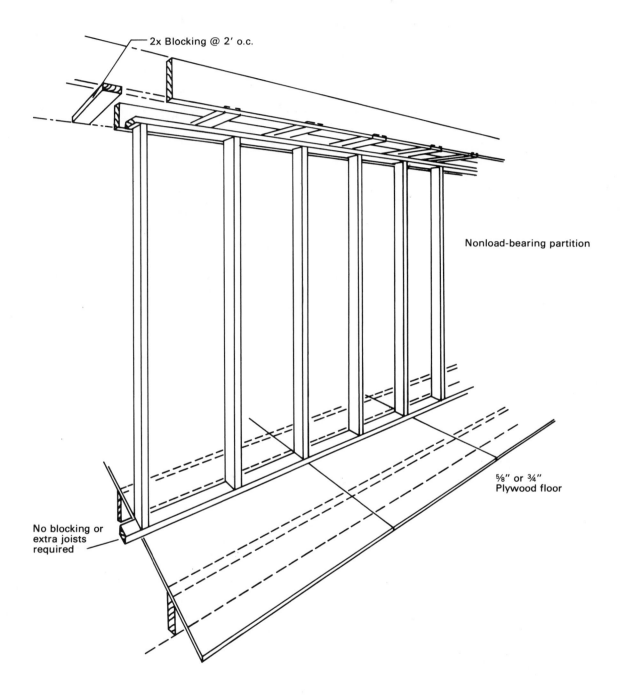

2x Blocking @ 2' o.c.

Nonload-bearing partition

⅝" or ¾"
Plywood floor

No blocking or
extra joists
required

**Figure 36. Nonload-bearing partitions (no extra floor framing
or blocking needed with ⅝-inch or thicker plywood floor)**

Table 9

Allowable spans for joists spaced 24 inches on center with ¾-inch glued plywood flooring

Allowable spans for living areas (40 lbs. per sq. ft. live load assumed)

Modulus of elasticity in 1,000,000 psi (E)[1]	0.6	0.8	1.0	1.2	1.4	1.6	1.8	2.0
2x6 Joists								
Minimum required Bending stress (f)[2]	1100	1270	1415	1545	1655	1755	1855	1950
Maximum span	8'1"	8'8"	9'2"	9'7"	9'11"	10'2"	10'6"	10'9"
2x8 Joists								
Minimum required Bending stress (f)[2]	1025	1180	1310	1430	1535	1630	1725	1810
Maximum span	10'3"	11'0"	11'7"	12'2"	12'7"	13'0"	13'4"	13'8"
2x10 Joists								
Minimum required Bending stress (f)[2]	970	1110	1230	1345	1445	1535	1625	1710
Maximum span	12'9"	13'8"	14'4"	15'0"	15'7"	16'0"	16'6"	16'11"
2x12 Joists								
Minimum required Bending stress (f)[2]	925	1060	1175	1280	1380	1470	1560	1640
Maximum span	15'2"	16'2"	17'1"	17'10"	18'6"	19'1"	19'8"	20'2"

Allowable spans for sleeping areas (30 lbs. per sq. ft. live load assumed)

Modulus of elasticity in 1,000,000 psi (E)[1]	0.6	0.8	1.0	1.2	1.4	1.6	1.8	2.0
2x6 Joists								
Minimum required Bending stress (f)[2]	1340	1540	1715	1865	2005	2130	2250	2360
Maximum span	8'11"	9'7"	10'1"	10'6"	10'11"	11'3"	11'7"	11'10"
2x8 Joists								
Minimum required Bending stress (f)[2]	1245	1430	1590	1730	1860	1975	2085	2190
Maximum span	11'4"	12'2"	12'10"	13'4"	13'10"	14'3"	14'8"	15'0"
2x10 Joists								
Minimum required Bending stress (f)[2]	1170	1345	1495	1625	1745	1860	1970	2070
Maximum span	14'0"	15'0"	15'10"	16'6"	17'1"	17'9"	18'2"	18'8"
2x12 Joists								
Minimum required Bending stress (f)[2]	1120	1280	1425	1550	1670	1780	1890	1985
Maximum span	16'8"	17'10"	18'10"	19'7"	20'4"	21'0"	21'8"	22'2"

Source: NAHB Research Foundation. *Reducing Home Building Costs with OVE Design and Construction.* 1977.

[1] The modulus of elasticity (E) measures stiffness and varies with the species and grade of lumber, as shown in Appendix A.

[2] The bending stress (f) measures strength and varies with the species and grade of lumber, as shown in Appendix A.

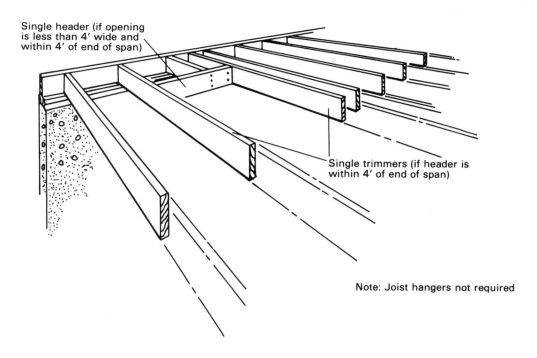

Single header (if opening is less than 4' wide and within 4' of end of span)

Single trimmers (if header is within 4' of end of span)

Note: Joist hangers not required

Figure 37. Floor opening framed with single header and single trimmer joists

joist depth not exceeding 12 inches. Even with tight-fitting, well-installed bridging there is no significant transfer of loads after the subfloor and finish floor are installed. Bridging also increases the likelihood of floor squeaking.

Details At Floor Openings

Large openings in the floor, such as stairwells and fireplaces or chimneys, usually interrupt one or more joists. Such openings should be planned so that their long dimension is parallel with joists in order to minimize the number of joists that are interrupted. The opening should not disrupt the center beam or bearing partition that supports the floor. Wherever possible, the opening should be coordinated with the normal joist spacing on at least one side to avoid the necessity for an additional trimmer joist to form the opening.

A single header is generally adequate for openings up to 4 feet in width. A single trimmer joist at each side of the opening is usually adequate to support single headers that are located within 4 feet of the end of joist spans (Figure 37). Tail joists under 6 feet in length may be fastened to the header with three 16d end nails and two 10d toe-nails, or equivalent

nailing. Tail joists over 6 feet in length should be attached with joist hangers. The header should be connected to trimmer joists in the same manner as tail joists are connected to the header.

Where wider openings are unavoidable, double headers are generally adequate up to 10 feet (Figure 38). Tail joists may be connected to double headers in the same manner and under the same conditions as specified previously for single headers. Tail joists that are end-nailed to a double header should be nailed before the installation of the second member of the double header, so that the nails penetrate adequately into the tail joist. A double header should always be attached to the trimmer with a joist hanger.

Trimmer joists at floor openings must be designed to support the concentrated loads imposed by headers where they attach to the trimmer. As noted previously, a single trimmer is adequate to support a single header located near the end of the span. All other trimmers should be at least doubled and should be engineered for specific conditions.

Floor Framing at Projections

The framing for wall projections such as bay windows, wood chimneys, or first- or second-floor

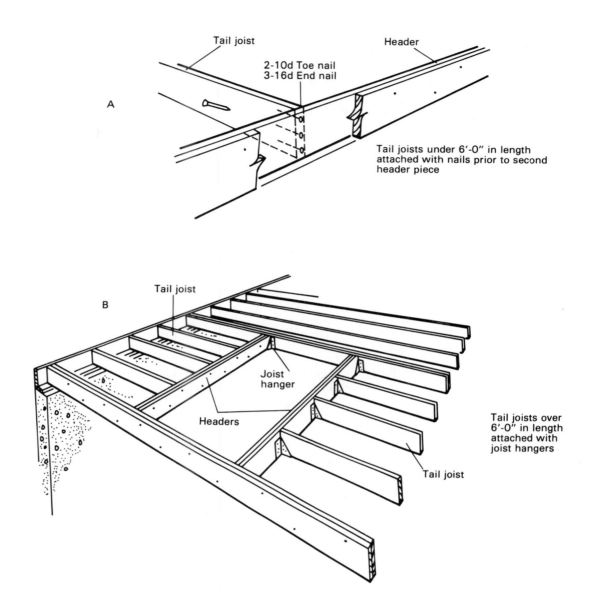

Figure 38. Floor opening framed with double header and double trimmer joists: (A) nailing tail joists under 6'10" in length; (B) joist hangers used for longer tail joists

extensions beyond the lower wall should consist of the projection of the floor joists (Figure 39). This extension normally should not exceed 24 inches. The subflooring is carried to and sawed flush with the outer framing member. Greater projections for special designs may require special anchorage at the opposite ends of the joists.

Projections at right angles to the length of the floor joists should generally be limited to small areas and extensions of not more than 24 inches. If the projecting wall carries any significant load, it should be carried by doubled joists (Figure 39B). Joist hangers should be used at the ends of members.

In two-story houses, there is often a projection or overhang of the second floor for architectural effect or to make second-floor siding flush with first-floor brick veneer. This overhang may vary from 2 to 15 inches or more and should ordinarily be on that side of the house where joist extensions can support the wall framing (Figure 40). This extension should be provided with insulation and a vapor retarder.

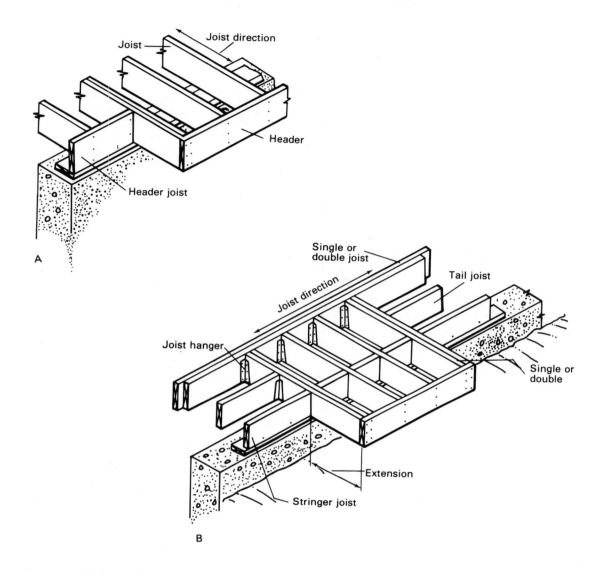

Figure 39. Floor framing at wall projections: (A) continuation of floor joists; (B) projection perpendicular to floor joists

When the overhang parallels the second-floor joists, a doubled joist should be located back from the wall at a distance about twice the width of the overhang to which overhang blocks are attached. These blocks rest on top of, and project beyond, the outside wall.

Framing Details for Plumbing, Heating, and Other Utilities

It is desirable to limit cutting of framing members for installation of plumbing lines and other utilities. This is more easily accomplished in one-story houses than in two-story houses. In single-story houses, most connections are made in the basement area; in two-story houses, they must be made within the second floor. When it is necessary to cut or notch joists, it should be done in a manner least detrimental to their strength, as is discussed in more detail under "Cutting Floor Joists."

Single-Layer Plywood Flooring

In the past, double floor construction consisting of subfloor and finish floor or underlayment has typically been employed. However, where carpet and/or resilient floorings are used throughout, a single layer of tongue-and-groove plywood, designed

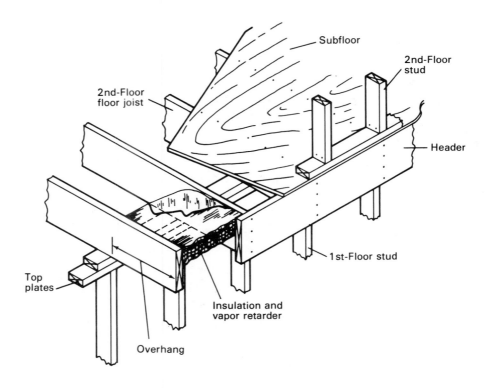

Figure 40. Floor framing at second-story wall projection

as a combination subfloor and underlayment, may be applied directly to floor joists.

Tongue-and-groove, ¾-inch-thick, Group 1 underlayment grade plywood is recommended for single-layer floors installed over joists spaced 24 inches on center, where the plywood is fastened only with nails. Either 8d common nails or 6d deformed-shank nails may be used. Nails should be spaced 6 inches apart at panel edges and 10 inches apart across the panel face. Edge blocking is not required with tongue-and-groove plywood.

Although this nailing will provide adequate attachment, the use of an approved construction adhesive provides additional benefits. Where glue is used, nail spacing can be increased to 12 inches, both along edges and across the face. Glue should also be used in the grooved joint of tongue-and-groove plywood.

As with plywood subfloors, glue-nailing of the plywood floor will increase the stiffness and/or allowable span of the floor system and can eliminate or reduce loose nails and squeaks, which can otherwise develop with even a small amount of joist shrinkage.

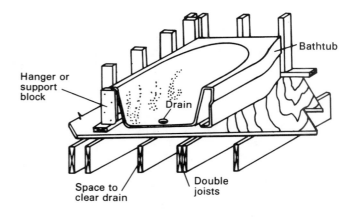

Figure 41. Framing for bathtub

Bathtub Framing

A bathtub full of water is heavy and may cause excessive deflection of floor joists. A doubled floor joist should be provided beneath the tub to support this load (Figure 41). The intermediate joist should be spaced to allow installation of the drain. Metal hangers or wood blocking should be used to support the edge of the tub at the wall.

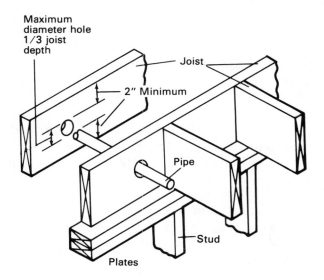

Figure 42. Drilled holes in joists

Cutting Floor Joists

It is sometimes necessary to cut, notch, or drill joists to conceal plumbing pipes or wiring in a floor. Joists or other structural members that have been cut or notched can sometimes be reinforced by nailing a reinforcing scab to each side or by adding an additional member.

Notching the top or bottom of the joist should only be done in the end one-third of the span and not more than one-sixth of the depth. When greater alterations are required, headers and tail joists should be added around the altered area similar to a stair opening (Figure 37). This need may occur where the closet bend must cross the normal joist locations.

When necessary, holes may be bored in joists if the diameter is no greater than one-third of the joist depth and the edge of the hole is at least 2 inches from the top or bottom edge of the joist (Figure 42).

Framing for Heating Ducts

Forced-air systems with large ducts for heating and air conditioning are becoming a standard part of house construction. Framing should be laid out with structural members located to accommodate the duct system where possible, and joists should be located so that they do not have to be cut when ducts are installed. When a load-bearing partition requires a doubled parallel floor joist as well as a warm-air duct, the joists can be spaced apart to allow room for the duct (Figure 43).

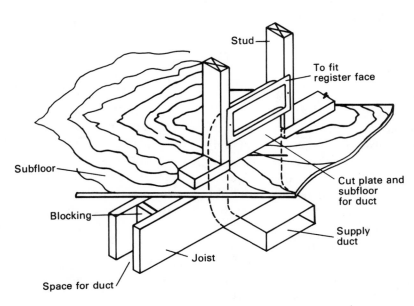

**Figure 43. Joists spaced to allow installation of
ductwork in load-bearing partitions**

Wiring

Wiring for electrical services is usually installed after the house has been closed in. The initial phase includes the installation of cable and switch, light, and outlet boxes. This rough-in work is done before insulation or drywall is installed.

The effect on floor framing is usually minor, consisting of holes drilled for the cable. Although these holes are of small diameter, they should comply with procedures specified above under "Cutting of Floor Joists" and as shown in Figure 42.

Switches or convenience outlet boxes on exterior walls must be sealed to prevent water vapor movement. Sealing of the vapor retarder around the box is important for maintaining the thermal protection of the home. This sealing may be accomplished by caulking the holes in the electrical box and by using duct tape to attach the vapor retarder to the box.

STAIRWAYS

Stairways should be designed to afford safety and adequate headroom as well as space for the passage of furniture. Two types of stairs are: (1) finished main stairs leading between the levels of the living areas of the house; and (2) service stairs leading to the basement or garage area. Main stairs are designed to provide easy ascent and descent and can be a feature of the interior design. Service stairs are usually constructed of less expensive materials, although safety and convenience are prime considerations in their design.

Construction

Both finished and service stairs may be ordered prebuilt from local millwork companies. Service stairs, however, are frequently constructed in place. Stairs assembled by millwork companies require accurate measurement of the rough framed stairway opening and floor-to-floor height to insure that the delivered stairs fit properly; therefore, it may be desirable for a millwork company representative to visit the home and perform the measurement. Service stairs can consist simply of 2x12-inch carriages or stringers, plank stair treads, and open risers (Figure 44). Construction and installation are discussed later in this section.

Stairway Design

Most stairway designs fall into two categories: straight run or stairway with landing. In the latter type, each flight should be considered as a separate run of stairs except that the individual riser height and tread width should be made the same on both flights.

Basic dimensions for stairway design include headroom clearance, stairway width, stair tread run and stair rise. Generally accepted dimensions (Figure 44) are:

- Minimum headroom clearance: 6 feet 8 inches
- Minimum stairway width: 36 inches
- Minimum stair tread run: 9 inches
- Maximum stair rise: 8¼ inches

Total rise is the height from floor surface to floor surface. Total run is the total horizontal distance spanned from the front edge of the bottom riser to the back of the top riser; it is equal to the number of steps multiplied by the individual stair tread run.

The stairway design should be completed before floor framing begins, since the stairwell opening must be framed at the time the floor is constructed. The rough-framed opening for a stairwell should be 1 inch wider than the desired finished stairway width. The length of the opening must be accommodated to tread run and stair rise, which in turn are governed by total rise.

An example will illustrate the method of calculation. In this example the bottom of the ceiling joists are 8 feet 1½ inches above the floor surface; the ceiling consists of 9¼-inch joists; and the upper floor sheathing consists of ¾-inch tongue-and-groove underlayment grade plywood. The total rise of the stairway between these two floors would be the sum of the ceiling height, the joist height, and the floor thickness, which totals 107½ inches.

The first estimate of the number of step risers is arrived at by dividing the total rise by the maximum allowable tread rise (e.g., 8¼ inches). The result is just over 13. Since it is unsafe to build a stairway with one short riser, the next larger whole number should be selected. In this example the choice would be 14 risers. The exact height of the 14 risers is then computed as the total rise of the stairway divided by 14. In this example, it is 107.5 divided by 14, or 7.68 inches.

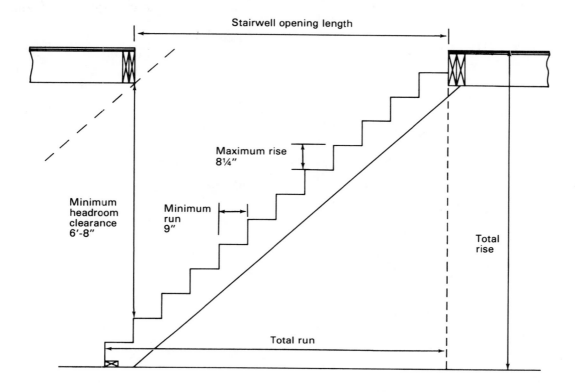

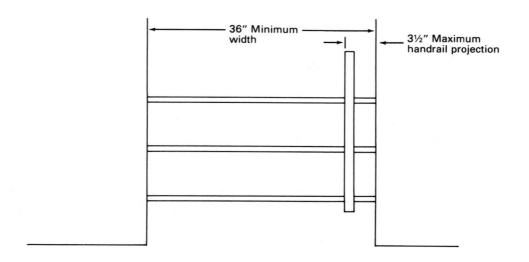

Figure 44. Stairway design requirements and terminology

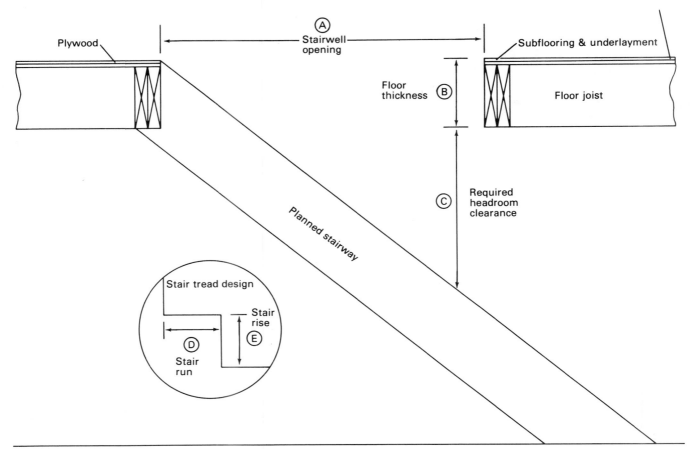

$$A = \frac{(B + C) D}{E}$$

where A is the length of the stairwell opening in inches.

B is the total thickness of the upper floor system including joist,
subflooring, and underlayment in inches.

C is the headroom clearance required in inches.

D is the planned stair tread run in inches.

E is the planned stair tread rise in inches.

Figure 45. Calculating length of stairway floor opening

Since the number of stair treads is one less than the number of risers, the stairway in the example above would have 13 treads. If the stair design calls for a 10-inch tread, the total run of the completed stairway will be 130 inches.

The final calculation is to determine the length of the stairwell opening in the floor framing so as to provide adequate headroom clearance. This calculation involves four dimensions: 1) the stair tread rise, 2) the stair tread run, 3) the required headroom clearance, and 4) the thickness of the upper floor including the joist and the layer(s) of the floor covering (excluding carpeting).

The stairwell opening length calculation is shown in Figure 45. Continuing with the example, the rise was calculated to be 7.68 inches and the tread run was set at 10 inches. The upper floor thickness of 10 inches was composed of a 9¼-inch joist plus a ¾-inch plywood underlayment. If the required headroom clearance is set at 6 feet 8 inches, and the equation in Figure 45 is applied, the stairwell opening length would have to be 9 feet 10 inches, plus 2 inches or more for finish trim. However, this minimum headroom clearance of 6 feet 8 inches will probably cause people over 6 feet tall to duck their heads when using the stairway. It may therefore be better to calculate the stairwell opening to allow headroom clearance of 7 feet or more.

Landings

The total run of the stairway is a critical value only when the direction of the stairs causes them to end close to a wall. If there is not enough space to construct a single straight-run stairway, a stairway with landing (Figure 46) must be considered. In some cases, such a stairway may also be desired for aesthetic reasons.

The platform frame for the landing (Figure 47) should be nailed to the adjacent walls and should be supported by a post under the unsupported corner. The dimensions should align the landing with the stairway width. If the stairway is 36 inches wide, the landing can be 36 inches square.

Framing for Stairs

The long dimension of stairway openings may be either parallel or at right angles to the joists. However, it is much easier to frame a stairway opening when its length is parallel to the joists. The opening is usually framed as shown in Figure 48A, when joists run perpendicular to the length of the opening, and as shown in Figure 48B, when joists run parallel to the length of the opening.

Utility Stairs

Utility stairs consist of the stair treads and the stringers or stair carriages that carry the treads and support the loads on the stairs. Utility stairs are usually constructed without risers, but are sometimes constructed with risers to improve their appearance and/or to facilitate cleaning.

Stringers are typically constructed of 2x12-inch lumber to provide a minimum of 3½ inches between the lower edge of the stringer and the back of the tread (Figure 49A). When the stairway is 3 feet wide and the treads are cut from nominal 2-inch lumber, one stringer on each side of the stairway is adequate to support most loads. When thinner material is used for the stair treads, an intermediate stringer positioned at the center of the tread is required. Risers provide additional support for the front and rear of the treads and are typically cut from nominal 1-inch boards.

The stringers can be toe-nailed to the joist header at the top of the stairway (Figure 49B). At the bottom of the stairway, the stringers rest on and can be anchored to a concrete footer or a basement floor. Alternatively, the stringers can be anchored to a 2x4-inch or 2x6-inch kicker plate of pressure-treated lumber firmly attached to the footer or basement floor as shown in Figure 49C.

There are two commonly used techniques for laying out the cuts on the stringers or carriages for service stairs: using a steel carpenter's square or using a specially made pitch board. In both techniques the stair stringers should be 2x10-inch or, preferably, 2x12-inch pieces of lumber. The choice of stringer dimension should be determined by the amount of lumber remaining between the bottom edge of the stringer and the apex of the notch cut out for the tread and riser. This remaining uncut portion of the stringer should be at least 3½ inches (Figure 50).

The carpenter's-square approach to stringer layout (Figure 50A) requires that the tread length be marked on one arm of the square and the riser height be marked on the other arm of the square. The square may then be placed on the stringer board with the two marks aligned with the edge of the board, and a pencil can be used to scribe a line on the board along the carpenter's square. This line forms the guide for cutting the stringer. The carpenter's square may be moved along the board until one of the marks is lined up with the scribe mark. Again, a pencil can be used to mark the cutout for the step. This process is repeated for the number of treads and risers required in the stair. The riser height at the bottom step should be reduced by the thickness of the stair tread material.

The second method involves the assembly of a pitch board which serves as a template for marking the tread and riser dimensions (Figure 50B). Either plywood or a nominal 1-inch board may be used as the triangular template material. One leg of the triangular template should be the tread depth and the other leg of the triangle should be the riser height. These two lines must meet in a 90° angle. A line connecting the ends of these two lines forms the long side of the triangle. The long side of the carefully cut triangular template should be screwed or nailed to the center of the flat side of a 2x4 to complete the pitch board. Using the 2x4 as a guide, the long edge of the pitch board should be placed along the edge of the stringer and the tread and riser

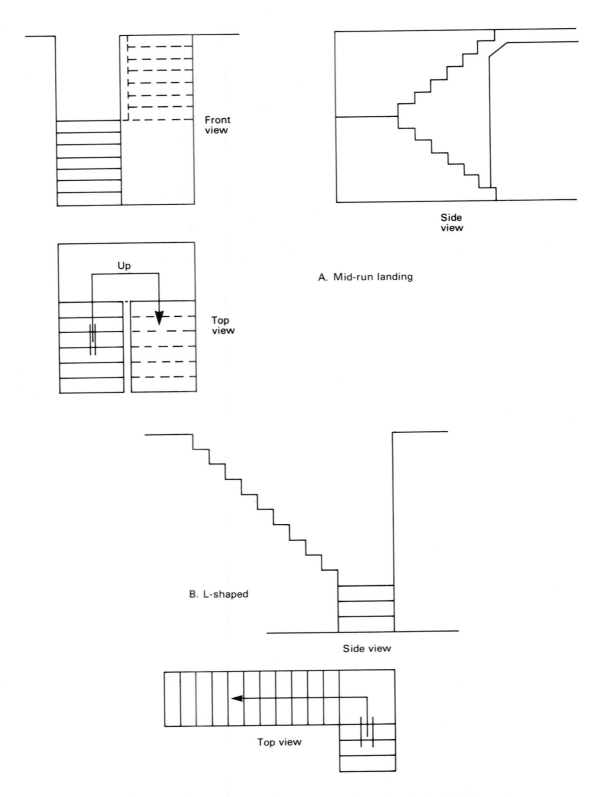

Figure 46. Space-saving stair design: (A) mid-run landing; (B) L-shaped

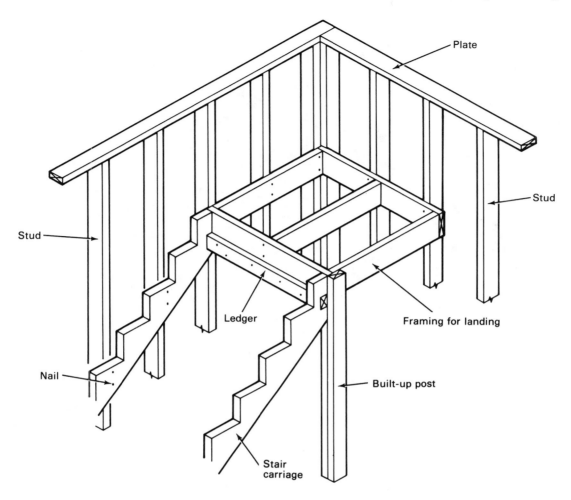

Plate

Stud

Stud

Ledger

Framing for landing

Nail

Built-up post

Stair
carriage

Figure 47. Framing for stair landing

outline scribed on the side of the stringer. The pitch board may then be moved along the stringer and the remaining tread and riser outlines scribed on the side of the stringer. The height of the riser from the bottom step should be reduced by the thickness of the tread material.

Both of these stringer-layout methods presume that the stringer will be cut so that the treads can be placed directly on the cuts. This type of stairway is referred to as an open-stringer design. The alternative is the closed-stringer stairway in which the stringer is not cut.

Either the carpenter's-square or the pitch-board technique may be used to mark the stringer for the location of the tread and riser dimensions for the closed stringer. Once this has been done, there are two commonly used methods for supporting the

stair treads without cutting the stringers: routing the stringer or attaching cleats.

In the routed-stringer approach (Figure 51A), a groove is routed across the stringer above each treadline. The width of the groove should be the thickness of the tread material, and the depth of the groove should be half the thickness of the stringer. When the grooves are completed in the two stringers, the stair treads should be inserted into the grooves and nailed at an angle through the tread into the stringer.

Perhaps the simplest technique for stair construction is to nail 1x3-inch or 2x2-inch cleats to the stringers below each tread line (Figure 51B). After treads are cut to the proper length, they are placed between the stringers on top of the cleats. When the treads are in place, they are nailed at an angle through the tread and cleat and into the stringer.

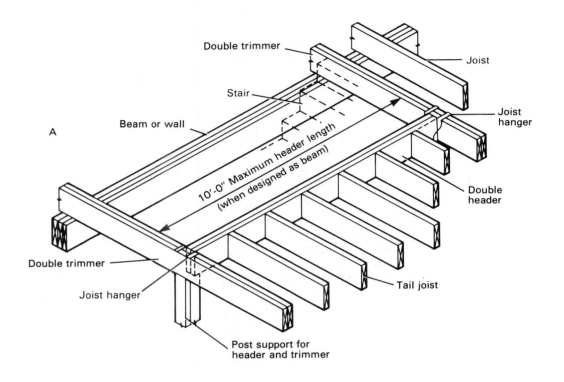

Double trimmer

Joist

Stair

Joist hanger

Beam or wall

A

10'-0" Maximum header length
(when designed as beam)

Double header

Double trimmer

Joist hanger

Tail joist

Post support for
header and trimmer

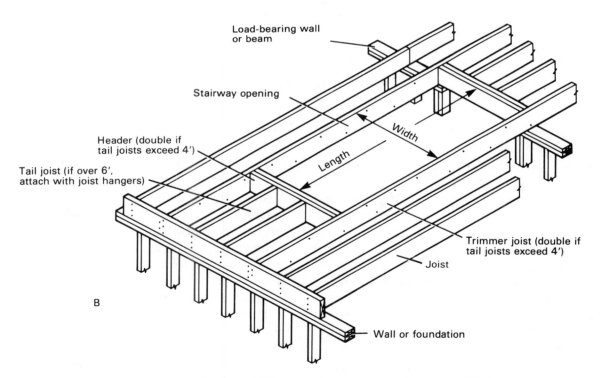

Load-bearing wall
or beam

Stairway opening

Width

Header (double if
tail joists exceed 4')

Length

Tail joist (if over 6',
attach with joist hangers)

Trimmer joist (double if
tail joists exceed 4')

Joist

B

Wall or foundation

**Figure 48. Floor framing for stairwell opening: (A) opening perpendicular
to floor joists; (B) opening parallel to floor joists**

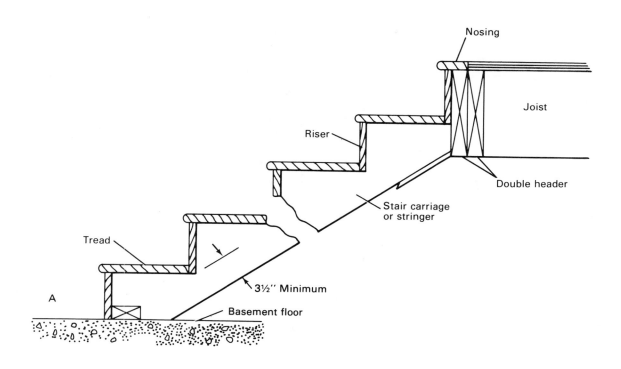

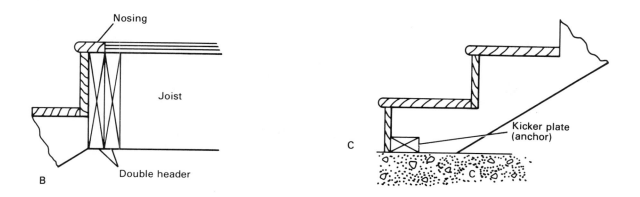

Figure 49. Utility stairs: (A) stair assembly; (B) attachment at top of stairway; (C) attachment at bottom of stairway

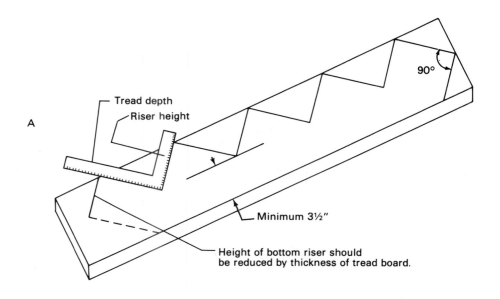

A

Tread depth

Riser height

90°

Minimum 3½"

Height of bottom riser should
be reduced by thickness of tread board.

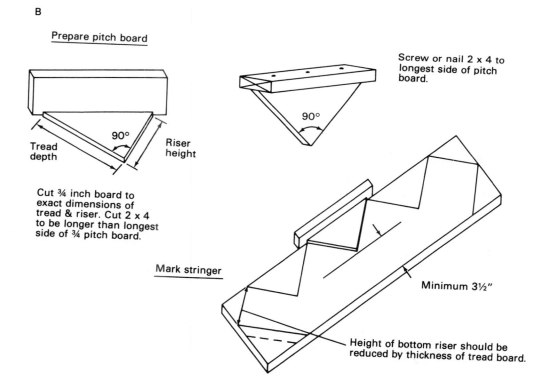

B

Prepare pitch board

Screw or nail 2 x 4 to
longest side of pitch
board.

90°

Tread
depth

90°

Riser
height

Cut ¾ inch board to
exact dimensions of
tread & riser. Cut 2 x 4
to be longer than longest
side of ¾ pitch board.

Mark stringer

Minimum 3½"

Height of bottom riser should be
reduced by thickness of tread board.

**Figure 50. Laying out a stringer: (A) using carpenter's square;
(B) using pitch board**

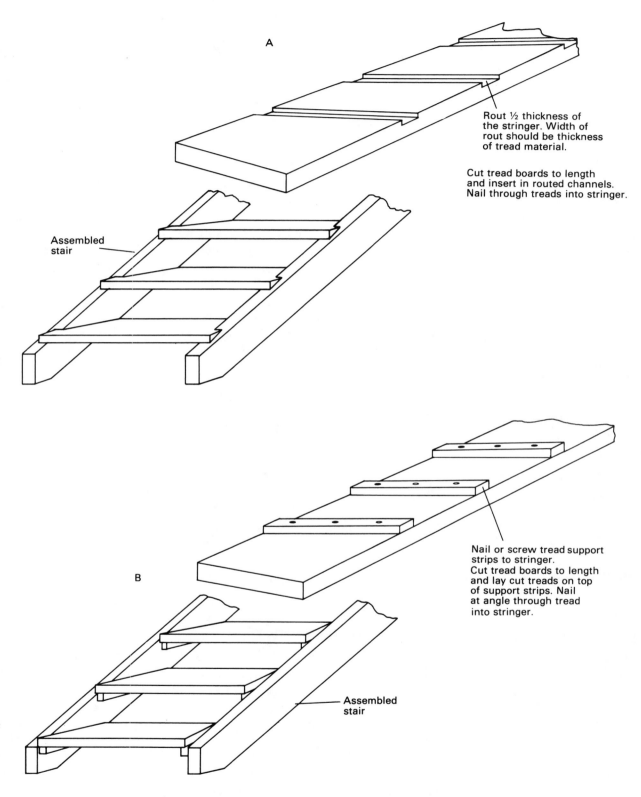

A

Rout ½ thickness of
the stringer. Width of
rout should be thickness
of tread material.

Cut tread boards to length
and insert in routed channels.
Nail through treads into stringer.

Assembled
stair

Nail or screw tread support
strips to stringer.
Cut tread boards to length
and lay cut treads on top
of support strips. Nail
at angle through tread
into stringer.

B

Assembled
stair

**Figure 51. Assembling stair treads and stringers: (A) treads set in routed stringers;
(B) treads on support strips**

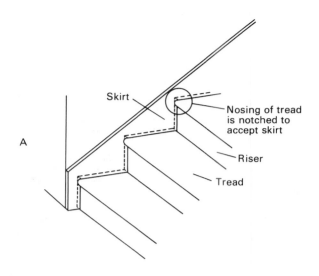

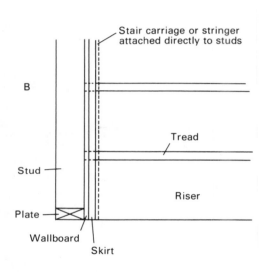

Figure 52. Stairway skirt board: (A) finished appearance; (B) front-view detail

Main Stairway

An open main stairway with railing and balusters ending in a newel post can be very decorative and pleasing, either in a traditional or contemporary house design. Main stairways generally differ from other types previously described, in such features as side trim boards; cove moldings nailed beneath stair tread nosing and between trim boards and wall; decorative railing and balusters; and the wood species, which is clear and can be given a durable natural finish.

Main stairs that are to be fully carpeted can be built with rough treads and risers and finished along both sides with trim board or skirt boards (Figure

52). The skirt boards should be nominal 1-inch boards, free of knots, and should be marked using the cut stringers as a pattern. The cut stringers are laid on top of the skirt boards, and each tread and riser outline is marked on the face of the skirt boards. The resulting step pattern is then carefully cut from the boards. After the stringers, treads, and risers are installed, a ¾-inch-wide notch is cut out of the nosing at each side of each stair tread. After all notches are cut out, the skirt boards are slipped into the notches and seated snugly against the faces of the treads and risers.

The trim work required to produce an attractive and safe main stairway is often best performed by a local millwork contractor. In addition to possessing the skills and equipment, these contractors are familiar with the local regulations that control stair design and construction. They will provide guidance on the measurements needed to construct the stairs. Some contractors may visit the house under construction to make the necessary measurements.

Attic Folding Stairs

Where attics are used for storage and space for a fixed stairway is not available, hinged or folding stairs are often used. These can be purchased ready to install. They operate through an opening in the ceiling and swing up into the attic space when not in use. Where such stairs are to be installed, the attic floor joists should be designed for limited floor loading. One common size of folding stairs requires only a 26x54-inch rough opening. These openings should be framed out as described for normal stair openings.

Exterior Stairs

Proportioning of risers and treads in laying out porch steps or approaches to terraces should be considered as carefully as the design of interior stairways. Similar riser-to-tread ratios can be used; however, the riser used in principal exterior steps should normally be between 6 and 7 inches in height. The need for a good support or foundation for outside steps is often overlooked. Where wood steps are used, the lumber should be pressure-treated to prevent insect and decay damage. Where the steps are located over backfill or disturbed soil, the footing should be carried down to undisturbed ground below the frostline.

FLOOR SHEATHING

Floor sheathing or subflooring is used over the floor joists to form a working platform and a base for finish flooring. It usually consists of: 1) square-edge or tongue-and-grooved boards no wider than 8 inches and not less than ¾-inch thick; 2) square-edge or tongue-and-grooved plywood ½-inch to ¾-inch thick, depending on species, type of finish floor, and spacing of joists; or 3) reconstituted wood panels such as particleboard or flakeboard, similar in application to plywood.

Boards

Subflooring boards, rarely used because of the extra labor they require, may be applied either diagonally or at right angles to the joists. If wood finish flooring is used over subflooring placed at right angles to the joists, the finish floor should be laid at right angles to the subflooring. Diagonal subflooring permits wood finish flooring to be laid either parallel or at right angles to the joists. The end joints of the boards should always be directly over the joists. Subflooring boards are nailed to each joist with two 8d nails for widths under 8 inches and three 8d nails for 8-inch widths.

The joist spacing should not exceed 16 inches on center when strip finish flooring is laid parallel to the joists or when tile or parquet finish flooring is used. An underlayment of plywood, particleboard, or hardboard is required over board subfloors where thin resilient floorings, carpet or other non-structural finish flooring is to be used.

Plywood

Plywood can be obtained in a number of grades to meet a broad range of requirements. Interior grades are suitable for most applications. They are available with a waterproof adhesive for uses involving exposure to moisture, such as in floors near plumbing fixtures or for subflooring that may be exposed for long periods during construction.

Plywood should be installed with the grain direction of the outer plies at right angles to the joists, and staggered so that end joints in adjacent panels break over different joists. Plywood should be nailed to the joists at each bearing using 8d common or 6d threaded nails or 1⅝-inch narrow crown staples for plywood ½-inch to ¾-inch thick. Nails should be spaced 6 inches apart along all edges and 10 inches apart along intermediate members. Whether used on the interior or exterior, plywood should not be installed with tight joints. The American Plywood Association recommends a ⅛-inch spacing at panel ends and edges for plywood subfloor applications.

Plywood suitable for subfloor, such as Rated Sheathing and Structural I or II grades, has a panel identification index marking on each sheet. These markings indicate the allowable spacing of rafters and floor joists for the various thicknesses when the plywood is used as roof sheathing or subfloor. For example, an index mark of 32/16 indicates that the plywood panel is suitable for a maximum spacing of 32 inches for rafters and 16 inches for floor joists.

When some type of underlayment or wood finish flooring is used over the plywood subfloor, a standard sheathing grade with square edges is generally used. The minimum acceptable thickness of plywood subfloor is generally ½ inch when joists are spaced 16 inches on center, and ¾ inch when joists are spaced 24 inches on center.

A Rated Sturd-I-Floor grade plywood can serve as combined subfloor and underlayment. Separate underlayment can be eliminated because the plywood functions as both a structural subfloor and a good substrate for the finish floor. This method applies to thin resilient flooring, carpeting, and other nonstructural finish flooring. Minimum thicknesses are similar to those for sheathing grade plywood subfloors used with underlayment. The plywood used in this manner must be tongue-and-grooved or blocked with 2-inch lumber along the unsupported edges.

Reconstituted Wood Panels

Several types of reconstituted wood panels are used for floor sheathing, including flakeboard, structural particleboard, oriented strand board, and composite panels (veneer faces bonded to reconstituted wood cores). These products are graded and installed in the same manner as plywood panels. Grade markings include the same index indicating allowable spacing of rafters and joists. The thickness of different products may vary for a given allowable spacing. This thickness is not important except that 8d threaded nails should be used for panels thicker than ¾ inch.

EXTERIOR WALL FRAMING

The floor framing and subfloor covering provide a working platform for construction of the wall framing. The term "wall framing" usually refers to exterior walls rather than interior partitions, and it includes vertical studs and horizontal members, (i.e., top and bottom plates and window and door headers). Exterior walls may be load-bearing (supporting ceilings, upper floor, and/or roof), or they may be nonload-bearing (i.e., not supporting a structural load, such as under the gable end of one-story houses). Wall framing also serves as a nailing base for wall covering materials.

Wall-framing members are generally 2x4-inch studs spaced 16 inches or 24 inches on center, depending on vertical loads and the support requirements of the covering materials. Top plates and bottom plates are also 2x4 inches in size. An alternative is the use of 2x6 lumber for wall framing, to provide space for greater amounts of insulation.

Headers over doors or windows in load-bearing walls consist of doubled 2x6-inch and deeper members, depending on the span of the opening.

Requirements

The requirements for wall-framing lumber are stiffness, good nail-holding ability, and freedom from warp. Species used may include Douglas fir, white fir, hemlocks, spruces, and pines. As noted in the section on "Floor Framing," the grades vary by species, but it is common practice to use a "Stud" grade for studs, and a "No. 2" or better grade for plates and for headers over doors and windows.

As with floor framing, the lumber for wall framing should be reasonably dry. The moisture content of wall-framing members, such as studs, plates, and headers, should not exceed 19 percent, and a maximum moisture content of 15 percent is much more desirable. If the moisture content of the lumber is in question, it is advisable to take the steps described in Chapter 1 under "Protection of Materials" to reduce moisture to in-service conditions before applying interior trim.

The ceiling height in most homes is nominally 8 feet. It is common practice to rough-frame the wall (subfloor to top of upper plate) to a height of 8 feet 1 inch. Precut studs are often supplied to a length of 92½ inches, allowing for a single bottom plate and a double top plate, each 1½ inches thick. If a single top plate is used, stud length will be 94 inches. This height allows the use of two 4-foot sheets of gypsum wallboard, applied horizontally, to finish the interior of the wall, along with clearance for the ceiling finish, which is applied first. A lower ceiling height can be used to reduce exterior wall finish or to reduce stair rise/run. However, the finished ceiling height should not be less than 7 feet 6 inches (rough height: 7 feet 7 inches). Areas under sloping ceilings may be as low as 5 feet, provided that one-half of the floor area has a clearance of at least 7 feet 6 inches.

Platform Construction

The wall framing in platform construction is erected over the subfloor which extends to the outer edge of the building (Figure 53). The most common method of framing is horizontal assembly on the subfloor and "tilt-up" of completed sections. When a sufficient work crew is available, full-length wall sections can be erected in this fashion. Otherwise, shorter sections easily handled by a smaller crew are preferable.

The horizontal assembly method involves laying down a top plate and a bottom plate with precut studs, window and door headers, window sills, and cripple studs (short-length studs) arranged between. Corner studs and headers are usually nailed together beforehand to form single units. Top and bottom plates are then nailed to studs. Headers and window aprons are nailed to adjoining studs with 12d or 16d nails. A 4x8 sheet of structural sheathing or siding should be installed at each end of the wall to provide resistance to racking. Alternative methods of providing racking resistance are to install let-in bracing, steel X-bracing, or rigid steel braces.

Wall sheathing and/or siding may be installed while the wall is in the horizontal position. Complete finished walls with windows and door units in place can also be fabricated in this manner. The entire section is then tilted up, plumbed, and braced (Figure 53). Bottom plates are then nailed to the floor joists through the subfloor and the corners are joined.

Where the structure is designed to have overhead roof or floor framing members bear directly over studs, a single top plate is used (Figure 54). However, if roof- or floor-framing members will bear on the top plate between studs, the top plate must be doubled. Where a double top plate is used, the second top plate is added so that it laps the first plate

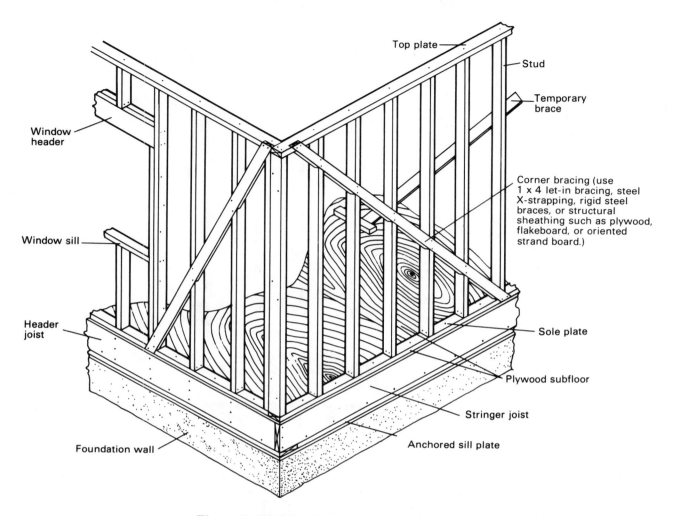

Top plate

Stud

Temporary brace

Corner bracing (use 1 x 4 let-in bracing, steel X-strapping, rigid steel braces, or structural sheathing such as plywood, flakeboard, or oriented strand board.)

Window header

Window sill

Sole plate

Header joist

Plywood subfloor

Stringer joist

Foundation wall

Anchored sill plate

Figure 53. Wall framing with platform construction

at corners and at wall intersections. This provides an additional tie for the framed walls. The second top plate can be fastened in place either when the wall is in a horizontal position or after it is erected. Top plates are nailed together with 12d or 16d nails spaced 24 inches apart and with two nails at each wall intersection.

In areas subject to hurricanes or high winds, it is often advisable to fasten wall and floor framing to the anchored foundation sill when sheathing does not provide this tie. Figure 55 illustrates one system of anchoring the studs to the floor framing with steel straps.

Several arrangements of studs at outside corners can be used in framing the walls. Blocking between two corner studs is the traditional method for providing a nailing edge for interior finish, as shown in

Figure 56A. A variation of the traditional method is shown in Figure 56B. A third method, which uses less lumber and provides more space for insulation, is the use of wallboard backup clips as shown in Figure 56C.

Interior walls should be fastened to all exterior walls where they intersect. This intersection should also provide backup support for the interior wall finish. Traditionally, this has been done by doubling the studs in the exterior wall at the intersection with the interior wall (Figure 57A). However, there is no structural requirement for extra studs at such an intersection. A mid-height block between exterior wall studs can be used to support the partition stud. This method requires the use of wallboard backup clips to support the drywall (Figure 57B).

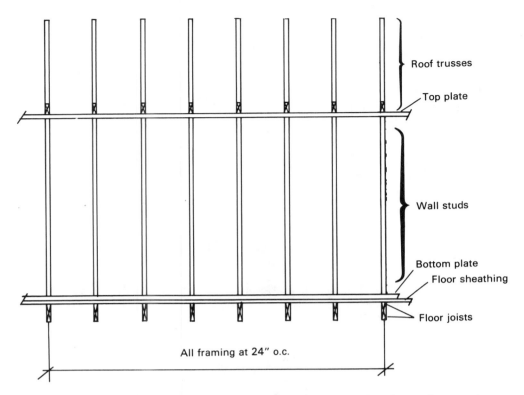

Figure 54. Vertical alignment of framing members simplifies framing and transmits loads directly down through structural members

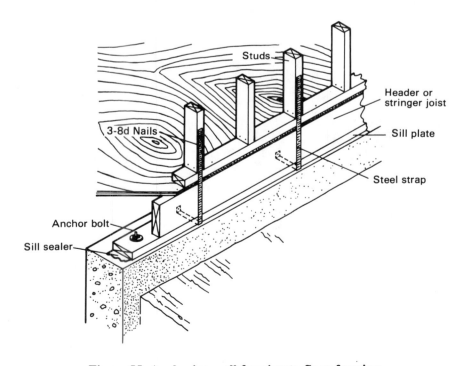

Figure 55. Anchoring wall framing to floor framing

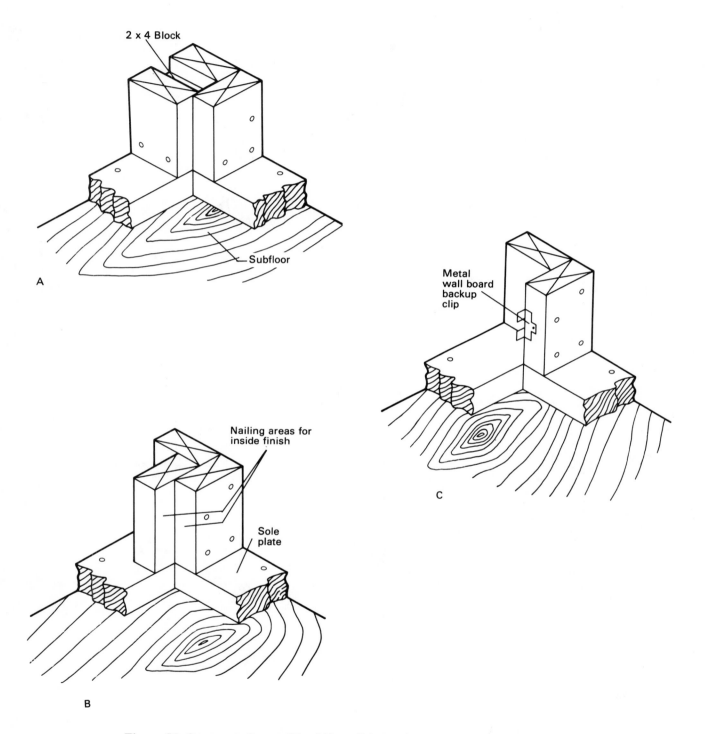

2 x 4 Block

Subfloor

A

Metal
wall board
backup
clip

C

Nailing areas for
inside finish

Sole
plate

B

**Figure 56. Corner stud assembly: (A) traditional three-stud corner with blocking;
(B) three-stud corner without blocking;
(C) two-stud corner with wallboard backup clips**

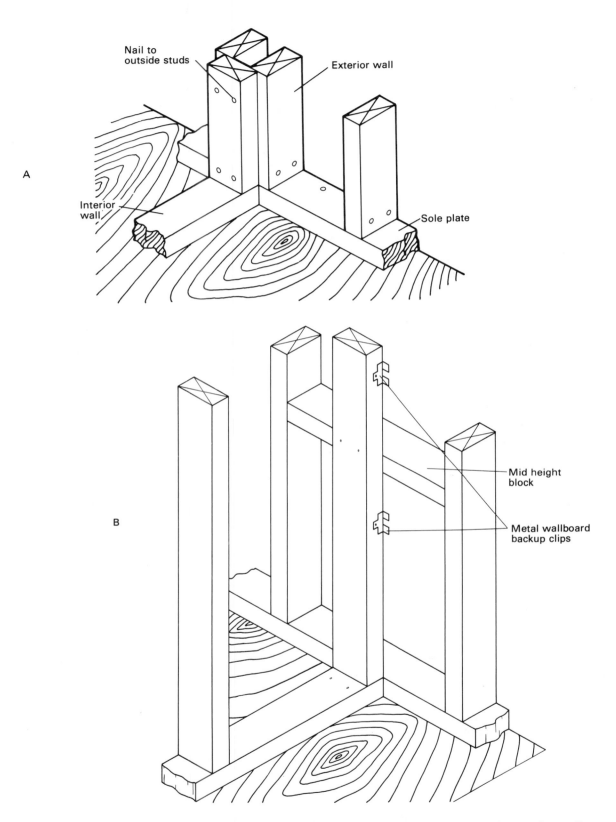

Figure 57. Intersection of interior partition and exterior wall: (A) double studs in exterior wall; (B) horizontal blocking to support partition

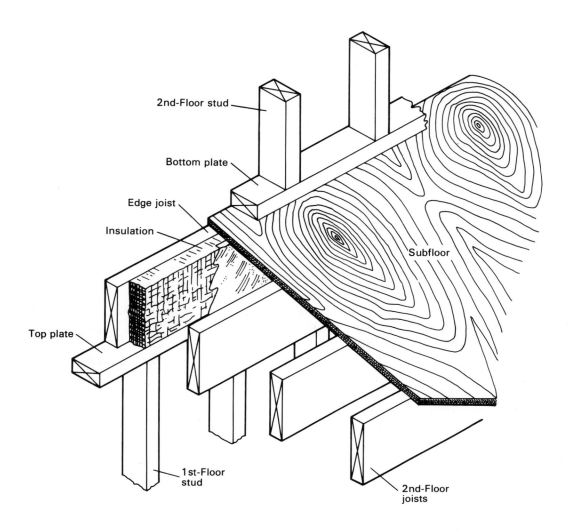

Figure 58. Second-story framing for platform construction

Second-Story Framing

Figure 58 shows a commonly used method of wall and ceiling framing for platform construction in 1½-story or 2-story houses with finished rooms above the first floor. The edge floor joist is toe-nailed to the top wall plate with 8d nails spaced 24 inches on center. The subfloor and wall framing are then installed in the same manner as for the first floor.

Window and Door Framing

The members used to span over window and door openings are called headers or lintels (Figure 59). As the span of the opening increases, it is necessary to increase the depth of these members to support the ceiling and roof loads. A header is traditionally made up of two 2-inch members spaced with ½-inch lath or plywood strips, all of which are nailed together for convenience in handling. However, from a structural point of view, it is not necessary to nail these members together, or even to space them apart. The lath or plywood spacers are used only to bring the faces of the header flush with the edges of the studs. In addition, lighter load conditions may only require a single header member.

Headers are supported at the ends by the inner studs or jack studs of the double stud assembly at each side of the window or door opening. Species and grades of wood normally used for floor joists are appropriate for headers. Table 10 shows an abbreviated list of allowable spans for 2x8 headers. It is good practice to ask the local building official to review in advance the species, grade, and dimension of material planned for headers.

A structural header can also be made by applying a plywood skin to framing members above openings in a load-bearing wall. Plywood ½-inch-thick may be nailed or glue-nailed to framing members to form a plywood box header over openings (Figure 60). The plywood may be applied to the inside or outside, or both sides, of the framing. AD interior grade plywood may be used on the interior side and may be taped and spackled to blend with standard ½-inch gypsum wallboard. CDX sheathing or better exterior-grade plywood should be used on the exterior side. As shown in Figure 60, stiffeners can be used to prevent the plywood skin from flexing.

One benefit of plywood box headers is that they can be fully insulated. Another benefit is that potential shrinkage with a lumber header is almost eliminated. Figure 60 shows a typical plywood header with the plywood nailed to the exterior side only.

The studs, headers, and aprons should provide a rough opening as recommended by the manufacturer of the door or window unit. The dimensions of the rough openings required for installation of doors and windows should be carefully checked. It is good practice to make a list of these dimensions and to keep the list available for quick reference during framing. The framing height to the bottom of the window and door headers should be based on the door heights, normally 6 feet 8 inches for the main floor. To allow for the thickness and clearance of the head jambs of window and door frames, the bottoms of the headers are usually located 6 feet 10 inches or 6 feet 11 inches above the subfloor, depending on the type of finish floor used. This dimension conveniently permits a 2x8-inch header to be installed immediately beneath a single top plate in a 7-foot 7-inch wall, eliminating the need for short cripples in a traditional 8-foot 1-inch wall.

EXTERIOR WALL SHEATHING

Exterior wall sheathing is the covering applied over the outside wall framework of studs, plates, and window and door headers. It forms a base upon which the exterior finish can be applied. Certain types of sheathing and methods of application can give the house great rigidity, eliminating the need for special corner bracing. Sheathing also serves to reduce air infiltration and, in certain forms, provides significant insulation. Some sheet materials serve both as sheathing and siding, eliminating the need for separate sheathing and siding layers.

Types of Sheathing

Types of sheathing include wood boards, insulating fiberboards, plywood, waferboard, oriented strand board, particleboard, composite panels of reconstituted wood cores between veneer facings, foil-faced laminated paperboards, gypsum boards, and a variety of rigid-formed plastic boards with or without facings. The oldest form of sheathing, now infrequently used, is *wood board*. This type of sheathing may not be available in some areas. When available, it is usually of nominal 1-inch thickness or resawn ⅝-inch boards in a square-edge pattern. The widths used are 6, 8, and 10 inches. The boards may be applied horizontally or diagonally; when they are applied diagonally, corner bracing can be eliminated.

Insulating fiberboard sheathings consist of an organic fiber coated or impregnated with asphalt or given other treatment for water resistance. Occasional wetting and drying that might occur during construction will not damage the sheathing significantly. Galvanized or other corrosion-resistant fasteners are recommended for installation.

Three types of insulating fiberboards are regular density, intermediate density, and nail base. Regular density is used for cover only, where no racking resistance or structural support is needed. Where structural support is required, intermediate density is used. Nail-base fiberboard will hold nails; it is well suited as a sheathing beneath sidings that require nailing at other than stud locations. Additional corner bracing is usually not required for intermediate and nail-base sheathing when they are properly applied with long edges aligned vertically. Shingles used for siding can be applied directly to nail-base sheathing if they are fastened with special annular-grooved nails.

Insulating boards are manufactured in ½-inch thickness and in 4x8-foot and 4x9-foot sizes for vertical applications of ½-inch regular, density sheathing. Insulating board sheathing should be fastened to the wall framing with 1½-inch roofing nails or with 1⅝-inch-wide crown staples.

Table 10
Allowable 2x8 header spans for different load conditions

Assumptions: Floor live and dead load of 50 lbs. per sq. ft.
Roof live and dead load of 30 lbs. per sq. ft.

Load carried by header	Minimum required Bending Stress (f)[1]	Minimum required Horizontal Shear (H)[2]	Header compo-sition	House depth in feet				
				24	26	28	30	32
Floor only	1000	75	1-2x8	3'8"	3'5"	3'3"	3'1"	2'11"
			2-2x8	6'8"	6'6"	6'3"	6'1"	5'10"
Roof only	1000	75	1-2x8	4'0"	3'9"	3'6"	3'3"	3'1"
			2-2x8	7'0"	6'9"	6'6"	6'4"	6'2"
Roof and floor	1000	75	1-2x8	2'1"	2'0"	—	—	—
			2-2x8	4'3"	4'0"	3'9"	3'6"	3'4"
Floor only	1000	90	1-2x8	4'5"	4'2"	3'11"	3'8"	3'6"
			2-2x8	8'2"	7'11"	7'8"	7'5"	7'0"
Roof only	1500	90	1-2x8	4'10"	4'6"	4'2"	3'11"	3'8"
			2-2x8	8'6"	8'3"	8'0"	7'9"	7'6"
Roof and floor	1500	90	1-2x8	2'6"	2'4"	2'3"	2'1"	2'0"
			2-2x8	5'0"	4'9"	4'5"	4'2"	4'0"

Assumptions: Roof live and dead load increased to 40 lbs. per sq. ft.

Load carried by header	Bending Stress	Horizontal Shear	Header composition	24	26	28	30	32
Roof only	1000	75	1-2x8	3'0"	2'10"	2'7"	2'5"	2'4"
			2-2x8	6'0"	5'7"	5'3"	4'11"	4'7"
Roof and floor	1000	75	1-2x8	—	—	—	—	—
			2-2x8	3'7"	3'4"	3'2"	3'0"	2'10"
Roof only	1500	90	1-2x8	3'7"	3'4"	3'2"	2'11"	2'9"
			2-2x8	7'3"	6'9"	6'3"	5'11"	5'7"
Roof and floor	1500	90	1-2x8	2'2"	2'0"	—	—	—
			2-2x8	4'4"	4'0"	3'9"	3'7"	3'4"

Assumptions: Roof live and dead load increased to 50 lbs. per sq. ft.

Load carried by header	Bending Stress	Horizontal Shear	Header composition	24	26	28	30	32
Roof only	1000	75	1-2x8	2'5"	2'3"	2'1"	2'0"	—
			2-2x8	4'9"	4'6"	4'2"	3'11"	3'8"
Roof and floor	1000	75	1-2x8	—	—	—	—	—
			2-2x8	3'2"	2'11"	2'9"	2'7"	2'5"
Roof only	1500	90	1-2x8	2'10"	2'8"	2'6"	2'4"	2'3"
			2-2x8	5'9"	5'4"	5'0"	4'8"	4'5"
Roof and floor	1500	90	1-2x8	—	—	—	—	—
			2-2x8	3'9"	3'6"	3'4"	3'1"	2'11"

Source: NAHB Research Foundation. *Reducing Home Building Costs with OVE Design and Construction.* 1977.

[1] The minimum Bending Stress (f) measures strength and varies with the species and grade of lumber, as shown in Appendix A.

[2] The Horizontal Shear is a measure of cross-grain breaking strength and varies with the species and grade of lumber, as shown in Appendix A.

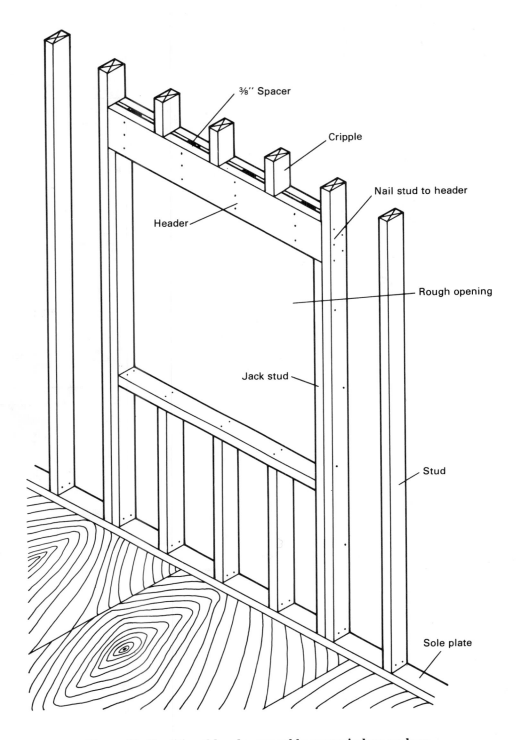

Figure 59. Traditional header assembly over window or door openings in load-bearing wall

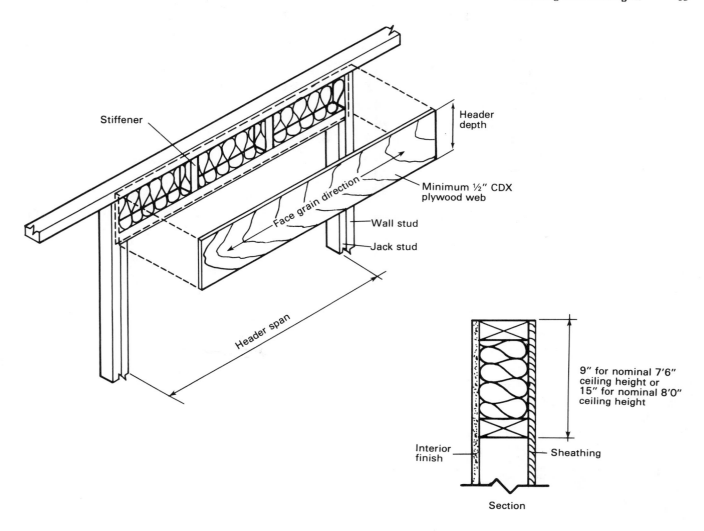

**Figure 60. Nail-only plywood open-box header for spans
up to 8 feet (plywood on exterior side)**

Plywood sheathing is available in thicknesses ranging from 5/16 inch to ¾ inch in various grades and constructions, for stud spacings of 16 inches and 24 inches on center. When plywood sheathing is adequately nailed, additional corner bracing is not required. Entire walls can be covered with 4x8-foot sheets applied vertically or horizontally. Alternatively, plywood sheathing can be used at corners only, with the remainder of the wall being covered with other sheathing materials. In this method, plywood panels replace corner bracing.

Specific recommendations on selection and use of plywood and reconstituted wood panel sheathing materials appear in American Plywood Association publications listed in the section on *Additional Reading.*

Waferboard is described in the section on "Roof Sheathing." Waferboard sheathing is commonly available in thicknesses ranging from 7/16 inch to ¾ inch. The most common panel size is 4x8 feet, but it can be obtained in sizes up to 4x16 feet or larger. Waferboard sheathing is installed in much the same manner as plywood sheathing, although many local codes require that the waferboard be ⅛-inch thicker than plywood for the same applications.

Oriented strand board, often called OSB, is a composite panel of compressed strandlike wood particles arranged in layers, usually three to five, oriented at right angles to each other in the same fashion as plywood. Bonding is accomplished with a phenolic resin, as with waferboard. Production thicknesses and panel sizes are similar to waferboard.

Structural particleboard sheathing is composed of small wood particles usually arranged in layers by particle size, but not usually with a particular strand orientation. As with other reconstituted wood panel sheathing materials, the particles are bonded together with a phenolic resin. Available thicknesses and panel sizes are similar to waferboard.

Composite sheathing consists of a reconstituted wood core bonded between wood veneer face and back plies. This material has a surface appearance similar to plywood and, like plywood, is available in various thickness and panel sizes.

Foil-faced laminated paperboard sheathing is available in structural grades from several manufacturers. This material is composed of a laminated paperboard core treated for water resistance, over which aluminum-foil facings are applied. Panels are available in 4x8-foot and 4x9-foot sizes. Some are produced in 48¾-inch widths overlapping. Thickness is commonly slightly less than ⅛ inch. When panels are nailed in accordance with the manufacturers' recommendations, corner bracing can be eliminated.

Gypsum sheathing is composed of treated gypsum filler faced on two sides with water resistant paper. Panels are ½-inch thick and are either 2x8 feet in size for horizontal application or 4x8 feet or 4x9 feet for vertical application. The 2x8-foot size either has one edge grooved and the other with a matched V edge, or has square-edged sides. The 4x8-foot and 4x9-foot sizes have square edges only. If panels are properly nailed, corner bracing is not required.

Rigid-foam plastic sheathing consists of polystyrene, urethane, isocyanurate, or phenolic foam panels, in some instances faced with aluminum foil, aluminum-foil-laminated craft paper, or polyethylene sheet on one or both sides. These materials, with thermal resistance (R) values ranging from less than R-4 to over R-8 per inch of material thickness, are used primarily to enhance the total thermal res-

istance values of wall construction. All are non-structural; that is, some form of wall corner bracing is required. Panels for wall sheathing are usually produced in thickness from ⅜ inch to 1 inch and in panel sizes of 2x8 feet, 4x8 feet, 4x9 feet, or longer.

Corner Bracing

Corner bracing gives the structure rigidity as well as resistance to the racking forces of wind or earthquakes. External corners of houses should be braced when the type of sheathing used does not provide the bracing required.

Corner bracing materials include structural sheathing panels, 1x4-inch boards, or patented light-gauge steel corner braces available in several configurations. Structural sheathing bracing consists of panels of ½-inch plywood, flakeboard, or oriented strand board, applied vertically at the corners. When 1x4-inch boards are used, they should be let in to the outside face of the studs and set at a 45° angle from the bottom of the sole plate to the top of the wall plate or corner stud (Figure 53). Where window openings near the corner interfere with 45° braces, the angle can be increased, but the full length of the brace should cover at least three stud spaces.

Installation of Sheathing

Minimum thickness of wood sheathing is generally ¾ inch, and widths are usually 6, 8, and 10 inches. Sheathing boards should be nailed at each stud crossing, with two nails for the 6-inch and 8-inch widths and three nails for the 10-inch and 12-inch widths.

Board sheathing is commonly applied horizontally because it is easy to apply in this fashion and because there is less lumber waste than in the diagonal pattern. Horizontal sheathing, however, requires diagonal corner bracing for wall framework. Diagonal wood sheathing should be applied at a 45° angle. This method of sheathing adds greatly to the rigidity of the wall and eliminates the need for corner bracing. When diagonal sheathing is used, one more nail can be used at each stud; for example, three nails for 8-inch sheathing. Joints should be placed over the center of studs.

Manufacturers usually recommend vertical application of structural insulating board in 4x8-foot sheets. When so specified by local building regulations, spacing nails 3 inches on edges and 6 inches at intermediate framing members can eliminate the requirement for corner bracing when ½-inch medium density or nail-base structural insulating board sheathing is used. Galvanized roofing nails of 1½ inch length or 1⅝-inch-long wide-crown staples should be used to attach the boards to the framing. Manufacturers usually recommend ⅛-inch spacing between sheets to allow the sheathing panel to expand without buckling. Joints should be centered on framing members.

Plywood, waferboard, and other reconstituted wood panel materials should be 4x8 feet or longer and should be applied vertically with perimeter nailing to eliminate the need for corner bracing. For plywood ranging from 5/16 inch through ½ inch in thickness, 6d nails or 1⅝-inch-long narrow-crown staples are used. Spacing of the fasteners should be 6 inches at all edges and 12 inches at intermediate framing members.

These sheathing materials may also be applied horizontally, but this somewhat reduces rigidity and strength. When it is done, some codes require blocking between studs for horizontal edge nailing to improve rigidity and eliminate the need for bracing. Edge spacing of ⅛ inch and end spacing of 1/16 inch between panel sheets should be maintained.

If this type of sheathing is installed only at corners to eliminate let-in wood bracing, ½-inch thickness should be used. The panels should be nailed with 1½-inch galvanized roofing nails spaced 4 inches on center along panel edges, and 8 inches on center at intermediate supports.

Structural grades of foil-faced laminated paperboard sheathing should be applied vertically on the framing in 4x8-foot or longer sheets. Manufacturer's recommendations generally specify the use of 1¼-inch-long galvanized roofing nails spaced at 3 inches on center around panel edges, and 6 inches on center on all intermediate members, for 16-inch stud spacing. Some manufacturers supply a heavier grade of sheathing for 24-inch stud spacing, with a similar nailing schedule. Corner bracing is not needed when these materials are fastened in accordance with the manufacturer's instructions.

Gypsum sheathing is generally ½-inch thick. It should be applied horizontally; vertical joints should be staggered. Sheathing in 2x8-foot sheets should be nailed to the framing with 1½-inch galvanized roofing nails spaced about 3½ inches apart to produce seven nails in the 2-foot height. This procedure will eliminate the need for corner bracing. If corner bracing is used, the nail spacing can be increased to 8 inches on center. With 4x8-foot or 4x9-foot sheets, 1½-inch galvanized roofing nails should be used, spaced 4 inches on center around the edges and 7 inches on center along intermediate members.

Sheathing Paper

Sheathing paper may be applied over the sheathing material. The sheathing paper should have a "perm" value of 6.0 or more, allowing the movement of water vapor but resisting the entry of water in liquid form and aiding in the control of air infiltration. Fifteen-pound asphalt felt paper is a satisfactory material.

Ordinarily, sheathing paper is not used over plywood, fiberboard, or other water-resistant material, except for 8-inch or wider strips applied around window and door openings to minimize air infiltration. Wood board sheathing must be covered with sheathing paper. When the house is to be covered by a stucco or masonry veneer, a sheathing paper should be installed regardless of the sheathing material used. Sheathing paper should be installed horizontally, starting at the bottom of the wall. Succeeding layers should lap about 4 inches.

Air Infiltration Barrier Materials

Air infiltration barrier sheet materials may consist of any of a variety of products, ranging from nonwoven fabrics to perforated plastic membranes. These materials are resistant to the passage of moving air but allow water vapor to escape. They can be used in all parts of the country, but are particularly effective in cold and/or windy climates. They are usually supplied in roll form in widths of 4 or 8 feet. Installation instructions are supplied by the manufacturer.

CEILING AND ROOF FRAMING

Roof frames provide structural members to which roofing, vents, and finish ceiling materials may be attached and within which insulation materials may be placed. Pitching of roof surfaces creates space for storage and living space that costs less than main floor space, because no additional foundation is required and because roof costs do not increase proportionately with the increase in living space.

Roof Designs

Roofs sometimes use one structural member as both ceiling and roofing support, as in flat or shed roofs in which the angle of the roof is the same as that of the ceiling. The most common roof configuration, however, is an isosceles triangle. Rafters or top chords of trusses form equal-length sloping sides to which roofing materials are attached. Ceiling joists or bottom truss chords form the horizontal base to which ceiling materials are fastened.

In a single-member roof, support must be provided on both ends by walls or beams. In the triangular roof, the ceiling joists require intermediate bearing support within the house, but the roof rafters usually do not. Since their weight and the weight they support is all transferred to the bottom, the rafters tend to push out at the bottom and fall in the center where they meet. They are restrained from doing so by the ceiling joists which are placed in tension and which consequently must be securely fastened to the rafters and to each other where spliced.

Most species of softwood framing lumber are acceptable for roof framing, subject to maximum allowable spans for the particular species, grade, and use. Because all species are not equally strong, larger sizes, as determined from the design, must be used for weaker species for a given span. All framing lumber should be well seasoned (dried). Lumber that is 2 inches thick or less should have a maximum moisture content not over 19 percent, with 15 percent being more desirable

The most commonly built roofs are made with triangular trusses in which the three sides of the triangle are fastened together with steel plates and reinforced with interior web members. Wood trusses can span up to 50 feet, and they are designed to require support only at the two ends of the base or bottom chord.

The slope of a roof is generally expressed as the number of inches of vertical rise in 12 inches of horizontal run. The rise is given first: for example, 4-in-12 or 4/12 pitch.

The architectural style of a house often determines the type of roof and roof slope. A contemporary design may have a flat or slightly pitched roof; a rambler or ranch type may have an intermediate slope; a Cape Cod cottage may have a steep slope.

Another consideration in roof slope is the type of roofing desired. For example, a built-up roof is permitted on flat roofs or slopes up to 2-in-12, depending on the type of asphalt or coal-tar pitch and aggregate surfacing materials used. Rolled roofing can be used on pitches of 1-in-12 or steeper. Wood or asphalt shingles are permitted on 4-in-12 pitches or steeper.

The most popular roof style is the gable roof, a triangular roof system in which the triangles are terminated at the ends of the house by triangular end walls called gables, which close in the attic space. Next most common is the hip roof — another triangular roof, in which the ends of the attic space are enclosed by sloping triangular roof sections set at right angles to the main roof planes and equal to them in pitch. Cape Cod and Saltbox styles use large second-floor shed dormers on the back and, often, eye dormers on the front to expand the attic space, admit light, and improve ventilation. Mansard, gambrel, and A-frame roofs use one frame member for both walls and roof. Post-and-beam, shed roofs, and flat roofs use one member to support both ceiling finishes and roofing.

On any roof, overhangs can be used to protect windows and siding from falling rain and to shade windows from the sun. Properly sized, overhangs allow sunlight to penetrate south-facing windows in the winter when solar heat is desired, but not in the summer when the sun is at a higher angle in the sky.

Manufactured Wood Roof Trusses

After exterior walls are plumbed and braced, manufactured wood roof trusses, when used, are normally placed across the width of the house and nailed to the top plates.

The roof truss is a rigid framework of triangular shapes which replaces rafters and ceiling joists. Roof sheathing is fastened to the top of the truss, and gypsum wallboard or other ceiling finish is fastened to the bottom. The truss is capable of supporting roof and ceiling loads over long spans without intermediate support. Typical roof truss spans for house construction are from 24 to 40 feet, but manufactured roof truss spans can range from 12 to 50 feet or more.

Trusses use less material than equivalent rafter/ ceiling joist systems. With the use of cranes, trusses require much less labor to erect and permit the house to be enclosed in a short time. Because no interior bearing walls are required, the entire house becomes one large workroom. Trusses also allow greater flexibility for interior planning, since partitions can be placed without regard to structural requirements.

Design and Fabrication. Trusses should be professionally engineered. Truss designs are based on analysis of the probable loadings of snow, wind, and roof and ceiling materials; the span over which the loads are to be carried; the shape of the truss; the location of bearing points; and the connectors used in joining the members. Assistance in truss design is available from truss dealers and fabricators. Most trusses are available with horizontal "return" blocks extending from the outer end of the overhang to the exterior of the wall to which soffit materials are fastened.

The purchaser normally specifies the span, pitch, spacing (normally 24 inches on center), style, and length of overhang; special loadings other than plywood roof sheathing, shingles, and ½-inch gypsum wallboard; and the quantities of trusses and gable trusses. The number of trusses required for a gable-roof house with the trusses installed on a 24-inch spacing equals the house length divided by two, rounded up, minus one. A gable end truss is required for each end of the roof. For example, a gable house 51 feet long requires 25 trusses plus two gable trusses.

Types of Trusses. Local prices, span, and design load requirements for snow, wind, and other conditions, determine the best type of truss to be used. Wood trusses most commonly used for houses include the Fink truss (web members form a W), the raised Fink, the gable, the King-post (one vertical web member), the Howe (web members form an M), the scissors (sloping bottom chords provide a vaulted ceiling), the hip (flat top), the attic (enclosing a rectangle of wall studs, bottom chord, and ceiling joist), and the floor truss (horizontal top and bottom chords). The general shapes of these common trusses are shown in Figure 61.

On L-shaped houses, trusses are used on most of the roof. A small portion of the roof joining the ridges and forming two valleys is completed by framing rafters on top of the trusses (Figure 62).

Trusses are commonly designed for 2-foot spacing. Three 12d common nails are used to fasten the bottom truss chord to each top wall plate. Plywood or waferboard sheathing ⅜-inch or ½-inch thick is nailed or stapled to the top with H-clip supports between the trusses on the sheathing edges.

The *Fink or W-type truss* (Figure 61A) is perhaps the most popular and extensively used of the light wood trusses. Two web members extending from the peak divide the bottom chord into three equal segments. From these points, web members return to the top chords, dividing them in half. The spans on the top chord are thus reduced, increasing their strength and stiffness and allowing them to be built of smaller size and/or lower grade lumber.

The *raised Fink or cantilevered truss* (Figure 61B) is a Fink truss in which the bottom chord cantilevers over the outside house walls and extends to the outer edge of the overhang. The weight of the roof is transferred to the walls by triangular heel wedges or compression blocks. This type of truss raises the height of the top chord where it passes over the outside wall. This permits a full thickness of ceiling insulation to be installed to the extreme outer edge of the exterior walls and allows additional vertical space for air to pass from soffit vents into the attic.

Gable trusses (Figure 61C) have flat, vertical members 16 inches or 24 inches apart to which sheathing and siding are attached. Since there is no triangular pattern of members, gable trusses are not as strong as other trusses and, if required to carry a load over a span, must be professionally engineered. Gable trusses normally are supported over their entire length by an exterior wall.

The *King-post* (Figure 61D), the simplest form of truss used for houses, is composed only of top and bottom chords and one center vertical web member or post. Lumber sizes must be greater and/or grades must be higher than those in the Fink (W-type) truss, since the span of the top chord is not broken by a web member and the bottom chord span is divided into two spans rather than three. For short and medium spans, the King-post truss is probably more economical than other types because is has fewer pieces and can be more easily fabricated.

The *Howe or M-type truss* (Figure 61E) is a King-post truss with additional web members starting at the bottom of the vertical center member, dividing the top chord, and returning vertically to the bottom chord. The Howe truss design divides the bottom chord into four equal segments. Assuming lumber of equal size and grade, the Howe truss can carry a heavier ceiling load than the Fink truss design,

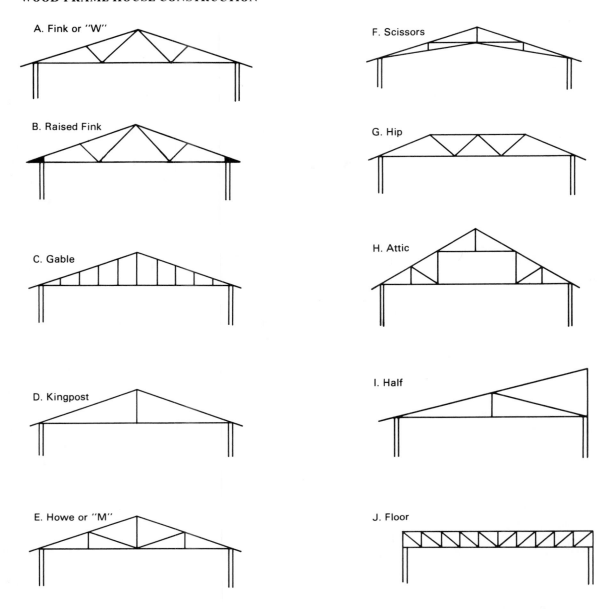

Figure 61. Common truss designs

which supports the bottom chord in two places instead of three.

The *scissors truss* (Figure 61F) provides a sloping interior ceiling without the need for center bearing for rafters on walls or ridge beams and posts. The top chords of the scissors truss are normally two or three pitches steeper than the bottom chords.

Hip trusses (Figure 61G) provide an easy way to construct a hip roof, which normally requires rafters of many different lengths with compound angle cuts. Hip trusses are trapezoids with equal pitch sides sloping up to flat tops. Each hip roof requires a

set of trusses ranging from a tall truss with a small flat top and long sloping sides to a short truss with a long flat top and short sloping sides. To complete the framing, short overhang rafters spaced 2 feet on center are extended at a right angle from the lowest truss over the end wall to the outer edge of the overhang.

The *attic truss* (Figure 61H) is a steep pitch truss designed to create second-story living or storage space. The bottom chord is normally a 2x8-inch or 2x10-inch floor joist, which must usually be supported by a wall or beam near the center. Vertical

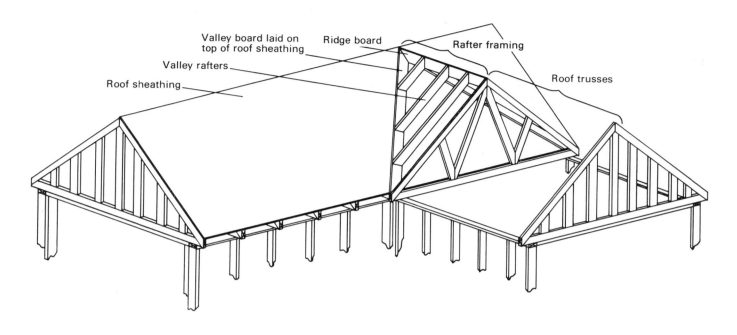

Valley board laid on top of roof sheathing   Ridge board   Rafter framing

Valley rafters

Roof sheathing

Roof trusses

Figure 62. Rafter framing joining perpendicular truss roof segments

studs run from the bottom chord to the sloping top chords, and a horizontal "ceiling joist" is positioned at a right angle to the top of the studs. The attic truss is sometimes too high for highway transportation. The top triangle of the truss is therefore sometimes made separately to reduce the truss height for shipment.

The *half truss* (Figure 61I) is a right triangle with the hypotenuse serving as the roof slope. It is frequently used in shed roof architecture.

Floor trusses (Figure 61J) can be used for "flat," slightly sloped roofs. These trusses have horizontal top and bottom chords and diagonal and vertical web members. The trusses are usually a minimum of 16 inches high. Some floor trusses are designed to provide space for ductwork.

Handling. Unusual stresses should not be placed on completed trusses during handling and storage. They are designed to carry roof loads in a vertical position and should be lifted and stored in an upright position. If they must be handled flat, enough workers or supports should be used to minimize lateral bending. Trusses should never be supported at the center, or only at each end, when in a flat position.

Erection. Five workers can install house trusses under 30 feet in length and up to 6-in-12 pitch. One sits on each wall to nail the trusses to the walls; another "rides" the ridge, standing on the bottom chord, to nail the top of the truss to a temporary 2x4-inch ridge brace on exact 2-foot centers; and the remaining members carry and hand the trusses up. With a crane, one less crew member is required on the ground.

The tops of the side walls and the temporary 2x4-inch ridge brace are marked on 2-foot centers. A gable truss is then set on top of the end wall, securely fastened to the wall on which it rests, and braced to the ground (Figure 63, step 1). Since all other trusses will be fastened to this gable truss by means of the ridge brace, gable bracing must be firm.

A 2x4-inch block is nailed in a horizontal position close to the top of the wall at the opposite end of the house from the gable truss. This block should extend out the precise width of, and at the exact height of, the planned roof overhang. A line is then strung the full length of the house between the end of this block and the end of the gable truss. Some builders set both gables first and string the line between the ends of their overhangs. Half-inch

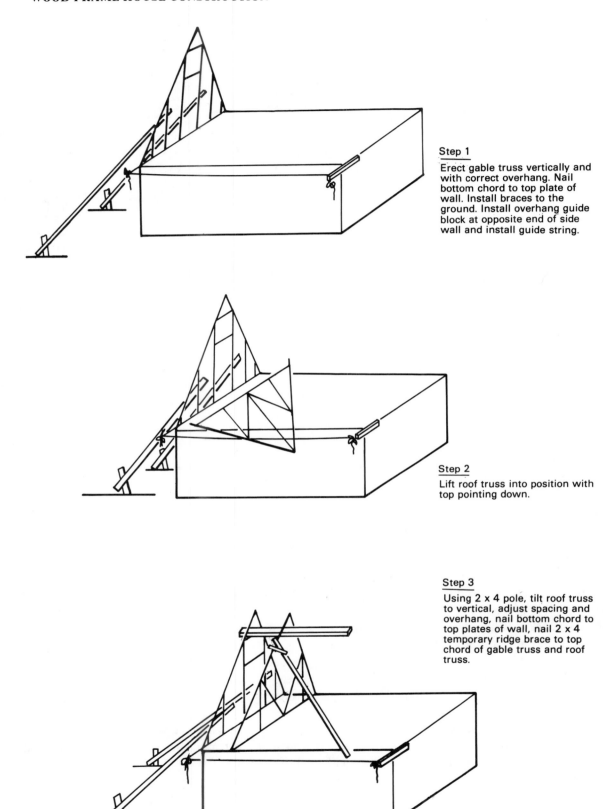

Step 1
Erect gable truss vertically and with correct overhang. Nail bottom chord to top plate of wall. Install braces to the ground. Install overhang guide block at opposite end of side wall and install guide string.

Step 2
Lift roof truss into position with top pointing down.

Step 3
Using 2 x 4 pole, tilt roof truss to vertical, adjust spacing and overhang, nail bottom chord to top plates of wall, nail 2 x 4 temporary ridge brace to top chord of gable truss and roof truss.

Figure 63. Erection of roof trusses

blocks are placed behind this string. Each truss, when it is installed, is brought to within ½-inch of the string using a ½-inch gauge block. The gauge block is used to prevent the trusses from pushing out on the string.

Next, a truss is slid horizontally over the top of the house wall and placed on the house, with the ends resting on the walls and the point facing down within the house (Figure 63, step 2). The truss is tipped up, using a long 2x4 with a short 2x4 nailed on the end to form a "Y." The truss is positioned on the 2-foot markings located on the wall and on the temporary 2x4 ridge brace; brought to the proper distance from the overhang guide string; nailed to the wall top plate with three 12d nails; and nailed to the temporary 2x4 ridge brace with one 10d duplex nail (Figure 63, step 3).

After six or seven trusses are erected, a temporary diagonal brace should be installed on top of the trusses running from the bottom of the gable truss to the top of the last truss on both sides of the house. This brace is then nailed into every truss with duplex nails. Temporary braces can prevent sudden gusts of wind from knocking down the trusses. These temporary braces should be removed in calm air, just before they are replaced with permanent braces and sheathing.

Trusses should be provided with permanent bracing according to the manufacturer's instructions. Diagonal braces are frequently placed at a 45° angle from the top of the gables to a bottom truss chord. In addition, continuous braces running the full length of the house are often required on top of the bottom chords beside the web members, and, on larger trusses, half-way up the web members.

In hurricane areas, twisted steel tie-down straps are recommended to secure the truss more firmly to the wall. These straps extend from the side of each truss to the face of the stud.

L-shaped houses have a perpendicular wing attached to the main house. Roof trusses are erected and sheathing installed on the main portion of the house. The roof trusses are then erected and the sheathing installed on the wing portion of the house. The two perpendicular roof lines are connected with rafter framing as shown in Figure 62. A 2x8 ridge board is installed between the peak of the roof trusses on the wing and the peak of the roof trusses on the main house. Valley boards of 2x8 lumber are installed on top of the main house roof sheathing

between the ridge board and the outer ends of the roof trusses on the house wing. Valley rafters of 2x6 lumber are installed on 16-inch centers between the ridge board and the valley boards. Roof sheathing is then applied on top of the rafter framing.

The ends of the main house roof trusses must be supported where the wing joins the main house. This support can be provided by an interior load-bearing wall. An alternative is to install a doubled or tripled roof truss on the wing at the exterior wall line of the main house. These trusses should be bolted together, and the main house roof trusses connected to and supported by their bottom chords with the aid of metal joist hangers. A truss manufacturer can provide the engineering necessary to determine the proper design of this configuration.

Ceiling Joists and Rafters

In lieu of manufactured trusses, roofs can be framed on site using rafters and ceiling joists. This method is usually more expensive and time consuming than using prebuilt trusses.

Ceiling Joists. Ceiling joists serve the same purpose as the bottom chords of a truss. They support ceiling finishes and serve as tension members to prevent the bottom of the roof rafters and tops of the walls from spreading outward. Ceiling joists often act as floor joists for second-story or attic floors, and as ties between exterior walls and interior partitions.

Ceilings can be framed on site from 2x6-inch or 2x8-inch lumber resting on exterior and interior walls. After the walls are plumbed and braced and the top plates added, ceiling joists are positioned and nailed into place. They are placed across the width of the house as are the rafters.

When possible, partitions should be located so that ceiling joists of even lengths such as 12, 14, 16 feet or longer can be used without waste to span from exterior walls to load-bearing interior walls. Joist sizes depend on span, wood species, spacing between joists, and the load they may support. Correct sizes for various conditions are designated by joist tables or local building code requirements.

Because ceiling joists serve as tension members to resist the thrust of the rafters on triangular roofs, they must be securely nailed to the plate at outer and inner walls. They are also nailed together, directly or with wood or metal cleats, where they lap or join at

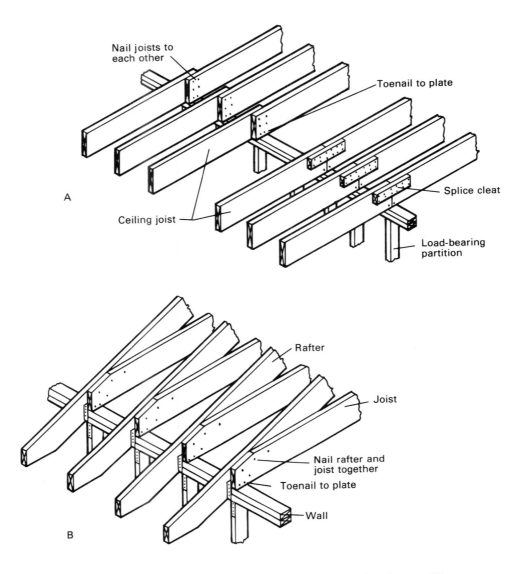

Figure 64. Ceiling joist connections: (A) at center bearing partition with joists lapped or butted; (B) at exterior wall

the interior load-bearing partition (Figure 64A), and to the rafter at the exterior walls (Figure 64B).

In areas with severe winds, it is good practice to use metal strapping or other systems of anchoring ceiling and roof framing to the wall.

The in-line joist system described in the section on "Floor Framing" can be adapted to ceiling or second-floor joists.

Flush Ceiling Joist Framing. In many house designs, the living room and the dining or family room form an open "L." A wide, continuous ceiling area between the two rooms is often desirable. This area can be created with a flush beam that replaces

the load-bearing partitions used in the remainder of the house. The ends of the joists are supported by nail-laminated built-up beams to carry the ceiling load. Joists are toe-nailed into the beam and further supported by metal joist hangers (Figure 65A) or 2x2-inch wood ledgers (Figure 65B).

Gable Roofs. The simplest form of triangular roof is the gable roof. The end walls of the house have triangular tops — gables — which close off the ends of the roof structure and attic space (Figure 66). All rafters are cut to the same length and pattern. Each pair of rafters is fastened at the top to a

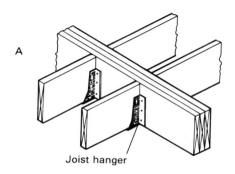

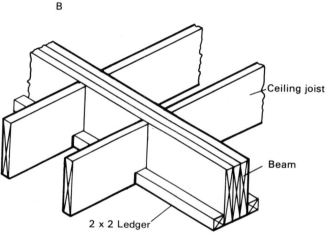

Figure 65. Framing of flush ceiling beam:
(A) joists attached with metal
joist hangers; (B) joists bearing
on 2x2-inch ledger

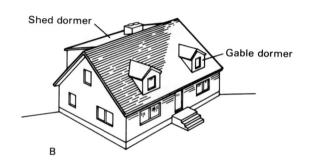

Figure 66. Pitched roof types:
(A) gable; (B) gable with dormers;
(C) hip

ridge board. The ridge board, usually a 1x8-inch member for 2x6-inch rafters, provides support and a nailing area for the rafter ends.

Rafters. In pitched-roof construction, the ceiling joists are nailed in place after the interior and the exterior wall framing are complete. Rafters should not be erected until ceiling joists are fastened in place, since the outward thrust of the rafters may push out the exterior walls.

Rafters are usually precut to length, with the proper angles cut at the ridge and eave and with

notches cut to rest on the top plates of the exterior walls (Figure 67). Rafters are erected in pairs. Studs for gable end walls are notched to fit under and past the end rafter and are nailed to the end rafter and the top plate of the end wall.

When roof spans are long and slopes are flat, it is common practice to use collar beams between opposing rafters. Steeper slopes and shorter spans may also require collar beams, but only between every third rafter pair. Collar beams can be 1x6-inch material. In 1½-story houses, 2x4-inch or larger collar beams are used at each pair of rafters and

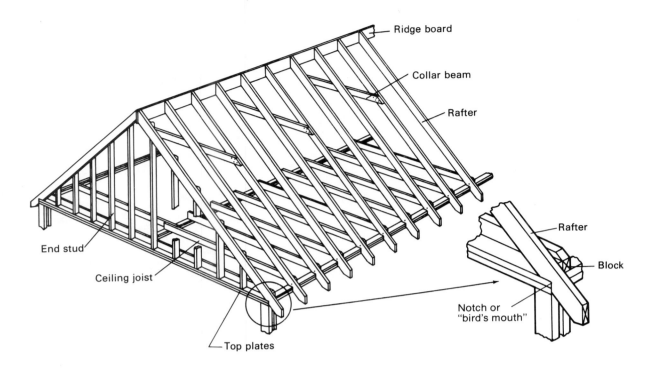

Figure 67. Typical rafter framing for pitched roof

serve also as ceiling joists for the upper-story finished rooms.

Overhang Rafters. With a gable (rake) overhang, an overhang or fly rafter is used beyond the end rafter and is fastened to the overhang blocking and to the sheathing. Additional construction details applicable to roof framing are given in the section on "Exterior Trim."

Valley Rafters. A valley is the internal angle formed by the juncture of the two sloping planes of perpendicular roof sections. The key member in valley construction is the valley rafter. In the intersection of two equal-size roof sections, the valley rafter is doubled (Figure 68) to carry the roof load and is 2 inches deeper than the other rafter members to provide full contact with jack rafters. Jack rafters are nailed to the ridge board and toe-nailed to the valley rafter with three 10d nails.

Hip Roof. The hip roof (Figure 66C) has no gable end. Center rafters are tied to the ridge board, and hip rafters (Figure 69) supply support for the shorter jack rafters. Cornice lines are carried around the entire perimeter of the building. Hip roofs are

framed in the same fashion as a gable roof at the center section of a rectangular house. The ends are framed with hip rafters that extend from each outside corner of the wall to the ridge board at a 45° angle. Jack rafters extend from the top plates to the hip rafters (Figure 69).

Cape Cod and Saltbox. A variation of the gable roof, used for Cape Cod or Saltbox house styles, includes the use of shed and gable dormers (Figure 66B). The ridgeline on the Cape Cod is in the center of the roof; on the Saltbox the ridgeline is off center. Both are 1½-story houses with about half as much living space upstairs as down. Second-floor space and light are provided by shed or gable dormers for bedrooms and bath. Roof slopes for this style may vary from 9-in-12 to 12-in-12 to provide the needed upper-story headroom.

Gable Dormers. In construction of small gable (eye) dormers, the rafters at each side of the dormer opening are doubled. The side studs and the short valley rafter rest on these members (Figure 70). Side studs can be carried past the rafters to bear on a bottom plate nailed to the floor framing and subfloor. This type of framing can be used for the

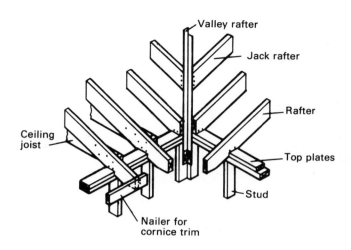

Figure 68. Framing at valley in rafter roof

sidewalls of shed dormers. The valley rafter is also tied to the roof framing at the roofline by a header. Methods of fastening at top plates conform to those previously described. Where future expansion is contemplated or where additional rooms may be built in an attic, consideration should be given to framing and enclosing such dormers when the house is built.

Joistless Post-and-Beam Framing. Sloping ceilings are often used in contemporary interior design. These can be constructed with scissors trusses or with single-member framing in which the ends of rafters bear on walls or beams at different elevations (Figure 71).

By replacing interior load-bearing partitions with beams bearing on posts, larger rooms can be formed. The combination of vaulted ceilings and fewer interior walls increases the feeling of spaciousness. Enough interior shear walls must be used, however, to provide sufficient racking strength.

The beams can be made of 4x8-inch, 4x10-inch, or 4x12-inch solid timbers; 2-inch boards nailed together; or, on long spans, plywood box construction, glue-laminated wood, or steel. Posts are usually 4x4 inches. Unusually long posts or those carrying unusually heavy loads may need to be 6x6 inches or larger. Post and beam sizes, grades, and configurations should be professionally determined.

Frequently, one end of the rafter bears on exterior walls and the other end bears on a ridge beam. Sometimes intermediate beams are also used.

Because the rafters are supported on both ends and the weight from the roof is carried to beams and posts in the center of the house as well as to the outside walls, there is no need for horizontal ties. Ceiling joists and collar ties can be eliminated.

Exposed 4x6-inch or 4x8-inch rafters may be installed on a 32-inch or 48-inch spacing. Decking of 2x6-inch tongue-and-groove material is frequently used to span from joist-to-joist, wall-to-beam, or beam-to-beam. This decking serves both as structural sheathing and as interior ceiling finish material. Rigid foam insulation can be placed on top of the decking and covered with shingles fastened with long nails.

In other cases, rafters are concealed. Insulation is placed between them with a minimum 1-inch ventilation space between the top of the insulation and the underside of the roof sheathing. This method should be combined with continuous soffit and ridge venting. Rigid foam insulation can be nailed to the bottom of the rafters with the finish ceiling material installed below the insulation (Figure 72).

Flat Roofs. Flat or low-pitched roofs, sometimes known as shed roofs, can take a number of forms (Figure 73). Roofs of this type require larger members than do steeper pitched roofs because they carry both roof and ceiling loads. A major concern

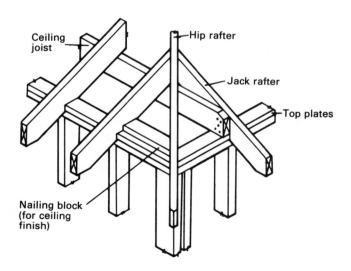

Figure 69. Framing at corner of hip rafter roof

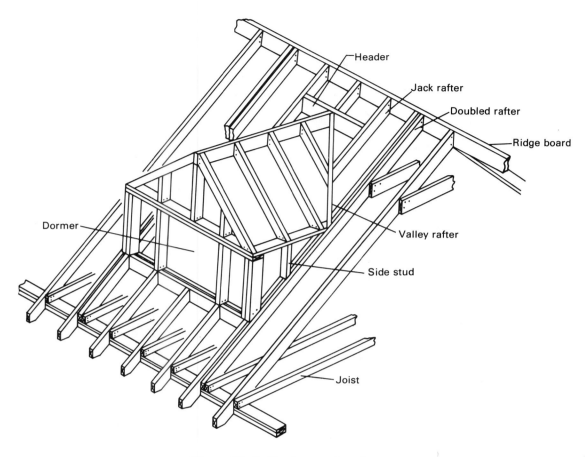

Header
Jack rafter
Doubled rafter
Ridge board
Valley rafter
Side stud
Dormer
Joist

Figure 70. Gable dormer framing

in flat-roof construction is the increased likelihood of roof leaks.

Roof joists for flat roofs are laid level or with a slight pitch. Roof sheathing and roofing are placed on top, and the underside supports the ceiling. A slight slope for roof drainage can be provided by tapering the joist or adding a cant strip to the top.

Flat-roof design usually includes an overhang of the roof beyond the wall. Insulation is installed with an airway directly under the roof sheathing to minimize condensation problems in winter.

When solid wood decking on beams is used, the beams eliminate the need for joists. Roof decking used between beams serves as supporting members, interior finish, and roof sheathing. It also provides a moderate amount of insulation (about R-2 for 1½-inch thick decking). In cold climates, rigid insulating materials are used over the decking to further reduce heat loss.

When flat roofs have an overhang on all sides, "lookout" rafters are ordinarily used (Figure 74).

These are nailed to a doubled header and toe-nailed to the wallplate. The distance from the doubled header to the wall line is usually twice the overhang width. Rafter ends may be finished with a nailing header for fastening soffit and facia boards. Care should be taken to provide ventilation for these soffit areas. (Refer to Chapter 4, section on "Attic Ventilation.")

While these roof types are the most common, others include such forms as the Mansard and the A-frame where the same members serve for wall and roof.

ROOF SHEATHING

Roof sheathing is the covering applied over roof rafters and trusses to give racking resistance to the roof framing and to provide surface for attachment of the roof covering materials. Plywood is the most

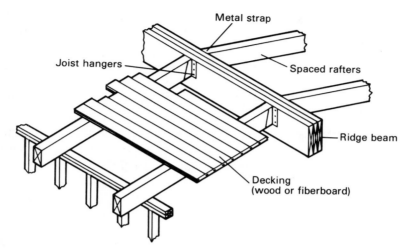

Figure 71. Sloping ceiling in post-and-beam construction

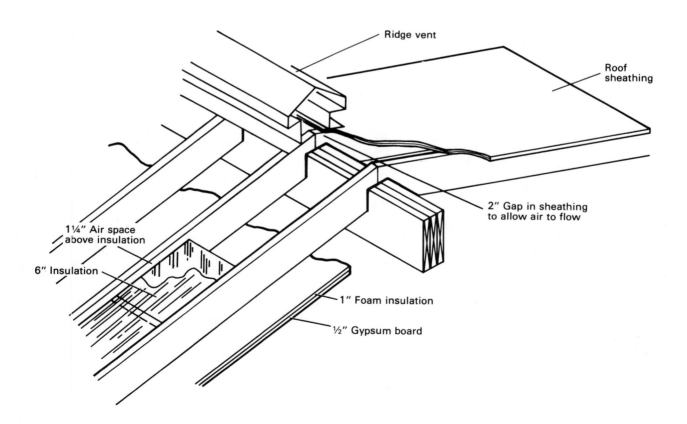

Figure 72. Sloping ceiling with concealed rafters

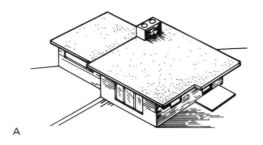

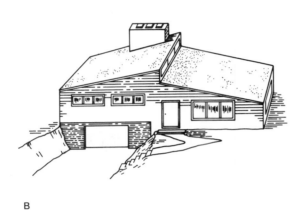

Figure 73. Roof types with single member construction: (A) flat roof; (B) low-pitched roof

commonly used material. Waferboard and 1-inch lumber can also be used. In some types of flat or low-pitched roofs, wood roof planking or fiberboard roof decking can be used. Regardless of material, sheathing must be thick enough to span between supports and to provide a solid base for fastening the roofing material.

Plywood and waferboard roof sheathing are commonly designated as standard sheathing grade. For lumber sheathing, lower grades of species such as pine, redwood, hemlock, western larch, fir, and spruces are commonly used. It is important that seasoned lumber be used with asphalt shingles. Unseasoned wood will dry out and shrink in width and may cause buckling or lifting of the shingles. Fifteen percent is usually considered to be the maximum allowable moisture content for wood sheathing.

Plywood Roof Sheathing

U.S. Voluntary Standard PS 1 specifies that standard plywood grades be marked for allowable spacing of rafters or trusses. For rafter spacing of 24 inches on center, ⅜-inch plywood is the minimum thickness where wood shingles or shakes or asphalt shingles are being used. For rafter spacing of 16 inches on center, 5/16-inch plywood sheathing is the minimum. To provide better penetration for nails used for the shingles, better racking resistance, and a smoother appearance, it is sometimes desirable to use material above the minimum thickness. For slate and similar heavy roofing materials, ⅝-inch plywood is considered minimum for 24-inch on-center rafter spacing, and ½-inch plywood for 16-inch on-center spacing.

Plywood roof sheathing should be laid with the face grain perpendicular to the rafters (Figure 75). Standard sheathing grade is commonly specified, but, where conditions are damp, it is desirable to use a standard sheathing grade with exterior glueline. It is unnecessary to stagger plywood end joints over alternate trusses. Full sheets can be applied, starting from either end. This procedure simplifies sheathing layout and application and may reduce the number of cuts.

Plywood should be fastened at each bearing, 6 inches on center along the edges of the panel and 12 inches on center along intermediate members. A 6d common nail, 5d threaded nail, or 1⅜-inch narrow crown staple should be used for 5/16-inch and ⅜-inch plywood. An 8d common nail, 7d threaded nail, or 1⅝-inch staple should be used for greater thicknesses.

Care should be taken during nailing to prevent "nailing in" a permanent set or deflection in the plywood between trusses. This deflection is caused by the weight of the installer standing or kneeling on the plywood while the nailing is being performed. It is better practice for the installer to stand either on the trusses or on adjacent plywood panels that have already been nailed into place.

Unless plywood has an exterior glueline, raw edges should not be exposed to the weather at the gable end or at the eave, but should be protected by the trim or an aluminum drip edge. A ⅛-inch edge space and a 1/16-inch end space should be left between sheets when installing to allow for possible expansion.

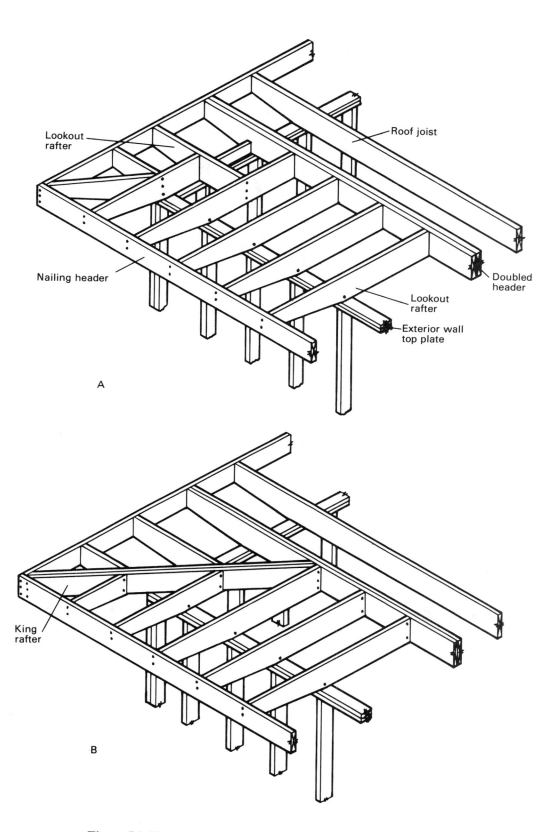

**Figure 74. Single-member roof construction with overhang:
(A) less than 3-foot overhang; (B) more than 3-foot overhang**

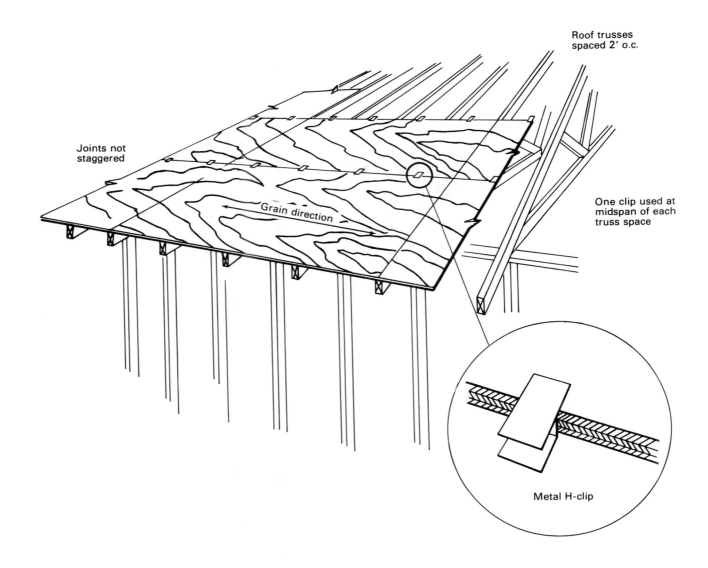

Roof trusses
spaced 2' o.c.

Joints not
staggered

Grain direction

One clip used at
midspan of each
truss space

Metal H-clip

Figure 75. Plywood roof sheathing with "H" clips for edge support

Most plywood roof sheathing edges that run perpendicular to the roof framing must be supported by wood blocking or fastened together with metal fasteners. These metal fasteners are called plyclips or "H" clips (Figure 75) and are the least costly method of providing the necessary edge support. No special edge support is required if the plywood roof sheathing has tongue-and-groove edges or if the plywood is ⅛-inch thicker than the minimum thickness required by the spacing of the roof framing. Blocking between trusses at the roof ridge and supporting the sheathing edges at the ridge are unnecessary.

Waferboard Sheathing

Waferboard is composed of waferlike particles or flakes, randomly or directionally oriented, interleafed together in thick mats, and bonded together with waterproof resins under heat and pressure. Waferboard panels are comparable to plywood in strength and water resistance, two key properties for exterior sheathing. Rafter or truss spacing, nailing, and edge treatments are the same as for plywood, and the same thicknesses are used. Some waferboard panels have fibers aligned to increase the directional

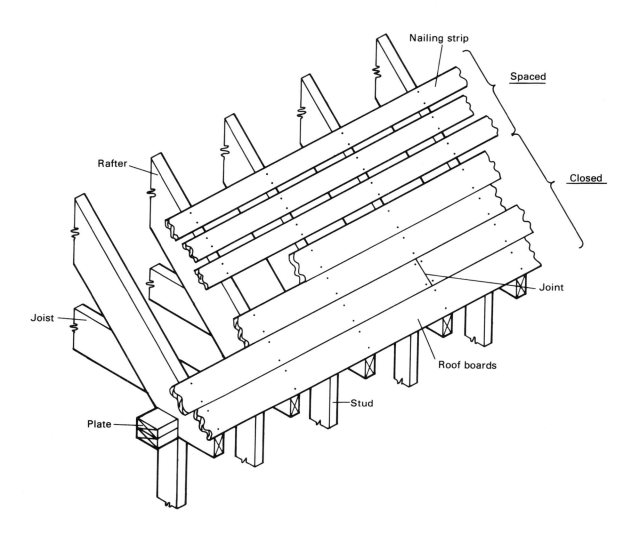

**Figure 76. Board roof sheathing showing both closed
and spaced boards**

strength parallel to the length of the panel. These products should be laid with the long alignment dimension perpendicular to supports.

Board Sheathing

Board sheathing used under such roofing as asphalt shingles, metal-sheet roofing, or other materials that require continuous support should be laid without spacing (Figure 76). Wood shingles can also be used over such sheathing.

Boards may be tongue-and-grooved, shiplapped, or square-ended. End joints should be made over the centerline of rafters. It is preferable to use boards no wider than 6 inches to 8 inches to minimize problems caused by shrinkage. Boards should have a minimum thickness of ¾ inch for rafter spacing of 16 inches to 24 inches and should be nailed with two 8d common or 7d threaded nails for each board at each bearing. End-matched tongue-and-groove boards can also be used and joints made between rafters. However, the joints of adjoining boards should not be made over the same rafter space. Each board should be supported by at least two rafters.

Spaced Sheathing

When wood shingles or shakes are used in damp climates, it is common to have spaced roof boards (Figure 76). Wood nailing strips in nominal 1x3-inch or 1x4-inch size are spaced the same distance

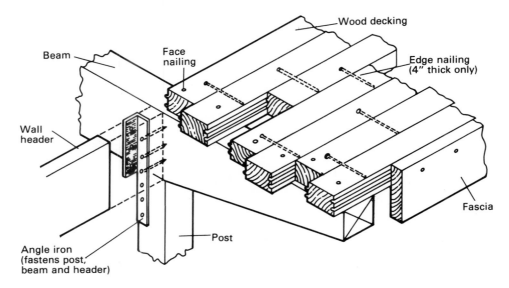

Figure 77. Plank roof decking common in post-and-beam construction

on centers as the shingle exposure. For example, if the shingle exposure to the weather is 5 inches and nominal 1x4-inch strips are used, there would be a space of 1⅜ inches to 1½ inches between adjacent boards.

Plank Roof Decking

Plank roof decking, consisting of nominal 2-inch and thicker tongue-and-groove wood planking, is often used in post and beam construction. Common sizes are nominal 2x6 inches, 3x6 inches, and 4x6 inches, the thicker planking being suitable for spans up to 10 or 12 feet.

The decking is nailed through the tongue and also face-nailed at each support. In the 4x6-inch size, it is predrilled for edge nailing (Figure 77). Maximum span for 2-inch planking is 8 feet when it is continuous over two or more supports. Special load requirements may reduce this allowable span.

Roof decking can serve both as an interior ceiling finish and as a base for roofing. However, due to the relatively low insulating value of plank roof decking, various types of rigid insulating sheathing are often laid over the decking. These include fiberboard, foam, and sandwiched insulation panels. A vapor retarder should also be used between the top of the plank and the roof insulation unless the insulation has an integral vapor retarder.

Fiberboard Roof Decking

Fiberboard roof decking is used the same way as wood-plank decking except that supports must be spaced closer together. Fiberboard decking is usually supplied in 2x8-foot "planks" with tongue-and-grooved edges. Thicknesses of planks and spacing of supports vary with the product, but are typically as follows:

Minimum thickness	Maximum joist spacing
1½ inches	24 inches
2 inches	32 inches
3 inches	48 inches

Fiberboard planks are fastened to the wood members with corrosion-resistant nails spaced not more than 5 inches on center. Nails should be long enough to penetrate the joist or beam at least 1½ inches.

Roof Sheathing at Gable Ends

The suggested method for installing board or plywood roof sheathing at gable ends of the roof is shown in Figure 78. Where there is no roof overhang at gable ends, roof sheathing is placed flush with the outside of the wall sheathing.

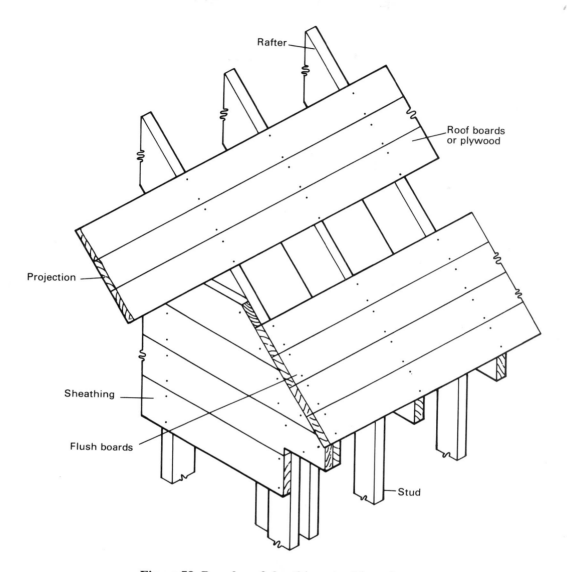

Figure 78. Board roof sheathing at gable ends

Roof sheathing that extends beyond gable end walls to form a rake overhang should span at least two rafter or truss spaces to insure proper anchorage (Figure 78). An overhang of 12 inches or less does not require special framing for support if the roof sheathing is at least ⅜-inch thick. When the projection is greater than 12 inches, ladder framing should be used to support the overhang as described in the section on exterior trim.

Plywood extension beyond the end wall can be adjusted to minimize waste. Thus, where rafters are spaced 16 inches on center, a 16-inch overhang might be most efficient; with 24-inch on-center spacing, a 12-inch overhang might be more efficient.

Sheathing at Chimney Openings

Where there are chimney openings in the roof, the roof sheathing should have a clearance of ¾ inch from the finished masonry on all sides (Figure 79). Rafters and headers around the opening should have a clearance of at least 2 inches from the masonry, or other clearance as specified by the local code for fire protection.

ROOF COVERINGS

The choice of roofing materials is influenced by initial cost, local code requirements, house design,

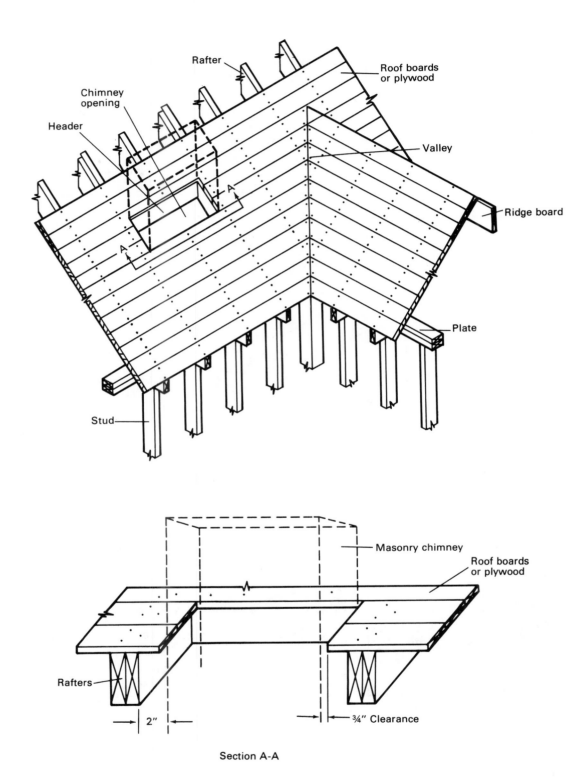

**Figure 79. Board roof sheathing at valley and chimney opening.
Section A-A shows clearance at chimney**

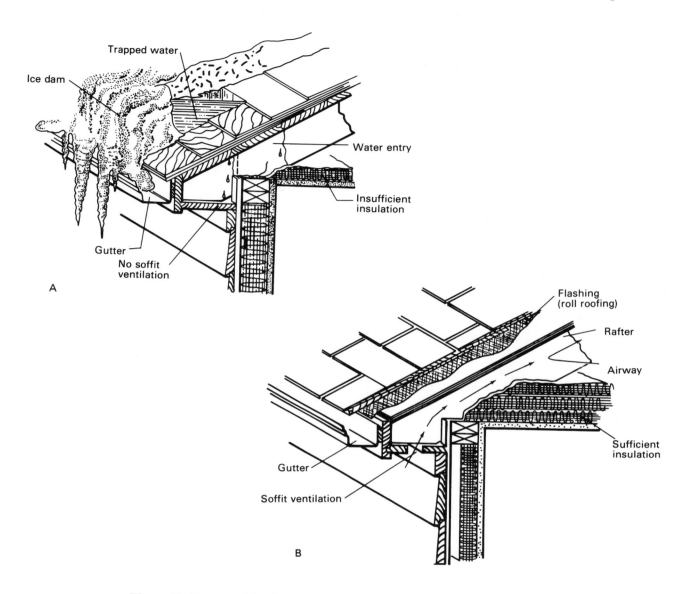

Figure 80. Snow and ice dams: (A) ice dam forming at roof overhang causing melting snow water to back up under shingles and facia board which damages ceilings inside and paint outside; (B) eave protection for snow and ice dams

and the builder's or owner's preferences. Wood and asphalt shingles, shakes, tile, slate, and sheet materials such as roll roofing, aluminum, copper and tin are used for pitched roofs. Flat or low-pitched roofs often employ built-up construction with a gravel topping or cap sheet. Plastic films can also be used on low-slope roofs.

Ice Dams

In areas with moderate to severe snowfall, "ice dams" can form along roof edges at the cornice

overhang. Ice dams form as a result of the melting of snow that has fallen on the warmer attic areas of the roof. The water from the melted snow runs down the roof to the colder cornice area where it refreezes, forming the ice dam. As more water runs down the roof, it gradually becomes deeper, backing up under the roof covering material and leaking through to the ceiling and walls (Figure 80A).

The possibility of leakage caused by ice dams is reduced by increasing the vertical distance the backed-up water must travel to reach the interior of the house or by tightening the seal between the layers of the roof covering materials.

The vertical distance the water must travel can be increased by increasing the overlap distance of successive layers of the roof covering or by making the pitch of the roof steeper, or both. The seal between the roof-covering layers can be accomplished by applying a sealer, such as roll-roofing adhesive, between the layers.

As an additional protection against water penetration, it is good practice to apply an underlay of 30-pound or heavier, smooth-surface roll roofing beneath the roof-covering materials. The underlay should be placed on top of the roof sheathing beginning at the eave line and extending up the roof sheathing to a point 24 inches inside the inner surface of the exterior wall (Figure 80B). If it is necessary to overlap the underlay, a double layer of 15-pound roll roofing should be lapped 18 inches on each side of the underlay joint and completely sealed with roll-roofing adhesive.

Good attic ventilation and sufficient ceiling insulation keep attic temperatures low enough to minimize snow melt and are important in eliminating the potentially harmful ice dams.

Shingles

With wood and asphalt shingles and shakes, the exposure distance is important. The amount of exposure generally depends on the roof slope and the type of material. This may vary from a 5-inch exposure for standard-size asphalt and wood shingles on a moderately steep slope, to about a 3½-inch exposure for flatter slopes, as specified by the manufacturer.

Roof underlay material of 15-pound or 30-pound asphalt-saturated felt is often used in moderate- and lower-slope roofs covered with asphalt, asbestos, or slate shingles or with tile roofing. Underlayment is not commonly used with wood shingles or shakes. Manufacturers' requirements for installation of underlay should be followed to insure warranty protection.

To reduce the likelihood of leakage if an ice dam should form, it is good practice to apply an underlay of 30-pound or heavier roll roofing along the eave line as described previously (Figure 80B).

Wood Shingles and Shakes. Wood shingles made entirely of heartwood give greater resistance to decay

Table 11
Recommended exposure for wood shingles[1]

Shingle length	Shingle thickness (green)	Maximum exposure	
		Slope (less than 4-in-12)	Slope (5-in-12 and over)
16″	5 butts in 2″	3¾″	5″
18″	5 butts in 2¼″	4¼″	5½″
24″	4 butts in 2″	5¾″	7½″

Note: Minimum slope for main roofs: 4-in-12.
Minimum slope for porch roofs: 3-in-12.

[1] As recommended by the Red Cedar Shingle and Handsplit Shake Bureau.

than do shingles that contain sapwood; wood shakes are 100 percent heartwood. Edge-grained shingles are less likely to warp than flat-grained. The tendency to warp is also less in thicker butted and narrower shingles. Western red cedar, northern white cedar, and redwood are the principal commercial shingle woods because their heartwood has high resistance to decay and low shrinkage. Shingles are of random widths, the narrower shingles being in the lower grades.

Table 11 shows recommended exposures for standard shingle sizes. Four bundles of 16-inch shingles laid with a 5-inch exposure will cover 100 square feet.

Figure 81 illustrates the proper method of applying a wood-shingle roof. Underlay or roofing felt is not required for wood shingles except for protection in ice-dam areas, as discussed previously. Spaced roof boards under wood shingles are common, although spaced or solid sheathing is a viable alternative.

The following general rules should be followed in applying wood shingles:

1. Shingles should extend about 1½ inches beyond the eave line and about ¾ inch beyond the rake (gable) edge.
2. Two rust-resistant nails should be used in each shingle, spaced about ¾ inch from the edge and 1½ inches above the butt line of the next course. Nails of 3d size should be used for 16-inch and 18-inch shingles and 4d nails

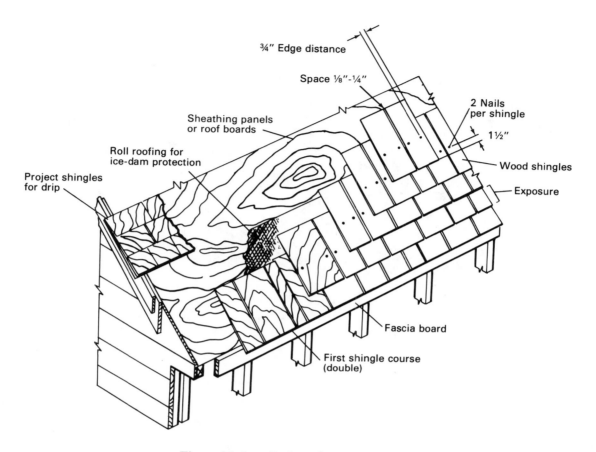

¾" Edge distance

Space ⅛"-¼"

2 Nails
per shingle

1½"

Sheathing panels
or roof boards

Roll roofing for
ice-dam protection

Wood shingles

Project shingles
for drip

Exposure

Fascia board

First shingle course
(double)

Figure 81. Installation of wood shingles

for 24-inch shingles in new construction. A ring-shank (threaded) nail is often recommended for plywood roof sheathing less than ½-inch thick.

3. The first course of shingles should be doubled. In all courses, ⅛ inch to ¼ inch of space between adjacent shingles should be allowed for expansion when wet. The joints between shingles should be offset at least 1½ inches from the joints between shingles in the course below so that they do not line up directly with joints in the second course below.

4. When valleys are present, shingling should proceed away from the valleys, selecting and precutting wide valley shingles.

5. A metal edging along the gable end should be considered to aid in guiding water away from the sidewalls.

6. In laying No. 1 all-heartwood edge-grain shingles, splitting of wide shingles is unnecessary.

Shakes are applied in much the same manner as wood shingles. Shakes are much thicker than shingles, with longer shakes having thicker butts, and long galvanized nails are therefore used. To create a rustic appearance, the butts are often laid unevenly.

Because shakes are also longer than shingles, they are applied with greater exposure. Exposure distance is usually 7½ inches for 18-inch shakes, 10 inches for 24-inch shakes, and 13 inches for 32-inch shakes. Shakes are not smooth on both faces and wind-driven snow might enter beneath them. In areas where such weather conditions are encountered, it is essential to use an underlay between successive courses. An 18-inch-wide layer of 30-pound asphalt felt should be used, with the bottom edge positioned above the butt edge of the shakes at a distance equal to double the weather exposure. A 36-inch-wide starting strip of asphalt felt is used at the eave line. Solid sheathing should also be used to protect against wind-driven snow.

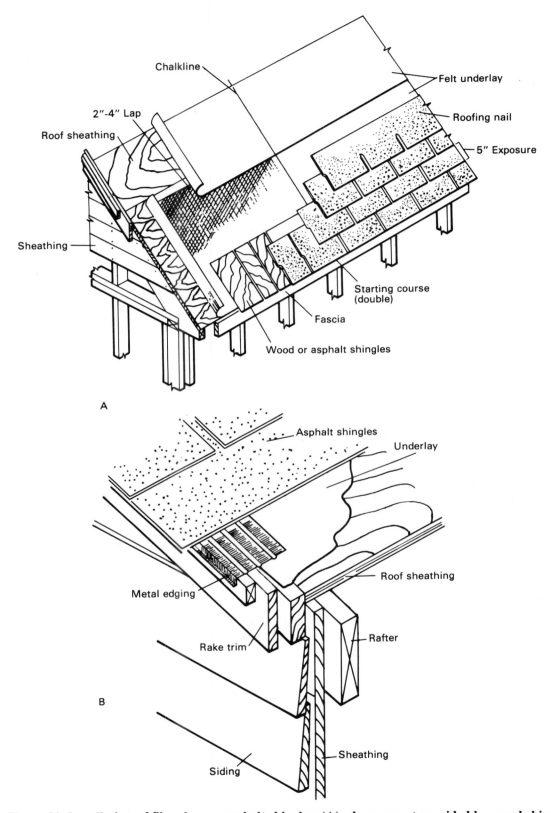

Figure 82. Installation of fiberglass or asphalt shingles: (A) edge support provided by wood shingle course; (B) edge support provided by metal edging

Asphalt and Fiberglass Shingles. Figure 82A shows the method of laying an asphalt or fiberglass shingle roof. Manufacturers' requirements for the underlayment beneath the shingles should be followed to insure warranty protection. The underlayment normally recommended is 15-pound asphalt saturated felt. In areas with moderate to severe snowfall, the precautions discussed with regard to ice dams should be taken.

Asphalt shingles consist of a felt base with asphalt coating. Concealed spots of adhesive called seal tabs glue the shingles together and thus provide greater wind resistance. Felt-base square-butt asphalt strip shingles should have a minimum weight of 240 pounds per "square." (A "square" is the amount of shingles required to cover 100 square feet of roof.)

Fiberglass shingles are made of an inorganic fiberglass base coated with asphalt. The usual minimum recommended weight is 220 pounds per square. Fiberglass shingles are generally considered more durable and fire resistant than felt-base shingles. Application methods are the same for both types.

The square-butt strip shingle is 12x36 inches, has three tabs, and is usually laid with 5 inches exposed to the weather. There are 27 strips in a bundle, and three bundles will cover a square. Bundles should be piled flat for storage so that strips will not curl when the bundles are opened.

Metal edging is often used around the entire perimeter of the roof. A starter course is used under the first shingle course. This starter course should extend downward about ½ inch beyond the metal or edging to provide a layer of roof covering under the tab cutouts and to provide uniform roof covering thickness. A ½-inch projection should also be used at the rake (Figure 82B).

Several chalk lines on the underlay will help align the shingles so that tab notches will be in a straight line for good appearance. Each shingle strip should be fastened securely according to the manufacturer's directions. It is good practice to use four 1¼-inch galvanized roofing nails for each 12x36-inch strip. The nails should be driven straight, they should not cut the shingle, and they should be driven to a depth that is flush with the surface of the shingle rather than below the surface. If a nail does not penetrate solid wood, another should be driven nearby.

Many builders use pneumatic staple guns rather than a hammer and nails to speed the process of fastening the shingles to the roof. If this method is chosen, 1⅝-inch wide crown staples should be used, and they should be installed parallel to the roof ridge line for maximum wind resistance.

Built-up Roofs

Built-up roof coverings are normally installed by roofing companies that specialize in this work. Such roofs may use three, four, or five layers of roofer's felt, each mopped down with tar or asphalt, with the final surface coated with asphalt and covered with gravel (Figure 83A). It is customary to refer to built-up roofs as 10-, 15-, or 20-year roofs, depending upon the method of application.

The cornice or eave line of projecting roofs is usually finished with metal edging or flashing, which acts as a drip. A metal gravel stop is used in conjunction with the flashing at the eaves when the roof is covered with gravel (Figure 83B). Where built-up roofing is finished against another wall, the roofing is turned up on the wall sheathing over a cant strip and is often flashed with metal (Figure 83C). This flashing generally extends about 4 inches above the bottom of the siding.

Other Roof Coverings

Other roof coverings, including slate, tile, and metal also require specialized applicators. They are less commonly used than wood, asphalt, or fiberglass shingles and built-up roofs. Several new materials, such as plastic films and coatings, show future promise as moderate-cost roof coverings. Currently, however, they are generally more expensive than the materials now in use.

Roofs made of galvanized steel, copper, or aluminum are sometimes used on flat decks over dormers, porches, or entryways. Joints should be watertight and the deck properly flashed at the juncture with the house. Nails should be of the same metal as that used for the roof covering. Special nails manufactured with rubber gaskets should be driven through the metal to the point at which the rubber gasket begins to expand in contact with the metal. This method provides a watertight seal around the nail hole.

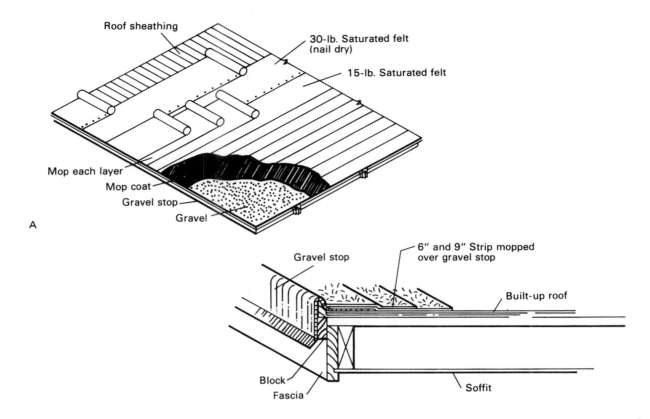

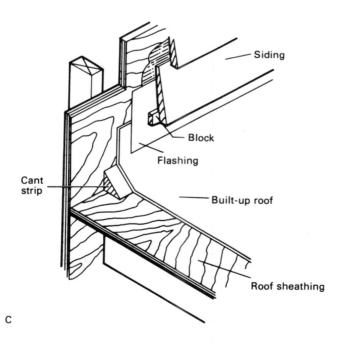

**Figure 83. Built-up roof: (A) installation of roof layers;
(B) gravel stop; (C) finishing at junction with vertical wall**

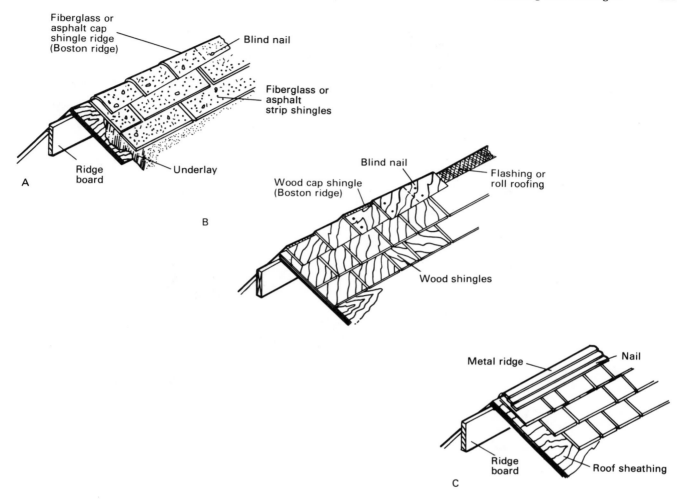

Figure 84. Finishing shingled roof ridge: (A) Boston ridge with fiberglass or asphalt shingles; (B) Boston ridge with wood shingles; (C) metal ridge

Finish at the Ridge and Hip

The most common type of ridge and hip finish for wood and asphalt shingles is called the Boston ridge. Asphalt or fiberglass cap-shingle squares (one-third of a 12x36-inch strip) are used over the ridge and blind-nailed (Figure 84A). Each cap shingle is lapped 5 to 6 inches to give double coverage, and the laps are turned away from the prevailing wind. In areas where there are driving rains, it is well to use metal flashing under the shingle ridge. The use of a ribbon of asphalt roofing cement under each lap will also reduce the chance of water penetration.

A wood-shingle roof (Figure 84B) can be finished in a Boston ridge with continuous flashing or roll roofing beneath the cap shingles. Flashing or roll roofing is first placed along the length of the ridge, as shown in Figure 84. Shingles 6 inches wide are alternately lapped, fitted, and blind-nailed. The shingles are nailed in place with exposed trimmed edges alternately lapped. Pre-assembled hip and ridge units, which can save both time and money, are available.

A metal ridge vent or ridge roll of copper, galvanized steel or aluminum, formed to the roof, can also be used on asphalt or fiberglass shingle or wood-shingle roofs (Figure 84C). Some metal ridge vents provide an outlet ventilating area and are designed with louvers and interior baffles to keep rain and snow out.

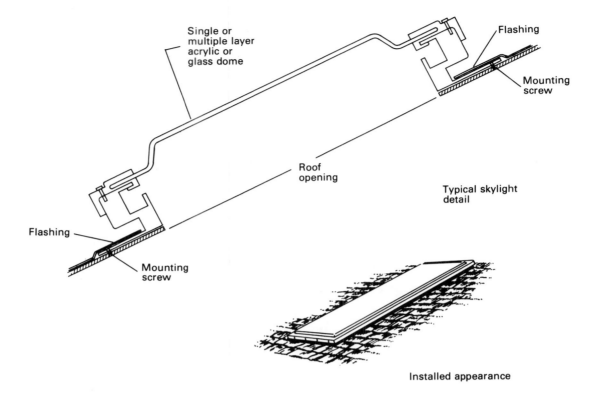

Single or
multiple layer
acrylic or
glass dome

Flashing

Mounting
screw

Roof
opening

Typical skylight
detail

Flashing

Mounting
screw

Installed appearance

Figure 85. Surface-mounted skylight

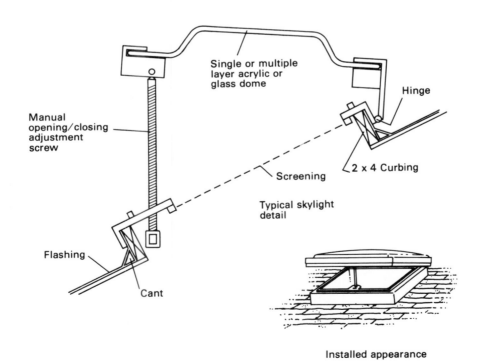

Single or multiple
layer acrylic or
glass dome

Hinge

Manual
opening/closing
adjustment
screw

Screening

2 x 4 Curbing

Typical skylight
detail

Flashing

Cant

Installed appearance

Figure 86. Curb-mounted skylight

SKYLIGHTS

Skylights have become popular for providing natural light and a sense of "outdoors" inside the home. Some can be opened for ventilation, while others are fixed. Ventilating skylights are usually manually operated, although motorized units are available. Skylights have sometimes been promoted as a way of providing passive solar heating. However, under most conditions, skylights are inefficient for this purpose and can very often be net energy losers.

Skylights are available in numerous shapes including flat, dome, and pyramid. They can have acrylic plastic or glass glazing, either clear or tinted, and can be single or double glazed. Skylight manufacturers provide installation specifications which should be followed to prevent leaks and to protect the warranty. The size of the hole in the roof sheathing to accommodate the skylight should conform to the mounting instructions.

There are three basic skylight frame types, as follows:

- *Surface-mounted skylights* (Figure 85) are fastened directly to the roof sheathing, usually with galvanized, aluminum, or stainless steel nails. Felt or aluminum flashing, and flashing cement, are required to make the skylight watertight.
- Built-up curbs are made by the installer in accordance with manufacturers' specifications. The skylight is installed atop the curb. Gaskets and flashing are usually included with the skylight to provide a weatherproof seal.
- Skylights with integral curbs (Figure 86) are common. Most operable skylights have integral curbs. The curb, which is an extension of the frame, raises the skylight off the roof. The skylight is fastened to the roof by means of a flange at the bottom of the curb.

Condensation often occurs on the inside of skylights, especially in areas of high humidity such as kitchens and bathrooms. Some skylights have built-in condensate gutters with weep holes in the frame to reduce moisture accumulation.

CHAPTER 4

Completing The Shell

The topics discussed in this chapter deal with specific tasks related to completing the construction of the shell of the house. Their order of presentation does not necessarily reflect the sequence of performance.

FLASHING AND OTHER SHEET-METAL WORK

Sheet-metal work normally consists of installing flashing, gutters, downspouts, and sometimes attic ventilators. Flashing is often provided to prevent wicking action by joints between moisture-absorbent materials. It can also be used to provide protection from wind-driven rain or melting snow. As previously indicated, damage from ice dams is often the result of inadequate flashing.

Gutters are installed at the cornice line of a pitched roof house to carry the rain or melted snow to the downspouts and away from the foundation area. They are especially needed for houses with narrow roof overhangs. Poor drainage away from the foundation wall is often the cause of wet basements.

Materials

Aluminum is the most commonly used material for sheet-metal work; other materials include zinc-coated (galvanized) steel, copper, and vinyl plastic. Aluminum flashing should have a minimum thickness of 0.019 inch. The thickness for gutters should be 0.027 inch and for downspouts, 0.020 inch. Copper for flashing and similar uses should have a minimum thickness of 0.020 inch. Aluminum is not normally used where it will come in contact with concrete or stucco, unless it is insulated with a coat of asphaltum or other protection against a reaction with the alkali in the cement.

Galvanized (zinc-coated) sheet metal is also frequently used. There are two weights of zinc coatings: 1.25 and 1.50 ounce per square foot (total weight of coating on both sides). When 1.25-ounce sheet is used for exposed flashing and for gutters and downspouts, 26-gage metal is required. With 1.50-ounce coating, a 28-gage metal is satisfactory for most metal work, except that gutters should be 26-gage.

In choosing accessory hardware such as nails, screws, hangers, and clips, it is important to avoid the potential for corrosion or deterioration that can occur when unlike metals are used together. With aluminum, only aluminum or stainless steel fasteners should be used. Galvanized sheet metal should be fastened with galvanized or stainless steel fasteners.

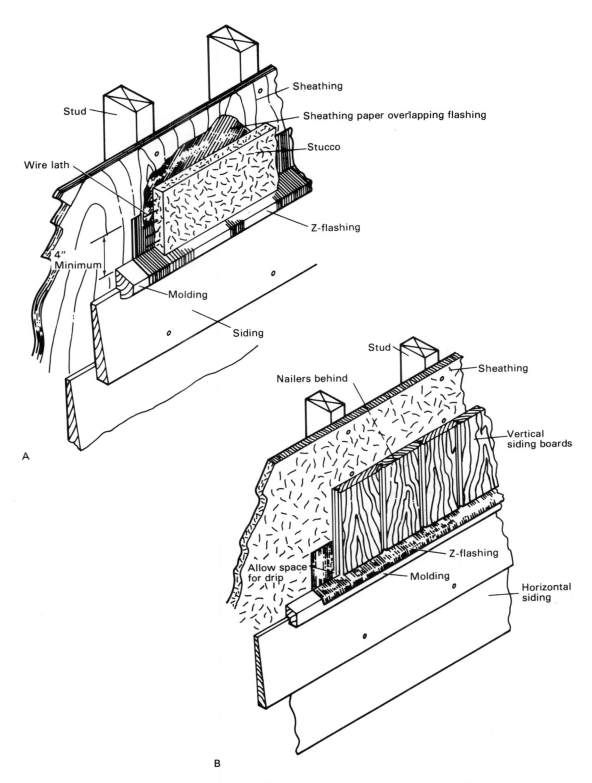

Figure 87. "Zee" flashing at material changes: (A) stucco above and siding below; (B) vertical siding above and horizontal siding below

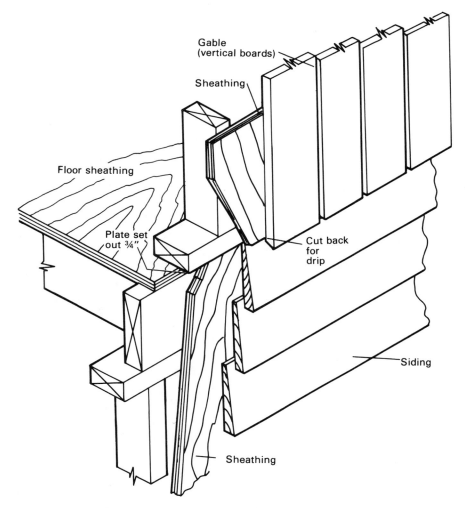

Gable
(vertical boards)

Sheathing

Floor sheathing

Plate set
out ¾"

Cut back
for
drip

Siding

Sheathing

**Figure 88. Gable-end projection material
transition without flashing**

Flashing

Flashing should be used at the junction of a roof and a wood or masonry wall, at chimneys, over exposed doors and windows, at places where siding material changes, in roof valleys, and in other areas where rain or melted snow might penetrate into the house.

Material Changes. Horizontal gaps formed at the intersection of two types of siding material often require "zee" flashing (Figure 87). For example, a stucco-finish gable end and a wood-siding lower wall should be flashed at their juncture (Figure 87A). An upper wall sided with vertical boards, with horizontal siding below, usually requires some type of flashing (Figure 87B). When the upper wall, such as a gable end, projects slightly beyond the lower wall (Figure 88), flashing is usually not required. The bottom edge of the siding is cut back at an angle to provide a drip edge, as shown in the illustration.

Doors and Windows. "Head" flashing, which is similar to "zee" flashing, should be used over door and window openings exposed to rain. Windows and doorheads protected by wide overhangs in a single-story house do not ordinarily require such flashing. "Head" flashing should be started behind the siding and should be bent out and down over the top molding over the window or door. When building paper is used on the sidewalls, it should lap the top edge of the flashing.

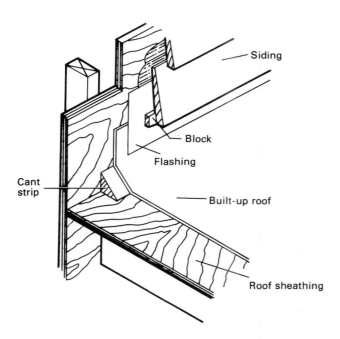

Figure 89. Flashing at junction of built-up roof and vertical building wall

Flat Roofs. Flashing is required at the junction of an exterior wall and a flat or low-pitched built-up roof (Figure 89). When a metal roof is used, the metal is turned up on the wall and covered by the siding. A clearance of 2 inches should be allowed at the bottom of the siding for protection from melted snow and water.

Ridges and Roofs. Ridge flashing or roll roofing should be used under a Boston ridge on wood shingle or shake roofs to prevent water entry (Figure 90). The flashing should extend about 3 inches on each side of the ridge and be nailed in place only at the outer edges. Ridge shingles or shakes, which are 6 to 8 inches wide, cover the flashing.

Vents. Stack vents and roof ventilators are provided with flashing collars, which are lapped by the shingles on the upper side. The lower edge of the collar laps the shingles. Sides are nailed to the shingles and caulked with roofing mastic.

Valleys. The valley formed by two intersecting roof planes is usually covered with metal flashing. Some building regulations allow the use of two thicknesses of mineral-surfaced roll roofing in place of metal flashing. As an alternative, one 36-inch-wide strip of roll roofing can be applied to the valley, and covered with asphalt or fiberglass shingles applied continuously from one plane of the roof to the other. This type of valley is normally used only on roofs with a slope of 10 in 12 or steeper. Widths of sheet-metal flashing for valleys should not be less than:

(a) 12 inches for roof slopes of 7-in-12 and steeper.
(b) 18 inches wide for roof slopes 4-in-12 to 7-in-12.
(c) 24 inches wide for slopes flatter than 4-in-12.

The width of the valley between shingles should increase from the top to the bottom (Figure 91A). The minimum open width at the top is 4 inches and should be increased at the rate of about ⅛ inch per foot. These widths can be chalklined on the flashing before shingles are applied.

When adjacent roof slopes vary, such as a low-slope porch roof intersecting a steeper main roof, a 1-inch-high crimped standing seam should be used (Figure 91B). This seam will keep heavy rains on the steeper slopes from overrunning the valley and being forced under the shingles on the adjoining slope. Nails for the shingles should be kept back as far as possible to eliminate holes in the flashing. A ribbon of asphalt-roofing mastic is often used under the edge of the shingles.

Roof-Wall Intersections. When shingles on a roof intersect a vertical wall, step flashing is used at the junction. Aluminum or galvanized steel is bent at a

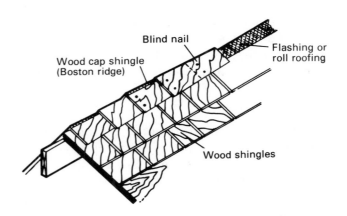

Figure 90. Flashing at Boston ridge with wood shingles

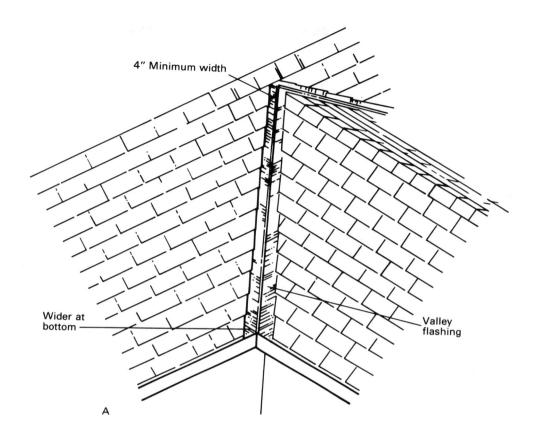

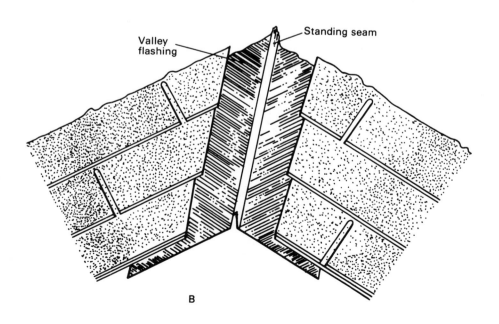

Figure 91. Flashing roof valley: (A) conventional valley flashing; (B) valley flashing with standing seam

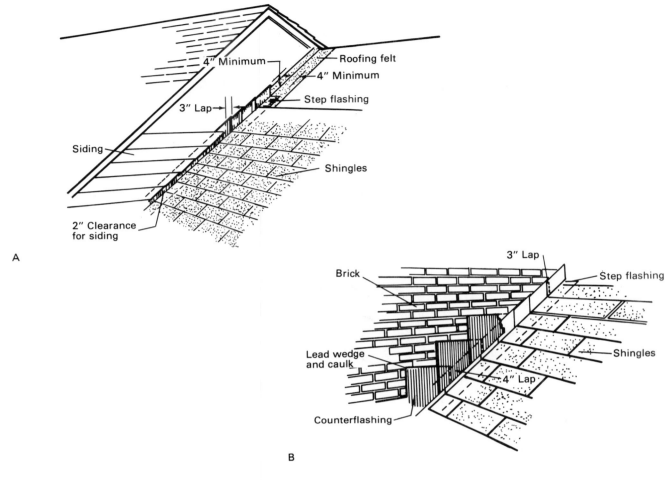

Figure 92. Flashing at roof-wall intersection:
(A) wood siding on wall; (B) brick wall

90° angle and extended up the side of the wall a minimum of 4 inches over the sheathing (Figure 92A). When roofing felt is used under the shingles, it is turned up on the wall and covered by the flashing. The siding is then applied over the flashing, allowing about a 2-inch vertical space between the level edge of the siding and the roof.

If the roof intersects a brick wall or chimney, the same type of metal flashing is used as that described for the wood-sided wall. In addition, counterflashing or brick flashing is used to cover the step flashing (Figure 92B). This counterflashing is often preformed in sections and is inserted in open mortar joints. All flashing joints should overlap the next lower piece.

In laying up the chimney or brick wall, the mortar is usually raked out for a depth of about 1 inch at flashing locations. Lead wedges driven into the joint above the flashing hold it in place. The joint is then caulked to provide a watertight connection. In chimneys, this counterflashing is often preformed to cover one entire side.

Around small chimneys, flashing often consists of simple counterflashing applied over step flashing on each side. For single-flue chimneys, the shingle flashing on the high side should be carried up under the shingles. This flashing should extend up the chimney about four inches above the roof sheathing (Figure 93A).

A saddle for better drainage is often constructed on the high side of wide chimneys. It is made of a ridgeboard and post and sheathed with plywood or boards (Figure 93B). It is then covered with metal that extends up on the brick and under the shingles.

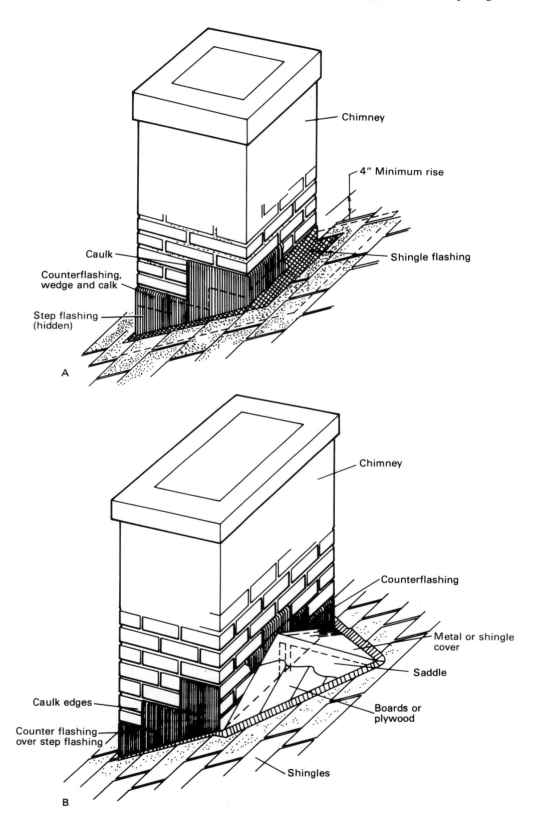

Chimney

4" Minimum rise

Caulk

Shingle flashing

Counterflashing, wedge and calk

Step flashing (hidden)

A

Chimney

Counterflashing

Metal or shingle cover

Saddle

Caulk edges

Boards or plywood

Counter flashing over step flashing

Shingles

B

Figure 93. Flashing at chimney: (A) single-flue chimney without saddle; (B) wide chimney with saddle

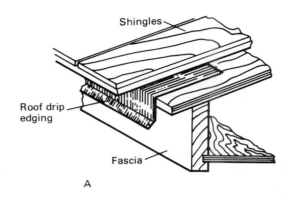

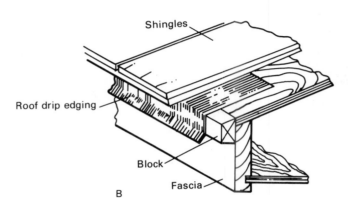

Figure 94. Roof drip edge: (A) drip edge on sheathing; (B) drip edge supported by molding

Counterflashing at the chimney is then used, as previously described, with lead plugging and caulking. A very wide chimney can have a partial gable on the high side, which can be shingled in the same manner as the main roof.

Roof Drip Edge. Aluminum drip edge flashing is often used around the entire perimeter of the roof to protect the edge of the sheathing and to reduce the amount of rainwater running down the fascia or blowing under the roof covering (Figure 94B).

Gutters and Downspouts

Several types of gutters are available to carry the rainwater to the downspouts and away from the foundation. The most commonly used gutter is the type hung from the edge of the roof or fastened to the edge of the cornice fascia. Gutters may be the half-round (Figure 95A) or the formed type (Figure 95B) and may be aluminum, galvanized steel, or vinyl. Some have a factory-applied enamel finish which minimizes maintenance.

Downspouts are round or rectangular (Figure 95C and 95D), the round type being used with the half-round gutters. They are usually corrugated to provide extra stiffness and strength. Corrugated patterns are less likely to burst when plugged with ice.

Size. One square inch of downspout cross-sectional area is required for each 100 square feet of roof area. The size of gutters should be determined by the size and spacing of the downspouts used. When downspouts are spaced up to 40 feet apart, the cross-sectional area of the gutter should be the same as that of the downspout. For greater spacing, the size of the gutter should be increased. On long runs of gutters, such as would be required around a hip-roof house, at least four downspouts are desirable.

Installation. Gutters should be installed with a slight pitch toward the downspouts, such as ¼ inch

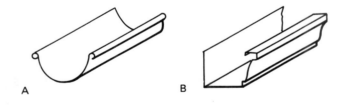

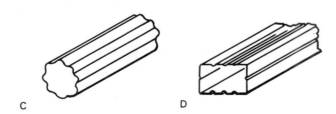

Figure 95. Gutters and downspouts: (A) half-round gutter; (B) formed gutter; (C) round downspout; (D) rectangular downspout

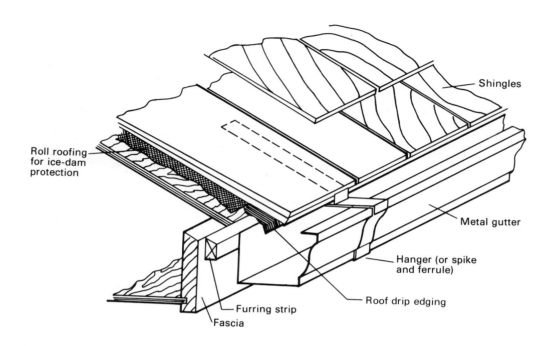

Roll roofing
for ice-dam
protection

Shingles

Metal gutter

Hanger (or spike
and ferrule)

Roof drip edging

Furring strip

Fascia

Figure 96. Gutter installation

in 10 feet. The points marking the ends of the gutter that produce the necessary slope should be established with a transit and marked on the fascia. A chalk line can be stretched tightly between the points and snapped. The resulting line on the fascia can be used to guide the installation of the gutter.

Gutters are often suspended from the edge of the roof with hangers (Figure 96). Hangers should be spaced 48 inches apart when made of galvanized steel and 30 inches apart when made of aluminum. Gutter splices, downspout connections, and corner joints should be soldered or sealed with a rubber caulk to provide watertight joints.

Downspouts, or conductor pipes, are fastened to the wall by straps (Figure 97A). Several patterns of fasteners allow a space between the wall and downspout. One common type consists of a metal strap with a spike and spacer collar. After the spike is driven through the collar and into the siding and backing stud, the strap is fastened around the pipe. Downspouts should be fastened at top and bottom. For long downspouts, a strap or hook should be used for every 6 feet of length. An elbow should be used at the bottom of the downspout, as well as a splash block, to carry the water away from the wall (Figure 97A). Alternatively, the downspout may be directly connected to the sewer system (Figure 97B).

ATTIC VENTILATION

Ventilation is required in most attic areas to aid the removal of water vapor and condensate. During cold weather, the warm, moist air from the heated rooms can work its way into these spaces around the places where pipes and electrical fixtures penetrate walls and ceilings, and through other inadequately protected areas. The use of vapor retarders in building construction can reduce this vapor migration. Although the total amount of vapor might be unimportant if equally distributed, it may be sufficiently concentrated in some cold spots to cause significant condensation and possibly damage. While wood-shingle and wood-shake roofs do not resist vapor movement, such roofings as asphalt shingles and built-up roofs are highly resistant, and this resistance can contribute to a buildup of vapor in the attic. The most practical method of removing the moisture is by adequately ventilating the roof spaces. During winter weather, a warm attic that is inadequately ventilated can foster the formation of ice dams at cornices or in roof valleys, as discussed in Chapter 3 under "Roof Coverings."

With a well-insulated attic floor and adequate ventilation, attic temperatures can be kept relatively

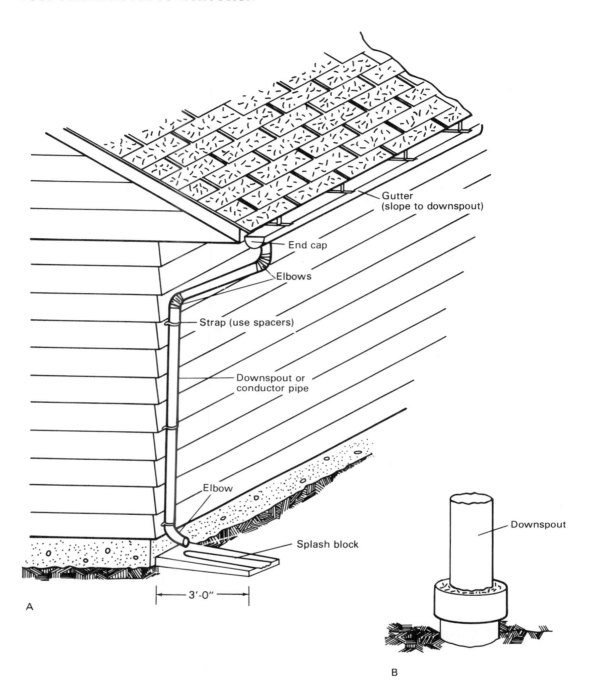

**Figure 97. Downspout installation: (A) downspout with splash block;
(B) downspout connected directly to storm sewer**

low, and melting of snow over the attic space can be reduced. In hot weather, ventilation of attic and roof spaces removes hot air and lowers temperatures in these spaces. Insulation should be used in the attic floor, or in the roof structure if there is no attic, to further retard the flow of heat into the rooms below.

Types and Location of Roof Ventilators

Small, well-distributed modular ventilators or a continuous slot in the soffit provide inlet ventilation. Small vents for easy installation in these locations can be obtained in most lumber yards or hardware stores (Figure 98). The small sections that

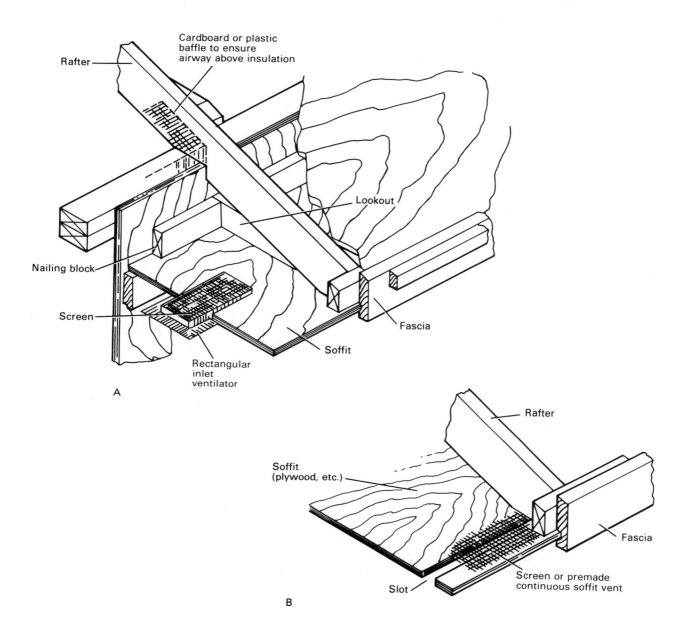

Cardboard or plastic
baffle to ensure
airway above insulation

Rafter

Lookout

Nailing block

Screen

Fascia

Soffit

Rectangular
inlet
ventilator

A

Rafter

Soffit
(plywood, etc.)

Fascia

Slot

Screen or premade
continuous soffit vent

B

**Figure 98. Soffit inlet ventilators: (A) rectangular ventilator;
(B) continuous soffit vent**

must be cut out of the soffit can be removed before the soffit is applied. Aluminum vent covers can be purchased to fit into the holes cut in the soffit or the holes can be covered with stapled screening. It is preferable to use a number of small, well-distributed ventilators rather than fewer large ones.

Blocking might be required between rafters at the wall line so as to leave an airway into the attic above the soffit vents. This airway should not be blocked with insulation. Cardboard or plastic baffles installed between the rafters at the wall line (Figure 98A) or the use of the raised Fink truss design help to ensure a free flow of air.

When a continuous screened slot is used for ventilation, it should be located near the outer edge of the soffit close to the fascia (Figure 98B) to minimize snow entrance. This type of ventilator can also be used under the extension of flat roofs.

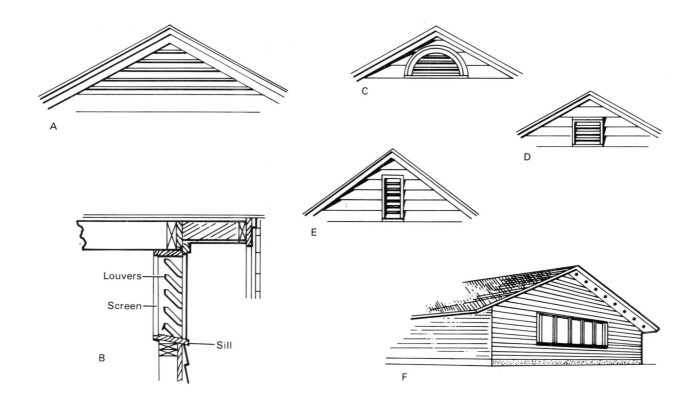

Figure 99. Outlet ventilators: (A) triangular gable vent; (B) gable vent cross-section; (C) half-circle gable vent; (D) square gable vent; (E) vertical gable vent; (F) soffit vents

Area of Ventilators

Minimum recommended ventilator sizes have been generally established for various types of roofs; most building codes specify these minimum sizes. The minimum net area is based on the projected ceiling area of the rooms below. This ratio, discussed for various roof types in the following paragraphs, determines the unobstructed or "net free vent area." When screening, louvers, or rain/snow shields cover the vents, the area of the vent opening should be increased to offset the area of the obstruction. Table 12 gives recognized conversion factors for determining the gross area of the vent opening related to the type of vent covering and the required net free ventilating area.

Louvered openings are generally provided in the end walls of gable roofs. These should be as close to the ridge as possible. The net free area for the vent openings should be 1/300 of the ceiling area or as required by local code. For example, where the ceiling area equals 1200 square feet, the minimum total net free area of the ventilators should be 4 square feet. Some building codes decrease the vent-area requirements for ventilators located close to the ridge or cornice.

Various styles of gable-end ventilators are available in metal and/or wood (Figure 99). One common type fits the slope of the roof and is located near the ridge (Figure 99A). In metal, it is often adjustable to conform to the roof slope. In wood, it is enclosed in a frame and placed in the rough opening, much as a window frame (Figure 99B).

Houses with a wide roof overhang at the gable end can use an attic ventilation system consisting of a series of small vents or a continuous slot on the underside of the soffit areas, in lieu of gable vents (Figure 99F). Several large openings located near the ridge can also be used. This system is especially desirable on low-pitched roofs where standard gable ventilators may not be suitable.

The roof framing at the wall line should not block ventilation to the attic area. Blockage can be avoided by use of a "ladder" frame extension.

Air movement through gable vent openings depends primarily on wind direction and velocity.

No appreciable movement can occur when there is no wind or when openings do not face the wind. Greater air movement can be obtained by providing openings in the soffit areas of the roof overhang in addition to openings at the gable ends or roof ridge. Minimum ventilation areas for this method are shown in Figure 100B.

Where there are rooms in the attic with sloping ceilings under the roof, the insulation should follow the roof slope and be placed so that there is a free opening of at least 1½ inches between the roof sheathing and insulation for air movement (Figure 100C).

Hip Roofs

Hip roofs should have air-inlet openings in the soffit area of the eaves and outlet openings at or near the peak. The differences in temperature between the attic and the outside will create an air movement independent of the wind and more positive movement when there is wind.

As shown in Figure 101A, minimum net free areas of vent openings are 0.5 square feet in each gable end or 1 square foot at the ridge for each 300 square feet of ceiling; and 0.5 square feet of vent area in each soffit or at each eave for each 300 square feet of ceiling, provided required ridge venting area is at least 3 feet above the eave or cornice vent.

The most efficient type of inlet is the continuous slot, which should be at least ¾-inch wide. The air outlet opening near the peak can be a globe-type metal ventilator or several smaller roof ventilators near the ridge. These can be located below the peak on the rear slope of the roof, so they will not be visible from the front of the house. Gabled extensions of a hip roof house are sometimes used to provide efficient outlet ventilators (Figure 101B).

Flat Roofs

A greater ratio of ventilating area is required in some types of flat roofs than in pitched roofs, because air movement there is less positive. There should be a clear open space above the ceiling insulation and below the roof sheathing to permit free air movement from inlet to outlet openings. Solid blocking should not be used for bridging or for bracing over bearing partitions if its use prevents air circulation.

A common type of flat or low-pitched roof is one in which the rafters extend beyond the wall, forming an overhang (Figure 102A). When soffits are used, this area can contain the combined inlet-outlet ventilators, preferably a continuous slot. When single ventilators are used, they should be distributed evenly along the overhang.

A parapet-type wall and flat roof combination may be constructed with the ceiling joists separate from or combined with the roof joists. When members are separate, the space between can be used as an airway (Figure 102B). Inlet and outlet are then located as shown, or a series of outlet stack vents can be used along the centerline of the roof in combination with the inlet vents. When ceiling joists and roof joists are served by one member in parapet construction, vents may be located as shown in Figure 102C.

WINDOWS AND EXTERIOR DOORS

Windows, exterior doors, and their frames are millwork items that are fully assembled and delivered to the building site ready for installation. Neither windows nor doors serve as structural elements of the house.

Window Materials and Styles

Windows are available in many styles including single- or double-hung, casement, stationary, awning, and horizontal sliding (Figure 103). They can be made of wood, metal, or vinyl, or a combination of wood or metal clad with vinyl. The window units may be purchased with either interior or exterior storm windows.

Glazing can consist of a single layer of glass or double- or triple-layer insulating glass. With insulating glass, the sheets are separated by a space that is evacuated and hermetically sealed. This type of glass offers better resistance to the flow of heat out of the house in the winter and into the house in the summer. The glass may also be tinted or coated to reduce the amount of solar heat that enters the house.

Wood window and door frames should be made from a clear grade of all-heartwood stock of a decay-resistant wood species. Such species include ponderosa and other pines, cedar, cypress, redwood, and spruce. Most manufacturers pretreat wood window and door frames with a water-repellant preservative for temporary protection.

Table 12
Multipliers for various vent coverings to determine net free vent area

Type of covering	Area of opening
¼″ hardware cloth	1 x required net free area
¼″ hardware cloth and rain louvers	2 x required net free area
⅛″ mesh screen	1.25 x required net free area
⅛″ mesh screen and rain louvers	2.25 x required net free area
1/16″ mesh screen	2 x required net free area
1/16″ mesh screen and rain louvers	3 x required net free area

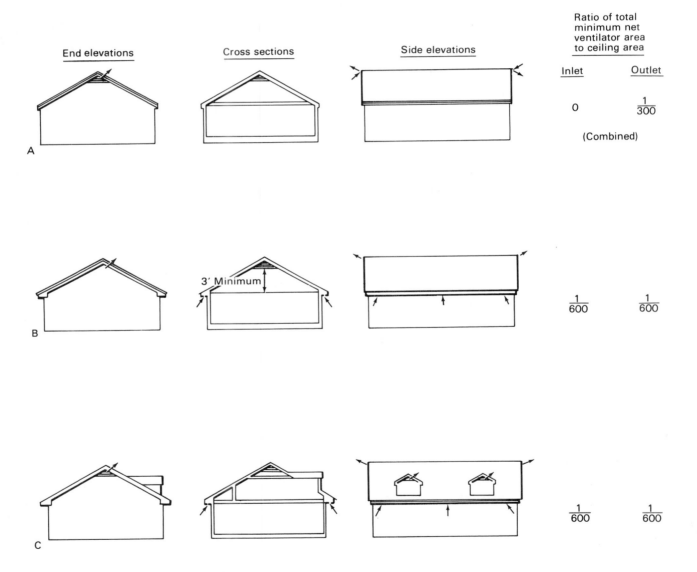

Figure 100. Ventilator areas for gable roofs: (A) louvers in end walls; (B) louvers in end walls with additional openings in eaves and soffit; (C) louvers at end walls with additional openings at eaves and dormers. (Note: Ratios of total minimum net ventilator area to ceiling area may be specified in local building codes.)

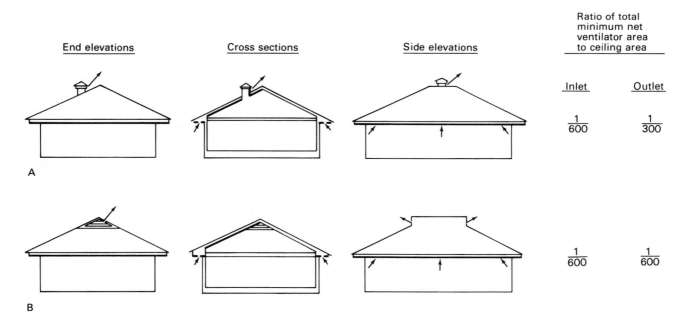

Figure 101. Ventilator areas for hip roofs: (A) inlet openings in eave soffit and outlet vent near peak; (B) inlet openings in eave soffit and outlet vent at ridge. (Note: Ratios of total minimum net ventilator area to ceiling area may be specified in local building codes.)

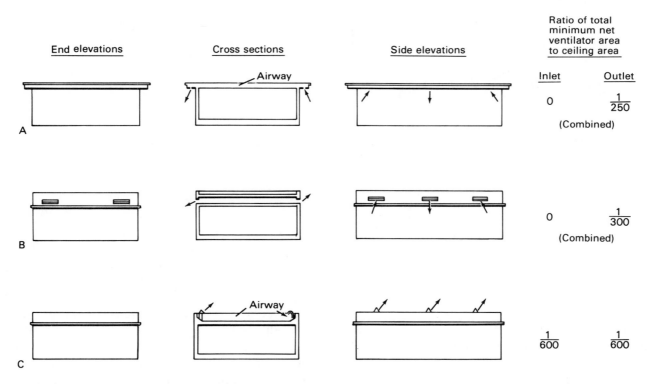

Figure 102. Ventilator areas for flat roofs: (A) vent openings in overhang soffit; (B) vent openings for roof with parapet where roof and ceiling joists are separate; (C) vent openings for roof with parapet where roof and ceiling joists are combined. (Note: Ratios of total minimum net ventilator area to ceiling area may be specified in local building codes.)

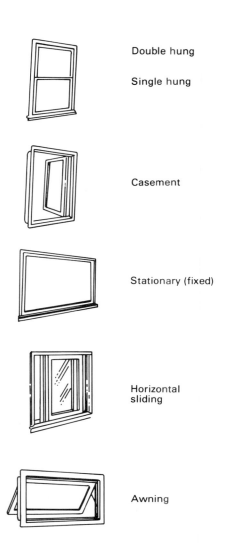

Double hung

Single hung

Casement

Stationary (fixed)

Horizontal sliding

Awning

Figure 103. Common window styles

Local building products suppliers have window manufacturers' catalogs that specify the various styles, sizes, and glass types. Catalog descriptions include the rough wall-opening dimensions required to install each window unit, as well as installation instructions.

Single- and Double-Hung Windows

Single- and double-hung windows are the most commonly used types of windows. In the single-hung style, the upper sash does not move; in the double-hung style, both the upper and lower sash are free to slide vertically. In both styles, moveable sashes are controlled by springs, balances, or compression weatherstripping to hold them at any posi-

tion. Compression weatherstripping offers the added benefit of reducing air infiltration. Several manufacturers offer units that permit removal of movable sashes for easy painting, cleaning, and repair.

The glass in window sashes may be divided into two or more smaller sections (called "lights") by small wood members called muntins. A ranch-type house may look best with top and bottom sash divided into two horizontal lights. A colonial or Cape Cod house may have each sash divided into six or eight lights. Some manufacturers provide preassembled dividers that snap into place over a single light, dividing it into two or more lights. These dividers may be made of plastic, wood, or metal. They give the appearance of muntins but can be removed for easier window cleaning.

Assembled frames are placed in the rough opening with the sash closed to maintain the window unit's squareness. The window unit should be leveled and plumbed before nailing it in place. Wedge-shaped strips of wood shingles may be used as shims to hold the window unit in place during leveling and plumbing. The shims should be positioned under each point where nails will be driven so that the nails do not cause the window casing to bend (Figure 104).

Hardware consists of sash locks or fasteners located at the meeting rail. They lock the window and draw the sash together to provide a tight fit.

Casement Windows

Casement windows consist of side-hinged sash, usually designed to swing outward because this type can be made more weathertight than the in-swinging style. An advantage of the casement window over the double-hung type is that the entire window area can be opened for ventilation.

Units are usually received from the factory entirely assembled with hardware, including weatherstripping, in place. Closing hardware consists of a rotary operator and sash lock. Variations in style are achieved by divided lights. Snap-in muntins provide a small, multiple-pane appearance for traditional styling. Screens are located inside out-swinging windows. Winter protection may be provided by storm sashes or by insulated glass in the sash.

Metal sash are sometimes used in casements. Because of the low insulating value of the metal, there may be condensation and frosting on the inte-

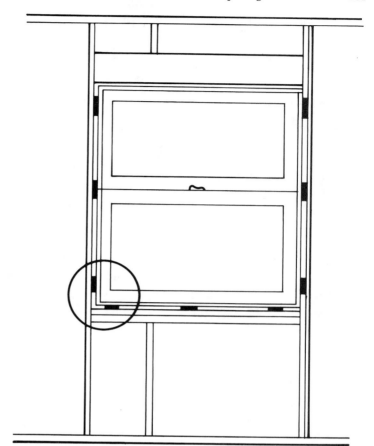

Figure 104. Installation of window unit in rough opening with detail at corner showing nailing

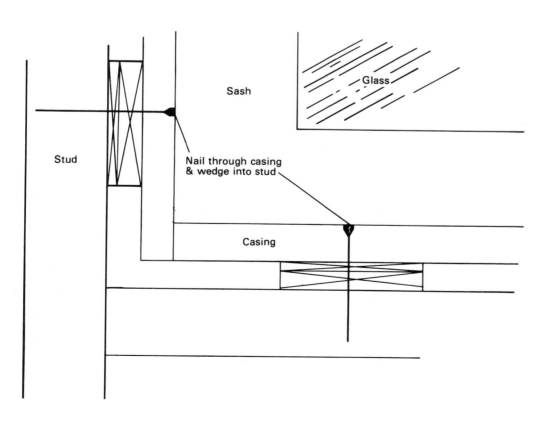

Sash

Glass

Stud

Nail through casing & wedge into stud

Casing

rior surfaces during cold weather. A full storm-window unit is sometimes necessary to eliminate this problem.

Stationary (Fixed) Windows

Stationary or fixed windows, used alone or in combination with vertical-opening or casement windows, usually consist of a wood sash with a large single light of insulating glass, fastened permanently into the frame. Because they may range up to 6 or 8 feet in width and because of the thickness of the insulating glass, 1¾-inch-thick sash is used to provide strength.

In some instances, stationary glazing is installed without a sash. The glass is set directly into rabbeted frame members and held in place with stops. As with window sash units, back puttying and face puttying of the glass provide moisture resistance.

Awning Windows

An awning window unit consists of a frame that may contain one or more fixed sash and includes sash of the awning type that swing outward at the bottom. A similar unit, called the hopper type, is one in which the top of the sash swings inward. Both types provide protection from rain when open.

Operable sash are provided with hinges, pivots, and sash-supporting arms. Weatherstripping, storm sash, and screens may be provided. The storm sash is omitted when the windows are glazed with insulating glass. Jambs are usually 1-1/16 inches or more thick because they are rabbeted, while the sill is at least 1-5/16 inches thick when two or more sash are used in a complete frame. Each sash may also be provided with an individual frame, so that any combination in width and height can be used.

Horizontal Sliding Window Units

With horizontal sliding windows, the sash slide horizontally in pairs in separate tracks or guides located in the sill and head jambs. Multiple window openings, consisting of two or more single units, can be used when a window-wall effect is desired. Weatherstripping, water-repellent preservative treatments, and hardware are included in these fully factory-assembled units.

Specialty Windows

Windows of various sizes and types may be grouped or ganged together to produce an architecturally pleasing effect. A common practice is to install a large stationary bay window with one smaller window unit at each side with movable sash. A wall of windows may be created by arranging awning-window units three across and three high.

Certain specialty window designs protrude from the wall of the house. Installation may require special floor framing, as shown in Figure 40. Bow windows consist of four or five individual window units that form a curve. The box bay is formed with three window units. The side units are installed perpendicular to the plane of the wall and the third unit is installed parallel to the wall. The angled bay is similar to the box bay except the two side window units are installed at either 45° or 30° to the plane of the wall.

Sliding Glass Doors

Sliding glass doors are similar to sliding windows in design and manufacture but are made from heavier material. They can be made with insulating glass, and the frames can be made of wood or aluminum. These units can be used for architectural effect as rear or side doors when space is at a premium or when more light is desired in a room.

Exterior Doors and Frames

Exterior doors are manufactured products which can be ordered prehung in frames and fully weatherstripped from local building-product suppliers. Exterior doors are commonly made of solid wood or metal skin. Metal-skin doors are foam-filled or contain a solid wood core. Most doors are equipped with compression weatherstripping similar to that used on refrigerator doors.

Detailed dimensions, rough opening requirements, and installation instructions are shown in catalogs available from local building-product suppliers. Residential exterior doors are typically 6 feet 8 inches high. Main entrance doors are usually 3 feet wide; rear doors and service doors are usually 2 feet 8 inches wide. The most common exterior door thickness is 1¾ inches. All exterior residential doors should open by swinging inward.

The two major door styles are flush and panel (Figure 105). The flush door has a smooth surface to which decorative molding can be applied, and may have one or more glass areas called doorlights. The panel door and its components are shown in Figure 106. Panels may be replaced by glass to form doorlights. An option available with either type is a fixed-pane window unit adjacent to the door, called a side light.

Installation of exterior doors begins with the setting of the unit — door, frame, and sill — in the rough opening. Space for the sill may have to be cut out of the floor sheathing and joists so that the top of the sill will be the correct distance above the rough floor to accommodate the finished floor covering. Once placed in the opening, the unit is centered and secured with a temporary brace. Blocks or wedges should be used to level the sill and to bring it to the proper height. A nail should be driven through the two side jambs near the bottom of the frame. Blocks or shingle wedges should then be used at the top of the side jambs to plumb and square the door frame. The frame should be secured by nailing through the side jambs and wedges. Additional blocks or wedges should then be nailed between the side jambs and studs to support the door frame and keep it straight.

EXTERIOR COVERINGS

Builders and homeowners have a wide choice of wood-base materials, masonry veneers, and metal or plastic sidings to cover exterior walls. Wood siding can be obtained in several patterns and can be finished naturally, stained, or painted. Wood shingles, plywood, and hardboard are other types of wood and wood-based exterior siding. Coatings and films applied to base materials, or certain base materials themselves, such as vinyl, eliminate the need for refinishing for many years.

Wood Siding

Important properties for wood siding include good painting characteristics, easy working qualities, and freedom from warp. Such properties are present to a high degree in cedars, eastern white pine, sugar pine, western white pine, cypress, and redwood; to a good degree in western hemlock,

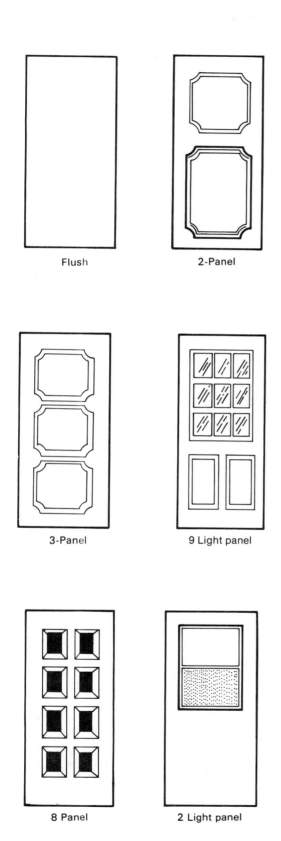

Flush   2-Panel

3-Panel   9 Light panel

8 Panel   2 Light panel

Figure 105. Common door styles

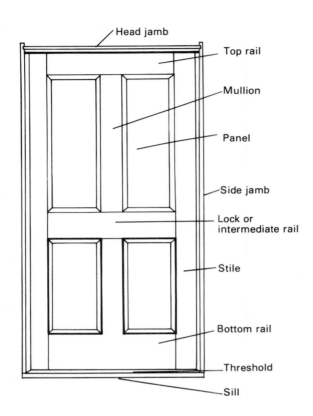

Figure 106. Panel door components

ponderosa pine, the spruces, and yellow poplar; and to a fair degree in Douglas fir, western larch, and southern pine.

Exterior siding that is to be painted should preferably be of a high grade and free from knots, pitch pockets, and waney edges. Edge grain (vertical grain) and mixed grain (in which some boards have edge grain and some have flat grain) are available in some species, such as redwood and western red cedar. Siding is subject to seasonal movement due to changes in moisture content. There is less movement in edge-grain siding than in flat-grain siding, and edge grain is therefore to be preferred. When the siding is to be painted, use of edge grain will result in longer paint life.

The moisture content of the siding at the time of application should match the general level that will be experienced in service. This content would be approximately 10 to 12 percent, except in the dry southwestern states where it should average about 8 to 9 percent.

Horizontal Siding

Several types of horizontal siding are shown in Figure 107 and are described in the following paragraphs.

Bevel Siding. Plain bevel siding with a ½-inch butt thickness can be obtained in widths from 4 to 8 inches, and with ¾-inch butt, from 8 to 10 inches wide. "Anzac" siding is ¾-inch thick by 12 inches wide. The finished width of bevel siding is usually about ½ inch less than the size listed.

One side of bevel siding has a smooth planed surface, while the other has a rough resawn surface. For a stained finish the rough or sawn side is exposed, since wood stain penetrates rough wood surfaces more fully and therefore lasts longer.

Other Horizontal Siding. Drop siding can be obtained in several patterns. This siding, with tongue-and-groove or shiplap edges, can be obtained in 1x6-inch and 1x8-inch sizes. It is commonly used for unconditioned buildings and for garages, usually without sheathing. Tests conducted at the Forest Products Laboratory have shown that the tongue-and-groove patterns have greater resistance to the penetration of wind-driven rain than shiplap patterns.

Hardboard lap siding is also available, both primed and prefinished, in various widths. Installation should be performed in accordance with the manufacturer's instructions as to spacing, nailing, and finishing.

Plywood and flakeboard are also available as 6-, 8-, and 12-inch horizontal lap siding in thickness from ½ inch to ⅝ inch.

Siding for Horizontal, Vertical, and Diagonal Applications

A number of sidings can be used horizontally, vertically, or diagonally. These are manufactured in nominal 1-inch thickness and in widths from 4 inches to 12 inches. Both matched and shiplapped edges are available. The narrow and medium widths are likely to be more satisfactory where changes in moisture content are moderate. When wide siding is used, vertical grain is desirable to reduce shrinkage. With tongue-and-groove siding, the correct moisture content at the time of installation is particularly important because of possible shrinkage to a point

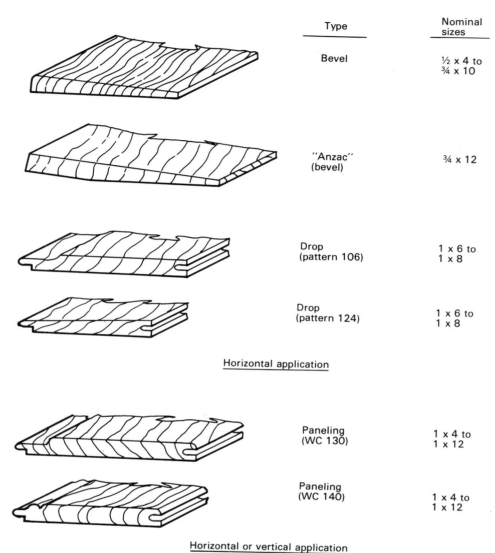

Type	Nominal sizes
Bevel	½ x 4 to ¾ x 10
"Anzac" (bevel)	¾ x 12
Drop (pattern 106)	1 x 6 to 1 x 8
Drop (pattern 124)	1 x 6 to 1 x 8

Horizontal application

Type	Nominal sizes
Paneling (WC 130)	1 x 4 to 1 x 12
Paneling (WC 140)	1 x 4 to 1 x 12

Horizontal or vertical application

Figure 107. Common wood-siding patterns

where the tongue is exposed or even totally withdrawn from the groove.

Treating the edges of drop siding with water-repellent preservative usually prevents moisture penetration of the wood. Under wide overhangs, or in porches or other protected areas, this treatment is not as important.

Siding for Vertical Application

A method of siding application popular for some architectural styles utilizes rough-sawn boards and battens applied vertically. These can be arranged in several ways: 1) board and batten; 2) batten and board; and 3) board and board (Figure 108). Nail vertical sidings to 2x4 horizontal wood blocking installed 16- to 24-inches on center between the studs.

Siding with Sheet Materials

Sheet materials are available for siding, including plywood, in a variety of face treatments and species, paper-overlaid plywood, and hardboard. Plywood or paper-overlaid plywood is often used without sheathing. Exterior grade particleboard and waferboard are also available for panel siding.

Sheets of these materials are usually 4x8 feet or longer. They are usually applied vertically, with intermediate and perimeter nailing to provide the desired rigidity. Some can be applied horizontally with appropriate vertical-joint treatment. Most other methods of applying sheet materials require some type of sheathing beneath. Horizontal joints should be protected by a "zee" flashing.

Exterior type plywood should be used for siding. It can be obtained in such surfaces as grooved, brushed, or saw-textured. These surfaces are usually finished with some type of stain. If shiplap or matched edges are not provided, some method of providing a waterproof joint should be used. This waterproofing often consists of applying caulking and a batten at each joint. A batten at each stud may be applied if closer spacing is desired for appearance. Another alternative is to install "zee" flashing along the joint (Figure 87). An edge treatment of water-repellent preservative will also help reduce moisture absorption. A minimum 1/16-inch edge and end spacing should be allowed for expansion when installing plywood in sheet form.

Paper-overlaid plywood provides a very satisfactory base for paint. A medium-density, overlaid plywood is most commonly used. Hardboard sheets are applied in much the same way as plywood. The manufacturer's recommendations for installation should be followed.

Many of these materials resist the passage of water vapor. When they are used, a well-installed vapor retarder should be applied on the warm side of the insulated walls.

Wood Shingles and Shakes

Wood shingles and shakes, discussed in Chapter 3 under "Roof Coverings," can be used for siding with many styles of houses. In Cape Cod or colonial houses, shingles can be painted or stained. For ranch or contemporary designs, wide exposures of shingles or shakes often add a desired effect and they are easily stained.

Grades and Species. Western red cedar, northern white cedar, bald cypress, and redwood are commonly used for shingles. The heartwood of these species has a natural decay resistance which is par-

ticularly desirable if shingles are to remain unpainted or unstained.

Western red cedar shingles can be obtained in three grades. The first grade (No. 1) is all heartwood, edge-grain, and knot-free. It is primarily intended for roofs but is desirable in double-course sidewall application where much of the face is exposed.

With second grade shingles (No. 2), three-fourths of the shingle length is blemish-free. A 1-inch width of sapwood and mixed vertical and flat grain are permissible in this grade. No. 2 shingles are most often used in single-course application for sidewalls.

Third grade shingles (No. 3) are clear for 6 inches from the butt. Flat grain and greater widths of sapwood are permissable. Third-grade shingles are likely to be somewhat thinner than the first and second grades. They are used for secondary buildings and sometimes as undercourse in double-course application. A lower grade than the third grade, known as undercoursing shingles, is used only as the under or completely covered course in double-course sidewall applications.

Shingle Sizes. Wood shingles are available in three standard lengths: 16, 18, and 24 inches. The 16-inch length has a butt thickness of slightly less than ½ inch, so that five butt thicknesses total 2 inches when green (designated as 5/2). These shingles are usually packed in bundles with 20 courses on each side. Four such bundles will cover 100 square feet (one square) of wall or roof with an exposure of 5 inches. The 18-inch and 24-inch shingles have thicker butts, five in 2¼ inches for the 18-inch shingles and four in 2 inches for the 24-inch lengths.

Shakes are usually available in several types, the most popular being the split-and-resawn. The sawed face is used as the back face. Butt thickness vary from ¾ inch to 1½ inches. They are usually packed in bundles of 20 square feet so that five bundles will cover one square.

Other Exterior Finishes

Some architectural designs use nonwood materials such as vinyl and metal sidings. Stucco or cement plaster, preferably over a wire mesh base, are most often seen in the Southwest and the West coast. Masonry veneers can be used in combination with wood siding in various finishes to enhance the appearance of both materials.

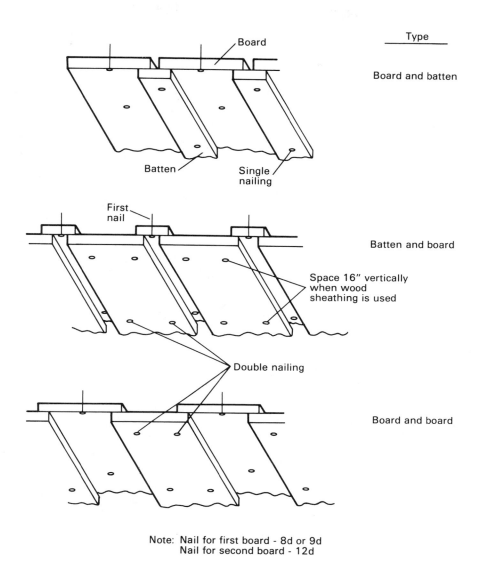

Type

Board and batten

Board

Batten

Single nailing

First nail

Batten and board

Space 16" vertically when wood sheathing is used

Double nailing

Board and board

Note: Nail for first board - 8d or 9d
Nail for second board - 12d

Figure 108. Common vertical board siding patterns

Installation

Corrosion-resistant nails made of galvanized steel, stainless steel, aluminum, or similar metals should be used to install siding. Ordinary steel-wire nails tend to rust very quickly and can cause disfiguring stains on the face of the siding. In some cases, small-head nails will show rust spots through the putty and paint.

Two types of nails are commonly used with siding: finishing nails with small heads and siding nails with moderate-size flatheads. Finishing nails should be set (driven with a nail set) about 1/16 inch below the face of the siding and the hole filled with putty after the prime coat of paint is applied. Flathead nails should be driven flush with the face of the siding and the head later covered with paint. In some types of prefinished sidings, nails with color-matched heads are supplied.

Nails with modified shanks can be used. These include annularly threaded shank (ring shank) nails and helically threaded shank nails. Both have greater withdrawal resistance than smooth-shank nails and, for this reason, a shorter nail can be used.

Exposed nails should be driven just flush with the surface of the wood. Overdriving may produce hammer marks and may split and crush the wood.

In sidings with prefinished surfaces or overlays, the nails should be driven so as not to damage the finished surface.

Bevel Siding. The lap for bevel siding should be at least 1 inch. The average exposure distance is usually determined by the distance from the underside of the window sill to the top of the drip cap (Figure 109). For weather resistance and appearance, the butt edge of the first course of siding above the window should coincide with the top of the window drip cap. In many one-story houses with an overhang, this course of siding is often replaced with a frieze board. It is also desirable that the bottom of a siding course be flush with the underside of the window sill. However, this may not always be possible because of varying window heights and types.

One system for determining siding exposure width so that it is about equal both above and below the window sill is to divide the overall height of the window frame by the approximate recommended exposure distance for the siding used (4 for 6-inch wide siding, 6 for 8-inch siding, 8 for 10-inch siding, and 10 for 12-inch siding). This method will give the number of courses between the top and bottom of the window. For example, if the overall height of a window from the top of the drip cap to the bottom of the sill is 61 inches and 12-inch siding is used, the number of courses would be 61/10 (= 6.1) or slightly more than six courses. To obtain the exact exposure distance, divide 61 by 6 (= 10-1/6 inches). The next step is to determine the exposure distance from the bottom of the sill to just below the top of the foundation wall. If this is 31 inches, three courses at 10-1/3 inches each would be used, and the exposure distance above and below the window would be about the same.

When this system is not satisfactory because of large differences in the two areas, an equal exposure distance for the entire wall height should be used and the siding at the window sill notched. The fit should be tight to keep moisture out.

Installation should begin at the bottom course. It is normally blocked out with a starting strip of the same thickness as the top of the siding board. Each succeeding course should overlap the upper edge of the lower course. Siding should be nailed to each stud with a 1½-inch minimum stud penetration. When plywood or wood is used over nonwood shea-

thing, 7d or 8d nails (2¼ inches and 2½ inches long) may be used for ¾-inch thick siding. For ½-inch-thick siding, nails may be ¼-inch shorter than those used for ¾-inch siding.

If rigid foam, gypsum, or nonnail-base fiberboard sheathing is used, the nail lengths must be adjusted to account for the thickness of the sheathing. Guidelines from the National Forest Products Association deal with the nailing of wood-bevel siding and hardboard lap siding over rigid-foam sheathing. For ½-inch wood-bevel siding installed over ½-inch rigid foam sheathing, a 9d (2¾-inch) smooth shank or a 7d (2¼-inch) ring shank wood siding nail is recommended. If ¾-inch rigid-foam sheathing is used, the nail sizes should be increased to a 10d (3-inch) smooth shank or 8d (2½-inch) ring shank. When ¾-inch wood-bevel siding is installed over ½-inch rigid-foam sheathing, the wood-siding nail sizes recommended are 10d smooth shank or 8d ring shank. If ¾-inch rigid-foam sheathing is used, the nail sizes should be increased to 12d (3¼-inch) smooth shank or 9d ring shank. The recommendation for 7/16-inch hardboard lap siding installed over either ½-inch or ¾-inch rigid-foam sheathing is to use a 10d smooth-shank hardboard siding nail.

Nails should be located far enough up from the bottom edge of the siding to miss the top edge of the lower siding course (Figure 110A). This clearance distance is usually ⅛ inch and will permit slight movement of the siding due to moisture changes without causing splitting. Such an allowance is particularly important for the wider sidings of 8 inches to 12 inches.

It is good practice to avoid butt joints whenever possible. Longer sections of siding should be used under windows and for other long stretches; shorter lengths should be used for areas between windows and doors. Where they are unavoidable, butt joints should be made over a stud and staggered between courses as much as possible.

Siding should be square-cut to provide good joints at windows and door casings and at butt joints. Open joints allow moisture to enter, often causing paint to deteriorate. It is good practice to brush or dip the fresh-cut ends of the siding in a water-repellent preservative before boards are nailed in place. Water-repellent preservative can be applied to end and butt joints after siding is in place by use of a small finger-actuated oil can.

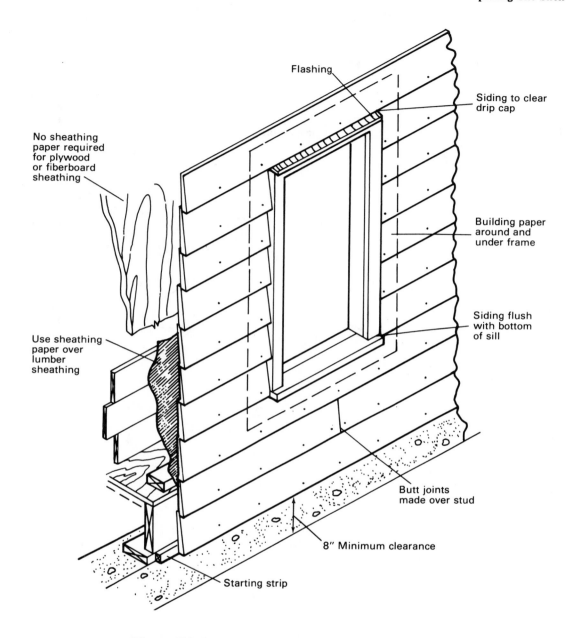

Flashing

Siding to clear drip cap

No sheathing paper required for plywood or fiberboard sheathing

Building paper around and under frame

Use sheathing paper over lumber sheathing

Siding flush with bottom of sill

Butt joints made over stud

8″ Minimum clearance

Starting strip

Figure 109. Installation of bevel-pattern wood siding

Drop and Similar Sidings. Drop siding is installed much the same fashion as lap siding except for spacing and nailing. Drop sidings have a constant exposure distance. Face width is normally 5¼ inches for 1x6-inch siding and 7¼ inches for 1x8-inch siding. One or two 8d nails should be used at each stud crossing, depending on the width (Figure 110). Two nails are used for widths greater than 6 inches.

Other materials such as plywood, hardboard, or medium-density fiberboard, which are used hori-zontally in widths up to 12 inches, should be applied in the same manner as lap or drop siding, depending on the pattern. Prepackaged siding should be applied according to the manufacturer's instructions.

Vertical and Diagonal Siding. Diagonally applied matched and similar siding having shiplap or tongue-and-groove joints is nailed to the studs in the same manner as when such materials are applied horizontally. When applied vertically, these sidings should be nailed to blocking inserted between studs.

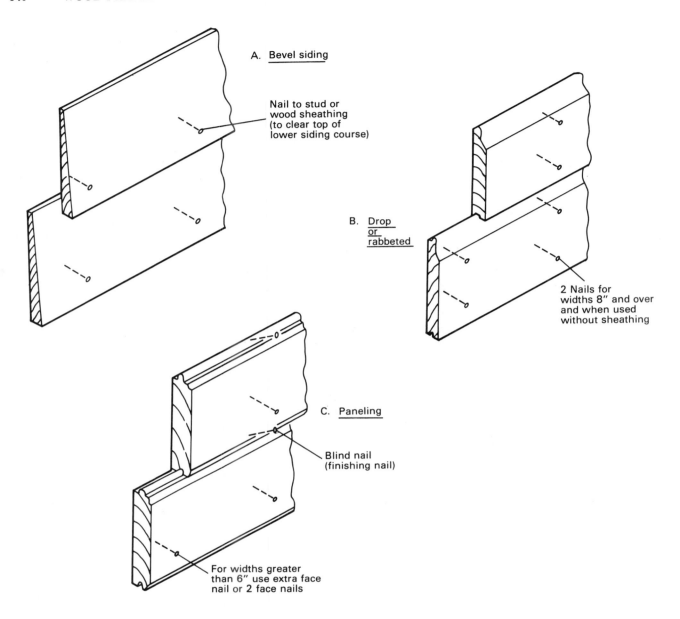

Figure 110. Nailing of wood siding: (A) bevel-pattern siding; (B) drop-pattern siding; (C) paneling-pattern siding

Blocking is installed horizontally between studs and spaced 16 to 24 inches apart.

When various combinations of boards and battens are used, they should also be nailed to horizontal blocking spaced from 16 to 24 inches apart between studs. The first boards or battens should be fastened with one 8d or 9d nail at each block to provide at least 1½-inch penetration. For wide underboards, two nails spaced about 2 inches apart may be used rather than a single row along the center. The second or top boards or battens should be nailed with 12d nails. Nails in the top board or batten should miss the underboards and not be nailed through them. Double nails should be spaced closely to prevent splitting if the board shrinks.

Plywood and Other Sheet Siding. Exterior type plywood, paper-overlaid plywood, hardboard, and similar sheet materials used for siding are usually applied vertically, although some plywood siding may be applied horizontally. All nailing should be over studs and effective penetration into wood should be at least 1½ inches.

Plywood should be nailed at 6-inch intervals around the perimeter and at 12-inch intervals at intermediate members. All types of sheet material should have joints caulked, unless the joints are of the overlapping or matched type or unless battens are installed. For all sheet-siding materials, manufacturer's recommended installation and finishing procedures should be followed.

Corner Treatment. The method of finishing wood siding or other materials at exterior corners is often influenced by the overall design of the house. The ends of the siding can be mitered as in Figure 111A.

A mitered corner effect (Figure 111B) on horizontal siding can be obtained by using metal corners at each course. Metal corners are easily placed over each corner as the siding is installed. They should fit tightly without openings, and should be nailed on each side to the sheathing or corner stud beneath. Most metal corners are made of aluminum and need no added treatment before painting. Those made of galvanized steel should be cleaned with a mild acid wash and primed with a metal primer before the house is painted, to prevent early peeling of the paint. Weathering of the metal will also prepare it for the prime paint coat.

Corner boards of various types and sizes can be used for horizontal sidings of all types (Figure 111C). They also provide a satisfactory termination for plywood and similar sheet materials. Corner boards are usually nominal 1-inch material and for purposes of appearance can be quite narrow.

Color-matched metal corners can be used with prefinished shingle or shake exteriors. Such corners can also be lapped over the adjacent corner shingle, alternating each course. This procedure is called "lacing." This type of corner treatment usually requires that flashing be used beneath.

When siding returns against a roof surface, such as at a dormer, there should be a clearance of about 2 inches (Figure 111D). Siding cut and installed tightly against the shingles retains moisture after rains and usually results in paint peeling. Shingle flashing extending well up on the dormer wall will provide the necessary resistance to the entry of rain. A water-repellent preservative should be used on the ends of the siding at the roofline.

Interior corners (Figure 111E) are butted against a square corner board of nominal 1¼-inch or 1⅜-inch size, depending on the thickness of the siding.

Material Transition. Different materials involving different application methods may be used in the gable ends and in the walls below. Good drainage should be assured at the juncture of the two materials. For example, if vertical boards and battens are used at the gable end and horizontal siding below, a drip cap or similar molding could be used (Figure 112). Flashing should be used over and above the drip cap so that moisture will clear the gable material. Alternatively, good drainage can be provided by extending the plate and studs of the gable end out from the wall a short distance, or by the use of furring strips to project the gable siding beyond the wall siding (Figure 113).

Wood Shingles and Shakes. Wood shingles and shakes are applied in a single-course or double-course pattern. They can be used over wood or plywood sheathing. If the sheathing is ⅜-inch plywood, threaded nails should be used. For nonwood sheathing, 1x3-inch or 1x4-inch wood nailing strips should be used as a base.

In the single-course method, one course is laid over the other in a manner similar to siding. The shingles can be second grade because one-half or less of the butt portion is exposed (Figure 114). Shingles should not be soaked before application, but should generally be laid up with about ⅛ inch to ¼ inch of space between adjacent shingles to allow for expansion during rainy weather. When a "siding effect" is desired, the shingles should be laid up so that the edges are lightly in contact. Prestained or pretreated shingles give the best results for this system.

In the double-course system, the undercourse is applied over the wall and the top course is nailed directly over the undercourse, with a ¼-inch to ½-inch projection of the butt below the butt of the undercourse (Figure 115). The first course should be nailed only enough to hold it in place while the outer course is being applied. The first shingles can be third grade or undercourse grade. The top course should be first grade.

Exposure distance for the various lengths of shingles and shakes can be guided by the recommendations in Table 14.

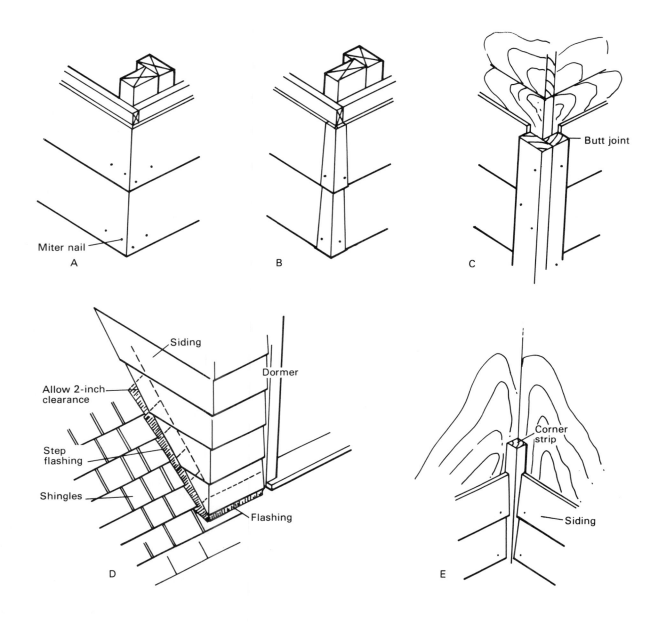

Figure 111. Siding installation details: (A) mitered corner; (B) metal corner; (C) corner boards; (D) siding return at roof; (E) interior corner strip

As with roof shingles, joints should be "broken" so that edge joints of the upper shingles are at least 1½ inches from the under-shingle joints. Closed or open joints can be used in the application of shingles to sidewalls at the discretion of the builder. Spacing of ¼ inch to ⅜ inch produces an individual effect, while close spacing produces a shadowline similar to bevel siding.

Shingles and shakes should be applied with rust-resistant nails that are long enough to penetrate into the wood-backing strips or sheathing. In single coursing, a 3d or 4d galvanized "shingle" nail is commonly used. In double coursing, where nails are exposed, a 5d galvanized nail with a small flathead should be used for the top course and 3d or 4d size for the undercourse.

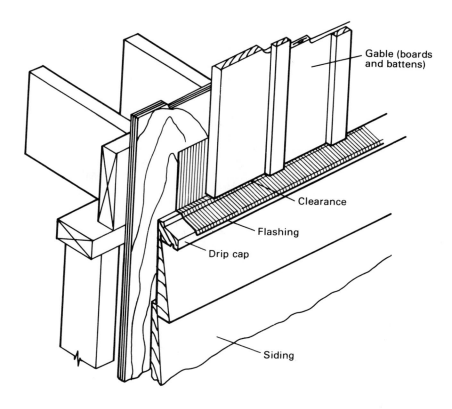

Gable (boards
and battens)

Clearance

Flashing

Drip cap

Siding

Figure 112. Siding transition at gable end

Nails should be placed ¾ inch from the edge of the shingle. Two nails should be used for shingles up to 8 inches wide and three nails for shingles over 8 inches. In single-course applications, nails should be placed 1 inch above the buttline of the next higher course (Figure 114). In double coursing, the use of a piece of shiplap sheathing as a guide allows the outer course to extend ½ inch below the undercourse, producing a shadowline (Figure 115). Nails should be placed 2 inches above the bottom of the shingle or shake. Rived or fluted processed shakes, usually factory-stained, produce a distinct effect when laid with closely fitted edges in a double-course pattern.

Stucco Finish. Stucco finishes are applied over a coated expanded metal lath and, usually, over some type of sheathing. In some areas where local building regulations permit, such a finish can be applied to. metal lath fastened directly to the braced wall framework. Waterproof paper should be used over the studs before the metal lath is applied.

When stucco is applied to platform-framed two-story houses, shrinkage of joists and sills may cause unsightly bulges or breaks in the stucco unless joists have reached moisture equilibrium. The proper moisture content of the framing members is important when this type of finish is used.

Masonry Veneer. Brick or stone veneer is used for all or part of the exterior wall finish in some styles of architecture. When possible, it is good practice to delay applying the masonry finish over platform framing until the joists and other members reach moisture equilibrium. Waterproof-paper backing and sufficient wall ties should be used. Figure 116 shows details of the installation of masonry veneer. It is normal practice to install the masonry veneer with a ¾-inch space between the veneer and the wall sheathing. This space provides room for the bricklayer's fingers when setting the brick.

Aluminum and Vinyl. Aluminum and vinyl can be purchased in a variety of qualities, and they

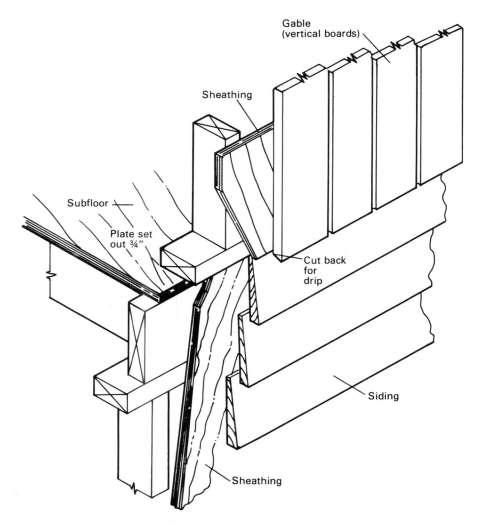

Figure 113. Gable-end siding projection to form drip edge without flashing

require little maintenance beyond periodic cleaning. Installation should be performed in compliance with the instructions provided by the manufacturers.

EXTERIOR TRIM

Exterior trim includes materials and products used for exterior finish other than siding or brick veneer. The term includes window and door trim, cornice moldings, fascia boards and soffits, rake or gable end trim, and porch trim and molding. Some exterior trim, in the form of finish lumber and moldings, is cut and fitted on the job. Other materials or assemblies such as shutters, louvers, railings, and posts, are shop-fabricated and are ready for installation.

Material Used for Trim

The properties desired in materials used for trim are good painting and weathering characteristics, easy working qualities, and maximum freedom from warp. Decay resistance is also desirable where materials may absorb moisture in such areas as the caps and the bases of porch columns, rails, and shutters. Pressure-treated lumber and the heartwood of cedars, cypress, and redwood have a high resistance to decay. Columns, shutters, and louvers are also available in aluminum and/or vinyl. Many

Table 13
Exposure distances for wood shingles and shakes on sidewalls

Material	Length	Single coursing	Double coursing	
			No. 1 grade	No. 2 grade
Shingles	16″	7½″	12″	10″
	18″	8½″	14″	11″
	24″	11½″	16″	14″
Shakes (hand split and resawn)	18″	8½″	14″	—
	24″	11½″	20″	—
	32″	15″	—	—

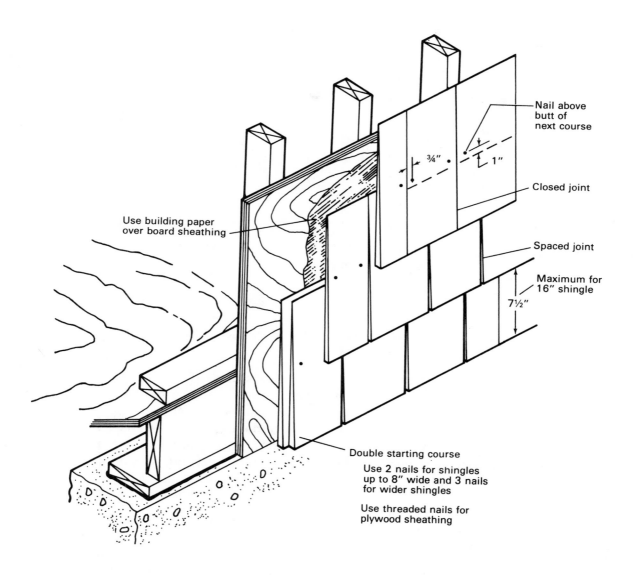

Nail above butt of next course

¾″   1″

Closed joint

Use building paper over board sheathing

Spaced joint

Maximum for 16″ shingle

7½″

Double starting course

Use 2 nails for shingles up to 8″ wide and 3 nails for wider shingles

Use threaded nails for plywood sheathing

Figure 114. Single-course application of wood shingles or shakes on sidewall

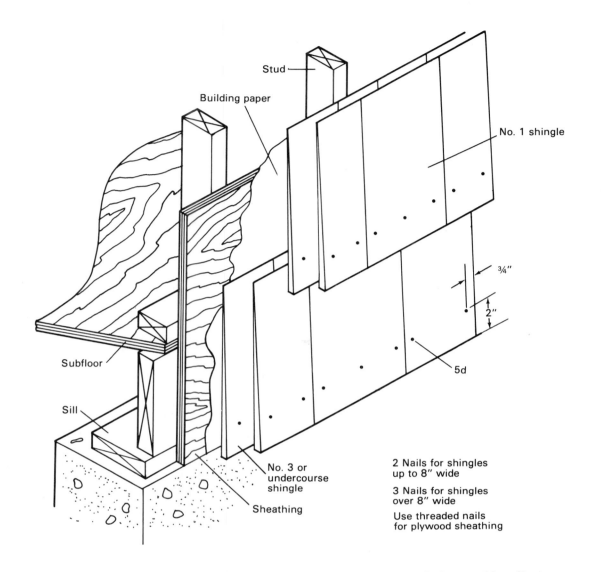

Figure 115. Double-course application of wood shingles or shakes on sidewalls

wood-trim manufacturers predip such materials as siding, window sash, window and door frames, and trim, using a water-repellent preservative. On-the-job dipping of end joints or miters is recommended for water resistance and decay protection.

Nails or screws used for fastening trim should be rust-resistant (i.e., aluminum, galvanized, or stainless steel) to reduce staining and discoloration. With a natural finish, only aluminum or stainless steel should be used. Cement-coated nails are not rust-resistant.

As with the installation of siding, trim is normally attached with standard nails; finish or casing nails can also be used. Most of the trim along the shingle line, such as at gable ends and cornices, is installed before the roof shingles are applied. Lumber used for exterior trim should be grade No. 1 or No. 2 and should have a moisture content of approximately 12 percent at the time of installation.

Cornice Construction

The cornice or eave of a building is the lower portion of the roof that overhangs the wall. In gable roofs, the cornice is formed on the long sides of a house; with hip roofs, it is continuous around the perimeter. Three common types of cornice are the

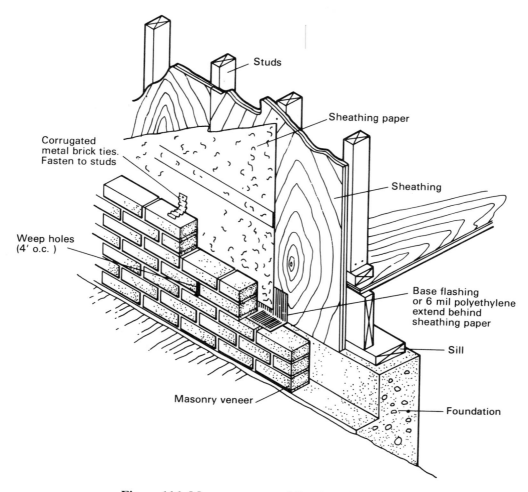

Figure 116. Masonry veneer siding installation

box, the close (no overhang), and the open (no soffit). The box cornice is the most widely used. Box and open cornices overhang and protect the sidewalls, windows, and foundation from rain. Properly sized, overhangs can shade south-facing windows in summer when the sun is at a high angle but will allow passive solar heating in winter when the sun is low in the sky. The close cornice, with little overhang, does not serve these functions. Exposed-beam roofs with wood roof decking and wide overhangs in contemporary or rustic designs commonly use the open cornice.

Narrow Box Cornice. With a narrow box cornice, the projection of a rafter is cut to serve as a horizontal nailing surface for the soffit and fascia (Figure 117A). The truss roof version has a small horizontal

return wedge to which the soffit is nailed (Figure 117B). The soffit provides a desirable area for inlet ventilators which allow good attic insulation and ventilation, keep the house and attic cooler in the summer, and minimize ice dams in winter. (Refer to the section on "Attic Ventilation.")

Soffit molding, often ¾-inch cove, is used to cover the crack between the siding and soffit. Metal roof drip edge is often used to cover the crack between the roof sheathing and fascia and to reduce the chance of water penetration and rotting.

Wide Box Cornice With Returns. A wide box cornice normally requires an additional horizontal member, attached to each truss, to which the soffit is nailed. Trusses can be ordered with these "returns"

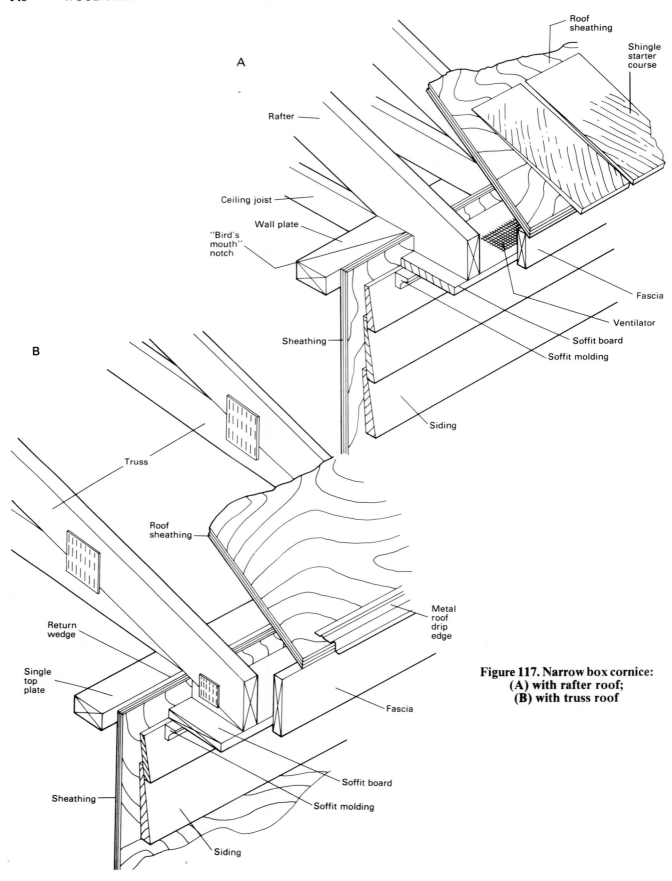

A

Roof
sheathing

Shingle
starter
course

Rafter

Ceiling joist

Wall plate

"Bird's
mouth"
notch

Sheathing

Fascia

Ventilator

Soffit board

Soffit molding

Siding

B

Truss

Roof
sheathing

Return
wedge

Single
top
plate

Metal
roof
drip
edge

Fascia

Sheathing

Soffit board

Soffit molding

Siding

**Figure 117. Narrow box cornice:
(A) with rafter roof;
(B) with truss roof**

attached (Figure 118A). When rafters are used, "lookouts" are toe-nailed to the wall and face-nailed to the ends of the rafter overhang (Figure 118B).

Soffits can be made of lumber, plywood, paper-overlaid plywood, hardboard, medium density fiberboard, or other sheet material. Soffits made of prefinished aluminum and vinyl are maintenance-free and have built-in ventilation holes. Thicknesses of wood soffit materials should be based on the distance between supports; ⅜-inch plywood and ½-inch fiberboard are often used for 24-inch truss spacing. Fascias are normally made of No. 1 wood boards but may also be aluminum or vinyl. Expansion of aluminum and vinyl fascia with high temperatures can give them a wavy look. A fascia backer at the ends of the trusses or rafters is sometimes used to provide additional nailing and support area for soffit and fascia (Figure 118A and 118B). The fascia backer is normally omitted in cornice extensions when a rabbeted fascia is used.

The projection of the cornice beyond the wall should not be so great as to prevent the use of a molding above the top casing of the windows. A combination of steep slope and wide projection will bring the soffit in this type of cornice too low. Alternatives include a box cornice without horizontal returns or lookouts, or a raised Fink roof truss.

Box Cornice Without Returns.

A wide boxed cornice without horizontal returns or lookouts, providing a sloped soffit, is sometimes used for houses with wide overhangs (Figure 119A and 119B). The soffit material is nailed directly to the underside of the rafter extensions. Inlet ventilators, singly or in a continuous strip, are installed in the soffit area.

Raised Fink Truss Box Cornice.

The raised Fink truss roof allows thick ceiling insulation, with an airspace above it, to extend to the outer edge of the exterior wall (Figure 120). It also permits construction of a steep slope roof with wide overhangs, without interfering with windows and doors. The soffit remains the same height as the interior ceiling regardless of the roof slope or projection of the cornice. The soffit is attached to the horizontal bottom truss chord, which extends to the end of the rafter projection. A compression wedge carries the weight of the roof from the top truss chord to the bottom chord directly over the wall.

Open Cornice.

An open cornice is structurally the same as a wide box cornice without returns or lookouts, except that the soffit is eliminated (Figure 121). Open cornices are often used in post-and-beam construction with large, widely spaced rafters and with 2x4-inch or 2x6-inch tongue-and-grooved decking used for roof sheathing. When rafters are more closely spaced, paper-overlaid plywood or V-grooved boards can be used for roof sheathing at the overhanging section. This method might require, for the rest of the roof, sheathing thicker than would normally be used. This type of cornice can also be used for conventionally framed houses, utility buildings, or cottages, with or without a fascia board.

The open cornice requires that blocking be toe-nailed in place between the rafters or trusses to close the space between the top of the wall and the bottom of the roof sheathing (Figure 121). If trim is desired, blocking is best placed vertically. The trim board must then be carefully notched to fit around the rafters. Roofing nails protruding through the exposed sheathing can be clipped with large bull-nosed snips, and a higher grade roof sheathing can be used around the perimeter of the roof to enhance the appearance of the underside of the overhang.

Close Cornice.

A close cornice is one is which there is no rafter or truss projection beyond the wall (Figure 122). Wall sheathing or sheet siding (plywood or hardboard) extends upward past the ends of the trusses or rafters to the bottom of the roof sheathing. The roof is terminated only by the fascia, siding, and, sometimes, a shingle molding. While this cornice is simple to build, it is unattractive, and it provides little weather protection to the sidewalls and no space for inlet ventilators. Its appearance can be improved and siding somewhat protected by the use of a gutter.

Rake or Gable-End Finish

A rake or gable overhang is the extension of a gable roof beyond the end wall of the house. The rake might be classed as 1) close, with little projection, 2) box or open, supported by the roof sheathing, and 3) wide box supported by special ladder-like roof framing. It is essentially nonfunctional since it provides little shade or protection from rain. Such overhangs are normally too high to shade windows, and wind renders their protection from

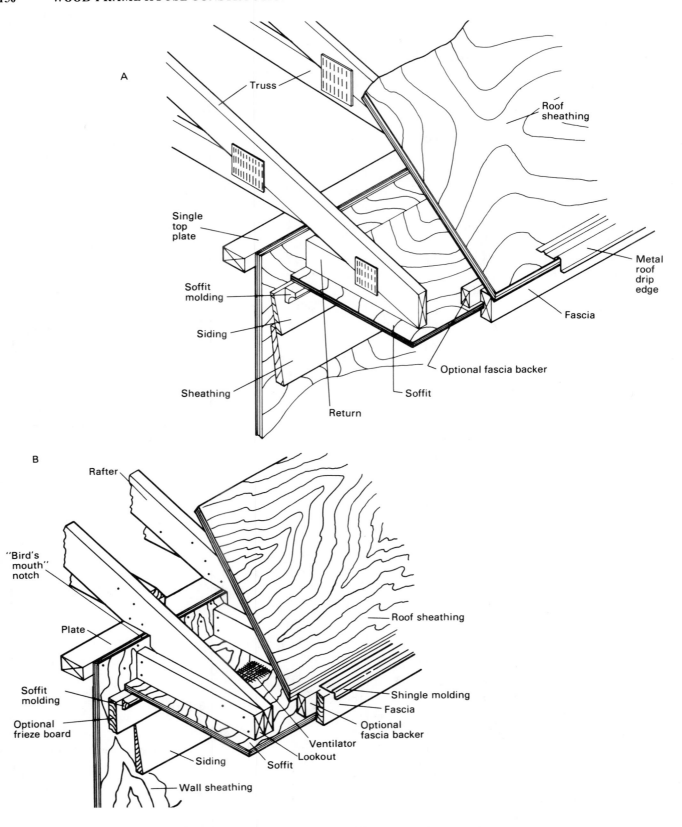

Figure 118. Wide box cornice with horizontal returns:
(A) with truss roof; (B) with rafter roof

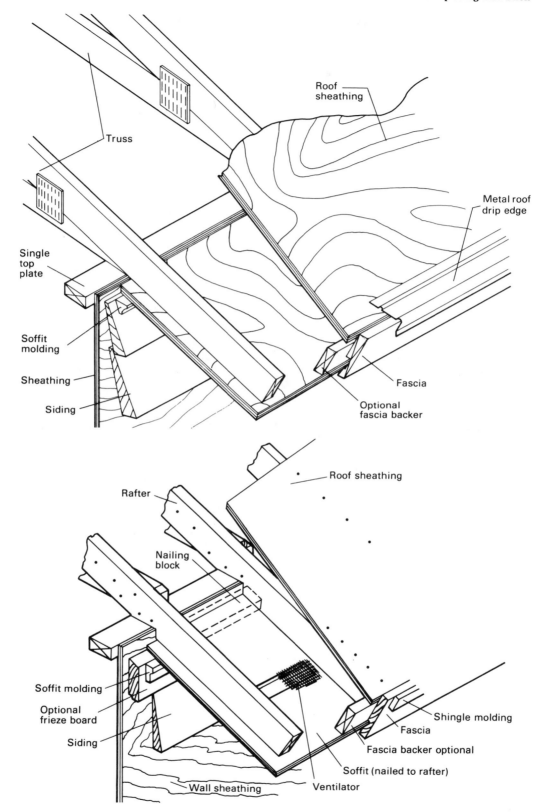

**Figure 119. Wide box cornice without returns:
(A) with truss roof; (B) with rafter roof**

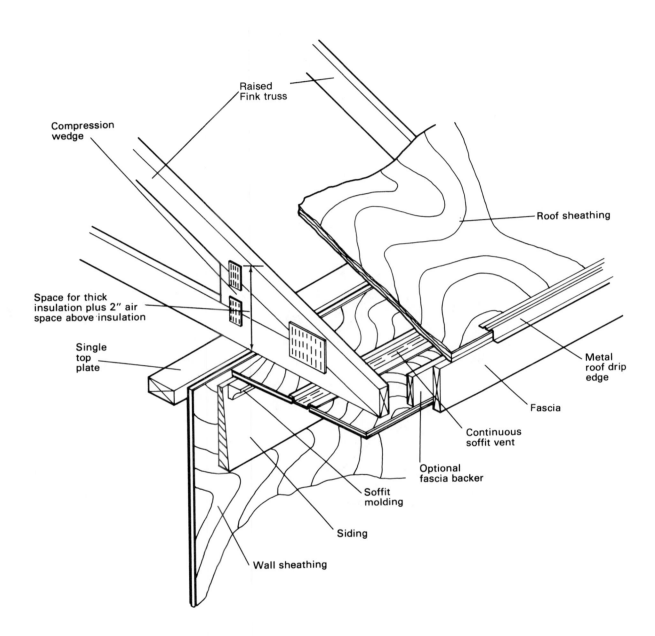

Figure 120. Wide box cornice with horizontal return and raised Fink trusses

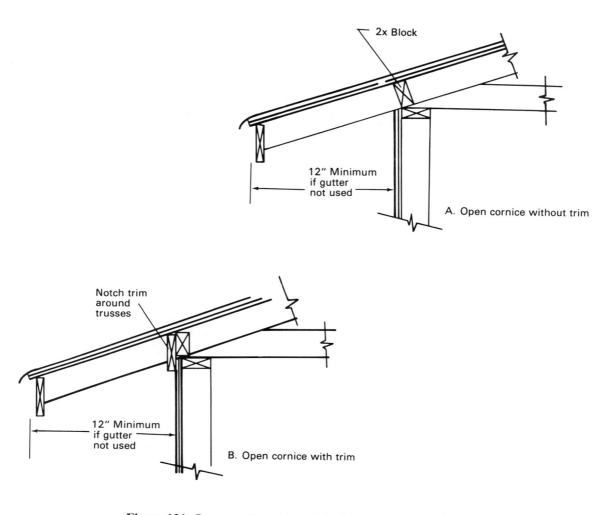

Figure 121. Open cornice detail: (A) without trim; (B) with trim

rain ineffective. In addition, no portion of the roof drains toward the gable overhang.

If no overhang is desired, the siding can be brought up to the underside of the roof sheathing and the crack covered by a metal roof drip edge. A small overhang can be provided by installing a fascia board (Figure 123B). A slightly greater overhang can be provided by attaching the fascia to a fascia block (Figure 123C). The siding can be terminated beneath the fascia block. When the rake extension is supported by the roof sheathing and is 6 to 8 inches wide, the fascia and soffit can be nailed to a series of short lookout blocks (Figure 124).

With an overhang of up to 12 inches, the extending sheathing supports the overhang, and a fly rafter (rake board) keeps the sheathing straight (Figure 125). Additional support for the fly rafter can be provided by extending the rafter ridge board and the fascia backers and fascia at the eaves. The roof sheathing boards or plywood should extend from inner rafters to the end of the gable projection to provide rigidity and strength. The roof sheathing is nailed to the fly rafter and to the lookout blocks, which aid in supporting the rake section and also serve as a nailing area for the soffit.

Gable extensions of more than 12 inches require rigid framing to resist roof loads and to prevent sagging of the rake section. This framing is usually provided by a series of purlins or lookout members nailed to a fly rafter at the outside edge. The purlins pass over and are supported by the gable wall and are nailed to an interior truss (Figure 126). This

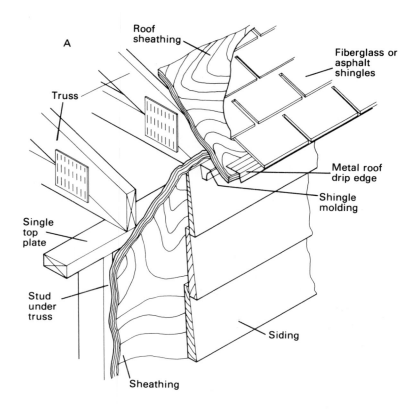

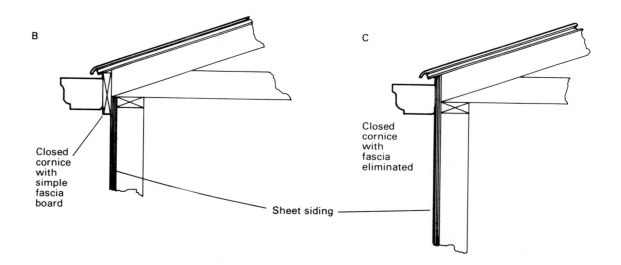

Figure 122. Close cornice detail: (A) assembly; (B) close cornice with simple fascia;
(C) close cornice with fascia eliminated

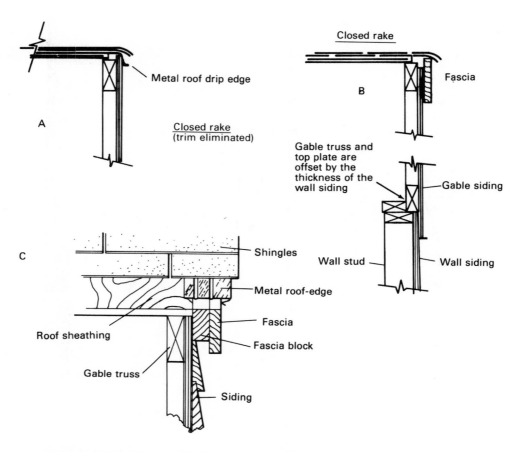

Figure 123. Close rake finish: (A) trim eliminated; (B) with fascia board; (C) with fascia and fascia block

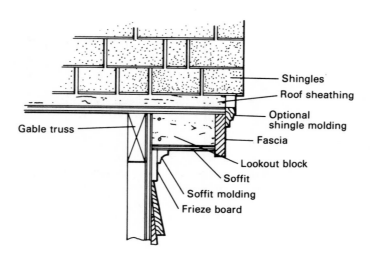

Figure 124. Short rake extension with lookout blocks

A

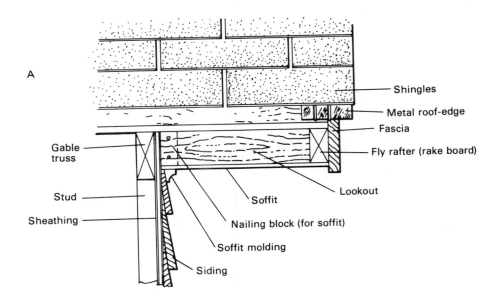

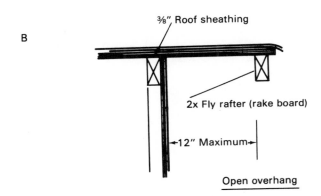

Figure 125. Moderate rake extension with fly rafter: (A) with enclosing lookout blocks, soffit, and fascia; (B) open overhang without trim

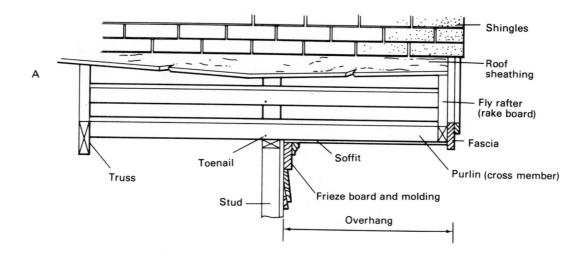

A

- Shingles
- Roof sheathing
- Fly rafter (rake board)
- Fascia
- Purlin (cross member)
- Soffit
- Frieze board and molding
- Toenail
- Truss
- Stud
- Overhang

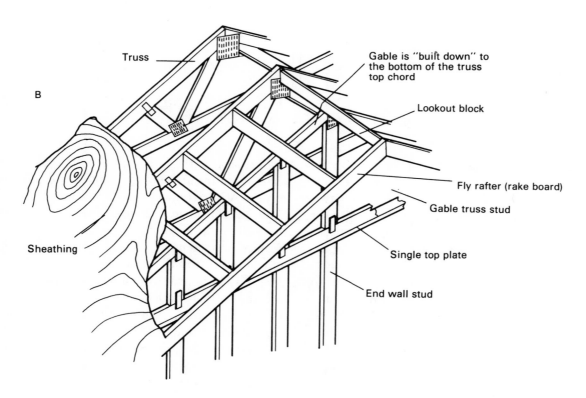

B

- Truss
- Sheathing
- Gable is "built down" to the bottom of the truss top chord
- Lookout block
- Fly rafter (rake board)
- Gable truss stud
- Single top plate
- End wall stud

Figure 126. Wide rake extension: (A) side view of ladder framing; (B) ladder framing details

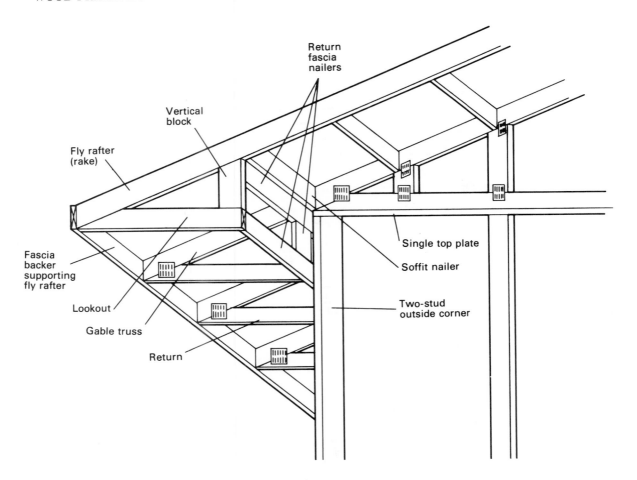

Figure 127. Cornice return framing detail

framing can be constructed either in place, or on the ground, and hoisted into place. For ease of construction, lookouts are often nailed between two rafters, giving the appearance of a "ladder." One side of the ladder is nailed to the interior truss. Although this practice wastes a rafter, it saves labor.

When ladder framing is used with a rafter roof, the rafter serving as the side of the ladder attached to the roof framing should be cut with a "bird's mouth" notch in the same fashion as the other rafters, to fit the wall plate. The lookouts should be spaced 16 to 24 inches apart, depending on the thickness of the soffit material.

Cornice Return

The cornice return is the finish where the cornice meets the rake on a gable roof. In hip roofs, the cornice is usually continuous around the entire house. In a gable house, it must be terminated or joined with the gable ends.

Cornices with horizontal soffits are usually changed to the angle of the roof by use of a cornice return. A horizontal lookout is attached to the fly rafter, and a vertical block connects the rafter with the lookout at a point in line with the house wall. Nailers are fastened from the lookout to the house and between the fly rafter and the gable (Figure 127). Fascia boards are nailed to vertical portions, and the soffit is nailed to the horizontal portions. The fascia board and shingle molding of the cornice are carried around the corners and up to the slope of the rake. On cornices without horizontal lookout members, the soffit continues its slope up the rake overhang (Figure 128).

The extra material and labor required for good cornice overhangs are usually justified by better sidewall and foundation protection, lower costs for paint maintenance, and, if soffit vents are used, a cooler house in summer and smaller ice dams in winter.

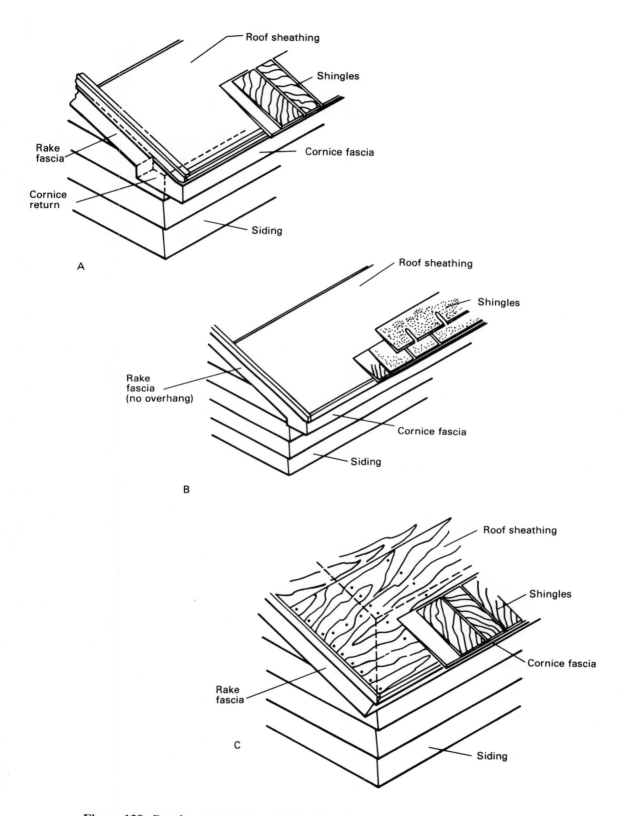

Figure 128. Cornice return types: (A) horizontal return; (B) horizontal return with no gable overhang; (C) sloped return

CHAPTER 5

Specialty Features

This chapter covers a variety of specialty features that are included in some, but not all, home construction plans.

FIREPLACES, WOOD STOVES, AND CHIMNEYS

There are significant structural considerations relating to both safety and efficiency in the installation of fireplaces and wood stoves and the chimneys that they require for operation. Basic information is provided in the following sections.

Fireplaces

From the standpoint of efficiency in heat production, which is estimated to be only 10 percent, fireplaces could be considered a luxury. However, they are often desired as a decorative feature. As indicated in the next two sections, their efficiency can usually be improved by installing a factory-made circulating fireplace. This metal unit, enclosed by masonry, allows heated air to be circulated throughout the room in a system separate from the direct heat of the fire.

Satisfactory fireplace performance can be achieved by following several rules relating the fireplace opening size to flue area, depth of the opening, and certain other measurements.

It is generally recommended that the depth of the fireplace should be about two-thirds the height of the opening. Thus, a 30-inch-high fireplace would be 20 inches deep from the face to the rear of the opening.

The flue area (inside length times inside width) should be at least one-tenth of the area of the fireplace opening (width times height) when the chimney is 15 feet or more in height. When less than 15 feet high, the flue area should be one-eighth of the area of the opening of the fireplace. This height is measured from the throat (Figure 129) to the top of the chimney. Thus, a fireplace with a 30-inch width and 24-inch height (720 sq. in.) would require an 8x12-inch flue, which has an inside area of about 80 square inches, when the chimney height is 15 feet or over. A 12x12-inch flue liner has an area of about 125 square inches and would be large enough for a 36x30-inch opening when the chimney height is 15 feet or over.

Steel angle iron should be used to support the brick or masonry over the fireplace opening. The bottom of the inner hearth, the sides, and the back should be built of a heat-resistant material such as firebrick. The outer hearth should extend at least 16

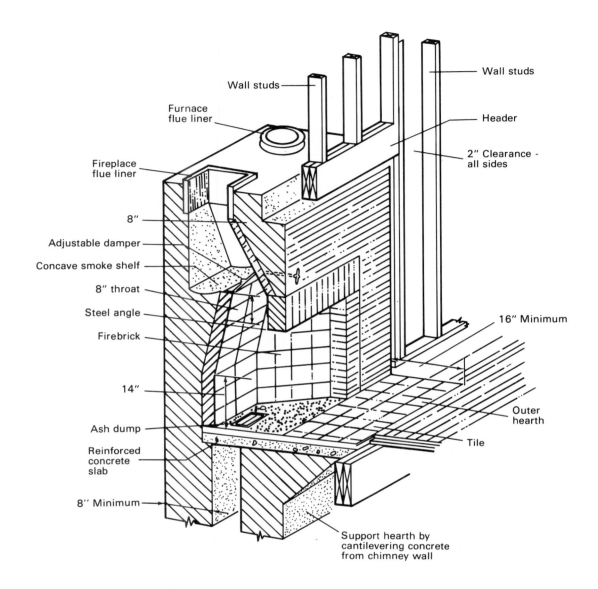

Figure 129. Masonry fireplace components

inches out from the face of the fireplace and be supported by a reinforced-concrete slab. This outer hearth provides protection against flying sparks and should be made of noncombustible materials such as glazed tile. Other details relating to clearance, framing of the wall, cleanout opening, and ash dump are also shown in Figure 129. Hangers and brackets for fireplace screens are often built into the face of the fireplace.

The back of the fireplace is usually 6 to 8 inches narrower than the front. This narrower width helps to guide the smoke and fumes toward the rear. A vertical backwall about 14 inches high tapers toward

the upper section or "throat" of the fireplace (Figure 129). The area of the throat should be about 1¼ to 1-1/3 times the area of the flue to promote better draft. An adjustable damper is used at this area for easy control of the opening.

The smoke shelf (top of the throat) is necessary to prevent back drafts. The height of the smoke shelf should be 8 inches above the top of the fireplace opening (Figure 129). The smoke shelf is concave to retain any slight amount of rain that may enter.

Fireplaces with two or more openings (Figure 130) require much larger flues than do conventional fireplaces. For example, a fireplace with two open adjacent faces (Figure 130A) would require a 12x16-inch flue for a 34x20x30-inch (width, depth, and height, respectively) opening. Local building regulations usually specify sizes for these types of fireplaces.

Air-Circulating Firebox Forms. The heating capacity of a fireplace can be increased by using steel air-circulating firebox forms. These usually form the firebox sides and rear, plus the throat, damper, smoke shelf, and smoke chamber. The sides and back of the circulator are double, enclosing a space within which air is heated. Cool air is introduced into this space near the floor level and, when heated by the hot steel, rises and returns to the room through registers located at a higher level.

Air-circulating firebox forms can also prevent smoke from entering the room. The volume of air drawn up the chimney is substantial and is normally replaced by cold air infiltrating through cracks in the house. In modern, "tight" house construction, however, the caulking and weatherstripping that reduce air infiltration also hamper the chimney draft, with the common result that smoke will be drawn into the room. This problem is solved by installation of an air circulating firebox, along with glass doors across the fireplace front that prevent room air from entering the firebox.

The firebox form is set on a firebrick floor laid on reinforced concrete. The chimney flue is begun at the top of the form and, facing the room, decorative masonry is laid around the unit opening. Small fans are often installed to increase the unit's heating efficiency, and the inlets and outlets are covered with decorative grates.

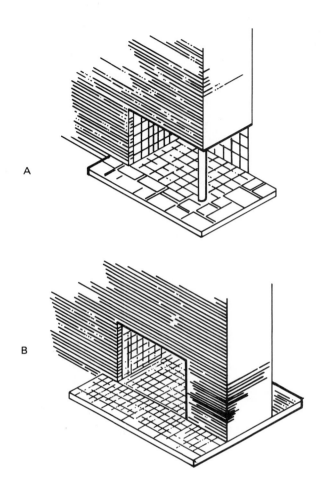

Figure 130. Dual-opening fireplace: (A) adjacent opening; (B) through fireplace

"Zero-Clearance" Prefabricated Fireboxes. Factory-built fireplace units can be ordered that include all fireplace and chimney components from the hearth to the chimney cap. These are called "zero-clearance units" because they can be installed on wood floors and against wood framing (Figure 131). The units have steel walls and include insulation that protects wood structures from excessive heat. They frequently include dampers, screens, glass doors, circulating fans, and external air supply ducts. Some are of free-standing contemporary type. Others can be placed on raised hearths and faced with stone or brick to provide a traditional appearance, or covered with sheetrock and trimmed in wood. Their insulated steel chimney pipe can be housed in a wood-stud chimney utilizing the same style of siding as the house.

Wood Stoves

Some types of wood stoves are free-standing; others are designed for insertion into fireplace openings. Their air intake is controlled to produce efficient slow and more complete combustion than is possible with fireplaces, with little loss of room air up the chimney. Airtight wood stoves can provide a combustion efficiency of 30 to 40 percent (a gas furnace is typically 80 percent efficient). Some models are made of steel or cast iron, which radiates heat. Others are enclosed in thin steel jackets, allowing air to circulate between the stove and the jacket. The cooler outer jacket provides a desirable safety feature. Air enters and leaves the space between stove and jacket through vents and heats the room

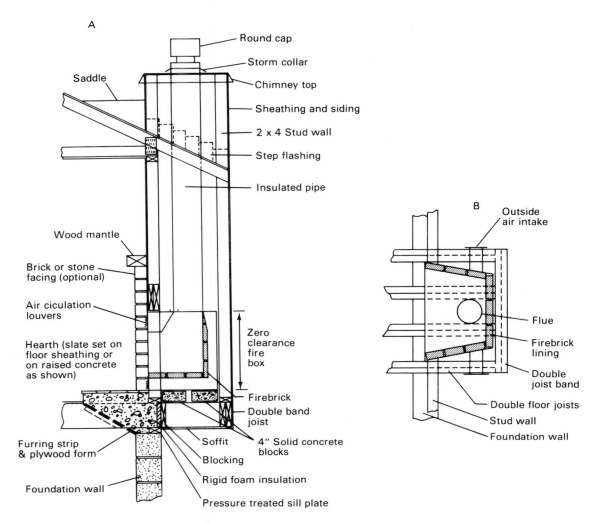

**Figure 131. Zero-clearance fireplace in external wood chimney:
(A) side view; (B) top view**

through convection. (Refer to Chapter 8, section on "Heat Flow and Insulation.") Fans are sometimes employed to improve circulation. In some systems, the heated air is collected in a plenum and distributed to other rooms through ducts.

Some models contain coils through which water circulates; the heated water can be employed for domestic uses or for space heating. Water can be pumped to various locations or circulated by convection.

Some wood stoves have glass doors that make them look more like a fireplace. They can be set on brick, tile, or stone hearths and surrounded with walls of the same materials. Wood stoves can be connected to either insulated steel or masonry flues (Figure 132).

As wood stoves have increased in popularity, failure to observe proper fire-safety precautions in construction and installation has resulted in fires and accidents. *It is especially important to remember that wood and other combustibles can be heated to the flash point even if there is no direct contact between the hot stove and the combustible material.* Sufficient heat to ignite combustibles can be passed from the stove across airspaces through convection and radiation, or through intervening noncombustible materials such as masonry that are in contact with the combustible material. Precautions that should be taken include the following:

1. When an uninsulated metal pipe or thimble passes through or comes in contact with

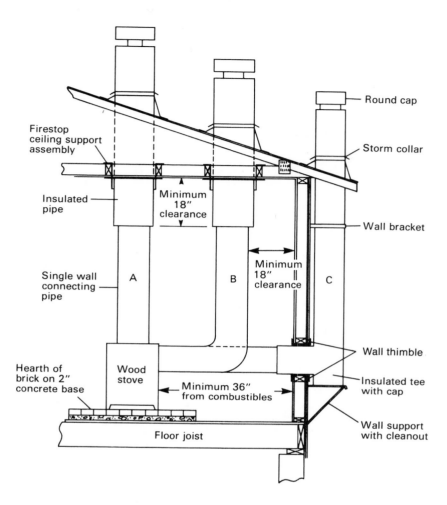

Figure 132. Wood stove: (A) top-mounted flue; (B) rear flue through ceiling; (C) rear flue through wall

walls, ceiling, or framing, at least 6 inches of fiberglass insulation should be packed between the pipe and such materials at all points of passage or contact. Fiberglass insulation with paper facings should not be used. Cement, stone, brick, or asbestos cannot serve as substitutes for such insulation, since all such materials can conduct sufficient heat to bring adjacent combustibles to the flash point.

2. Clay thimbles should not be run directly through concrete block or other nonflammable masonry. The thimble, masonry, or both, may crack, allowing heat to rise within the masonry cavities and ignite the wood sill. For passage through nonflammable block or masonry, an insulated steel pipe should be used. Alternatively, a steel pipe can be passed through the thimble, with any of various techniques being used to maintain an airspace between the two pipes. This airspace should be open to the basement room.

3. Manufacturers of various types of stoves specify minimum safe distances for their stoves from walls and other combustible materials. These specifications should be carefully followed. In general, free-standing wood stoves should be kept at least 3 feet from combustibles, including wood studs covered with gypsumboard and half-bricks. If a stove is placed closer to a wall or other combustible material than the minimum distance specified by the manufacturer, a steel heat shield should be placed between the stove and such materials, with airspace on both sides of the shield.

4. Uninsulated steel flue pipes should not be closer than 3 feet from ceilings.

5. Free-standing wood stoves should be set on brick or concrete hearths. Bricks of standard 2¾-inch thickness or 3 inches of concrete should be used.

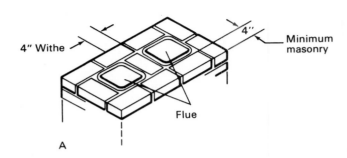

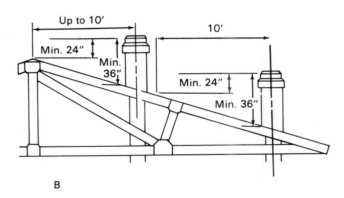

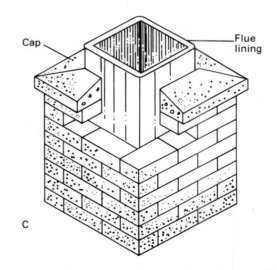

**Figure 133. Chimney details: (A) spacer between flues;
(B) height of chimneys;
(C) chimney cap**

Chimneys

Chimneys can be constructed of masonry units supported on a suitable foundation or of lightweight insulated stainless steel pipe. They must be structurally safe and capable of producing sufficient draft for fireplaces, stoves, and/or other fuel-burning equipment. Steel flue pipe should bear a label signifying approval by Underwriters Laboratories, Inc.

The chimney should be built on a concrete footing of sufficient area, depth, and strength for the imposed load. It is usually free standing and is constructed in such a way that it neither supports nor is supported by the structural framework of the house. The chimney footing should be below the frostline. For houses with a basement, the footings for the walls and fireplace are usually poured together and at the same elevation.

The size of the chimney depends on the number of flues, the presence or absence of fireplaces, and the design of the house. Each fireplace should have a separate flue. For best performance, flues should be separated by a 4-inch-wide brick spacer (withe) placed between them (Figure 133A).

Certain house designs include a room-wide brick or stone fireplace wall that extends through the roof. While only two or three flues may be required for heating units and fireplaces, several "false" flues may be added at the top for appearance.

Flue sizes conform to the width and length of a brick so that full-length bricks can be used to enclose the flue lining. Thus, an 8x8-inch flue lining (about 8½ inches by 8½ inches in outside dimensions) with the minimum 4-inch thickness of surrounding masonry will use six standard bricks for each course (Figure 134A). An 8x12-inch flue lining (8½ inches by 13 inches in outside dimensions) will be enclosed by seven bricks at each course (Figure 134B), and a 12x12-inch flue (13 inches by 13 inches in outside dimensions) by eight bricks (Figure 134C).

The height of the chimney and the size of the flue are important factors in providing sufficient draft. In addition, the greater the difference in temperature between chimney gases and the outside atmosphere, the better the draft. A chimney constructed within the house framework will have better draft then a chimney constructed in an exterior wall because the masonry will retain heat longer.

The height of a chimney above the roofline usually depends on its location in relation to the roof

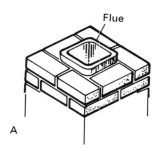
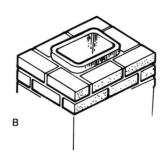
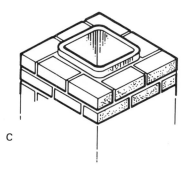

Figure 134. Chimney brick and flue combinations: (A) 8x8-inch flue lining; (B) 8x12-inch flue lining; (C) 12x12-inch flue lining

ridge. If the chimney is within 10 feet of the roof ridge, the top of the flue liner must extend a minimum of 24 inches above the ridge and must be a minimum of 36 inches above the highest part of the roof next to the chimney. When the chimney is more than 10 feet from the roof ridge, the top of the chimney must extend a minimum of 24 inches above the highest point on the roof within 10 feet of the chimney and at least 36 inches above the highest point on the roof next to the chimney (Figure 133B). For flat or low-pitched roofs, the chimney should extend at least 3 feet above the highest point of the roof.

To prevent moisture from entering between the brick and flue lining, a concrete cap is usually poured over the top course of brick (Figure 133C). Precast or stone caps with a cement wash are also used.

Flashing for chimneys is illustrated in Figures 93 and 135. Masonry chimneys should be separated from wood framing, subfloor, and other combustible materials. Framing members should have at least a 2-inch clearance and should be fire-stopped at each floor with a noncombustible material (Figure 136). Subfloor, roof sheathing, and wall sheathing should have a ¾-inch clearance.

A cleanout door is included in the bottom of the chimney where there are fireplaces or other solid fuel burning equipment, as well as at the bottom of other flues. The cleanout door for the furnace flue is usually located just below the smokepipe thimble, with enough room for a soot pocket.

Flue Linings. Rectangular fire-clay linings or round vitrified (glazed) tile are normally used for chimney flues. Local codes usually require vitrified tile or a stainless-steel lining for gas-burning equipment.

Rectangular flue lining is made in 2-foot lengths and in various sizes from 8x8 inches to 24x24 inches. Wall thicknesses vary with the size of the flue. Smaller linings have a ⅝-inch thick wall, and larger sizes vary from ¾ inch to 1⅜ inches in thickness. Vitrified tiles 8 inches in diameter are most commonly used for the flues of the heating unit, although larger sizes are also available. This type of tile has a bell joint.

Flue lining should begin at least 8 inches below the thimble for a connecting smokepipe or vent pipe

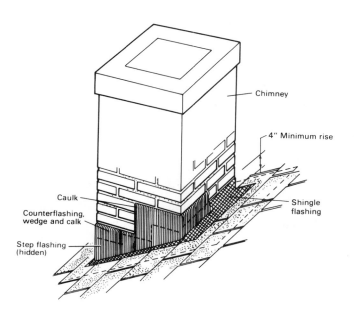

Figure 135. Chimney flashing

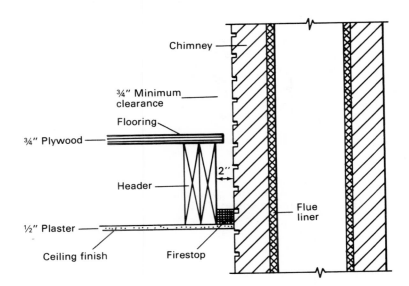

Figure 136. Chimney clearances for wood frame construction

from the furnace. For fireplaces, the flue liner should start at the top of the throat and extend to the top of the chimney.

Flue liners should be installed sufficiently ahead of the brick or masonry work, as it is carried up, so that careful bedding of the mortar will result in a tight, smooth joint. When diagonal offsets are necessary, the flue liners should be beveled at the directional change in order to have a tight joint. It is also good practice to stagger the joints in adjacent tile.

Standard flue blocks are available for building less expensive chimneys. These blocks are 8 inches high by 16 inches square or larger, with holes in the center sized to fit standard flue liners. Other blocks have half-circular holes on one side; two of these form a circular hole through which a thimble can be placed.

Insulated Steel Chimneys. Insulated steel chimneys are made in tubular sections from 12 to 36 inches long, which are fastened together to form a long pipe. Triple-wall pipe consists of three pipes with spaces between them through which air circulates to remove heat. The inner pipe is made of stainless steel; the outer pipes are galvanized. Another type consists of double-wall stainless-steel pipe with asbestos insulation between the walls.

Both types come with a full line of accessories including tees, wall supports and brackets, roof

supports and flashing, storm collars, caps to keep rain from going down the flue, and spark arrestors. Both types can be fully exposed to weather or enclosed in wood chimneys. Wood chimneys normally consist of conventional stud walls covered with sheathing and siding. The entire top, 2 feet square or larger, is covered with galvanized flashing through which the last section of insulated steel pipe extends.

Unlike clay flues, which could crack in flue fires, steel chimneys do not crack when subjected to the heat of such fires. If creosote buildup is ignited in a steel flue, the fire can burn until the creosote burns off and, if the manufacturer's installation recommendations have been followed, the flue should not be damaged.

GARAGES AND CARPORTS

Garages can be classified as attached, detached, or basement. A carport is a roofed, open structure for sheltering vehicles. The attached garage offers a number of advantages. It can give better architectural lines to the house, it is warmer during cold weather, and it provides convenient space for storage. It also provides covered protection for people who enter or leave vehicles, as well as a short, direct entrance to the house. An attached garage is also less expensive to build than a detached garage because it shares a wall with the house. Detached garages are independent structures which are built on a slab foundation. The specifications for the slab foundation are generally the same as those for an attached garage.

Where there is considerable slope to a lot, basement garages may be desirable. Such garages will generally cost less than those above grade. Carports are usually attached to the house. To improve their appearance and utility, storage cabinets are often built on the open side or at the end.

Size

Many car models are up to 215 inches long and the larger, more expensive models are usually over 230 inches — almost 20 feet — in length. While the garage need not necessarily be designed to take all sizes with adequate room around the car, it is good practice to provide a minimum distance of 21 to 22 feet between the inside faces of the front and rear walls. If additional storage or work space at the back is desired, greater depth is required.

The inside width of a single garage should never be less than 11 feet; 13 feet is better. The recommended minimum outside size for a single garage, therefore, would be 14 by 22 feet. A double garage should be not less than 22 by 22 feet in outside dimensions to provide reasonable clearance. The addition of a shop or storage area would increase these dimensions.

For an attached garage, the foundation wall should extend below the frostline and about 8 inches above the exterior final grade level. It should be not less than 6 inches thick. The sill plate should be anchored to the foundation wall with anchor bolts spaced about 8 feet apart, with at least two bolts in each sill piece. Extra anchors may be required at the sides of the main door.

If fill is required below the floor, it should be sand or gravel. If some other type of soil fill is used, it should be well compacted. If these precautions are not taken, the concrete floor may settle and crack.

The concrete floor should be not less than 4 inches thick. It should be laid with a pitch of about 2 inches from the back to the front of the garage. Welded wire mesh is often used to help control surface

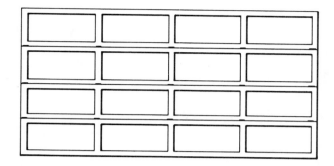

Figure 137. Sectional overhead garage door

cracks; however, unless it is placed in the top one-third of the concrete, it has little value. The garage floor should be set about 1 inch above the drive or apron level. It is desirable to have an expansion joint between the garage floor and the driveway or apron.

The framing of the sidewalls and roof and the application of the exterior covering material should be similar to that of the house. Interior studs can be left exposed or covered with some type of sheet material. Building codes require that the wall between the house and the attached garage be covered with fire-resistant material. Local building regulations and fire codes should be consulted before construction is begun.

Garage Doors

Garage doors most commonly used are of the overhead sectional type (Figure 137). They are made in four or five horizontal hinged sections and have a track extending along the sides under the ceiling framing with a roller for each side of each section. They are opened by lifting and are adaptable to automatic electric opening with remote-control devices. The standard size for a single door is 9 feet wide by 6½ feet or 7 feet high. Doors for two-car garages are usually 16 feet wide.

Doors vary in design, but those most often used are the panel type with solid stiles, rails, and panel fillers. A glazed panel section is often included; translucent fiberglass and embossed steel or aluminum are also available. Clearance from the top of the door to the ceiling must usually be about 12 inches, although low-headroom brackets are available that can reduce the required clearance to 6 inches.

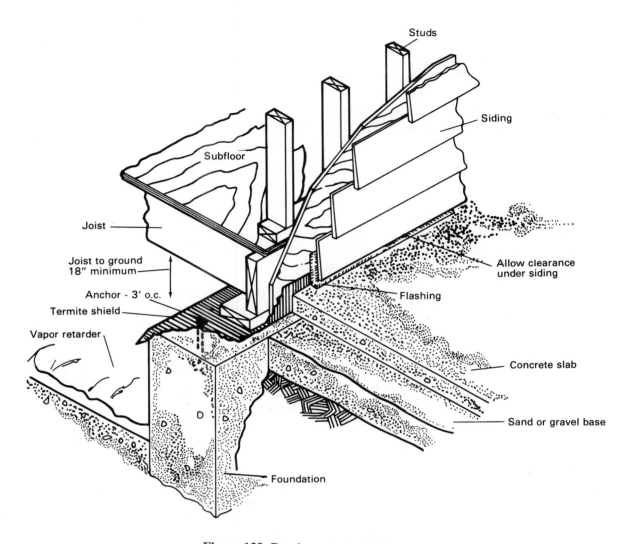

Figure 138. Porch concrete-slab floor

The header beam over garage doors should be designed for the dead load and live load that might be imposed by the roof above. If this header also carries floor loads, the floor live loads must also be considered. Three 2x12-inch boards, 18 feet long, are often required for 16-foot doors. Garage doors in trussed gable end walls have no roof loads to consider.

To keep the garage warmer in cold climates, overhead door units can be ordered with insulation kits and weatherstripping for the perimeter of the door. Weatherstripping is typically made of vinyl for head and side jambs and rubber or vinyl for contact with the floor.

Carports

Carports are often built with 4x4-inch solid wood posts, or 6x6-inch posts in heavy snow-load areas, at all corners and at other intermediate points determined by the size of the load-bearing headers. Typically, there will be four posts (three spaces) in the long direction. The headers that span between the posts are normally 2x8 inches or 2x12 inches on 2-car ports in areas of heavy snow.

Metal post bases are often used to fasten posts to the concrete slab. The load-bearing header is either bolted or nailed to the posts. Connectors must be able to resist strong wind uplift forces. Clearances for automobiles should be the same as for garages, to allow for the possibility that the carport will be closed in at a later date.

PORCHES AND DECKS

Porches or decks should be joined to the main house by means of the framing members and roof sheathing. Rafters, ceiling joists, and studs should be securely attached by nailing, bolting, or lag-screwing to the house framing.

When additions are made to an existing house, it may be desirable to remove siding or other exterior finish so that the framing members of the addition can be easily fastened to the house. In many instances, siding can be cut to the outline of the addition and removed only where necessary. Metal joist hangers are sometimes applied directly to wood or plywood siding, but only at points where the attachment will be to framing members behind the siding at the point of application. Footings should be of sufficient size, with bottoms located below the frostline, and the foundation walls should be anchored to the house foundation when possible.

All lumber used outside, especially joists, flooring, posts, and lattices, should either be pressure-treated or should be of species that offer natural resistance to decay, such as redwood, cypress, and cedar.

Porches

Some porches have roof slopes continuous with the roof of the house. Other porch roofs may have just enough pitch to provide drainage and may require continuously sealed roofing or hot-tar built-up roofing rather than shingles. Basic construction principles for porches are, however, similar, and a general description can cover various types.

Figure 138 shows the construction details for the juncture of a concrete slab floor and the house foundation wall. An attached porch can be open or fully enclosed. It can be constructed with a concrete-slab floor, insulated or uninsulated, or with wood floor framing over a crawl space (Figure 139). Construction details should conform to those previously outlined for various parts of the house itself.

Porch Framing and Floors. Porch floors, whether wood or concrete, should have sufficient slope away

from the house to provide good drainage. Weep holes or drains should be provided in any solid or fully sheathed perimeter wall. Open wood balusters with top and bottom railings should be constructed so that the bottom rail is free of the floor surface.

Wood floor framing should be at least 18 inches above the soil. It is good practice to use a soil cover of polyethylene or similar material under a partially open or a closed porch.

Lattice or grillwork around an open crawl space should be made with a removable section for entry in areas where termites may be present. (Refer to Chapter 8, section on "Protection Against Decay and Termites."). A fully enclosed crawl-space foundation should be vented or have an opening to the basement.

Wood for porch flooring should have good resistance to decay and wear, be nonsplintering, and be resistant to warping. Species commonly used are cypress, Douglas fir, western larch, southern pine, and redwood.

Porch Columns. Roof support for enclosed porches usually consists of fully framed stud walls. Because both interior and exterior finish coverings are used, the walls are constructed much like the walls of the house. However, in open or partially open porches, solid or built-up posts or columns are used. Solid posts, normally 4x4 or 6x6 inches, are used mainly for open porches. A more finished column can be made up of doubled 2x4-inch lumber covered with 1x4-inch boards on two opposite sides and 1x6-inch boards on the other sides (Figure 140A). An open railing may be used between posts.

A large house entrance often includes columns topped by capitals. These columns are factory-made and ready for installation when they reach the building site.

The bases of posts or columns in open porches should be designed so that no pockets are formed to retain moisture. In single posts, a steel pin can be used to locate the post, and a large galvanized washer or similar spacer can be used to keep the bottom of the post above the concrete or wood floor (Figure 140B). Alternatively, a variety of metal post bases are available at lumber yards. The type selected should provide space for drainage under the end of the post (Figure 140C). The bottom of the post should be treated with a moisture-repellant preservative to minimize moisture penetration. Sin-

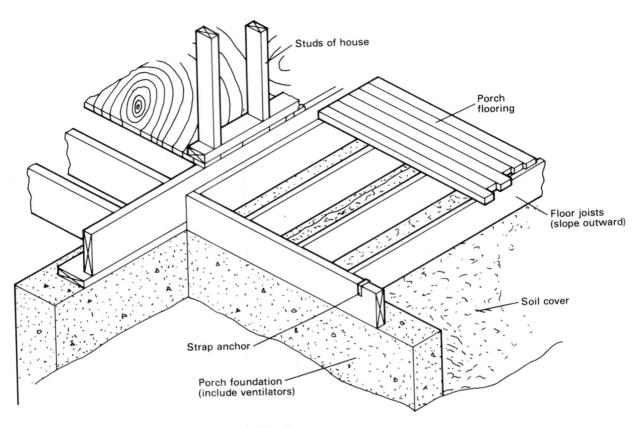

Figure 139. Porch crawl-space floor

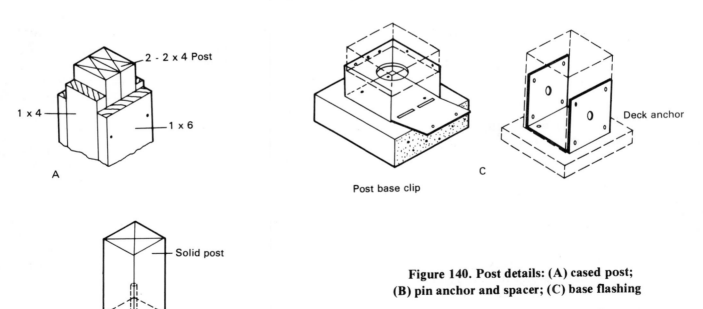

Post base clip

Figure 140. Post details: (A) cased post; (B) pin anchor and spacer; (C) base flashing

gle posts of this type are often made from a decay-resistant wood species or pressure-treated wood.

Balustrades. Porch balustrades usually consist of one or two railings with balusters between them. A closed balustrade can be used in combination with screens or combination windows (Figure 141A). A balustrade with decorative railings can be used for an open porch (Figure 141B). This type can also be used with full-height removable screens.

All balustrade members that are exposed to water and snow should be designed to shed water. The top of the railing should be tapered, and connections with balusters should be protected as much as possible (Figure 142A). Railings should not contact a concrete floor, but should be blocked to provide a small space beneath. When wood such as the blocks must be in contact with the concrete, it should be pressure-treated to resist decay.

The connection of the railing to a post should be made in a way that prevents moisture from being trapped. One method provides a small space between the post and the end of the railing (Figure 142B). When the railing is painted or treated with water-repellent preservative, this type of connection should provide good protection. Exposed members, such as posts, balusters, and railings, should be all heartwood stock of decay-resistant or pressure-treated wood.

Decks

A variety of wood species can be used for building decks. For long life and reduced maintenance, either pressure-treated wood or wood with natural resistance to decay (such as redwood, cedar, or cypress) should be used. Some woods that are easy to work (such as hemlock, most pines, spruce, and Douglas fir) have either low resistance or only moderate resistance to decay and insect attack. Such species can be used for deck construction if they are pressure-treated.

Decks should be designed to withstand heavy loads since they tend to be places where many people congregate. Local building codes should be checked, because they may specify minimum loading requirements. If there are no code requirements, a 40-pounds-per-square foot (psf) live load (people, snow, furniture, equipment, etc.) and a 10 psf dead load (the weight of the deck itself) should be assumed. The spacing of posts, beams, and joists should be based on these requirements. Span tables for floor joists, as shown in the section on "Floor Framing," should be consulted.

Layout. Most decks are attached to the house, although some are free-standing. For those that are attached to the house, the top of decking should be located 1 inch below the inside floor level. If no doorway is in place so that easy measurements can be made, some other point of reference should be used that can be transferred to the outside. For example, the measurement from the top of the inside floor to the bottom of a window sash can be transferred to the outside from the bottom of the same window sash. One inch should be added to this measurement to locate the top of the decking.

Next, a measurement should be made down from the top of the deck to a distance equal to the thickness of the deck flooring plus the height of the deck joists. This point will represent the bottom of the deck joists. The bottom of the deck joists can be located in this manner at both ends of the proposed deck, and a chalkline snapped through the points.

Joist spacing should be marked along the length of the chalkline. The outside face of the first-floor joist will be in line with the end of the deck. Beginning with the outside face of the first-floor joist, a distance of 15¼ inches should be measured to mark the beginning face of the second joist. Thereafter, the beginning faces of the floor joists should be marked at 16-inch intervals. The final mark at the end of the deck marks the outside face of the final floor joist.

One of several methods can be used to attach the deck floor joists to the house along the chalkline. The simplest method is to attach joist hangers directly to the siding with lag screws (Figure 143). The lag screws must penetrate either the floor framing members or the wall studs of the house. The bottoms of the joist hangers are aligned with the chalkline, and the sides of the hangers are aligned with the marks indicating the spacing of the joists.

Another method is to attach a header joist to the side of the house with lag screws that are long enough to penetrate the floor framing or wall studs of the house (Figure 144). The bottom of the header joist should be aligned with the chalkline; its height is the same as the deck floor joists. Metal joist

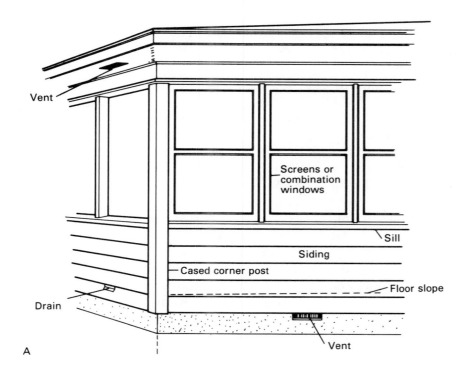

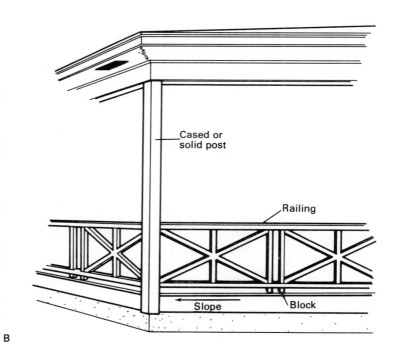

Figure 141. Types of balustrades: (A) closed; (B) open

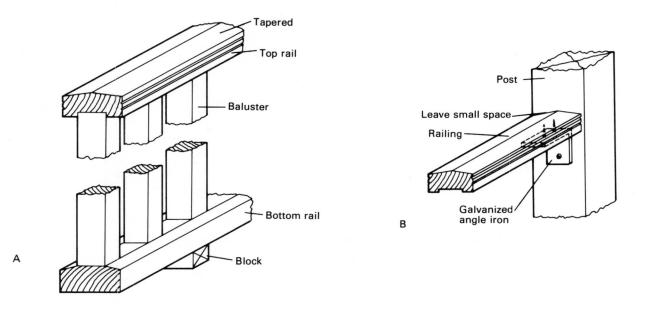

**Figure 142. Railings: (A) balustrade assembly;
(B) rail-to-post connection**

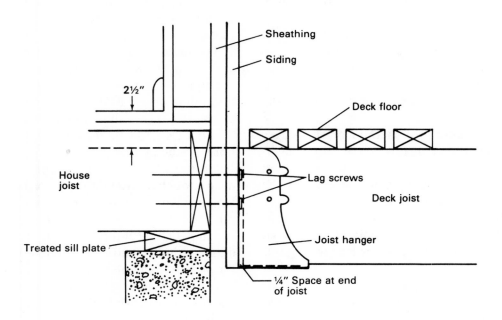

Figure 143. Deck attachment to house with joist hangers

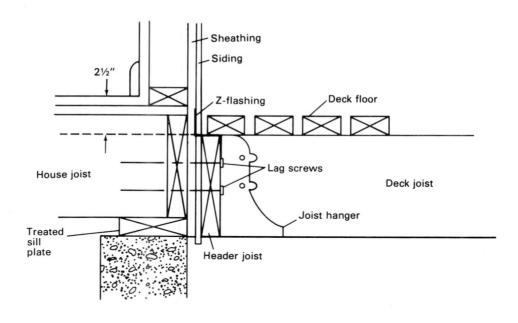

Figure 144. Deck attachment to house with header joist

hangers should be nailed to the header joist with their bottoms aligned with the bottom edge of the joist. The sides of the joist hangers should be aligned with the marks indicating the spacing of the deck floor joists.

A third method is to attach a 2x4- or 2x6-inch wood ledger to the side of the house with lag screws (Figure 145). The top of the ledger should be aligned with the chalkline. No joist hangers are required because the deck floor joists will rest on top of the ledger.

If either the header-joist method or the ledger method is chosen for use against wood siding, flashing must be installed. A circular saw should be used to cut through the siding at the top and along the entire length of the header or ledger. The siding should be pried out with a flat bar, and "zee" flashing installed to prevent water accumulation between the wood siding and the header or ledger (Figures 144 and 145).

If the deck floor framing is attached to a brick or block wall, lead anchors and expansion bolts should be used in place of lag screws.

The deck floor framing should be assembled on the ground by nailing a header joist to the ends of the floor joists on the side of the deck away from the house, using 16d hot-dipped galvanized nails, 3 per

joist. A second header joist should then be nailed to the first. The floor joists should be lifted and the ends placed into the joist hangers or onto the ledger. The header joist should be raised until the deck floor framing is level, and temporarily braced with 2x4 posts.

The deck should be squared with diagonal measurements and a temporary brace placed across the framing to maintain squareness. From a ladder, a plumbline should be dropped to locate footings and posts, and stakes should be driven at these points. The deck should be set on the ground while post holes are being dug.

Footings for the deck's support posts should be deep enough to extend to undisturbed soil below the frostline (Figure 146). One method of digging footing holes is to use a post-hole digger. A 6-foot steel bar may be useful for loosening the soil. An 8-inch diameter hole is sufficient for 4x4-inch posts. When the post footing holes are dug, the deck should again be raised, levelled, and temporarily braced. The joist ends at the house should then be permanently nailed to the hangers or ledger.

If concrete footings are used, the holes should be filled with concrete and post anchors fastened in the concrete. It may be worthwhile to check the location of the anchor with the plumbline. It should be

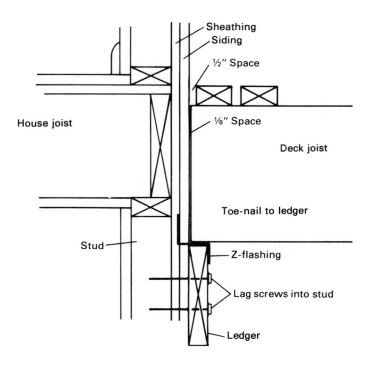

Figure 145. Deck attachment to house using ledger

remembered that the plumb line will probably be at the outside corner of the post, and the anchor should be positioned accordingly. Then, 4x4-inch pressure-treated posts should be cut to fit between the anchor and the deck joists and nailed to the joists (Figure 146A). Curing of the footings requires about seven days. When they are cured, the temporary deck bracing can be removed and the support posts set on and nailed to the anchors.

As an alternative to the use of a concrete footing, about 4 inches of gravel can be placed in the bottom of the hole, its depth measured, and the post cut, set in the hole on top of the gravel, and nailed to the deck floor framing. The hole should then be back-filled with gravel and the gravel tamped (Figure 146C).

Flooring. Starting from the house, string lines should be snapped for placement of deck flooring. If 2x4-inch lumber is used, marks should be made every 4 inches; if 2x6-inch lumber is used, marks should be made every 6 inches. For a 12-foot-deep deck, 36 2x4s or 24 2x6s will be needed. This marking provides a ½-inch space between boards. The first ½-inch space should be adjacent to the house, to allow rain water to drain past the decking.

Corrosion-resistant nails should be used. Two 16d nails should be driven at each deck/joist intersection. If nails are driven at about a 30° angle, they are less likely to loosen. Three 16d nails should be used at butt joints.

Decking boards should be inspected visually for straightness while they are being placed. Any boards having a slight edgewise crook can be straightened somewhat by nailing one end and bending the board into place as it is nailed. Occasionally, a pry bar may be needed to straighten difficult boards. Boards that are slightly bowed should be laid with the crown up. Boards that are "cupped" should be laid with the convex side up to prevent the accumulation of water. It may be necessary to discard boards that are badly deformed.

Railings. Railings must be sturdy enough to withstand the weight of people leaning against them. They should also be designed to prevent children from falling through. Local codes may specify minimum height and opening sizes.

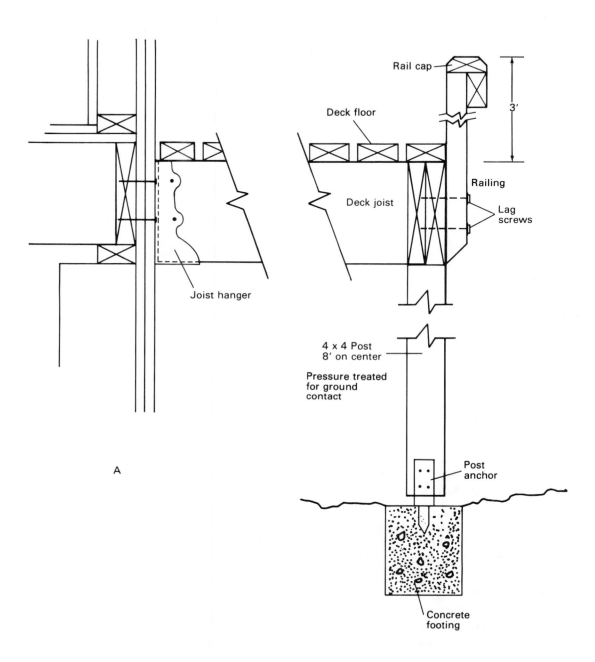

A

Figure 146. Deck post and footing: (A) concrete footing and separate railing;

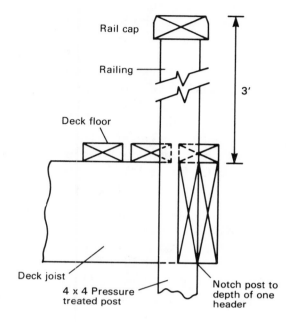

Rail cap

Railing

3'

Deck floor

Deck joist

4 x 4 Pressure treated post

Notch post to depth of one header

B

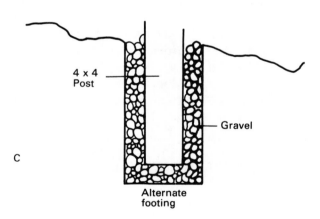

4 x 4 Post

Gravel

C

Alternate footing

Figure 146. Deck post and footing: (B) integral post and railing; (C) alternate gravel footing

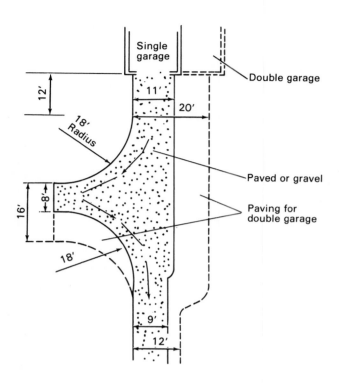

Figure 147. Driveway with turnaround

In the extended post deck method of building railings, the posts extend 36 inches up through the deck flooring and serve as the major rail posts. Many builders use 2x2-inch rail posts, spaced 6 inches on center and lag-screwed to the deck header or to an edge joist. A vertical 2x4-inch board at the top of the 2x2s and a horizontal cap board complete the top of the railings. Edges of the cap board can be routed to give the board a more finished look and to minimize splinters (Figure 146).

DRIVEWAYS AND WALKWAYS

Driveways and walks should be installed before such landscaping as final grading, planting of shrubs and trees, and seeding or sodding of the lawn areas. Concrete and bituminous pavement are most commonly used in the construction of walks and drives, especially in areas where snow removal is important. In some areas of the country, a gravel driveway and a flagstone or precast-concrete walk may be satisfactory, thereby reducing cost.

Driveways

The grade, width, and radius of curves in a driveway are important factors in establishing a safe entry to the garage. When attached garages are located near the street on relatively level property, driveway width is the basic consideration. Driveways that are long and require an area for a turnaround require careful planning and design. Figure 147 shows a driveway and turnaround that allow the driver to back out of a single or double garage into the turnaround and then drive to the street or highway in a forward direction. This approach to traffic is much safer than having to back onto the street or roadway, particularly in areas of heavy traffic. As shown in the Figure 147, a double garage should be serviced by a wider entry and turnaround.

Driveways that must be steep should have a near-level area 12 to 16 feet in front of the garage for safety. Driveways that have a grade more than 7 percent (7-foot rise in 100 feet of length) should have some type of pavement to prevent erosion.

Two types of paved driveways are the more common slab or full-width type and the ribbon type (Figure 148). When driveways are fairly long or steep, the full-width type is the most practical. The ribbon driveway is cheaper and perhaps less conspicuous, because of the grass center strip between the two concrete runners. However, it is not practical if there is a curve or turn involved or if the driveway is long.

The width of the slab-type driveway should be 9 feet, although 8 feet is often considered acceptable (Figure 148A). When the driveway is also used as a walk, it should be at least 10 feet wide to allow for a parked car as well as a walkway. The width should be increased by at least 1 foot at curves. The radius of the drive at the curb should be at least 5 feet. Relatively short double driveways should be at least 18 feet wide and 2 feet wider when they are also to be used as a walk from the street.

The concrete strips in a ribbon driveway should be at least 2 feet in width and located so that they are 5 feet on center (Figure 148B). When the ribbon is also used as a walk, the width of strips should be increased to at least 3 feet.

A 5-bag or 5½-bag commercial concrete mix is ordinarily used for driveways. However, a 5½-bag

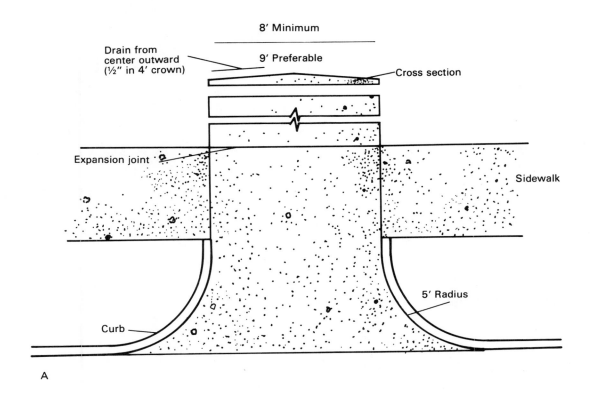

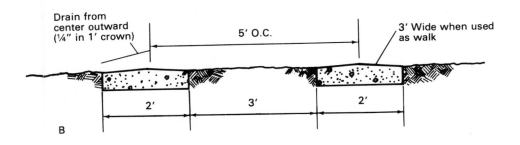

**Figure 148. Driveway details: (A) single-slab driveway
(B) ribbon driveway**

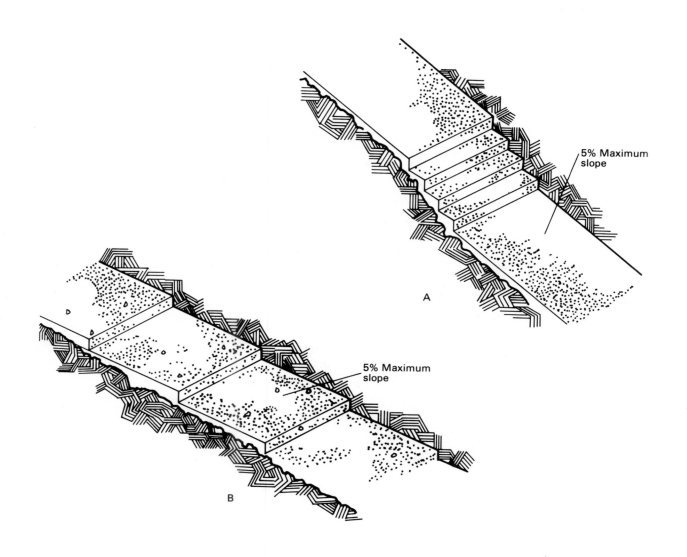

**Figure 149. Sidewalks on slopes: (A) with stairs;
(B) with stepped ramp**

to 6-bag mix containing an air-entraining mixture should be used in areas that have severe winter climates. Pouring a concrete driveway over an area that has been recently filled is poor practice unless the fill, preferably gravel, has settled and is well tamped. A gravel base is not ordinarily required on sandy undisturbed soil, but should be used under all other conditions. Concrete should be about 4 inches thick. A 2x4 is often used for a side form and will produce a 3½-inch-thick slab. The side forms establish the elevation and alignment of the driveway and are used for striking off the concrete.

Under most conditions, steel reinforcing should be used. Steel mesh, 6x6 inches in size and installed in the upper one-third of the poured concrete, will normally prevent or minimize cracking.

Isolation joints, sometimes called expansion joints, should be used 1) at the junction of the driveway with the public walk or curb, 2) at the junction with the garage slab, and 3) about every 40 feet on long driveways. The purpose of the isolation joint is to separate two adjacent concrete sections that may move relative to each other. The isolation joint should be filled with a material such as asphalt-impregnated fiber sheathing. The joint filler material should be set ½-inch below the concrete surface, to allow placing of a sealant at the top to make the joint watertight.

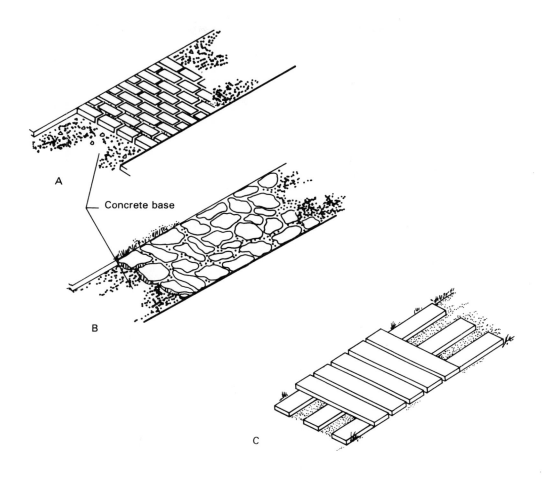

**Figure 150. Other sidewalks: (A) brick;
(B) flagstone; (C) pressure-treated wood**

Control joints should be provided at 10-foot to 12-foot intervals. These crosswise grooves, cut into the partially set concrete, will allow the concrete to crack in a controlled fashion along these lines during the cold weather rather than forming irregular cracks in other areas. To be effective, the control-joint depth should be approximately one-fourth of the concrete thickness.

Blacktop driveways, normally constructed by paving contractors, should also have a well-tamped gravel or crushed rock base. The top should be slightly crowned for drainage.

Walkways

Main walkways generally extend from the front entry to the street or front sidewalk, or to a driveway leading to the street. A 5-percent grade is considered maximum for sidewalks; any greater slope usually requires steps. Walks should be at least 3 feet wide.

Concrete walkways should be constructed in the same general manner as concrete driveways. They should not be poured over filled areas unless such areas have settled and are well tamped, especially in areas near the house after basement excavation backfill has been completed.

The thickness of the concrete over normal undisturbed soil should be about 4 inches. A 2x4 is commonly used as a side form. As described for concrete driveways, control joints should be used and spaced on 4-foot centers. Isolation joints should be used to separate the walkways from steps, driveway, and the public sidewalk.

When slopes to the house are greater than a 5-percent grade, stairs or steps should be used, such as a flight of stairs at a terrace, a continuing sidewalk (Figure 149A), or a ramp sidewalk (Figure 149B). Such stairs should have 11-inch treads and 7-inch risers when the total stair size is 30 inches or less. When the rise is more than 30 inches, the tread should be 12 inches and the riser 6 inches.

For a moderately uniform slope, a stepped ramp may be satisfactory (Figure 149B). Generally, the rise should be about 6 to 6½ inches and the length between risers sufficient for two or three normal paces.

Walks can also be made of brick, flagstone, or other types of stone. Brick and stone are often placed directly over a well-tamped sand base. However, this system is not completely satisfactory where freezing of the soil is possible. For a more durable walk in cold climates, the brick or stone topping should be embedded in a freshly laid reinforced-concrete base (Figure 150).

As with all concrete sidewalks and curbed or uncurbed driveways, the walk should include a slight crown for drainage. Joints between brick or stone may be filled with a cement mortar mix or with sand.

Walkways made of pressure-treated wood can be used in conjunction with decks. Two 2x4-inch boards can be fastened to the ground, 24 inches on center, with steel rebar stakes, to which 2x6 decking is attached. Such a walkway can lead to the wood steps of the deck.

CHAPTER 6

Working Inside

The sections in this chapter discuss the work to be done inside the house after the shell is complete.

INTERIOR WALL FRAMING

Some interior partitions, called load-bearing partitions, support the joists of the roof or second floor. The others are called nonload-bearing partitions. Interior load-bearing partitions are framed in the same way and with the same types of studs, plates, and headers as exterior load-bearing walls. Wood stud framing is commonly used for nonload-bearing partitions because of its cost effectiveness, simplicity, and efficiency. It requires no special fastening and can be finished with a variety of easily available materials.

Most building codes accept 2x3-inch studs spaced 24 inches on center with single top and bottom plates for nonload-bearing partitions. Alternatives include use of 2x3-inch studs spaced 16 inches on center, or 2x4-inch studs with either 16-inch or 24-inch on-center spacing. These methods require more material.

It is not necessary to coordinate the placement of nonload-bearing partitions with either ceiling or floor framing members. Partitions may be located either parallel with, or perpendicular to, such members. When located perpendicularly, the partitions may be anchored by nailing through the top and bottom plates directly into the ceiling and floor framing as shown in Figure 151A.

Partitions running parallel to ceiling or floor framing can be located between the framing members. In such instances, top anchoring can be done by installing precut 2x3-inch or 2x4-inch blocks between the overhead joists or trusses (Figure 151B). These blocks should be spaced no more than 24 inches apart to provide adequate backup for ceiling finish. Nails should be driven through the block into the top plate of the partition.

Nonload-bearing partitions running parallel to and between floor framing members are adequately supported by ⅝-inch or ¾-inch plywood subflooring. They may be anchored by nailing directly through the bottom plate into the plywood flooring.

Interior partitions can be attached directly to studs in intersecting walls at the point where the walls meet. If the juncture occurs between the studs of the intersecting wall, a 2x3-inch or 2x4-inch block should be installed at mid-height between the studs (Figure 152). The end stud of the interior partition can be anchored to this block by nailing directly through the stud into the block. When two interior partitions meet to form a corner, they can be joined

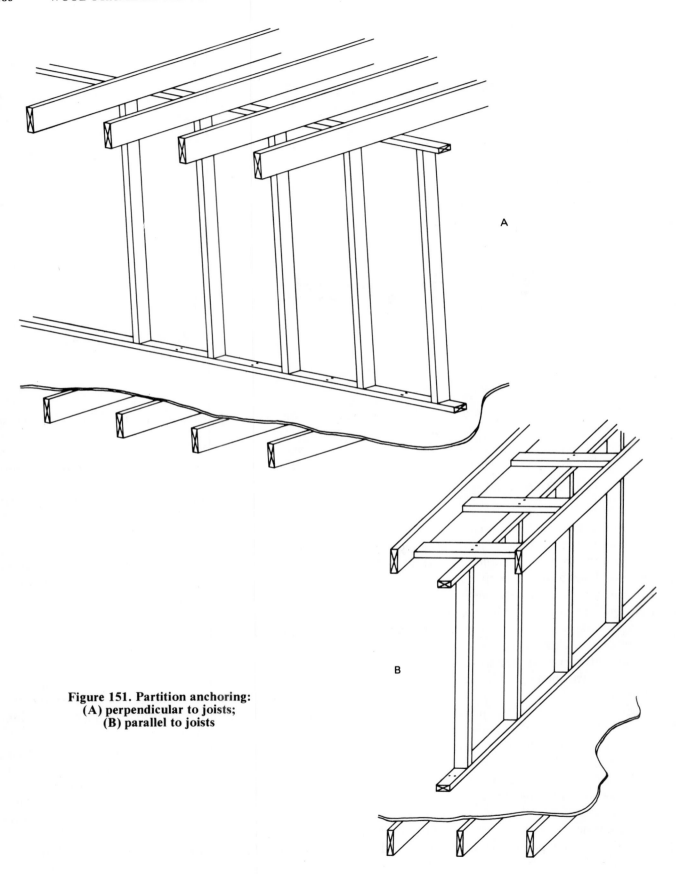

**Figure 151. Partition anchoring:
(A) perpendicular to joists;
(B) parallel to joists**

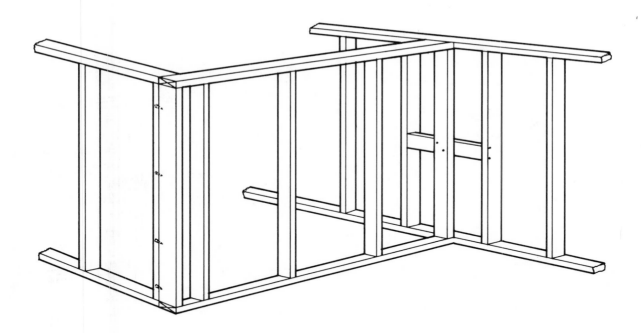

Figure 152. Anchoring partition intersections

and anchored by nailing the end studs of the partitions together.

Studs and plates used in framing partitions form the backup structure to which interior wall finish is attached. Additional backup is required at corners and intersections. Supplementary backup for standard gypsum wallboard or drywall (Figure 153) can consist of cleats of ⅜-inch plywood or metal backup clips spaced up to 24 inches apart. Strips of 1x3-inch or 1x4-inch lumber 36 to 48 inches long can also be used. The gypsum wallboard is not fastened to these clips or wood backers. The drywall sheet supported by the backers should be installed first, so that the adjacent sheet will wedge it into place. This technique provides the recommended nonrigid drywall joint which will minimize cracking.

Similar methods are used to provide backup for ceiling gypsum wallboard at the top of partitions. Such backup should not be necessary for partitions running parallel with overhead members if 24-inch on-center blocking has been installed.

Backup for other types of interior finish, such as wood paneling or plaster-base lath, may require other methods or materials. Instructions provided by the manufacturer of the interior finish material should be followed.

Installation of drain, waste, or vent plumbing within interior partitions can require special fram-ing. Figure 154A shows an interior partition that has a 2x6-inch or 2x8-inch top and bottom plate to accommodate large-diameter pipes. The arrangement of the 2x4-inch studs is designed to accommodate the plumbing laterals. It is also possible to use 2x4-inch framing materials with pipe diameters up to 3 inches. However, it is necessary to reinforce the top plates penetrated by these pipes by applying a double scab (Figure 154B). The scabs should be well nailed on each side of the pipe and should extend over two studs. Small angle irons can also be used.

PLUMBING, HEATING, AND ELECTRICAL INSTALLATION

Utilities must be installed while the wall cavities are open and accessible. This is commonly called "roughing in" plumbing lines, heating ducts, and electrical wiring, which will eventually be concealed in the walls. Because of this concealment, inspection by a code authority is usually required for the roughed-in utilities while the wall cavities are still visible. Wiring for other services is not mandatory, but is much easier to accomplish while the walls are open. These items include thermostat, telephone, doorbell, intercom, and cable TV. All of this

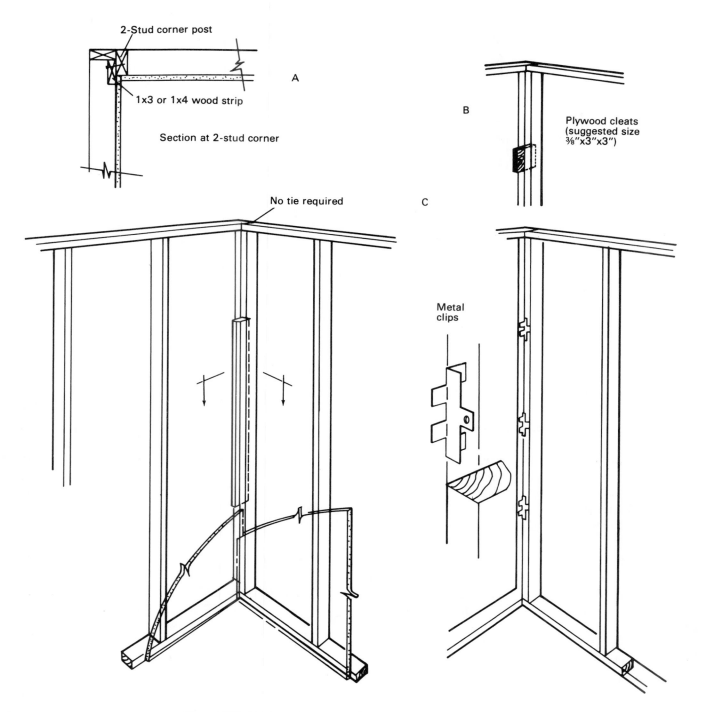

2-Stud corner post

A

1x3 or 1x4 wood strip

Section at 2-stud corner

No tie required

B

Plywood cleats
(suggested size
3/8"x3"x3")

C

Metal
clips

**Figure 153. Backup for wall finish: (A) wood strip backup;
(B) plywood cleat backup; (C) metal backup clips**

requires advance planning of room use and the typical placement of furniture to be most effective. At
least one telephone jack in each room may be advisable. Where cable TV is available, TV jacks should
be placed in several locations.

INSULATION AND VAPOR RETARDERS

Following the utility rough-in, insulation should
be installed. The most widely used home insulation
is made of mineral fibers and is called rock wool or
fiberglass. It is composed of very fine inorganic
fibers made from rock, slag, or glass, with other
materials added to enhance service properties.
Available forms include flexible batts and blankets
(with and without facings), semirigid and rigid
boards (with and without facings), and a loose form
for blowing or pouring.

Batt and blanket insulations usually have a kraft
vapor retarder paper facing, with stapling flanges.
Sometimes an enclosure or "breather" paper is used
on the back side. Batts and blankets are also available with aluminum-foil facings including stapling
flanges and in an unfaced form held in place by
pressure.

Blown mineral wool must be installed with
pneumatic equipment; this requires the service of an
insulation contractor. Pouring wool may be used by
home owners to increase the performance level of
attic insulation. As an alternative, many homeowners prefer to use faced or unfaced batts or
blankets.

Mineral-wool board insulation can be used on the
inside face of crawl space walls. Mineral-wool
blankets and boards are also available for use as
duct insulation. (Building blankets should not be
used for this purpose.) Preformed mineral-wool
pipe insulation is also available through industrial
insulation contractors for both hot and cold water
piping.

Other types of insulation used in residential construction include foamed plastic insulation boards
or sheets; these are sometimes used as exterior wall
sheathing, foundation insulation, and quite commonly as perimeter edge insulation for slab-on-
grade construction. Cellulose-fiber insulation, which
should be pneumatically installed, is used primarily
in ceilings and in walls of existing homes, and is
preferably installed by an insulation contractor.

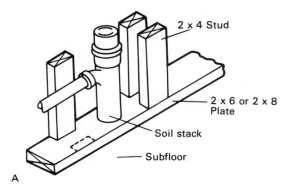

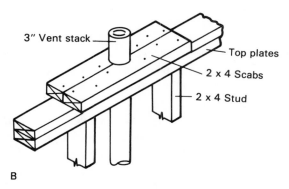

**Figure 154. Plumbing inside of partitions:
(A) Thick wall for 4-inch soil stack;
(B) reinforcing scabs for 3-inch
vent stack in 2x4 wall**

Multiple-layer aluminum-foil insulation is sometimes used between furring strips on masonry wall
construction. It is fragile and must be installed with
great care if it is to be effective. Whatever the insulating material, once it is installed, it becomes a
permanent part of the home.

Combustible vapor-retarder facings on insulation
should not be left exposed. They should be covered
with finish materials. Breather paper is combustible
and, when exposed in accessible space, should be
either covered or stripped off after the batts are in
place.

Effective locations for installing insulation are:

1. *Exterior Walls.* Sections sometimes over-
    looked are the wall between living space and
    an unheated garage or storage room, dormer
    walls, and the portion of wall above ceiling of
    an adjacent section of a split-level home.
    Stuff insulation in the narrow spaces around
    window and door openings between jambs
    and framing.

2. *Ceilings beneath cold spaces and dormer ceilings.* The attic access panel can be insulated by stapling the edges of a piece of blanket insulation to its top. The use of adhesive-backed foam tape on the bottom side around the edge of the attic access panel is a convenient method of weatherstripping this opening.

3. *Knee walls when attic space is finished as living space.*

4. *Between collar beams and rafters above attic space that is finished as living space,* leaving open space above for ventilation.

5. *Around the perimeter of a slab-on-grade when required.*

6. *Floors above vented crawl spaces.* When a crawl space is used as a plenum, insulation should be applied to crawl-space walls instead of the floor above.

7. *Floors of habitable rooms over an unheated or an open space,* such as over a garage or a porch and the cantilevered portion of a floor.

8. *Basement walls,* especially when below-grade space is finished for living purposes. Sill sealer (insulation) between the sill and foundation provides an effective wind infiltration barrier.

9. *On the inside of band or header joists.*

10. *In an annular space around pipes and wires penetrating top plate framing,* to prevent cold attic air from streaming down into interior and exterior wall cavities. If the spaces are small, it may be easier to caulk them rather than to stuff them with insulation.

Installing Insulation

Proper installation of insulation is essential for good performance, and quality control of the installation is necessary to ensure that the expected performance is delivered. Installation techniques vary somewhat with different constructions, but the fundamentals of application are essentially the same. While these are not complicated, certain details are important. Some general guidelines and installation tips are:

- Insulate all large and small spaces of the building walls, floors, and ceilings.
- Place insulation on the cold side (in winter) of pipes and ducts or partially tear or slit the back of the insulation batt so the pipe or wire can be surrounded with insulation without compressing the batt.
- Install insulation so the vapor retarder side faces the interior of the home.
- Apply batt or blanket flanges snugly against the framing members.
- Butt ends of batts or blankets tightly to each other and to framing as appropriate.
- Repair major rips or tears in the vapor retarder.

Ceiling Insulation. There are three methods of installing blanket insulation in ceilings: 1) stapling from below, 2) installing unfaced (no vapor retarder) pressure-fit blankets, or 3) laying the insulation in from above after the ceiling finish material is in place.

Staple flanges to the ceiling joists when installing ceiling insulation from below. Extend the insulation entirely across the top wall plate, keeping the blanket as close to the plate as possible. If necessary, stuff the gap between the blanket and plate with loose insulation. Where eave vents exist, the insulation should not block the movement of air from the eaves into the attic.

Wedge unfaced, pressure-fit blankets between ceiling joists. Allow insulation to overlap the top plate of the exterior wall, but not enough to block eave ventilation. The insulation should touch the top of the plate to avoid heat loss and wind penetration beneath the insulation.

Fit separate batt sections snugly together at the intersection of rafters and collar beams, insulating the collar beams first. If there is no continuous space for ventilation between the back of the rafter batts and the roof sheathing, apply a separate polyethylene vapor retarder, stapling it to the faces of the rafters and the beams.

Ceiling batts should be butted together snugly, with adjoining vapor retarders in the same plane. A poor fit substantially reduces the effectiveness of the vapor retarder. At ceiling joist plates over interior bearing partitions, fit separate sections of batts at framing offsets. A batt or a blanket should not be continuously run through the offset area; this practice results in poor vapor-retarder coverage and excessive heat loss and gain. Vapor retarders of all three batt sections should be in the same plane.

When insulating a sloped or cathedral ceiling, the insulation should extend over the wall plate with the vapor retarder stapled to the plate. When the back of the insulation touches the roof sheathing, a continuous polyethylene sheet should be stapled to the faces of the rafters.

Specific guidelines for installing blanket ceiling insulation are:

- Vapor retarders should face the heated-in-winter side.
- Insulation should cover as much of the top wall plate as possible, leaving at least 1 inch clearance between the top of the insulation and the underside of roof sheathing when eave vents are installed.
- With no soffit vents, adequate gable ventilation is essential.
- With two-layer insulation, run the second layer perpendicular to the framing whenever possible to cover thermal "short circuits" caused by framing members.
- The top layer of two layers of blankets should be unfaced or have the vapor retarder facing removed.
- Butt the ends of insulation pieces snugly together where they meet.
- Stuff insulation between the vapor-retarder face and the top wall plate as necessary.
- Use enough staples to eliminate gaps between stapling flanges and the sides of ceiling framing.
- Use two separate pieces of blanket or cut the blanket or roll at the framing offsets. Do not run the insulation continuously at the offset, as gaps and buckling will result at the joint.
- Where collar beams meet rafters and rafters meet knee walls, separate insulation pieces should be snugly butted together. If rafter insulation requires that the full rafter depth be filled, ventilation above the collar beams is a must.
- Stuff pieces of mineral wool insulation in ceiling voids such as those around vent pipes and chimneys. (Check the local code for the chimney-framing clearance requirement.)
- Do not cover recessed lighting fixtures with insulation. The heat they generate by their operation must be dissipated to the attic.
- Take special care to ensure that dropped soffit areas above built-in cabinets are insulated. If blankets cannot be installed between the ceiling framing and separately down the exterior wall behind the soffit, they should be installed

at the inside face and across the bottom face of the soffit construction, making sure that there are no gaps at the intersection of the exterior sidewall insulation.

- Insulate and weatherstrip the attic access panel.

Many variable factors pertaining to blown attic insulation can cause differences in installed resistance value. For a given manufacturer's insulation, the installed resistance depends on the thickness and weight of insulating material applied per square foot. For this reason, the current federal specification for mineral-fiber insulation requires that each bag of insulation be labeled to show the minimum thickness, the maximum net coverage, and the minimum weight required per square foot to produce specified resistance values. Most manufacturers also provide instructions on each bag for determining the number of bags (required for a given attic area) that are necessary to achieve a specific resistance value. These procedures must be followed. The amount of blown attic insulation to be installed must not be specified (or purchased) solely on the basis of the number of inches of thickness.

Specific guidelines for installing loose-fill attic insulation are:

- Proper coverage per bag, weight per square foot, and no less than the thickness indicated on the bag are a must if full R-value is to be achieved. Most blowing wool bag labels show the minimum number of bags per 1,000 square feet for several different R-values.
- With gable-roof construction, baffles or pieces of blanket insulation should be installed adjacent to the top exterior wall plates at the eaves.
- When eave ventilation is installed with low-slope hip roof constructions, blanket insulation should be installed around the entire periphery of the ceiling area, since corners of hips and ceiling periphery areas of such roofs are difficult to blow properly.
- A separate polyethylene ceiling vapor retarder may be needed.
- Careful application is important to ensure adequate coverage at the far side of chimneys and vent pipes.
- Small spaces between framing members around chimneys or at obstructions should be

hand-packed with mineral wool before the ceiling is blown.

- Do not cover recessed lighting fixtures with insulation.
- Dropped soffits and other lowered ceiling areas should be covered with plywood or similar material before blowing, or should be blown full.
- Insulate and weatherstrip the attic access panel.

Wall Insulation. Blankets should be pushed into stud spaces so that they touch the sheathing or siding. Working from the top down, staples should be spaced 8 inches apart, pulling flanges to fit snugly against the studs. Blanket ends should then be cut to fit tightly against the top and bottom wall plates. As an alternative, the blankets can be cut slightly over-length and the staples driven through the vapor retarder to the plates by compressing the insulation.

When pressure-fit blankets without a vapor retarder are used, they should be wedged into place, and the inside face of wall studs covered with a 4-mil-thick polyethylene vapor retarder that is stapled to the top and bottom plates. The sheet should be unrolled across the entire wall area including window and door openings, and the openings cut out later. Foil-backed gypsumboard may be used as a vapor retarder instead of a polyethylene sheet. Insulation must be pushed behind pipes, ducts, and electrical boxes. As an alternative, the space may be packed with loose insulation, or a piece of insulation of the proper size can be cut to fit. Small spaces between rough framing and door and window heads, jambs, and sills should be stuffed with pieces of insulation and the spaces should be covered by stapling insulation vapor-retarder paper or polyethylene over them.

Nonstandard-width stud or joist spaces can be filled by cutting the insulation and vapor retarder an inch or so wider than the space to be filled. Staple the uncut flange as usual. Pull the vapor retarder on the cut side to the other stud, compressing the insulation behind it, and staple through the vapor retarder to the stud. Unfaced blankets are cut slightly oversize and wedged into place. Heat loss and gain at exterior corners may be minimized by constructing two-stud corners, thus providing space for the insulation.

Masonry walls may be insulated by using nominal 1x2-inch furring strips or 2x3-inch studs. Furring strips may be 16 or 24 inches on center, depending on the thickness and type of wall finish. Masonry wall insulation, nominally 1-inch thick (about R-3), is available without a vapor retarder; use 4-mil polyethylene film or foil-backed gypsumboard as the vapor retarder.

For colder climates the most cost-effective method of providing more thermal protection for masonry walls is to build a frame wall with 2x3-inch studs placed 24 inches on center and with 1x3-inch bottom and top plates. Set the frame one inch from the foundation wall, nail the top plate to the underside of the joists (or blocking between the joists), and fasten the bottom plate to the concrete floor with masonry nails or power-actuated fasteners. Staple R-11 insulation batts between the studs.

Specific guidelines for installing blanket wall insulation are:

- Vapor retarders should face the side that is heated in the winter.
- Blankets should be snugly butted to each other and at horizontal framing members. If the insulation is too short, cut another small piece to fill the gap. If the insulation is too long, it should not be doubled over or compressed at the framing member, rather it should be cut to fit properly.
- For nonstandard width spaces, insulation should be cut about 1 inch wider than the space. The vapor retarder on the cut side should be pulled to the side or face of the stud and stapled.
- Enough staples should be used to avoid gaps when stapling to the sides of studs.
- Insulation should be wedged behind electric boxes and wiring. If excessive compression will result, the blanket may be cut or split so that the full installed thickness will be achieved. If the vapor retarder is cut, tape over the cut.
- Water piping must be protected in locales where freezing temperatures may occur. The blanket insulation should be wedged behind the piping.
- Insulate behind all exterior-wall ductwork.
- Narrow areas between framing members around window and door areas should be stuffed with insulation. Cover these areas with vapor retarder material.

- At exterior corners and intersections of exterior and interior walls, insulation should be placed in openings between studs. This must be done before exterior sheathing is applied.
- When stapling insulation flanges to the sides of studs (inset stapling), do not compress the insulation at the stapling flange more than is absolutely necessary. The greater the compression, the more the reduction in R-value. Do not staple flanges to the face of studs.
- Wedge insulation or caulk around any penetrations through the top and bottom wall plates.
- A separate small piece of insulation behind electrical boxes will minimize heat loss in these areas. The insulation blanket and vapor retarder should then be carefully cut to fit snugly at the top, bottom, and sides of the box.
- Be sure to insulate portions of walls separating conditioned and unconditioned spaces in multilevel homes.
- Overhanging cantilevered soffit areas should be carefully insulated. A single blanket length may be extended horizontally and turned up at the exterior band joist, or two separate pieces may be used. The vapor retarder should face the interior of the home.
- Sill sealer between the bottom wall plate and the subfloor is desirable to cut air infiltration.
- Areas behind bath/shower units installed at exterior walls must be insulated before the units are installed.

Floor, Basement, and Crawl-Space Insulation.
Floors over crawl spaces may be insulated either by insulating the foundation walls if the crawl space is unvented or by placing insulation between the joists if the crawl space is vented. Place the vapor retarder (polyethylene film) covering the crawl-space ground against the wall, using tape to hold it against the wall until the insulation has been put into place. Place one edge of the insulation on top of the foundation wall, taping it temporarily in place as needed. The remainder of the insulation should be draped over and against the inside of the wall. Insulation is held permanently in place by the sill plate or by the header joist if no sill plate is used. At the bottom, where the insulation stands away from the wall, use stones, bricks, or blocks spaced as needed to hold

the insulation against the wall. The vapor retarder on the insulation should face inward (the warm side in winter). In this method of installation, the insulation also serves as a sill sealer.

Walls of unvented crawl spaces may also be insulated by fastening rigid insulation board to the inside face of the wall, extending from the ground to the top of the wall. Follow the manufacturer's instructions for the method and type of adhesive or fasteners to attach the insulation to the wall.

Floors over vented crawl spaces can be insulated by installing insulation between the joists and holding it in place as follows:

1. By using heavy-gauge wires pointed at both ends (they are made especially for this purpose). Bow the wires and wedge them under the insulation and between the joists.
2. Lacing wire back and forth between nails placed in the bottom of joists.
3. Nailing chicken wire to bottoms of joists.

In all cases, the vapor retarder side of the insulation should face the floor above.

Polyethylene may be used as a vapor retarder to cover the ground. If the insulation is to be protected from the weather, as may be the case in open crawl spaces, nail interior-grade softwood plywood, nail-base insulation board, or similar covering to the bottom of the floor joists. Be sure the water pipes are on the interior (warm-in-winter) side of the insulation envelope in all cases.

In basement and unvented crawl space constructions, sill sealer insulation may be used if necessary to prevent air infiltration between sill and foundation or between the header joist and foundation. The sill sealer is merely unrolled on top of the foundation wall and temporarily taped in place as necessary.

Wedge or staple short pieces of blanket insulation behind the band or header joists. As an alternative, when using insulation at the bottom of joists, the header joist may be insulated by folding the end of the blanket up and pushing it against the header.

Headers in cantilevered floor construction can be insulated as mentioned previously. Insulate soffits below cantilevered floors by cutting blankets to fit and wedging them in place, vapor retarder up. As an alternative, these headers and soffits can be insulated by folding the end of the blanket against the header.

Specific guidelines for installing insulation under floors, in basements, and in crawl spaces are:

- Insulation installed in floors over unheated basements and vented and unvented crawl spaces should be applied with the vapor retarder side facing up. When floor insulation is applied over a partially heated basement, the vapor retarder may face down.

- Commercially available wire fasteners with pointed ends or galvanized lacing wire may be used to support insulation blankets between the joists with vapor retarder facing up.

- If the bottom surface of the blanket is at the bottom of the floor joists, separate pieces of blanket should be installed at the band-joist area with the vapor retarder facing in.

- Sill sealer should be applied over the top of the foundation wall before the sill plate, if any, is placed to minimize infiltration at the joint.

- Openings around ductwork, pipes, and wiring between heated and unheated spaces should be stuffed with insulation.

- Exposed vapor retarder facings in floors above partially heated basements or on basement walls should be covered, as they are to some degree combustible. Gypsumboard, paneling and ceiling tiles, or panels with acceptable flame-spread ratings may be used.

- To ensure full R-value when insulating basement walls with R-11 blankets, 2x3-inch studs may be installed 1 inch from the surface of the wall, thus achieving a full 3½-inch cavity.

- When needed, rigid perimeter insulation should be installed at the edges of slab-on-grade floors. The insulation should extend either down the foundation wall or down the wall and horizontally under the slab for at least 24 inches. The ground cover vapor retarder membrane should be below any horizontal perimeter insulation.

Vapor Retarders

Vapor retarders are used in walls, ceilings, and sometimes in floors to help limit water vapor from migrating to a cold surface where it may condense or freeze. The term "vapor barrier" is common construction language. However, construction vapor barriers such as polyethylene and facings on insulation batts and blankets do not completely bar the transmission of moisture vapor. As a result, the term "vapor retarder" is used in this book.

A typical home with a family of four produces about two to three gallons of water per day. About half of this is due to the moisture exhaled from the body in the normal breathing process. The other half is a result of showering, bathing, cooking, washing dishes, washing clothes, and similar water-consuming tasks. Water vapor from these activities increases the indoor relative humidity.

The ability of air to retain water in the vapor state decreases as the air temperature drops. When the water-vapor content (humidity) in the air becomes high enough or the temperature becomes low enough, the water vapor saturation point of the air is reached. The relative humidity becomes 100 percent. The dew point has then been reached, and water vapor in the air condenses to the liquid state. Condensation can also occur at relative humidities well below 100 percent when moisture-laden air comes in contact with a cold surface. This condition is the reason condensation sometimes occurs in winter on colder inside surfaces such as window glass, the inside surface of metal grilles of exhaust fans, and even the inside surfaces of exterior walls. A little such condensation is only a nuisance, but a lot of it can cause deterioration of some building materials.

In older homes, winter problems with condensation of moisture were relatively rare because enough dry winter air leaked into and out of the home to remove the moisture that was produced. Because energy-conserving homes are being built to reduce air infiltration, it is necessary to pay careful attention to vapor retarders and ventilation to avoid winter moisture problems.

There are good reasons to minimize the migration of warm, moisture-laden air through building sections such as exterior walls or ceilings. There the temperature progressively decreases in winter from the warmer inside to the colder outside of the building section. It may become low enough to cause the water vapor to condense and accumulate in the framing and building materials. This condition can ultimately cause deterioration if such moisture condensation is frequent or continuous. Sometimes the water vapor freezes as it comes in contact with a colder surface, such as the inside of the roof sheathing in the attic. If so, on a warm day, the ice melts and there can be substantial water problems.

There are three ways to minimize potential water vapor problems in walls, floors, and attics: 1) vapor retarders can be used to limit the transmission of water vapor; 2) sufficient ventilation can be provided to reduce excessive water vapor in the habitable space; or 3) the building section can be ventilated so that excessive water vapor is dissipated by outdoor air. Providing sufficient ventilation of the habitable space to do away with the need for vapor retarders would waste energy.

Ventilation of floor and wall sections is generally not necessary and causes some additional heat loss. So it is advisable to use vapor retarders on the warm-in-winter side of insulated floor sections over crawl spaces and on exterior walls. In attic spaces that can be adequately ventilated, a vapor retarder in the ceiling may not be necessary or even desirable. Where the roof pitch is low, or in flat- or cathedral-roof constructions where adequate ventilation is difficult to achieve, vapor retarders in the ceiling are generally advisable.

It is desirable to use a vapor retarder in the ceiling and adequate attic ventilation when winter design temperatures are -20°F or lower. If there is adequate attic ventilation, it is believed that vapor retarders are not usually necessary in climates with winter temperatures higher than -20°F. Hundreds of thousands of homes have been built in relatively cold climates, such as occur in Chicago, Cleveland, and Denver, without vapor retarders in the ceiling and with blown insulation. Experience indicates that water-vapor condensation problems in these attics and ceilings are very rare and that in almost every case inadequate attic ventilation or excessive moisture production in the home is the cause. Such high moisture production is usually related to the excessive use of humidifiers, water seepage into basements, the lack of a vapor retarder over damp ground in crawl spaces, water seepage into heating ducts located under a slab, unvented gas space heaters, or similar items.

When it is possible to provide adequate attic ventilation, it may even be undesirable to install a ceiling vapor retarder in homes where no combustion air is required. Combustion air and air escaping through gas or oil furnace and hot-water heater flues (resulting in an equal amount of infiltration makeup air) help to remove substantial amounts of indoor water vapor. Electrically heated homes (no combustion air needed) with low air-infiltration rates, normal rates of household vapor production, and a vapor retarder in the ceiling may have sufficient moisture buildup to require periodic operation of a dehumidifier.

There is no precise formula for when and where to use vapor retarders in ceilings. There are too many variables and only a limited amount of applied research information is available. Local experience is the best guide.

As an alternative for the vapor retarder on a batt or blanket, 4-mil polyethylene film can be stapled to the inside faces of wall plates and studs or to the bottom of ceiling joists or trusses. As installed, this may be considered a more effective vapor retarder than batts or blankets with vapor retarder facings. Other vapor retarders include:

1. Foil-backed gypsumboard on the inside surface of exterior walls or ceilings.
2. Two coats of a paint resistant to vapor penetration on the inside surface of exterior walls or ceilings. One major manufacturer of household paints has determined that two coats of its alkyd semigloss interior paint, having a dry film thickness of 2.4 mils, has a vapor permeance of 0.9 perm. Typical latex paints have a relatively high vapor permeance.

A vapor retarder, such as 4- or 6-mil polyethylene film, is usually desirable over the ground in a crawl space. Four mils is adequate, but 6-mil film is more puncture resistant. Stretch the film over the ground and turn up the edges a few inches at the walls. Periodically tape the film to the wall. Rocks, bricks, blocks, or similar (nonwood) weights can also be used to hold the film in place. If a lap is necessary, about 12-inches is adequate. Place a few weights on the lapped films.

Two factors related to condensation in a thermally well-protected home tend to offset each other. Because such homes have significantly lower amounts of air infiltration, the vapor-diluting effect of dry (winter) infiltrating air is reduced, the relative humidity is increased, and condensation is more likely to occur. However, because such homes have warmer inside surface temperatures, there is less tendency for condensation to occur.

In homes that have low amounts of air infiltration, condensation may occur on double glass or

Table 14
Gypsumboard thickness (single-layer)

Long dimension of sheet installed:	Gypsumboard thickness	Maximum spacing of supports (on center) for application to:	
		Walls	Ceilings
Parallel to framing members	⅜″	16″	—
	½″	24″	16″
	⅝″	24″	16″
Right angles to framing members	⅜″	16″	16″
	½″	24″	24″
	⅝″	24″	24″

metal sash in cold climates. Thermal breaks in the metal sash and/or triple glazing usually solve the problem, unless there is some excessive moisture source. If so, it must be curtailed or eliminated.

INTERIOR WALL AND CEILING FINISHING

The most widely used wall and ceiling finish is gypsumboard. It has the advantages of being economical, noncombustible, and easy to install and repair. Another popular wall covering is paneling in 4x8-foot sheets which may be plywood, hardboard, or particleboard. Often this paneling is applied over a base of gypsumboard. More costly and labor intensive paneling is in the form of tongue-and-groove or shiplap boards.

Gypsumboard

Gypsumboard is available in a number of types to satisfy specific needs. Regular board is most commonly used, but other types include fire-rated, water-resistant, and sound-deadening boards. Regular gypsumboard is faced with a strong paper which will accommodate almost any type of decorative treatment. The edges may be tapered, square, beveled, or tapered with a round edge. The tapered edges are designed to be finished with joint compound and tape. Square edges are used where another finish surface such as wallpaper, paneling, or tile will be applied. Beveled edges give a paneling effect. Gypsumboard is available in 4-foot widths and in lengths up to 16 feet.

Although all gypsumboard is noncombustible and thus provides some fire protection, fire-rated

board gives added protection. The core is reinforced so that it remains intact even after the chemically combined water has been released from the gypsum. This type of board is primarily used where a rated firewall is required or where major structural members require fire protection. Such protection is not normally required in single-family dwellings, except that some codes may require fire-rated board on a wall between the garage and the house. It may also be required in multifamily or special types of buildings. Fire-rated board may provide a finished surface or be used as a backer board for some other type of finish.

Water-resistant board is most often used as a backer for tile, but could be used with other finishes in high-moisture areas such as bathrooms or kitchens. It is particularly important that it be used around bathtubs and showers, where leaks could develop and cause deterioration of regular gypsumboard. The water resistance is provided by an asphalt wax emulsion combined with the gypsum.

Sound-deadening board is normally used between living units in multifamily dwellings, but can also improve privacy for single-family houses. This board is also primarily a backer with regular gypsumboard applied over it.

The regular and fire-rated boards are also available with a variety of finishes laminated to the face. The most widely used finish is vinyl with colors, textures, or patterns imprinted. The patterns may be wood grain applied with a photographic process that gives the appearance of wood paneling. These usually have a finished beveled edge, so that no further finish is required.

Table 14 lists maximum member spacing for the various thicknesses of gypsumboard. When the single-layer system is used, the 4-foot-wide gypsum sheets are applied vertically or horizontally on the walls after the ceiling has been covered. Vertical application covers three stud spaces when studs are spaced 16 inches on center, and two when spacing is 24 inches. Edges should be centered on studs, and only moderate contact should be made between edges of adjacent sheets.

With ½-inch gypsumboards, 5d cooler-type nails (1⅝ inches long) should be used, and 4d (1⅜ inches long) with the ⅜-inch-thick material. Ring-shank nails, about ⅛ inch shorter, can also be used. Many builders prefer to use screws rather than nails in order to avoid nail pops (nails working their way out of framing) due to changes in moisture content of the framing. Screws should be 1¼ inches long. If moisture content of the framing members is less than 15 percent when gypsumboard is applied, nail pops will be greatly reduced. It is good practice, when framing members have a high moisture content, to allow them to approach moisture equilibrium before the gypsumboard is applied. Nails should be spaced 6 to 8 inches for sidewalls and 5 to 7 inches for ceiling application (Figure 155). Minimum edge distance is ⅜ inch.

The horizontal method of application is best adapted to rooms in which full-length sheets can be used, as it minimizes the number of vertical joints. Where joints are necessary, they should be made at windows or doors. Nail spacing is the same as that used in vertical application. Horizontal nailing blocks between studs are not normally required when stud spacing is not greater than 16 inches on center and gypsumboard is ⅜ inch or thicker. However, when spacing is greater, or an impact-resistant joint is required, nailing blocks may be used (Figure 155).

Another method of gypsumboard application (laminated two-ply) includes an undercourse of ⅜-inch material applied vertically and nailed in place. The finish ⅜-inch sheet is applied horizontally, usually in room-size lengths, with an adhesive. This adhesive is either applied in ribbons or spread with a notched trowel. The manufacturer's recommendations should be followed in all respects. Gypsumboard with a laminated finish may also be applied on walls with an adhesive so that the surface is left undisturbed. An alternative is the use

of nails with heads that are coated to match the finish. In either case, the boards are 4x8 feet and applied vertically, similar to paneling. Edges are finished, so no additional finishing is required.

Nails and screws in the regular gypsum wallboard should be driven with the heads slightly below the surface. The crowned head of the hammer will form a small dimple in the wallboard (Figure 156A). A nail set should not be used and care should be taken to avoid breaking the paper face.

Joint cement (spackle) is used to apply the tape over the tapered edge joints and to smooth and level the surface. It comes in powder form, and is mixed with water to a soft putty consistency so that it can be easily spread with a trowel or putty knife. It can also be obtained in premixed form. The general procedure for taping (Figure 156B) is as follows:

1. Use a wide spackling knife (5 inches) and spread the cement in the tapered edges, starting at the top of the wall.
2. Press the tape into the recess with the putty knife until the joint cement is forced through the perforations.
3. Cover the tape with additional cement, feathering the outer edges.
4. Allow to dry, sand the joint lightly, and then apply the second coat, feathering the edges. A steel trowel is sometimes used in applying the second coat. For best results, a third coat may be applied, feathering beyond the second coat.
5. After the joint cement is dry, sand it smooth (an electric vibrating sander works well).
6. For hiding hammer indentations, fill with joint cement and sand smooth when dry. Repeat with a second coat when necessary.

Interior corners may be treated with tape. Fold the tape down the center to a right angle (Figure 156C) and apply cement at the corner, press the tape in place, and finish the corner with joint cement. Sand it smooth when dry and apply a second coat. The interior corners between walls and ceiling may also be concealed with some type of molding (Figure 156D). When moldings are used, taping this joint is not necessary. Wallboard corner beads (metal) at exterior corners will prevent damage to the gypsumboard (Figure 156E). They are fastened in place and covered with the joint cement.

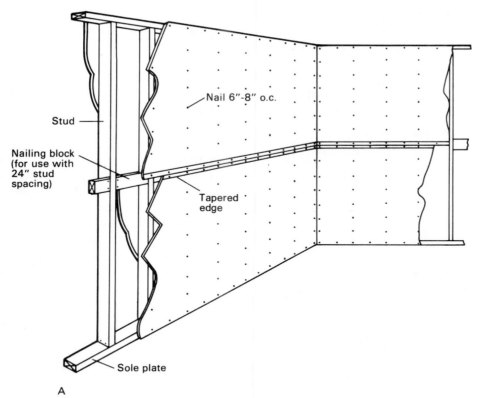

Nail 6"-8" o.c.

Stud

Nailing block
(for use with
24" stud
spacing)

Tapered
edge

Sole plate

A

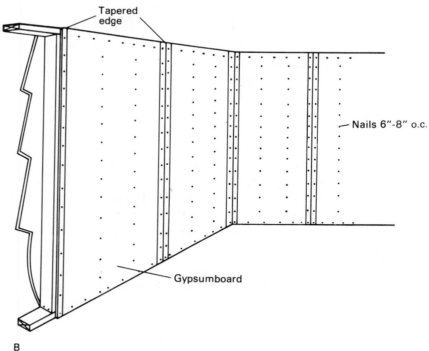

Tapered
edge

Nails 6"-8" o.c.

Gypsumboard

B

**Figure 155. Installing gypsumboard on walls:
(A) horizontal application; (B) vertical application**

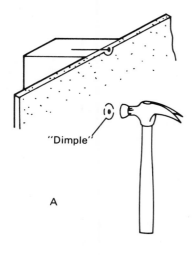

"Dimple"

A

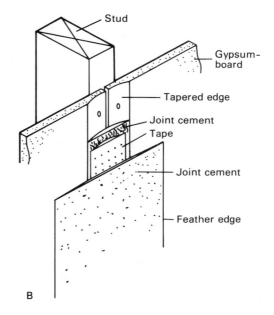

Stud

Gypsum-
board

Tapered edge

Joint cement

Tape

Joint cement

Feather edge

B

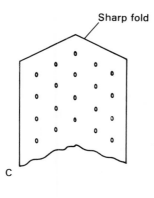

Sharp fold

C

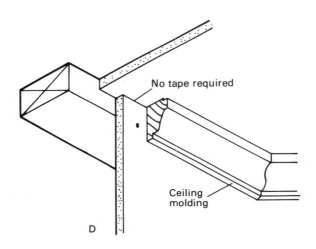

No tape required

Ceiling
molding

D

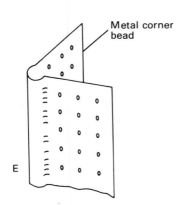

Metal corner
bead

E

**Figure 156. Finished
gypsumboard: (A) nail set with
crowned hammer; (B) cementing
and taping joint; (C) taping at
inside corners; (D) alternate
finish at ceilings; (E) metal
corner bead at exterior corner**

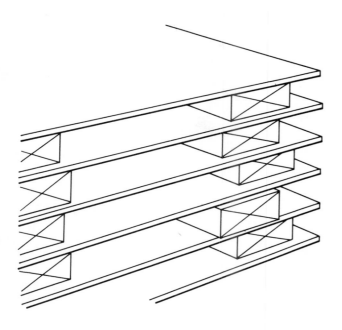

**Figure 157. Stacking panels for conditioning
to room environment prior to use**

Paneling

Plywood, hardboard, and particleboard are usually in 4x8-foot sheets for vertical application. However, 7-foot-long panels can sometimes be purchased for use in basements or other low-ceiling areas. Plywood can be purchased in a number of species and finishes with wide variation in costs. Hardboard and particleboard imprinted with a wood grain pattern is generally less expensive than plywood. A photograph of wood is used to imprint a facing material, which produces a very realistic pattern. Both smooth and textured facings are also available in solid colors as well as designs. Facings are usually materials that clean easily.

Paneling material should be delivered to the site and placed in the conditioned space at least 24 hours before installation to allow it to assume the moisture and temperature conditions of the room. Stack the panels, separated by full-length strips, to allow air to get to all panel faces and backs (Figure 157). Conditioning can also be accomplished by standing panels around the room.

Installation of the first panel is critical for establishing vertical edges and locating edges over a stud. Place the first panel butted against a corner of the room. Make sure the outer edge is vertical by hold-

ing a plumb bob at the top corner; then if the outer edge is over a stud, the panel can be secured. If there is no stud at that point, measure the width that must be cut off for the edge to coincide with a stud. Then mark or scribe the amount to be cut off, measuring from the corner. The use of an art compass to scribe the panel (Figure 158) will assure the right cut even if the corner is uneven or not vertical. After the cut is made, fit the panel snugly into the corner and secure it. Successive panels are placed with moderate contact against the preceding one, and 16-inch or 24-inch stud spacing should assure that all edges will be over a stud.

Cutouts for doors and windows or heat registers require careful measurements. Take dimensions from the edge of the last applied panel for width, and from the ceiling or floor for height. Transfer these to the panel and proceed with cutting. For electrical boxes, paint or run chalk around the box edges. Next, carefully position the panel and press it firmly over the box, transferring the outline to the back of the panel (Figure 159), and cut out the section.

Panels can be fastened with nails or adhesive. Adhesive is sometimes preferable because there are no nailheads to mar the finish. Most adhesives include instructions for application and these should be followed carefully. Use an adhesive that allows enough open assembly time to adjust the panel for a good fit. Where panels are nailed, use small finish-

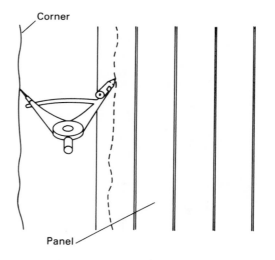

**Figure 158. Scribing of cut at panel edge to provide
exact fit in a corner or at ceiling**

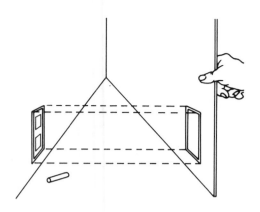

**Figure 159. Chalk outlet box
for marking cutout**

ing nails (brads). Use 1½-inch-long nails for ¼- or ⅜-inch-thick materials and space 8 to 10 inches apart on edges and at intermediate supports. Many panels are grooved, and nails can be driven in these grooves. Set nails slightly with a nail set. Many prefinished materials are furnished with small nails having heads that match the color of the finish; thus no setting is required.

The right moldings add the final decorative accent for fine paneling. They also cover seams and joints at ceiling and floor and protect the corners. Moldings also provide a variety of midwall transitions from one sheet of paneling to the next.

Measure each piece of molding separately for the area it will occupy. For example, do not assume that lengths at the floor and ceiling are identical. Remember when you measure to allow for mitering — molding will be longer than its corresponding wall section if there is an outside corner at either end, and shorter if it is framed by two inside corners.

Molding should be cut with a fine-tooth saw and miter box for accuracy. To splice molding sections along a wall, 45° cuts are made in the same direction on both pieces. Where moldings meet at right angles, trim both pieces at opposite 45° angles so that they will join to form a tight right angle. Finish moldings with stain or paint after cutting and before installing in place. Use 3d nails (finish or colored), countersink, and cover with matching putty stick.

Wood paneling is tongued-and-grooved or ship-lapped and is available in various widths. Wood is usually limited to no more than 8 inches in nominal width. This paneling should also be stacked in the room to be paneled, as recommended for 4x8-foot panels, to stabilize at the temperature and moisture conditions of the room. Paneling is usually applied vertically, but at times is applied horizontally for special effects.

Vertically applied paneling is nailed to horizontal furring strips or to nailing blocks between studs (Figure 160). Nail with 1½- to 2-inch finishing or casing nails. Blind nail through the tongue and, for 8-inch boards, face nail near the opposite edge. Where adhesive is used, the only nailing is the blind nail in the tongue. Moldings can also be used with wood paneling.

Wainscot

Wainscoting is a lining applied to the lower 3 to 4 feet of a wall. It is used in specific types of rooms to protect that portion of the wall, but may be decorative as well as functional.

In dining rooms, studies, or offices, the wainscot is about the height of chair backs to protect the wall when chairs are pushed against it. The traditional height for this is 36 inches; however, 32 inches is often used to make optimum use of 4x8-foot panels. A molding or cap is applied at the top of the wainscot and is sometimes referred to as a chair rail. Application of this type of wainscot is similar to installing paneling, except that longer nails may be required to go through the wall covering under the wainscot and still penetrate the studs adequately.

Wainscoting is also used in wet areas such as bathrooms or rooms with swimming pools or hot tubs. Ceramic tile is the usual material for this application. Application in these areas should always be over water-resistant gypsumboard. Tile should be installed around bathtubs, behind sinks or laundry tubs, and in any other area where water may be splashed.

Tile is commonly applied with an adhesive to a gypsumboard base. The gypsumboard should have all joints taped and nail heads covered with two coats of joint compound similar to preparation for painting. In wet areas, water-resistant gypsumboard must be used and installed on framing not to exceed 16 inches on center. A ¼-inch gap should be left between the paper edge of the gypsumboard and a bathtub or shower receptor. This gap must be filled with a nonhardening caulk.

Where tile is applied to a plywood base, use underlayment-grade plywood with exterior glue or

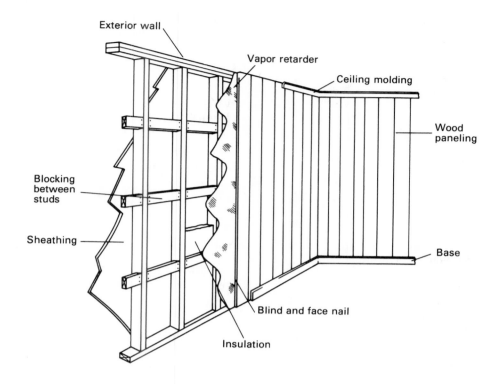

Figure 160. Blocking between studs for vertical wood paneling

exterior-type C-C plugged or better. Use ⅜-inch or thicker plywood with face grain perpendicular to studs or ½-inch or thicker with face grain parallel to studs. Allow ⅛-inch expansion joints between sheets. Provide 2x4-inch solid blocking between framing members at horizontal edges. Prior to installation, seal all plywood edges with a quality exterior primer or aluminum paint.

FLOOR COVERINGS

A wide variety of floor coverings are available for application over wood subfloor. In some cases, special preparation may be required for installation on a concrete slab. The usual considerations in making a selection are maintenance, durability, comfort, esthetics, and initial cost. Commonly used floor coverings include carpet, sheet vinyl, vinyl tile, hardwood, and ceramic tile.

Regardless of the type of floor covering, installation should not begin until the work of all other trades has been completed and the area cleared of extraneous materials. If it is necessary to install floor covering before all other work is finished, the installed covering should be immediately covered with heavy paper or other suitable protective covering.

Carpet

Carpeting is often desired because it absorbs sound, resists impact, and is attractive and easy to maintain. It can be installed over almost any type of subfloor, or directly to a concrete slab. The thickness of carpet and padding help to even out slight roughness or discontinuities, so little preparation is required. Installation is usually done by a professional with appropriate tools and skills for cutting to a precise size and stretching between tack strips at the room perimeter.

Sheet Vinyl and Resilient Tile

A smooth underlayment is required for these resilient floor coverings, since they will conform to the contour of the surface under them. Plywood should meet the requirements of *U.S. Product Standard PS1 83* published by the American Plywood Association and be in grades and thicknesses recommended by the floor covering manufacturer.

Table 15
Hardwood flooring grades

Unfinished oak	Unfinished beech, birch, and hard maple	Unfinished pecan	Prefinished oak
Clear	First grade white hard maple	First grade red	Prime
Select and better	First grade red beech and birch	First grade white	Standard and better
Select	First grade	First grade	Standard
No. 1 Common	Second and better	Second grade red	Tavern and better
No. 2 Common	Second grade Third and better Third grade	Second grade Third grade	Tavern

Hardboard must meet the requirements of *ANSI Standard A135.4* (Basic Hardboard, Class 4, underlayment grade with a 0.215- + 0.005-inch thickness tolerance), published by the American Hardboard Association. The subfloor/underlayment assembly must be solid, well-nailed at the joists, and free from springiness. Install plywood underlayment with cross-joints staggered at least 16 inches. Nail the center of the panel first, working out to the edges. Leave a space between underlayment sheet edges equal to the thickness of a dime (approximately 1/32 inch). Drive fasteners flush or set not more than 1/16 inch below the surface. Fill any low spots, holes, splits, or openings of more than 1/16 inch with a hard-set, nonshrinking latex compound. Sand after drying.

The installation of resilient materials is usually done by a contractor specializing in that type of flooring. In any case, it should be installed according to manufacturer's instructions. The flooring and adhesive must be maintained at a minimum temperature of 70° F for at least 24 hours before, during, and 24 hours after the application.

Wood Flooring

Wood flooring is available in a variety of species and types. While some softwood flooring is used, most strip flooring in new construction is hardwood. Species graded for flooring use include oak, beech, birch, hard maple, and pecan. In addition, some foreign species are used for parquet flooring.

Appearance alone determines the grades of hardwood flooring since all grades are equally strong and serviceable in any application. Oak, the most popular of the hardwoods, has four basic grades (Table 15). Flooring that is practically free of defects and made mostly of heartwood is known as "Clear," though it still may contain minor imperfections. "Select" is almost clear, but this grade contains more of the natural characteristics such as knots and color variations. The "Common" grades (No. 1 and No. 2) have more markings than either of the other two grades and are often specified because of the character these natural features bring to the installation. Grades are sometimes combined (i.e., "Select and better") and special combinations are made for "shorts," the short pieces produced in manufacturing. The grades for other species are also shown in Table 15. Usual strip flooring is 1½, 2, or 2¼ inches wide, and thickness may vary from ½ to ¾ inch. Planks are available up to 8 inches wide.

Installation on Wood Joist Construction. In joist construction with no basement, outside cross-ventilation through vents or other openings in the foundation walls must be provided, with no dead-air areas. A ground cover of 6-mil polyethylene film is essential as a moisture barrier.

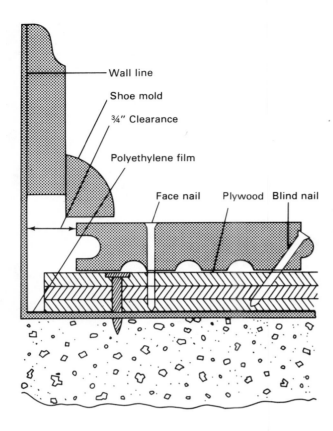

**Figure 161. Plywood-on-slab method of installing
strip oak flooring**

Use exterior plywood, common pine, or other softwood suitable for subfloors. The plywood must be at least ½-inch thick. Lay panels with the grain of faces at right angles to joists. Use appropriate nail sizes and nail spacing, and leave expansion space between plywood panels as recommended by the American Plywood Association. Mark the location of the joists on the plywood so that flooring can be nailed into them.

Installation Over Concrete Slab. Hardwood flooring can be installed successfully over a slab that is on grade or above grade. Below-grade installations are not recommended. The slab must be constructed properly.

Watch out for water. New concrete is heavy with moisture, an inherent enemy of wood. Proper on-grade slab construction requires a vapor retarder between the gravel fill and the slab. While this retards moisture entry through the slab, it also retards curing of the slab. So test for dryness, even if the slab has been in place over two years. The following tests may be used:

1. *The Rubber Mat Test.* Lay a flat, noncorrugated rubber mat on the slab, place a weight on top to prevent moisture from escaping, and allow the mat to remain overnight. If there is "trapped" moisture in the concrete, the covered area will show water marks when the mat is removed. Note that this test is worthless if the slab surface is other than light in color originally.
2. *The Polyethylene Film Test.* Tape a 1-foot square of heavy clear polyethylene film to the slab, sealing all edges with plastic packaging tape. If, after 24 hours, there is no "clouding" or drops of moisture on the underside of the film, the slab can be considered dry enough to install wood floors.
3. *The Calcium Chloride Test.* Place a quarter teaspoonful of dry (anhydrous) calcium chloride crystals, available at drug stores, inside a 3-inch-diameter putty ring on the slab. Cover with a glass so that the crystals are totally sealed off from the air. If the crystals dissolve within 12 hours, the slab is too wet for hardwood flooring to be installed.
4. *The Phenolphthalein Test.* Put several drops of a 3-percent phenolphthalein solution in alcohol at various spots on the slab. If a red color develops in a few minutes, there is a moist alkaline substance present, and it would be best not to install hardwood flooring. These products are available at drug or chemical stores.

NOTE: Whichever test is used, the test should be made in several areas of each room on both old and new slabs. The remedy for a moist slab is to wait until it dries naturally or to accelerate drying with heat and ventilation.

If the slab is sufficiently dry, the installation process starts with a good vapor retarder. To give added assurance that moisture does not reach the finished floor, a vapor retarder must be used on top of each slab. Where this is placed will depend on the type of nailing surface and/or the type of wood flooring used. In all cases, prepare the slab by sweeping it clean. The slab must be sound, level, and free of grease, oil stains, and dust.

Plywood-on-slab method. This system uses ¾-inch or thicker exterior plywood as the subfloor nailing base (Figure 161). Roll out 4-mil or heavier polyethylene film over the entire slab, overlapping edges 4 to 6 inches and allowing enough to extend under the baseboard on all sides. Imbedding the mastic is not required.

Lay plywood panels out loose over the entire floor. Cut the first sheet of every run so that end joints in adjacent runs will be staggered 4 feet. Leave a ¾-inch space at all wall lines and ¼ to ½ inch between panels. At doors and other vertical obstructions where molding will not be used to cover the void, cut the plywood to fit, leaving about ⅛ inch of space.

Fasten the plywood to the concrete with a powder-actuated concrete nailer or hammer-driven concrete nails. Use a minimum of nine nails per panel, starting at the center of the panel and working toward the edges to be sure of flattening out the plywood and holding it securely.

An alternate method is to cut the plywood into 4x4-foot squares, score the back, and lay in mastic. However, this will require the use of moisture retarders laid in mastic.

Screeds method. This method uses flat, dry, 2x4-inch screeds (sometimes called sleepers) of random lengths from 18 to 48 inches. They must be preservative-treated with a product other than creosote, which might bleed through and stain the finish floor, and they must be dried after each treatment if the treatment process involves saturation with water, as in waterborne preservatives.

Sweep the slab clean, prime with an asphalt primer, and allow it to dry. Apply hot (poured) asphalt mastic and imbed the screeds, 12 inches on center, at right angles to the direction of the finished floor. Stagger joints and lap ends at least 4 inches. Leave a ¾-inch space between ends of screeds and walls (Figure 162).

Over the screeds spread a vapor retarder of 4- or 6-mil polyethylene film with edges lapped 6 inches or more. It is not necessary to seal the edges or to affix the film with mastic, but avoid bunching or puncturing it, especially between screeds. The finish flooring will be nailed through the film to the screeds.

Some installers prefer to use two-membrane asphalt felt or building paper with cut-back or cold-stick adhesive as a vapor retarder. The screeds are laid in rivers of mastic on the asphalt felt or building

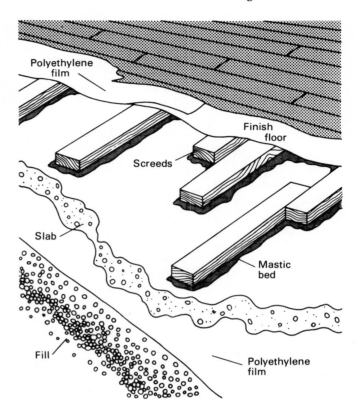

Figure 162. Screed method of installing strip oak flooring over a concrete slab

paper. In this system, the polyethylene film over the screeds is recommended for the extra moisture protection provided at nominal cost.

The screeds method alone — that is, without a subfloor and spaced 12 inches on center — is satisfactory for all strip flooring and plank flooring to 4-inch width. Plank flooring wider than 4 inches requires either the plywood-on-slab subfloor or screeds plus a wood subfloor to provide an adequate nailing surface. The subfloor may be ⅝-inch or thicker plywood or ¾-inch boards.

Parquet, herringbone, and similar flooring. These floors are normally laid in asphalt mastic and thus do not require a nailing surface on top of the slab. However, a good moisture retarder is most important, and it can be achieved by either of the two following methods:

Polyethylene method. Prime the slab with an asphalt primer and allow to dry. Apply cold-type cut-back asphalt mastic with a straight-edge trowel to the entire slab surface. Allow to dry 30 minutes.

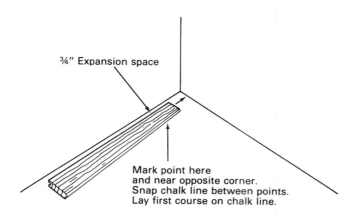

¾" Expansion space

Mark point here
and near opposite corner.
Snap chalk line between points.
Lay first course on chalk line.

**Figure 163. Start nailing strip flooring
¾-inch from the wall**

Unroll 4-mil polyethylene film over the slab, covering the entire area and lapping edges 4 inches. "Walk in" the film, stepping on every square inch of the floor, to insure proper adhesion. Small bubbles are of no concern.

Two-membrane asphalt felt or building paper method. Prime in the polyethylene method and apply mastic with a notched trowel at the rate of 50 square feet per gallon. Let set 2 hours. Roll out 15-pound asphalt felt or building paper, lapping the edges 4 inches. Butt the ends. Apply another coating of mastic with the notched trowel and roll out a second layer of asphalt felt or building paper. Lay both layers in the same direction, but stagger the overlaps to achieve a more even thickness.

The finish floor will be laid in mastic on the vapor retarder. The second method applies only to tongued-and-grooved parquet flooring where tongues and grooves are engaged. Other flooring types require a retarder applied to the slab by the first method.

Laying and Fastening the Finish Floor.

Strip flooring. The following instructions apply to strip flooring laid on plywood-on-slab, on screeds, and on plywood or board subfloors.

Where a plywood or board subfloor is used, start by renailing any loose area and sweeping the subfloor clean. Then cover it with a good grade of 15-pound asphalt felt or building paper, lapped 4 inches at the seams. This covering helps keep out dust, retards moisture from below, and helps prevent squeaks in dry seasons.

For best appearance, lay the flooring in the direction of the longest dimension of the room or building (across, or at right angles, to the joists). If a hallway parallels the long dimension of the room, begin the flooring by snapping a chalk line through the center of the hall and work from there into the room. Use a slip-tongue or spline to reverse direction when you complete the hall later.

The location and straight alignment of the first course are important. When starting within a room, place a strip of flooring ¾ inch (Figure 163) from the starter wall (or leave as much space as will be covered by base and shoe mold), groove side toward wall, and mark a point on the subfloor at the edge of the flooring tongue. Do this near both corners of the room, and then snap a chalk line between the two points. Nail the first strip with its tongue on this line. The gap between that strip and the wall is needed for expansion space and will be hidden by the shoe mold.

When working with screeds on slab, it will not be possible to snap a satisfactory chalk line on the loose polyethylene film laid over the screeds. Make the same measurements and stretch a line between nails at the wall edges. Remove the line after the starter board is in place.

Lay the first strip along the starting chalk line, tongue out, and drive an 8d finishing nail at one end of the board near the grooved edge. Drive additional nails at each joist or screed and at midpoints between joists, keeping the starter strip aligned with the chalk line. (Predrilling the nail holes will prevent splits.) The nail heads will be covered by the shoe molding. Nail additional boards in the same way to complete the first course.

Rack the floor. Lay out seven or eight loose rows of flooring end-to-end in a staggered pattern with the end joints at least 6 inches apart. Find or cut pieces to fit within ½ inch of the wall at the end of boards. Watch the pattern for even distribution of long and short pieces and to avoid clusters of short boards.

Fit each board snug, groove-to-tongue, and blind nail through the tongue (Figure 164) according to the schedule shown in Table 16. Countersink all nails. Begin the nailing process with a hammer. After the second or third course is in place, a floor-nailing machine can be used. The floor-nailing machine is easier to use, does a much better job, and automatically sets the nail. Various nailing machines

Table 16
Nailing schedule for flooring

Flooring material	Fasteners	Fastener spacing
Tongue-and groove flooring (Must be blind-nailed)		
¾″x1½″, 2¼″, and 3¼″	2″ machine driven fasteners, 7d or 8d spirally grooved or plain shank nail.	10″ to 12″ apart[1]
¾″x3″ to 8″ squared plank[2]	2″ machine driven fasteners, 7d or 8d spirally grooved or plain shank nail.	8″ apart
Tongue-and-groove flooring (Must be blind-nailed and laid on a subfloor)		
½″x1½″ and 2″	1½″ machine driven fastener, 5d screw, cut steel or wire casing nail.	10″ apart
⅜″x1½″ and 2″	1¼″ machine driven fastener, or 4d bright wire casing nail.	8″ apart
Square-edge flooring (Face-nailed through top face)		
5/16″x1½″ and 2″	1″ 15-gauge fully barbed flooring brad.	Two nails every 7″
5/16″x1-1/3″	1″ 15-gauge fully barbed flooring brad.	One nail every 5″ on alternate sides of strip.

[1] If subfloor is ½-inch plywood (actual thickness), fasten into each joist with additional fastening between.

[2] Plank flooring over 4″ wide must be installed over a subfloor.

use either a barbed fastener or staples, fed into the machine in clips. Fasteners are driven through the tongue of the flooring at the proper angle.

When using the nailing machine to fasten ¾-inch-thick strip or plank flooring to plywood laid on a slab, be sure to use a 1¾-inch cleat, not the usual 2-inch cleat (barbed fastener) which may come out the back of the plywood and prevent nails from countersinking properly. In all other applications the 2-inch cleat is preferred.

Continue the nailing process across the room, ending up on the far wall with the same ¾-inch space allowed on the beginning wall. It may be necessary to rip a strip to fit. Avoid nailing into a subfloor joint. If the subfloor is at right angles to the finish floor, don't let ends of the finish floor meet over a subfloor joint.

When nailing directly to screeds (no subfloor), nail at all screed intersections and to both screeds where a strip passes over a lapped screed joint. Since flooring ends are tongued and grooved, all end joints do not need to meet over screeds, but end joints of adjacent strips should not break over the same void between screeds.

Some long boards may have horizontal bends or "sweeps" resulting from a change in moisture content. A simple lever device can be made on the job to force such boards into position, as well as pull up several courses. An alternative is to hammer against a short strip of flooring fitted against the crooked piece. Shoe molding should be nailed to the baseboard, not the flooring, after the entire floor is in place (Figure 161).

Plank flooring. This flooring is normally made in 3- to 8-inch widths and may have countersunk holes for securing planks with wood screws. These holes are then filled with wood plugs that are supplied with the flooring (Figure 165).

Plank flooring is installed in the same manner as strip flooring, alternating courses by widths. Start

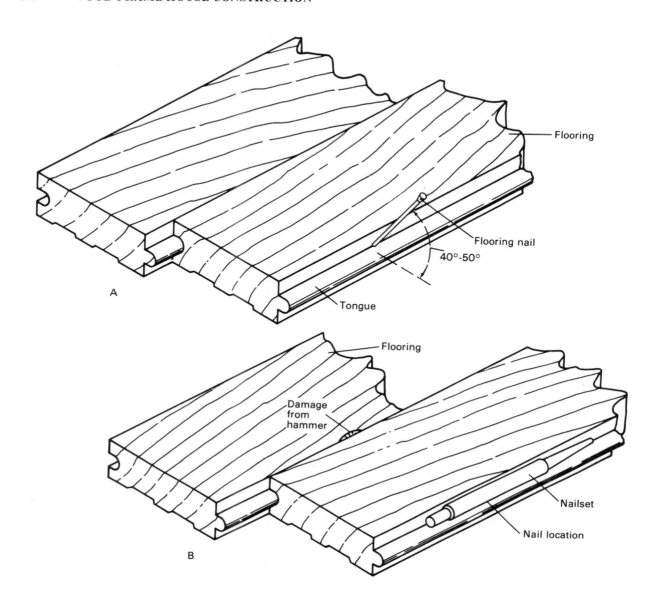

**Figure 164. Nailing of flooring: (A) nail angle;
(B) setting of nail**

with narrowest boards, then the next width, etc., and repeat the pattern. Manufacturers' instructions for fastening the flooring vary and should be followed. The general practice is to blind nail through the tongue as with conventional strip flooring; then countersink one or more No. 9 or No. 12 screws (depending on width of the plank) at each end of each plank and at intervals along the plank to hold it securely. Cover the screws with wood plugs glued into the holes. Take care not to use too many screws which, with the plugs in place, will tend to give the flooring a "polka-dot" appearance.

Be sure the screws are the right length. Use 1-inch screws if the flooring is laid over ¾-inch plywood on a slab; use 1- to 1¼-inch screws in wood-joist construction or over screeds. Some manufacturers recommend face nailing in addition to other fastenings. Consult the manufacturer's installation instructions for details. Another practice sometimes recommended is to leave a slight crack, about the thickness of a putty knife, between planks.

Parquet, herringbone, and similar flooring. The styles and types of block and parquet flooring as well as the recommended procedures for application vary somewhat among the different manufacturers. Detailed installation instructions are usually provided with the flooring or are available from the manufacturer or distributor.

Use a cold, cut-back asphalt mastic spread at the minimum rate of 50 square feet per gallon. Use the notched edge of the trowel. Allow the mastic to harden a minimum of 2 hours or up to 48 hours as directed by the manufacturer; this is referred to as open time. The surface will be solid enough after 12 hours to allow working lines to be "snapped" on it. Use blocks of the flooring as stepping stones on the mastic to snap lines and begin the installation.

There are two ways to lay out parquet. The most common is with edges of parquet units (and thus the lines they form) square with the walls of the room. The other way is a diagonal pattern, with lines at a 45° angle to walls.

For a square pattern, never use the walls as a starting line because walls are almost never truly straight. Instead, use a chalk line to snap a starting line about 3 feet or so from the handiest entry door to the room, roughly parallel to the nearest wall. Place this line exactly equal to four or five of the parquet units from the center of the entry doorway (Figure 166).

Next find the center point of this baseline (line A, Figure 166) and snap another line at an exact 90° angle to it from wall to wall. This line will become the test line to help keep the pattern straight as the installation proceeds. A quick test for squareness is to measure 4 feet along one line from where they intersect, and 3 feet along the other. The distance between these two points will be 5 feet if the lines are truly square (Figure 166).

For a diagonal pattern, measure equal distances from one corner of a room, along both walls, and snap a chalk line between these two points to form the baseline. (This pattern need not be at a precise 45° angle to walls in order to give satisfactory appearance.) A test line should again intersect the center of the baseline at an exact 90° angle from the corner of the room (Figure 167).

For a herringbone pattern, unlike most existing parquet patterns which can be laid out with two working lines, two test lines will be required. One will be at the 90° line already described; the other crosses the intersection of the first two lines, but at a 45° angle to both.

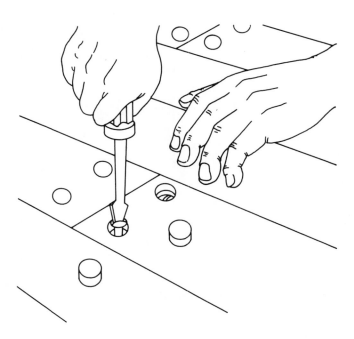

Figure 165. Countersink screws in plank flooring and cover with plugs

If such elaborate preliminary layout preparation seems a bit overdone, keep in mind that the material being installed is wood. Each piece must be carefully aligned with all of its neighbors, and small variations in size, natural to wood, must be accommodated during installation to keep the overall pattern squared up. A "creeping" pattern cannot be corrected after it develops. The more carefully laid out floor prevents larger problems during field work.

Wood parquet must always be installed in a pyramid, or stair-step, sequence rather than in rows. Again, this procedure prevents the small inaccuracies of size in all wood from magnifying, or "creeping," to give an appearance of misalignment. Place the first parquet unit carefully at the intersection of the base and test lines. Lay the next units ahead and to the right of the first one along the lines. Then continue the stair-step sequence, carefully watching the corner alignment of new units with those already in place. Install in a quadrant of the room, leaving trimming at the walls until later. Then return to the base and test lines and lay another quadrant, repeating the stair-step sequence. Install the last quadrant from the baseline to the door. A reducer strip may be required at the doorway.

Most wood-floor mastics, regardless of type or open time, will allow the tiles to slip or skid for

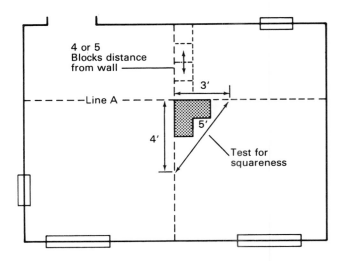

Figure 166. Working lines for laying block in a square pattern

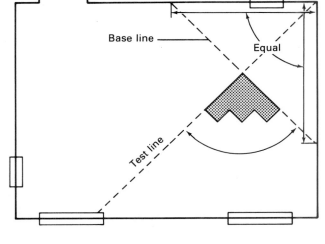

Figure 167. Working lines for laying block in a diagonal pattern

awhile after open time has elapsed when sidewise pressure is applied. By working from "knee boards" or plywood panels laid on top of the installed area of flooring, this sidewise pressure can be avoided. For the same reason, heavy furniture should not be allowed on the finished parquet floor for about 24 hours. Some mastics also require rolling.

Cut blocks or parquetry pieces to fit at walls, allowing ¾-inch expansion space on all sides. Use cork blocking in 3-inch lengths between flooring edge and wall to permit the flooring to expand and contract by compressing and relaxing the cork. With blocks, a diagonal pattern is recommended in corridors and in rooms where the length is more than 1½ times the width. This diagonal placement minimizes expansion in high humidity.

Ceramic Tile

Where ceramic tile is used over a wood-joist floor, the maximum joist spacing is 16 inches on center. Plywood (⅝ inch thick) is required for the subfloor. An underlayment of ⅜-inch plywood is secured to the subfloor with an adhesive or by nailing with 6d ring-shank nails at 6-inch spacing along panel edges and 8-inch spacing at interior supports. Plywood can serve as a combination subfloor underlayment if the plywood is ⅝-inch Group 1, ¾-inch Group 2 or 3, or ⅞-inch Group 4. The face grain of the plywood must be at right angles to the joists, and the edges

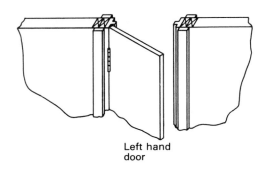

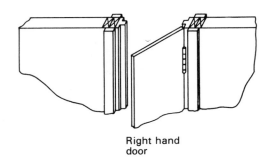

Figure 168. Direction of swing of right- and left-hand doors

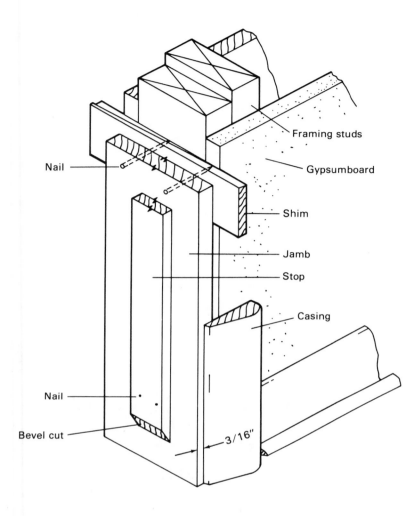

Figure 169. Installation of door frame in rough opening

must be either tongue-and-groove or supported by 2x4 blocking. Leave a ¼-inch-wide space between underlayment sheet edges and between all materials that they abut, such as walls, drains, and posts.

A variety of mortars and adhesives is available for setting the tile. Follow the manufacturer's instructions for application of these materials. Also follow tile manufacturer's recommendations for type of setting material and for exposure to various traffic and environmental conditions.

INTERIOR DOORS

Interior doors are usually purchased prehung, hinged to a sidejamb, and with stops and latch hardware in place. The main installation required is nailing to the rough framing. Hollow-core doors are commonly used except where fire resistance or sound transmission are critical, such as between the garage and the house. Hollow-core doors consist of thin facings glued to a perimeter frame and to a core material such as expanded paper honeycomb between the framing. Where a natural wood finish is desired, plywood with an attractive veneer face is used. Where doors are to be painted, paper-overlaid plywood or hardboard are used. Hardboard may also be overlaid with a simulated wood-grain pattern or be molded to give the appearance of a colonial-style panel door. Traditionally constructed panel doors are available at higher costs, and louvered doors can be used where air circulation is desirable.

Rough openings in the stud walls for interior doors are usually framed out to be 2 inches more than the door height and 2 inches more than the

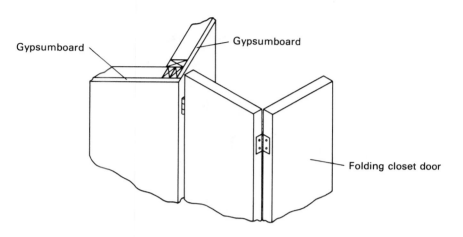

Gypsumboard

Gypsumboard

Folding closet door

**Figure 170. Folding closet door mounted directly on finished wall
with hinges secured to wall framing**

door width. The standard door height is 6 feet 8 inches. Common minimum widths for single interior doors are a) bedroom and other habitable rooms, 2 feet 6 inches; b) bathrooms, 2 feet 4 inches; c) small closet and linen closets, 2 feet. These sizes vary a great deal, and sliding doors, folding door units, and similar types are often used for full-width access to closets.

Folding closet doors can also be purchased in 8-foot height so that full floor-to-ceiling access is given and no header is required. The standard jamb width is 4-9/16 inches to fit a 2x4 stud wall with ½-inch gypsumboard each side. While it may not be necessary to lock many interior doors, privacy locks are often used on bathroom and bedroom doors.

Doors must be purchased as left-hand or right-hand depending on the direction of swing. The right-hand door has hinges on the right as the door swings toward you. Hinges are on the left of the left-hand door as the door swings toward you (Figure 168).

The frame is set in place and jambs are nailed to the rough framing. Where there is a gap between jambs and rough framing, place shims in the gap before nailing. Use two 8d finishing nails about 16 inches apart over the length of the jambs (Figure 169). Folding closet doors can be installed by mounting hinges on the gypsumboard at the opening with screws secured into the framing behind the gypsumboard (Figure 170).

CHAPTER 7

Finishing Touches

After the interior wall, ceiling, and floor coverings have been installed, it will be necessary to apply the finishing touches: interior trim, cabinetry, and painting and staining both inside and outside.

INTERIOR TRIM

A variety of moldings are available to provide a finished trim around doors and windows and at the intersection of walls with the floor or the ceiling. Typical molding patterns are shown in Figures 171 to 174. Moldings that receive a natural finish are often oak or other hardwood species. The usual softwood molding is ponderosa pine, and it is used where the finish will be paint, but sometimes it is stained and given a natural finish. Molded particleboard with a wood-grain vinyl overlay is also used in some cases.

Casing is the edge trim around interior door openings and it is also used to finish the room side of exterior door frames. Casing usually varies in width from 2¼ to 3½ inches, depending on the style. Casing may be obtained in thicknesses from ½ to ¾ inch, although 11/16 inch is standard in many of the narrow-line patterns. Door casings are nailed to both the jamb and the framing studs or header,

allowing about a 3/16-inch edge distance from the face of the jamb (Figure 169). Finish or casing nails in 6d or 7d sizes, depending on the thickness of the casing, are used to nail into the stud. Finishing nails (4d or 5d) or 1½-inch brads are used to fasten the thinner edge of the casing to the jamb. In hardwood, it is usually advisable to predrill to prevent splitting. Nails in the casing are located in pairs (Figure 175) and spaced about 16 inches apart along the full height of the opening and at the head jamb.

Casing with any form of molded shape must have a mitered joint at the corners (Figure 175A). When casing is squared-edged, a butt joint may be made at the juncture of the side and head casing (Figure 175B). If the moisture content of the casing is well above that recommended, a mitered joint may open slightly at the outer edge as the material dries. This condition can be minimized by using a small glued spline at the corner of the mitered joint. Actually, use of a spline joint under any moisture condition is considered good practice, and some prefitted jamb, door, and casing units are provided with splined joints. Nailing into the joint after drilling will help retain a close fit (Figure 175).

The casing around the window frames on the interior of the house should be the same pattern as that used around the interior door frames. Other

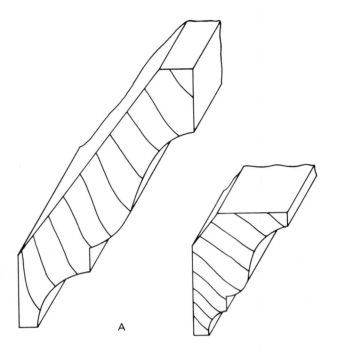

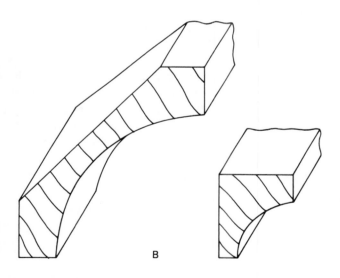

Figure 171. Moldings for intersection of walls and ceilings: (A) crowns; (B) coves

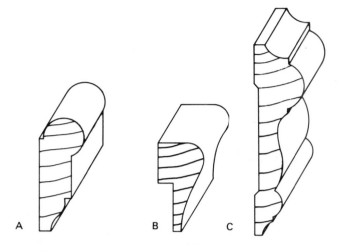

Figure 172. Wall moldings: (A) picture molding; (B) wainscot cap; (C) chair rail

trim that is used for a double-hung window frame includes the sash stops, stool, and apron (Figure 176A). In another method of using trim around windows, the entire opening is enclosed with casing (Figure 176B). The stool is then a filler member between the bottom sash rail and the bottom casing.

The stool is the horizontal trim member that laps the window sill and extends beyond the casing at the sides, with each end notched against the wall. The apron serves as a finish member below the stool. The window stool is the first piece of window trim to be installed and is notched and fitted against the edge of the jamb and the gypsum board, with the outside edge being flush against the bottom rail of the window sash (Figure 176A). The stool is blind-nailed at the ends so that the casing and the stop will cover the nail heads. Predrilling is usually necessary to prevent splitting. The stool should also be nailed at midpoint to the sill and to the apron with finishing nails. Face-nailing to the sill is sometimes used instead of, or in combination with, toe-nailing of the outer edge to the sill.

The casing is applied and nailed as described for door frames (Figure 175), except that the inner edge is flush with the inner face of the jambs so that the stop will cover the joint between the jamb and casing. The apron is cut to a length equal to the outer width of the casing line. It is nailed to the window sill and to the 2x4-inch framing sill below.

When casing is used to finish the bottom of the window frame as well as the sides and top, the narrow stool butts against the side window jamb. The casing is then mitered at the bottom corners (Figure 176B) and nailed as described previously.

Base molding serves as a finish between the finished wall and the floor. It is available in several

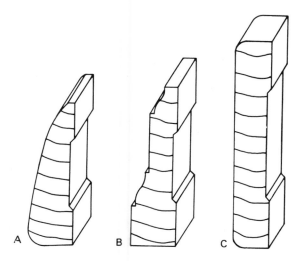

Figure 173. Casings: (A) ranch; (B) traditional; (C) combination casing or base molding

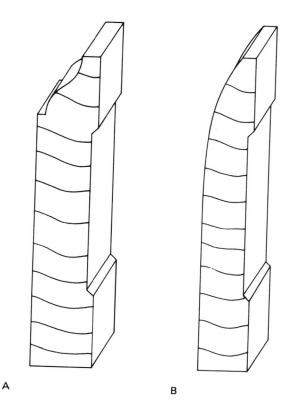

Figure 174. Base moldings: (A) traditional; (B) ranch

widths and forms. Two-piece base consists of a baseboard topped with a small base cap (Figure 177A). When the wall finish is not straight and true, the small base molding will conform more closely to the variations than will the wider base alone. A common size for this type of baseboard is ⅝ by 3¼ inches or wider. One-piece base (Figure 177B and 177C) varies in size from 7/16 by 2¼ inches to ½ by 3¼ inches and wider. Although a wood member is desirable at the junction of the wall and carpeting to serve as a protective "bumper," wood trim is sometimes eliminated entirely.

Most baseboards are finished with a base shoe, ½ by ¾ inch in size (Figure 177D). A single-base molding without the shoe is sometimes placed at the wall-floor junction, especially where carpeting might be used.

Square-edged baseboard should be installed with a butt joint at inside corners and a mitered joint at outside corners (Figure 177). It should be nailed to each stud with two 8d finishing nails. Molded single-piece base, base moldings, and base shoe should have a coped joint at inside corners and a mitered joint at outside corners. A coped joint is one in which the first piece is square-cut against the wall or base and the second molding coped. This is accomplished by sawing a 45° miter cut, and trimming the molding along the inner line of miter with a coping saw (Figure 177). The base shoe should be nailed into the subfloor with long slender nails and not into

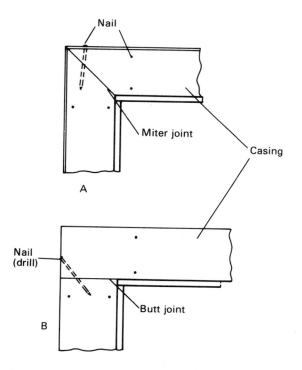

Figure 175. Casing joints: (A) mitered; (B) butt

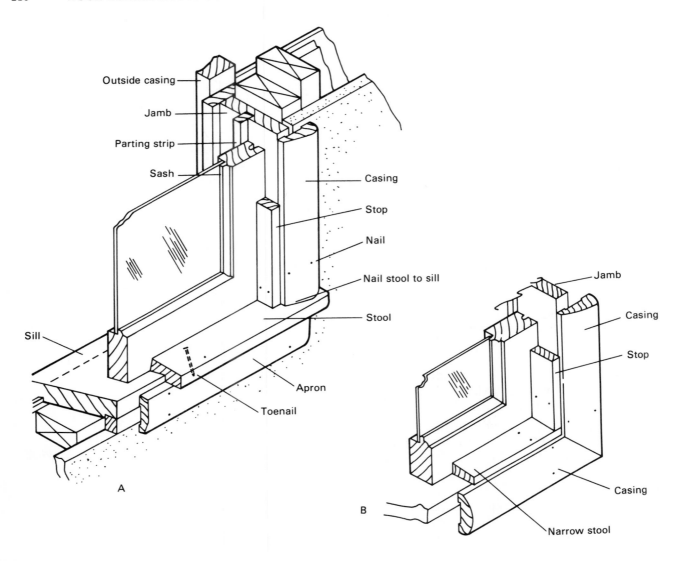

**Figure 176. Installation of window trim: (A) with stool and apron;
(B) enclosed with casing**

the baseboard itself. Thus, if there is a small amount of shrinkage of the joints, no opening will occur under the shoe.

Ceiling moldings (Figure 171) are sometimes used at the junction of wall and ceiling for an architectural effect or to terminate paneling, gypsumboard, or wood (Figure 178). As in the base moldings, inside corners should also be cope-jointed. This technique insures a tight joint and retains a good fit if there are minor moisture changes.

A cutback edge at the outside of the molding will partially conceal any unevenness of the finish and make painting easier where there are color changes (Figure 178). Finish nails should be driven and set

into the upper wallplates and also into the ceiling joists for large moldings.

CABINETS AND OTHER MILLWORK

Millwork, as a general term, usually includes most of those wood materials and house components that require manufacturing. These components include not only the interior trim, doors, and other items previously described, but also such items as kitchen cabinets, fireplace mantels, china cabinets, and similar units. Most of these units are produced in a millwork manufacturing plant and

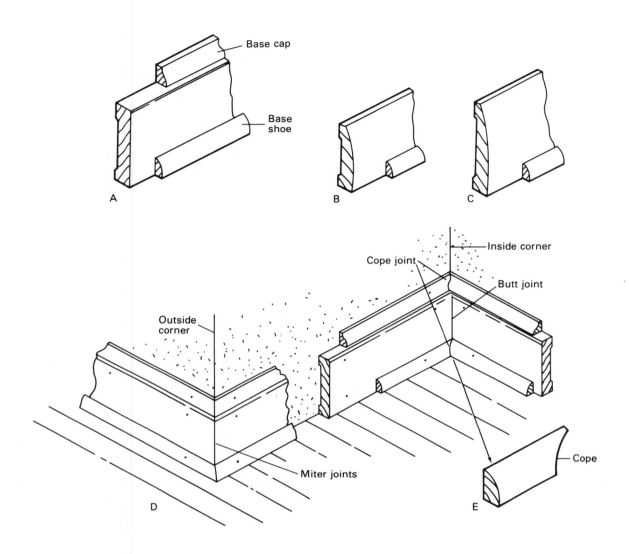

Figure 177. Base molding: (A) square-edge base; (B) narrow ranch base; (C) wide ranch base; (D) installation; (E) cope

are ready to install in the house. They usually require only fastening to the wall or floor.

While many units are custom made, others can be ordered directly from stock. For example, kitchen cabinets are often stock items which may be obtained in 3-inch increments of width, usually beginning at widths of 12 or 15 inches and on up to 48 inches.

As in the case of interior trim, the cabinets, shelving, and similar items can be made of various wood species. If the millwork is to be painted, ponderosa pine, southern pine, Douglas fir, gum, and similar species may be used. Birch, oak, redwood, and knotty pine, or other species with attractive surface variations, are some of the woods that are finished with varnish or sealers.

The recommended moisture content for bookcases and other interior millwork varies from 6 to 11 percent in different parts of the country.

Kitchen Cabinets

The kitchen usually contains more millwork than the rest of the rooms combined. This millwork is in the form of wall and base cabinets, broom closets, and other items. An efficient plan with properly arranged cabinets will not only reduce work and

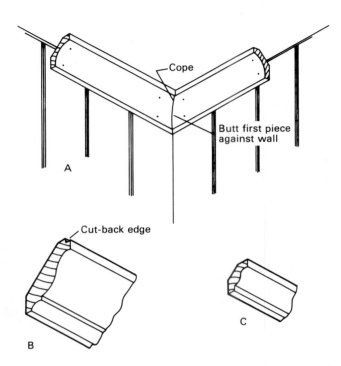

Figure 178. Ceiling moldings: (A) installation (inside corner); (B) crown molding; (C) small crown molding

cabinets may be obtained in full-door or full-drawer units or with both drawers and doors. Sink fronts or sink-base cabinets, corner cabinets, broom closets, and desks are some of the special units that may be used in planning the kitchen. Cabinets are fastened to the wall through cleats located at the back of each cabinet. It is good practice to use long screws to penetrate well into each wall stud.

Four basic layouts are used in the design of a kitchen. The U-type, with the sink at the bottom of the U and the range and refrigerator on opposite sides, is very efficient (Figure 180A).

The L-type (Figure 180B), with the sink and refrigerator on one leg and the range on the other, is sometimes used with a dining space in the opposite corner.

The galley kitchen plan (Figure 180C) is often used in narrow kitchens and can be quite efficient with a sink near the center of one side and the range and refrigerator near opposite ends on the other side.

save steps for the user, but will often reduce costs because it allows the use of a smaller area. Location of the refrigerator, sink, dishwasher, and range, together with the cabinets, is also important from the standpoint of plumbing and electrical connections. Good lighting, both natural and artificial, is also important in designing a pleasant kitchen.

Kitchen cabinets, both base and wall units, should be constructed to specific standards of height and depth. Figure 179 shows the common counter heights and depths for base cabinets, as well as clearances for wall cabinets. While the counter height limits range from 30 to 38 inches, the standard height is usually 36 inches. Wall cabinets vary in height depending on the type of installation at the counter. The tops of wall cabinets are located at the same height, either free or under a 12- to 14-inch drop ceiling or storage cabinet. Wall cabinets are normally 30 inches high, but not more than 21 inches when a range or sink is located under them. Wall cabinets can also be obtained in 12-, 15-, 18-, and 24-inch heights. The shorter wall cabinets are usually placed over refrigerators.

Narrow wall cabinets are furnished with single doors and the wider ones with double doors. Base

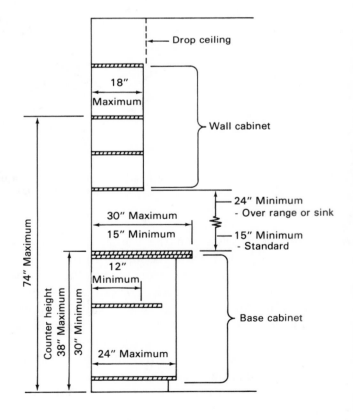

Figure 179. Kitchen cabinet dimensions

The sidewall type (Figure 180D) usually is preferred for small apartments. All cabinets, the sink, range, and refrigerator are located along one wall. Counter space is usually somewhat limited in this design when kitchens are small.

Counter tops are often plastic laminate and are available in a wide range of colors and textures. The counter top is usually purchased with the laminate already applied. Where ceramic tile is used, it must be applied on the site after the top is installed. Another popular counter top is molded plastic that simulates marble.

Bathroom Cabinets

Cabinets are frequently used in the bathroom and can be purchased prebuilt to a number of standard sizes, just as for the kitchen. Counter tops are similar, but where molded plastic is used the sink may also be molded as an integral part of the counter top. While natural wood cabinets are available, plastic laminates are often used because of the severe exposure to moisture. These cabinets are usually purchased as a complete unit for either one or two sinks.

Closet Shelving and Rod

Shelving can be simple 1-inch boards supported at ends by 1x2 cleats; however, manufactured units are often used to save installation time. Metal shelves and clothes rods that telescope allow adjustment to fit any space. Another popular shelving is fabricated from steel rod welded to form an open mesh and in a self-supporting configuration. The entire assembly is then coated with vinyl. These units are easy to install and have the advantage of not collecting dust as the solid shelves do.

Mantels

The type of mantel used for a fireplace depends on the style and design of the house and its interior finish. The contemporary fireplace may have no mantel at all or at best a simple wood molding used as a transition between the masonry and the wall finish. However, the colonial or formal interior usually has a well-designed mantel framing the fireplace opening. This mantel may vary from a simple to a more elaborate unit combining paneling and built-in cabinets along the entire wall. In each design, however, it is important that no wood or other combustible material be placed within 3½ inches of

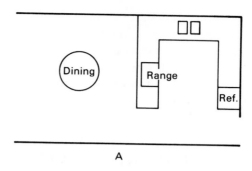
A

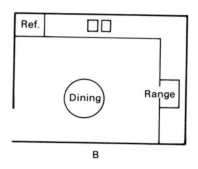
B

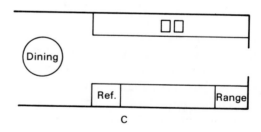
C

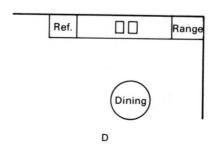
D

Figure 180. Kitchen layouts: (A) U-type; (B) L-type; (C) galley type; (D) sidewall type

the edges of the fireplace opening. Furthermore, any projection more than 1½ inches in front of the fireplace, such as the mantel shelf, should be at least 12½ inches above the opening. Mantels are fastened to the header and framing studs above and on each side of the fireplace.

INTERIOR PAINTS AND STAINS

Interior wood finishing differs from exterior finishing chiefly in that interior woodwork usually requires much less protection against moisture but more exacting standards of appearance and cleanability. Good finishes used indoors should last much longer than paint or other coatings on exterior surfaces. Veneered panels and plywood, however, present special finishing problems because of the tendency for lathe checks to become more prominent.

Opaque Finishes

Interior surfaces may be easily painted by procedures similar to those for exterior surfaces. As a rule, however, smoother surfaces, better color, and a more lasting sheen are demanded for interior woodwork, especially wood trim; therefore, enamels or semigloss enamels are used rather than flat paints.

Before enameling, the wood surface should be sanded extremely smooth and the surface dust removed by a tack cloth. Imperfections such as planer marks, hammer marks, and raised grain are accentuated by enamel finish. Raised grain is especially troublesome on flat-grained surfaces of the denser softwoods because the hard bands of latewood are sometimes crushed into the softer earlywood in planing and later expand when the wood changes moisture content. To achieve the smoothest surface, it is helpful to sponge softwoods with water, allow them to dry thoroughly, and then sand them lightly with new sandpaper before enameling. In new buildings, woodwork should be allowed adequate time to come to its equilibrium moisture content in the heated building before finishing.

To effectively finish hardwoods with large pores, such as oak and ash, the pores must be filled with wood filler. (Refer to section on "Fillers.") After filling and sanding, successive applications of interior primer and sealer, undercoat, and enamel are used. Knots in the white pines, ponderosa pine, or

southern pine should be sealed with shellac or a special knot sealer before priming. A coat of pigmented shellac or special knot sealer is also sometimes necessary over white pines and ponderosa pine to retard discoloration of light-colored enamels by colored matter present in the resin of the heartwood of these species.

One or two coats of enamel undercoat are next applied; this application should completely hide the wood and also present a surface that can be easily sandpapered smooth. For best results, the surface should be sanded just before applying the finish enamel; however, this step is sometimes omitted. After the finishing enamel has been applied, it may be left with its natural gloss or rubbed to a dull finish. When wood trim and paneling are finished with a flat paint, the surface preparation need not be as exacting.

Transparent Finishes

Transparent finishes are used on most hardwood and some softwood trim and paneling, according to personal preference. Most finishing consists of some combination of the fundamental operations of sanding, staining, filling, sealing, surface coating, and waxing. Before applying the finish, planer marks and other blemishes on the wood surface that would be accentuated by the finish should be removed.

Stains. Both softwoods and hardwoods are often finished without staining, especially if the wood has a pleasing and characteristic color. When stain is used, however, it often accentuates color differences in the wood surface because of unequal absorption into different parts of the grain pattern. With hardwoods, such emphasis of the grain is usually desirable; the best stains for the purpose are dyes dissolved either in water or solvent. The water stains give the most pleasing results, but raise the grain of the wood and require an extra sanding operation after the stain is dry.

The most commonly used stains are the "non-grain-raising" ones in solvents which dry quickly; these often approach the water stains in clearness and uniformity of color. Stains on softwoods color the earlywood more strongly than the latewood, reversing the natural gradation in color unless the wood has been sealed first with a wash coat. Pigment-oil stains, which are essentially thin paints, are less subject to this problem and are therefore more suitable for softwoods. Alternatively, the softwood may be coated with penetrating clear sealer before applying any type of stain, in order to give more nearly uniform coloring.

Fillers. In hardwoods with large pores, the pores must be filled, usually after staining and before varnish or lacquer is applied, if a smooth coating is desired. The filler may be transparent and without effect on the color of the finish, or it may be colored to contrast with the surrounding wood.

For finishing purposes, the hardwoods may be classified as follows:

Hardwoods with large pores	Hardwoods with small pores
Ash	Alder, red
Butternut	Aspen
Chestnut	Basswood
Elm	Beech
Hackberry	Cherry
Hickory	Cottonwood
Lauans	Gum
Mahogany	Magnolia
Mahogany, African	Maple
Oak	Sycamore
Sugarberry	Yellow poplar
Walnut	

Birch has pores large enough to take wood filler effectively when desired, but small enough as a rule to be finished satisfactorily without filling. Hardwoods with small pores may be finished with paints, enamels, and varnishes in exactly the same manner as softwoods.

A filler may be a paste or liquid, natural or colored. It is applied by brushing first across the grain and then brushing with the grain. Surplus filler must be removed immediately after the glossy wet appearance disappears. Wipe first across the grain to pack the filler into the pores; then complete the wiping with a few light strokes along the grain. Filler should be allowed to dry thoroughly and sanded lightly before the finish coats are applied.

Sealers. Sealers are thinned varnish or lacquer. They are used to prevent absorption of surface coatings and also to prevent the bleeding of some stains and fillers into surface coatings, especially lacquer coatings. Lacquer sealers have the advantage of drying very rapidly.

Surface Coats. Transparent surface coatings over the sealer may be gloss varnish, semigloss varnish, shellac, nitrocellulose lacquer, or wax. Wax provides protection without forming a thick coating and without greatly enhancing the natural luster of the wood. Coatings of a more resinous nature, espe-

cially lacquer and varnish, accentuate the natural luster of some hardwoods and seem to permit the observer to look down into the wood. Shellac applied by the laborious process of French polishing probably achieves this impression of depth most fully, but the coating is expensive and easily marred by water. Rubbing varnishes made with resins of high refractive index for light (ability to bend light rays) are nearly as effective as shellac. Lacquers have the advantages of drying rapidly and forming a hard surface, but require more applications than varnish to build up a lustrous coating.

Varnish and lacquer usually dry with a highly glossy surface. To reduce the gloss, the surfaces may be rubbed with pumice stone and water or polishing oil. Waterproof sandpaper and water may be used instead of pumice stone. The final sheen varies with the fineness of the powdered pumice stone; coarse powders make a dull surface and fine powders produce a bright sheen. For very smooth surfaces with high polish, the final rubbing is done with rottenstone and oil. Varnish and lacquer made to dry to semigloss or satin finish are also available.

Flat oil finishes commonly called Danish oils are also very popular. This type of finish penetrates the wood and forms no noticeable film on the surface. Two or more coats of oil are usually applied and may be followed with a paste wax. Such finishes are easily applied and maintained but are more subject to soiling than a film-forming type of finish. Simple boiled linseed oil or tung oil are also used extensively as wood finishes.

Finishes for Floors

Wood has a variety of properties that make it a highly desirable flooring material for homes and industrial and public structures. A variety of wood-flooring products permits a wide selection of attractive and serviceable wood floors. Selection is available not only from a variety of different wood species and grain characteristics, but also from a considerable number of distinctive flooring types and patterns.

The natural color and grain of wood floors make them inherently attractive and beautiful. Floor finishes enhance the natural beauty of wood, protect it from excessive wear and abrasion, and make the floors easier to clean. A complete finishing process may consist of four steps: sanding the surface, applying a filler for open-grain woods, applying a stain to achieve a desired color effect, and, finally, applying a finish. Detailed procedures and specified materials depend largely on the species of wood used and individual preference in type of finish.

Careful sanding to provide a smooth surface is essential for a good finish because the finish will magnify any irregularities or roughness in the wood surface. Development of a top-quality surface requires sanding in several steps with progressively finer sandpaper, usually with a machine sander unless the area is small. The final sanding is usually done with a 2/0-grade paper. When sanding is complete, all dust must be removed with a vacuum cleaner and then a tack rag. Steel wool should not be used on floors unprotected by finish because minute steel particles left in the wood may later cause staining or discoloration. A filler is required for wood with large pores, such as oak and walnut, if a smooth, glossy, varnish finish is desired.

Stains are sometimes used to obtain a more nearly uniform color when individual boards vary too much in their natural color, or they may also be used to accent the grain pattern. If the natural color of the wood is acceptable, staining is omitted. The stain should be oil-based or a nongrain-raising type. Stains penetrate wood only slightly; therefore, the finish should be carefully maintained to prevent wearing through the stained layer. It is difficult to renew the stain at worn spots in a way that will match the color of the surrounding area.

Finishes commonly used for wood floors are classified either as sealers or varnishes. Sealers, which are usually thinned varnishes, are widely used in residential flooring. They penetrate the wood just enough to avoid formation of a surface coating of appreciable thickness. Wax is usually applied over the sealer; however, if greater gloss is desired, the sealed floor makes an excellent base for varnish. The thin surface coat of sealer and wax needs more frequent attention than do varnished surfaces. However, rewaxing or resealing and waxing of high-traffic areas is a relatively simple maintenance procedure — much simpler than the maintenance of varnish coatings.

Varnish may be based on phenolic, alkyd, epoxy, or polyurethane resins. Varnish forms a distinct coating over the wood and gives a lustrous finish. The kind of service expected usually determines the type of varnish. Varnishes especially designed for homes, schools, gymnasiums, or other public build-ings are available. Information on types of floor finishes can be obtained from the flooring associations or the individual flooring manufacturers.

The durability of floor finishes can be improved by keeping them waxed. Paste waxes generally give the best appearance and durability. Two coats are recommended and, if a liquid wax is used, additional coats may be necessary to get an adequate film for good performance.

EXTERIOR PAINTS AND STAINS

The primary functions of any wood finish (paint, varnish, wax, stain, oil, etc.) are to protect the wood surface, help maintain appearance, and make cleaning easier. Unfinished wood can be used both outdoors and indoors without further protection. However, wood surfaces exposed to the weather without any finish change color, are roughened by photodegradation and surface checking, and erode slowly.

Wood and wood-based products in a variety of species, grain patterns, textures, and colors can be finished effectively by many different methods. The choice of an exterior finish will depend on the appearance and degree of protection desired and on the substrates used. Because different finishes give varying degrees of protection, the type of finish, its quality, quantity, and the application method must be considered in selecting and planning the finishing or refinishing of wood and wood products used outdoors.

Moisture-Excluding Effectiveness of Finishes

Changes in moisture content cause shrinking, swelling, and the accompanying stresses in wood that cause warping and checking and that contribute to weathering. Such changes occur whenever wood is exposed to varying atmospheric conditions. Effective protection against such moisture changes is furnished by coatings of various moisture-retardant finishes, provided that the coating is applied to all surfaces of wood through which moisture might gain access. No coating is entirely moistureproof, however, and as yet there is no way of completely keeping moisture out of wood that is exposed to dampness constantly or for prolonged periods.

The protection afforded by coatings depends on a great number of variables. Among them are the thickness of the coating film, defects and voids in the film, type of pigment, chemical composition of the vehicle, volume ratio of pigment to vehicle, the vapor-pressure gradient across the film, and the length of the exposure period. The degree of protection also depends on the kind of exposure. For example, a water-repellent treatment, which may have 0 percent effectiveness against water vapor after 2 weeks at 80° F and 90 percent relative humidity, would have an effectiveness of over 60 percent when tested after immersion in water for 30 minutes. The high degree of protection provided by water repellents and water-repellent preservatives to short periods of wetting by liquid water is the major reason they are recommended for exterior finishing.

Porous paints — such as the latex paints and low-luster (flat) or breather-type oil-based paints formulated at a pigment volume concentration usually above 40 percent — afford little protection against moisture. These paints permit rapid entry of water vapor and water from dew and rain unless applied over a nonporous primer.

The moisture-excluding effectiveness of many coatings improves slightly with age. Good exterior coatings either retain their maximum effectiveness for a considerable time or lose effectiveness slowly. As long as the original appearance and integrity of the coatings are retained, most of the effectiveness remains. Paint that is slowly fading or chalking remains effective if vigorous rubbing will remove the chalk and disclose a glossy film underneath. Deep chalking, checking, or cracking indicates serious impairment of the effectiveness.

Factors Affecting Finish Performance

Exterior wood finishes perform well when full consideration is given to the many factors that affect them. These factors include the effect of the wood substrate, the properties of the finishing material, details of application, and severity of exposure.

Wood Properties. Wood surfaces that shrink and swell the least are best for painting. Wood shrinks less across annual ring than in the direction of the annual rings. For this reason, vertical- or edge-grained surfaces (Figure 181) are far better than flat-grained surfaces of any species, especially for exterior use where wide ranges of relative humidity and periodic wetting can produce wide ranges of swelling and shrinking.

Also, because the swelling of wood is directly proportional to density, low-density species are preferred. However, even high-swelling and dense wood surfaces with flat grain can be stabilized with a resin-treated paper overlay (overlaid exterior plywood and lumber) to provide excellent surfaces for painting. Medium-density, stabilized fiberboard products with a uniform, low-density surface or paper overlay are also good substrates for exterior use. However, vertical-grained heartwood of western red cedar and redwood are most widely used for exterior siding and trim that is to be painted. These species are classified in Group I, woods easiest to keep painted (Table 17). Vertical-grain surfaces of all species actually are considered excellent for painting, but most species are generally available only as flat-grain lumber.

Species that are normally cut as flat-grained lumber, that are high in density and swelling, or have defects such as knots or pitch are classified in Groups II through V, depending upon their general paint-holding characteristics. Many species in Groups II through IV are commonly painted, particularly the pines, Douglas fir, and spruce, but these species generally require more care and attention than the vertical-grain surfaces of Group I. Exterior paint will be more durable on vertical-grain boards than on flat-grain boards for any species with marked differences in density between earlywood and latewood, even if the species are rated in Group I. Flat-grain boards that are to be painted should be installed in areas protected from rain and sun.

Plywood for exterior use nearly always has a flat-grain surface. In addition, cycles of wetting and drying with subsequent swelling and shrinking tend to open lathe checks on the face veneer of plywood. This checking sometimes extends through paint coatings to detract from their appearance and durability. Plywood with a resin-treated paper overlay does not check. It has excellent painting qualities and would be equal to, or better than, vertical-grain lumber of Group I.

Types of Wood Products Used Outdoors. Three general categories of wood products are commonly used in exterior construction: 1) lumber, 2) plywood, and 3) reconstituted wood products such as hardboard and particleboard. Each product has unique characteristics that will affect the durability of any finish applied to it.

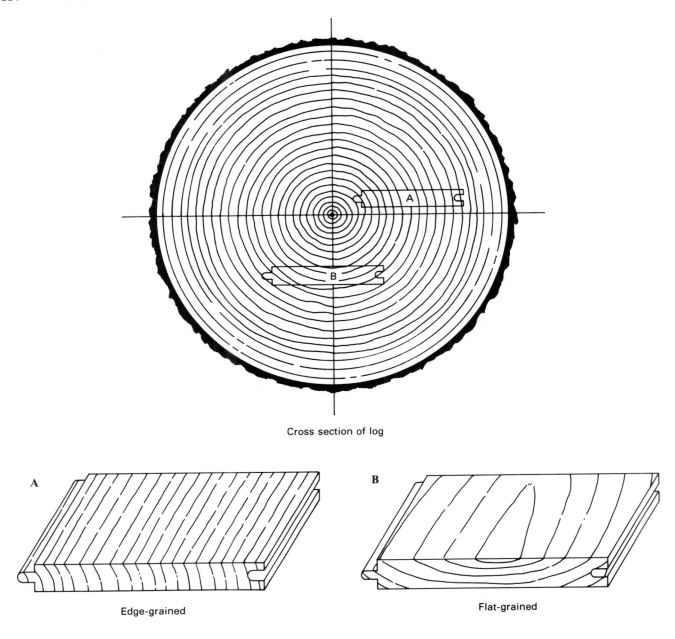

Cross section of log

Edge-grained

Flat-grained

Figure 181. Wood grain in lumber: (A) edge-grained, vertical-grained, or quartersawed;
(B) flat-grained, slash-grained, or plainsawed

Many older homes have wood siding. The ability of lumber to retain and hold a finish is affected by species, by ring direction with respect to the surface (vertical versus flat grain), and by smoothness.

The weight of wood varies tremendously between species. Some common construction woods such as southern pine are dense and heavy compared with the lighter weight ones such as redwood and cedar. The weight of wood is important because heavy woods shrink and swell more than light ones. This dimensional change in lumber occurs as the wood gains or loses moisture. Excessive dimensional change in wood constantly stresses a paint film and may result in early failure.

Some species have wide bands of earlywood and latewood. Wide, prominent bands of latewood are characteristic of southern pine and most Douglas fir, and paint will not hold well on these species. By contrast, redwood and cedar do not have wide late-wood bands and these species are preferred when paint will be used.

Ring direction also affects paint-holding characteristics and is determined at the time lumber is cut from a log. Most standard grades of lumber contain a high percentage of flat grain. Lumber used for board-and-batten siding, drop siding, or shiplap is frequently flat grained. Bevel siding is commonly produced in several grades. In some cases, the highest grade is required to be vertical grained and all heartwood over most of the width for greater paint durability. Other grades may be flat grained, vertical grained, or mixed grain and without requirements as to heartwood.

Exterior plywood with a rough-sawn surface is commonly used for siding. Smooth-sanded plywood is not recommended for siding, but it is often used in soffits. Both sanded and rough-sawn plywood will develop surface checks, especially when exposed to moisture and sunlight. These surface checks can lead to early paint failure with oil-based or alkyd paint systems. Quality acrylic latex primer and topcoat paint systems generally perform better. The flat-grained pattern present in nearly all plywood can also contribute to early paint failure. Therefore, if smooth or rough-sawn plywood is to be painted, special precautions should be taken. Penetrating stains are often more appropriate for rough-sawn exterior plywood surfaces, but quality acrylic latex paints also perform very well.

Reconstituted wood products are those made by forming small pieces of wood into large sheets, usually 4x8 feet or as required for a specialized use such as beveled siding. These products may be classified as fiberboard or particleboard, depending upon the nature of the basic wood component.

Fiberboards are produced from mechanical pulps. Hardboard is a relatively heavy type of fiberboard, and its tempered or treated form, designed for outdoor exposure, is used for exterior siding. It is often sold in 4x8-foot sheets but is also available in narrow strips as a substitute for solid-wood beveled siding.

Particleboards are manufactured from whole wood in the form of splinters, chips, flakes, strands, or shavings. Waferboard and flakeboard are two types of particleboard made from relatively large flakes or shavings.

Some fiberboards and particleboards are manufactured for exterior use. Film-forming finishes such as paints and solid-color stains will give the most protection to these reconstituted wood products. Some reconstituted wood products may be factory-primed with paint and some may even have a factory-applied topcoat. Also, some may be overlaid with a resin-treated paper to provide a superior surface for paint.

Treated wood is sometimes used in severe outdoor situations where special treatments and finishes are required for proper protection and best service. These situations involve the need for protection against decay (rot), insects, fire, and harsh exposures such as marine environments.

Although not generally classified as wood finishes, preservatives in wood do protect against weathering (in addition to decay), and a great quantity of preservative-treated wood is exposed outdoors without any additional finish. There are three main types of preservatives: l) the preservative oils (e.g., coal-tar creosote); 2) the organic solvent solutions (e.g., pentachlorophenol); and 3) waterborne salts (e.g., chromated copper arsenate). These preservatives can be applied in several ways, but pressure treatment generally gives the greatest protection against decay.

Water-repellent preservatives introduced into wood by a vacuum-pressure or dipping process can be painted. Coal-tar creosote or other dark oily preservatives tend to stain through paint, especially light-colored paint, unless the treated wood has weathered for many years before painting.

Fire-retardant treatment of wood does not generally interfere with adhesion of decorative paint coatings, unless the treated wood has an extremely high moisture content because of its increased hygroscopicity. It is most important that only those fire-retardant treatments specifically prepared and recommended for outdoor exposure be used for that purpose. These treated woods are generally painted according to recommendations of the manufacturer rather than being left unfinished, because the treatment and subsequent drying often darken and irregularly stain the wood.

Extractives in Wood. Water-soluble colored extractives occur naturally in the heartwood of such species as western red cedar, cypress, and redwood. It is to these substances that the heartwood of these

Table 17
Characteristics of woods for painting and weathering

Wood [1]	Ease of keeping well painted (I=easiest V=most exacting[1])	Weathering		Appearance	
		Resistance to cupping (1=best; 4=worst)	Ease of checking (1=best; 2=most)	Color of heartwood (sapwood is light)	Degree of figure on surface (flat grain)
Softwoods:					
Cedar:					
Alaska	I	1	1	Yellow	Faint
California incense	I	—	—	Brown	Faint
Port-Orford	I	—	—	Cream	Faint
Western red cedar	I	—	—	Brown	Distinct
White	I	—	—	Light brown	Distinct
Cypress	I	1	1	Light brown	Strong
Redwood	I	1	1	Dark brown	Distinct
Products[2] overlaid with resin-treated paper	I	—	1	—	—
Pine:					
Eastern white	II	2	2	Cream	Faint
Sugar	II	2	2	Cream	Faint
Western white	II	2	2	Cream	Faint
Ponderosa	III	2	2	Cream	Distinct
Fir, commercial white	III	2	2	White	Faint
Hemlock	III	2	2	Pale brown	Faint
Spruce	III	2	2	White	Faint
Douglas-fir (lumber and plywood)	IV	2	2	Pale red	Strong
Larch	IV	2	2	Brown	Strong
Lauan (plywood)	IV	2	2	Brown	Faint
Pine:					
Norway	IV	2	2	Light brown	Distinct
Southern (lumber and plywood)	IV	2	2	Light brown	Strong
Tamarack	IV	2	2	Brown	Strong

Table 17 (continued)
Characteristics of woods for painting and weathering

Wood [1]	Ease of keeping well painted (I=easiest; V=most exacting) [1]	Weathering		Appearance	
		Resistance to cupping (1=best; 4=worst)	Ease of checking (1=best; 2=most)	Color of heartwood (sapwood is light)	Degree of figure on surface (flat grain)
Hardwoods:					
Alder	III	—	—	Pale brown	Faint
Aspen	III	2	1	Pale brown	Faint
Basswood	III	2	2	Cream	Faint
Cottonwood	III	4	2	White	Faint
Magnolia	III	2	—	Pale brown	Faint
Yellow-poplar	III	2	1	Pale brown	Faint
Beech	IV	4	2	Pale brown	Faint
Birch	IV	4	2	Light brown	Faint
Cherry	IV	—	—	Brown	Faint
Gum	IV	4	2	Brown	Faint
Maple	IV	4	2	Light brown	Faint
Sycamore	IV	—	—	Pale brown	Faint
Ash	V or III	4	2	Light brown	Distinct
Butternut	V or III	—	—	Light brown	Faint
Chestnut	V or III	3	2	Light brown	Distinct
Walnut	V or III	3	2	Dark brown	Distinct
Elm	V or IV	4	2	Brown	Distinct
Hickory	V or IV	4	2	Light brown	Distinct
Oak, white	V or IV	4	2	Brown	Distinct
Oak, red	V or IV	4	2	Brown	Distinct

Note: Omissions in the table indicate inadequate data for classification.

[1] Woods ranked in Group V for ease of keeping well painted are hardwoods with large pores that must be filled with wood filler for durable painting. When so filled before painting, the second classification in the table applies.

[2] Plywood, lumber, and fiberboard with overlay or low-density surface.

species owes its attractive color, stability, and natural resistance to decay. However, paint may discolor when the extractives are dissolved and leached from the wood by water. This water may be from vapor condensing or from rain. When the solution of extractives reaches the painted surface, the water evaporates, leaving the extractives as a yellow to reddish-brown stain. The water that gets behind the paint and causes moisture blisters also causes migration of extractives. The discoloration produced when water wets siding from the back frequently forms a rundown or streaked pattern.

Finishing Wood Exposed Outdoors

Weathering. The simplest finish for wood is that created in the weathering process. Without paint or treatment of any kind, wood surfaces gradually change in color and texture and then may stay almost unaltered for a long time if the wood does not decay. Generally, the dark-colored woods become lighter and the light-colored woods become darker. As weathering continues, all woods become gray, accompanied by photodegradation and gradual loss of wood cells at the surface. As a result, exposed unfinished wood will slowly wear away (erode).

The weathering process is a surface phenomenon and is so slow that softwoods erode at an average rate of about 1/4 inch per century. Dense hardwoods will erode at a rate of only 1/8 inch per century. Low-density softwoods such as western red cedar may erode at a rate as high as 1/2 inch per century. In cold northern climates, erosion values as low as 1/32 inch per century have been reported.

Weathering is usually accompanied by the growth of dark-colored spores and mycelia of fungi or mildew on the surface, which give the wood a dark gray, blotchy, and unsightly appearance. In addition, highly colored wood extractives in such species as western red cedar and redwood add to the variable color of weathered wood. The dark-brown color of extractives may persist for a long time in areas not exposed to the sun and where the extractives are not removed by the washing action of rain.

Types of Exterior Wood Finishes. The outdoor finishes described in this section, their properties, treatment, and maintenance are summarized in Table 18. The suitability and expected life of the most commonly used finishes on several wood and wood-based products is summarized in Table 19. The information in Tables 18 and 19 should be considered as general guidelines only. Many factors affect the performance and lifetime of wood finishes as described earlier.

Paints may be either oil or latex based. Latex-based paints and stains are waterborne, and oil-based or alkyd paints are organic solvent-borne.

Paints are applied to the wood surface and do not penetrate it deeply. The wood grain is completely obscured, and a surface film is formed. Paints perform best on smooth, edge-grained lumber of lightweight species. This surface film can blister or peel if the wood is wetted, or if inside water vapor moves through the house wall and wood siding because of the absence of a vapor-retarding material.

Latex paints are generally easier to use because water is used in the cleanup process. Also, these paints are porous and thus will allow some moisture movement. In comparison, oil-based paints require organic solvents for cleanup and some are resistant to moisture movement.

Of all the finishes, paints provide the most protection for wood against surface erosion and offer the widest selection of colors. A nonporous paint film retards penetration of moisture and reduces the problem of discoloration by wood extractives and checking and warping of the wood. *Paint is not a preservative. It will not prevent decay if conditions are favorable for fungal growth.* Original and maintenance costs are often higher for a paint finish than for a water-repellent preservative or penetrating stain finish.

Solid-color stains are opaque finishes (also called hiding, or heavybodied) that come in a wide range of colors and are made with a much higher concentration of pigment than the semitransparent penetrating stains. As a result, they will totally obscure the natural wood color and grain. Oil-based solid-color stains tend to form a film much like paint and as a result can also peel away from the substrate. Latex-based solid-color stains are also available and form a film, as do the oil-based solid-color stains. Both these stains are similar to thinned paints and can usually be applied over old paint or stains.

Semitransparent penetrating stains are only moderately pigmented and, thus, do not totally hide

Table 18
Exterior wood finishes: Types, treatment, and maintenance[1]

Finish	Initial treatment	Appearance of wood	Cost of initial treatment	Maintenance procedure	Maintenance period of surface finish	Maintenance cost
Preservative oils (creosotes)	Pressure, hot and cold tank steeping	Grain visible. Brown to black in color, fading slightly with age	Medium	Brush down to remove surface dirt	5-10 years only if original color is to be renewed; otherwise no maintenance is required	Nil to low
	Brushing	Grain visible. Brown to black in color, fading slightly with age	Low	Brush down to remove surface dirt	3-5 years	Low
Waterborne preservatives	Pressure	Grain visible. Greenish in color, fading with age	Medium	Brush down to remove surface dirt	None, unless stained, painted, or varnished as below	Nil, unless stains, varnishes, or paints are used. See below
	Diffusion plus paint	Grain and natural color obscured	Low to medium	Clean and repaint	7-10 years	Medium
Organic solvents preservatives[2]	Pressure, steeping, dipping, brushing	Grain visible. Colored as desired	Low to medium	Brush down and reapply	2-3 years or when preferred	Medium
Water repellent[3]	One or two brush coats of clear material or, preferably, dip applied	Grain and natural color visible, becoming darker and rougher textured	Low	Clean and apply sufficient material	1-3 years or when preferred	Low to medium
Stains	One or two brush coats	Grain visible. Color as desired	Low to medium	Clean and apply sufficient material	3-6 years or when preferred	Low to medium
Clear varnish	Four coats (minimum)	Grain and natural color unchanged if adequately maintained	High	Clean and stain bleached areas, and apply two more coats	2 years or when breakdown begins	High
Paint	Water repellent, prime, and two topcoats	Grain and natural color obscured	Medium to high	Clean and apply topcoat; or remove and repeat initial treatment if damaged	7-10 years[4]	Medium to high

[1] This table is a compilation of data from the observations of many researchers.

[2] Pentachlorophenol, bis (tri-n-butyltin oxide), copper naphthenate, copper-8-quinolinolate, and similar materials.

[3] With or without added preservatives. Addition of preservatives helps control mildew growth and gives better performance.

[4] Using top-quality acrylic latex topcoats.

Table 19
Suitability of finishing methods for exterior wood surfaces[1]

Type of exterior wood surfaces	Water-repellent preservative		Stain		Paints	
	Suitability	Expected life[2] (Years)	Suitability	Expected life[3] (Years)	Suitability	Expected life[4] (Years)
Siding:						
Cedar and redwood						
Smooth (vertical grain)	High	1-2	Moderate	2-4	High	4-6
Rough sawn or weathered	High	2-3	Excellent	5-8	Moderate	3-5
Pine, fir, spruce, etc.						
Smooth (flat grain)	High	1-2	Low	2-3	Moderate	3-5
Rough (flat grain)	High	2-3	High	4-7	Moderate	3-5
Shingles						
Sawn	High	2-3	Excellent	4-8	Moderate	3-5
Split	High	1-2	Excellent	4-8	—	—
Plywood (Douglas-fir and Southern pine)						
Sanded	Low	1-2	Moderate	2-4	Moderate	3-5
Rough sawn	Low	2-3	High	4-8	Moderate	3-5
Medium-density overlay[5]	—	—	—	—	Excellent	6-8
Plywood (cedar and redwood)						
Sanded	Low	1-2	Moderate	2-4	Moderate	3-5
Rough sawn	Low	2-3	Excellent	5-8	Moderate	3-5
Hardboard, medium density[6]						
Smooth						
Unfinished	—	—	—	—	High	4-6
Preprimed	—	—	—	—	High	4-6
Textured						
Unfinished	—	—	—	—	High	4-6
Preprimed	—	—	—	—	High	4-6

Table 19 (continued)

Type of exterior wood surfaces	Water-repellent preservative		Stain		Paints	
	Suitability	Expected life[2] (Years)	Suitability	Expected life[3] (Years)	Suitability	Expected life[4] (Years)
Millwork (usually pine):						
Windows, shutters, doors, exterior trim[7]	High	—	Moderate	2-3	High	3-6
Decking:						
New (smooth)	High	1-2	Moderate	2-3	Low	2-3
Weathered (rough)	High	2-3	High	3-6	Low	2-3
Glue-Laminated Members:						
Smooth	High	1-2	Moderate	3-4	Moderate	3-4
Rough	High	2-3	High	6-8	Moderate	3-4
Waferboard:						
Waferboard	—	—	Low	1-3	Moderate	2-4

[1] This table is a compilation of data from the observations of many researchers. Expected life predictions are for an average continental U.S. location; expected life will vary in extreme climates or exposure (desert, seashore, deep woods, etc.)

[2] Development of mildew on the surface indicates a need for refinishing.

[3] Smooth, unweathered surfaces are generally finished with only one coat of stain, but rough-sawn weathered surfaces, being more absorptive, can be finished with two coats, with the second coat applied while the first coat is still wet.

[4] Expected life of two coats, one primer and one topcoat. Applying a second topcoat (three-coat job) will approximately double the life. Top-quality acrylic latex paints will have best durability.

[5] Medium-density overlay is generally painted.

[6] Semitransparent stains are not suitable for hardboard. Sloid-color stains (acrylic latex) will perform like paints. Paints are preferred.

[7] Exterior millwork, such as windows, should be factory treated according to Industry Standard IS4-81. Other trim should be liberally treated by brushing before painting.

the wood grain. These stains penetrate the wood surface, are porous, and do not form a surface film as paints do. As a result, they will not blister or peel even if moisture moves through the wood. Penetrating stains are alkyd- or oil-based, and some may contain a fungicide as well as a water repellent. Moderately pigmented latex-based (waterborne) stains are also available, but they do not penetrate the wood surface as do the oil-based stains.

Stains are most effective on rough lumber or rough-sawn plywood surfaces, but they also give satisfactory performance on smooth surfaces, although they will require frequent renewal. They are available in a variety of colors and are especially popular in the brown or red earth tones because these give a "natural or rustic wood appearance." They are an excellent finish for weathered wood. Semitransparent stains are not effective when applied over a solid-color stain or over old paint.

An effective stain of this type is the Forest Products Laboratory natural finish. The finish has a linseed oil vehicle; a fungicide to protect the oil and wood from mildew; and a water repellent, paraffin wax, to protect the wood from excessive penetration of water. Durable red and brown iron-oxide pigments simulate the natural colors of redwood and cedar. A variety of other colors (except pure white) can also be achieved with this type of finish.

A water-repellent preservative may be used as a natural finish. It contains a fungicide or mildewcide, a small amount of wax as a water repellent, a resin or drying oil, and a solvent such as turpentine or mineral spirits. Water-repellent preservatives do not contain any coloring pigments. Therefore, the resulting finish will vary in color depending on the wood itself. The preservative also prevents wood from darkening (graying) as a result of mildew and mold.

The initial application to smooth surfaces is usually short lived. When a surface starts to show a blotchy discoloration due to extractives or mildew, it should be cleaned with liquid household bleach and detergent solution and retreated after drying. During the first few years, the finish may have to be applied every year or so. After the wood has gradually weathered to a uniform color, the treatments are more durable and need refinishing only when the surface starts to become unevenly colored by fungi.

CAUTION: Because of the toxicity of some fungicides in water-repellent preservative solutions and some semitransparent stains, avoid excessive contact with the solution or its vapor or with the treated wood. Shrubs and other plants should also be protected from accidental contamination.

Water-repellent preservatives may also be used as a treatment for bare wood before priming and painting or in areas where old paint has peeled, exposing bare wood, particularly around butt joints or in corners. This treatment keeps rain or dew from penetrating into the wood, especially at joints and end grain, and thus decreases the shrinking and swelling of wood. The fungicide inhibits decay.

Water repellents are water-repellent preservatives with the preservative left out. Water repellents are not effective natural finishes by themselves because they do not control mildew. They can be used as a stabilizing treatment before priming and painting.

Transparent or clear coatings of conventional spar, urethane, or marine varnishes, which are film-forming finishes, are not generally recommended for exterior use on wood. Such coatings become brittle with exposure to sunlight and develop severe cracking and peeling, often in less than two years. Areas that are protected from direct sunlight by an overhang or that are on the north side of the structure can be finished with exterior-grade varnishes. However, even in protected areas, at least three coats of varnish are recommended and the wood should be treated with water-repellent preservative before finishing. The use of pigmented stains and sealers as undercoats also will contribute to greater life of the clear finish. In marine exposures, six coats of varnish should be used for best performance.

Many commercial fire-retardant coatings are available to provide varying degrees of protection of wood against fire. These paint coatings generally have low surface flammability; they "intumesce" to form an expanded low-density film upon exposure to fire, thus insulating the wood surface below from heat and retarding pyrolysis reactions. The paints have added ingredients to restrict the flaming of any released combustible vapors. Chemicals may also be present in these paints to promote decomposition of the wood surface to charcoal and water rather than forming volatile flammable products.

Most fire-retardant coatings are intended for interior use, but some are available for exterior application. Conventional paints have been applied over the fire-retardant coatings to improve their durability. Most conventional decorative coatings will in themselves slightly reduce the flammability of wood products when applied in conventional film thicknesses.

Application of Exterior Finishes. Proper surface care and preparation before applying paint to wood is essential for good performance. Wood and wood-based products should be protected from the weather and wetting on the job site and after they are installed. Surface contamination from dirt, oil, and other foreign substances must be eliminated. It is most important to paint wood surfaces within one week, weather permitting, after installation.

To achieve maximum paint life, follow this procedure:

1. Wood siding and trim should be treated with a paintable water-repellent preservative or water repellent. These treatments help protect the wood against the entrance of rain and dew and thus help to minimize swelling and shrinking. They can be applied by brushing or dipping. Lap and butt joints and the edges of panel products such as plywood, hardboard, and particleboard should be especially well treated because paint normally fails in these areas first. Allow at least two warm, sunny days for adequate drying before painting the treated surface. If the wood has been dip-treated with a water repellent or water-repellent preservative, allow at least one week of favorable weather.

2. After the water-repellent preservative or water repellent has dried, the bare wood must be primed. Because the primer coat forms a base for all succeeding paint coats, it is very important that it be applied properly. For woods with water-soluble extractives such as redwood and cedar, the best primers are good-quality oil-based and alkyd-based paints or stain-blocking acrylic latex-based paints. The primer seals in the extractives so that they will not bleed through the top coat. A primer should be used whether the top coat is oil-based or latex-based. For species that are predominantly sapwood and free of extractives, such as pine, a high-quality acrylic latex top coat paint may be used as both a primer and top coat. Enough primer should be applied to obscure the wood grain; it should not be spread too thinly. Follow the application rates recommended by the manufacturer. A primer coat that is uniform and of the proper thickness will distribute the swelling stresses which develop in wood with changes in moisture content and thus help to prevent premature paint failure.

3. Two coats of a good-quality acrylic latex house paint should be applied over the primer. Other paints that are used include the oil-based, alkyd-based, and vinyl acrylic. If it is not practical to apply two top coats to the entire house, consider two top coats for fully exposed areas on the south and west sides as a minimum for good protection. Areas fully exposed to sunshine and rain are the first to deteriorate and therefore should receive two coats. On those wood surfaces best suited for painting, one coat of a good house paint over a properly applied primer (a conventional two-coat paint system) should last four to five years, but two coats over the primer can last up to ten years (Table 19).

4. One gallon of paint will cover about 400 square feet of a smooth wood surface area. However, coverage can vary with different paints, surface characteristics, and application procedures. Research has indicated that the optimum thickness for the total dry paint coat (primer and two top coats) is 4 to 5 mils, or about the thickness of a sheet of newspaper. The quality of paint is usually, but not always, related to price. Brush application is always superior to roller or spray application, especially for the first coat.

5. To avoid future separation between paint coats, the first top coat should be applied within two weeks after the primer and the second top coat within two weeks of the first. As certain paints weather, they can form a soaplike substance on their surface that may prevent proper adhesion of new paint coats. If more than two weeks elapse before applying another coat, scrub the old surface with water using a bristle brush or sponge. If

necessary, use a mild detergent to remove all dirt and deteriorated paint. Then rinse well with water and allow the surfaces to dry before painting.

6. To avoid blistering caused by temperature, oil-based paints should not be applied on a cool surface that will be heated by the sun within a few hours. This blistering is most common with thick coats of dark colors of paints applied in cool weather. The blisters usually show up in the last coat of paint, from a few hours to as much as a day or two after painting.

7. Oil-based paint may be applied when the temperature is 40°F or above. A minimum of 50°F is desired for applying latex-based waterborne paints. For proper curing of these latex paint films, the temperature should not drop below 50°F for at least 24 hours after paint application. Low temperatures will result in poor coalescence of the paint film and early paint failure.

8. To avoid wrinkling, fading, or loss of gloss of oil-based paints and to avoid streaking of latex paints, the paint should not be applied in the evenings of cool spring and fall days. Heavy dews tend to form during the night before the surface of the paint has thoroughly dried. Serious water absorption problems and major finish failure can also occur with some latex paints when applied under these conditions.

Solid-color stains may be applied to a smooth surface by brush, spray, or roller application; but brush application is best. These stains act much like paint. One coat of solid-color stain is considered adequate for siding, but two coats will provide significantly better protection and longer service. These stains are not generally recommended for horizontal wood surfaces such as decks and window sills.

Unlike paint, lap marks may form with a solid-color stain. Latex-based stains are particularly fast-drying and are more likely to show lap marks than those with an oil base. To prevent lap marks, follow the procedures suggested for the application of semitransparent penetrating stains.

Semitransparent penetrating oil-based stains may be brushed, sprayed, or rolled on. Brushing will give the best penetration and performance. These stains

are generally thin and runny, so application can be messy. Lap marks may form if stains are improperly applied. They can be prevented by staining only a small number of boards or one panel at a time. This method prevents the front edge of the stained area from drying out before a logical stopping place is reached. Working in the shade is best because the drying rate is slower. One gallon will usually cover about 200 to 400 square feet of smooth wood surface and from 100 to 200 square feet of rough or weathered surface.

For long life with penetrating oil-based stain on rough-sawn or weathered lumber, use two coats and apply the second coat before the first is dry. (If the first coat dries completely, it may seal the wood surface so that the second coat cannot penetrate into the wood.) Apply the first coat to a panel or area in a manner to prevent lap marks. Then work on another area so that the first coat can soak into the wood for 20 to 60 minutes. About an hour after applying the second coat, use a cloth, sponge, or dry brush lightly wetted with stain to wipe off the excess stain that has not penetrated into the wood. Otherwise areas of stain that did not penetrate may form an unsightly surface film and glossy spots will appear. Avoid intermixing different brands or batches of stain. Stir stain occasionally and thoroughly during application to prevent settling and color change.

CAUTION: Sponges or cloths that are wet with oil-based stain are particularly susceptible to spontaneous combustion. To prevent fires, bury them, immerse them in water, or seal them in an airtight metal container immediately after use.

A two-coat system on rough wood may last as long as six to eight years in certain exposures due to the large amount of stain absorbed. By comparison, if only one coat of penetrating stain is used on new smooth wood, its life expectancy is two to four years; however, succeeding coats will last longer.

The most effective method of applying a water repellent or water-repellent preservative is to dip the entire board into the solution. However, brush treatment is also effective. When wood is treated in place, liberal amounts of the solution should be applied to all lap and butt joints, edges and ends of boards, and edges of panels where end grain occurs. Other areas especially vulnerable to moisture, such as the bottoms of doors and window frames, should not be overlooked. One gallon will cover about 250 square feet of smooth surface or 150 square feet of rough surface. The life expectancy is only one to two years as a natural finish, depending on the wood and exposure. Treatments on rough surfaces are generally longer lived than those on smooth surfaces. Repeated brush treatment to the point of refusal will improve durability and performance. Treated wood that is painted will not need to be retreated unless the protective paint layer weathers away.

Finishing porches and decks. Exposed flooring on porches and decks is sometimes painted, and the recommended procedure for treating, using water-repellent preservative and primer, is the same as for wood siding. After the primer, an undercoat (first top coat) and matching second top coat of porch and deck enamel should be applied. These paints are especially formulated to resist abrasion and wear.

Many fully exposed decks are more effectively finished with only a water-repellent preservative or a penetrating-type semitransparent pigmented stain. These finishes will need more frequent refinishing than painted surfaces, but this is easily done because there is no need for laborious surface preparation as when painted surfaces start to peel. Solid-color stains should not be used on any horizontal surface such as decks because early failure may occur.

Finishing treated wood. Wood pressure-treated with waterborne chemicals, such as copper, chromium, and arsenic salts (CCA-treated wood) that react with the wood or form an insoluble residue, presents no major problem in finishing if the wood is properly redried and thoroughly cleaned after treating. Wood treated with solventborne or oilborne preservative chemicals, such as pentachlorophenol, cannot be painted until all the solvents have evaporated. Solvents such as methylene chloride or liquified petroleum gas evaporate readily. When heavy oil solvents with low volatility are used to treat wood under pressure, successful painting is usually impossible. Even special drying procedures (that use highly volatile solvents) for wood pressure-treated with the water-repellent preservative formulas do not restore complete paintability.

Woods that have been pressure-treated for decay or fire resistance sometimes have special finishing requirements. All the common pressure preservative treatments (creosote, pentachlorophenal, water-repellent preservatives, and waterborne) will not significantly change the weathering characteristics of woods. Certain treatments, such as waterborne treatments containing chromium, reduce the degrading effects of weathering. Except for esthetic or visual reasons, there is generally no need to apply a finish to most preservative-treated woods. If necessary, oil-based, semitransparent penetrating stains can be used, but only after the preservative-treated wood has weathered for one to two years depending on exposure. The only preservative-treated woods that can be painted or stained immediately after treatment and without further exposure are CCA-treated woods, but only if they are dry and clean. Because CCA is waterborne, the wood must be dried after treatment. Manufacturers generally have specific recommendations for good painting and finishing practices for fire-retardant and preservative-treated woods.

Refinishing Wood. Exterior wood surfaces need to be refinished only when the old finish has worn thin and no longer protects the wood. In repainting with oil-based paint, one coat may be adequate if the old paint surface is in good condition. Dirty paint can often be freshened by washing with detergent. Too frequent repainting with oil-based systems produces an excessively thick film that is likely to crack abnormally across the grain of the wood. Complete paint removal and repainting is the only cure for cross-grain cracking.

In refinishing an old paint coat (or solid-color stain), proper surface preparation is essential if the new coat is to give the expected performance. First, scrape away all loose paint. Use sandpaper on any remaining paint to "feather" the edges smooth with the bare wood. Then scrub any remaining old paint with a brush or sponge and water. Rinse the scrubbed surface with clean water. Wipe the surface with your hand. If the surface is still dirty or chalky, scrub it again using a detergent. Mildew should be removed with a dilute solution of liquid household bleach. Rinse the cleaned surface thoroughly with fresh water and allow it to dry before repainting. Areas of exposed wood should be treated with a water-repellent preservative or water repellent, allowed to dry for at least two days, and then primed. Top coats can then be applied.

It is particularly important to clean areas protected from sun and rain, such as porches, soffits, and side walls protected by overhangs. These areas tend to collect dirt and water-soluble materials that interfere with adhesion of the new paint. It is probably adequate to repaint these protected areas every other time the house is painted.

Latex paint can be applied over freshly primed surfaces and on weathered paint surfaces if the old paint is clean and sound. Where old sound paint surfaces are to be repainted with latex paint, a simple test should be conducted first. After cleaning the surface, repaint a small, inconspicuous area with latex paint and allow it to dry at least overnight. Then, to test for adhesion, firmly press one end of a an adhesive bandage onto the painted surface. Snap it off. If the bandage is free of paint, the latex paint is well bonded and the old surface does not need priming or additional cleaning. If the new latex paint adheres to the tape, the old surface is too chalky and needs more cleaning or the use of an oil-based primer. If both the latex paint and the old paint coat adhere to the tape, the old paint is not well bonded to the wood and must be removed before repainting.

Semitransparent penetrating oil-based stains are relatively easy to refinish. Heavy scraping and sanding are generally not required. Simply use a stiff-bristle brush to remove all surface dirt, dust, and loose wood fibers, and then apply a new coat of stain. The second coat of penetrating stain often lasts longer than the first, because it penetrates into small surface checks that open up as wood weathers.

Water-repellent preservatives used for natural finishes can be renewed by a simple cleaning of the old surface with a bristle brush and an application of a new coat of finish. To determine if a water-repellent preservative has lost its effectiveness, splash a small amount of water against the wood surface. If the water beads up and runs off the surface, the treatment is still effective. If the water soaks in, the wood needs to be refinished. Refinishing is also required when the wood surface shows signs of graying. Gray discoloration can be removed with liquid household bleach.

NOTE: Steel wool and wire brushes should not be used to clean surfaces to be finished with semitransparent stains or water-repellent preservatives because small iron deposits may be left behind. The small iron deposits can react with certain water-soluble extractives in woods such as western red cedar, redwood, Douglas fir, and the oaks to yield dark blue-black stains on the surface.

CHAPTER 8

Special Topics

This chapter discusses of a variety of topics whose importance varies from region to region and from home to home. The final section, "Maintenance and Repair," is included because it is influenced by the choices made during the construction process.

PROTECTION AGAINST DECAY AND TERMITES

Wood used under conditions where it will always be dry, or even where it is wetted briefly and rapidly redried, will not decay. However, all wood and wood products in construction use are susceptible to decay if kept wet for long periods under temperatures favorable to the growth of decay organisms. Most of the wood as used in a house is not subjected to such conditions. There are places where water can work into the structure, but such places can be protected. Protection is accomplished by methods of design and construction, by use of suitable materials, and in some cases by using treated material.

Wood is also subject to attack by termites and some other insects. Termites can be grouped into two main classes: subterranean and dry-wood. In the northernmost states, subterranean termites are confined to scattered, localized areas of infestation (Figure 182). The Formosan subterranean termite has been discovered (1966) in several locations in the South. It is a serious pest because its colonies contain large numbers of the worker caste and they can cause damage rapidly. Though presently in localized areas, it could spread. Controls are similar to those for other subterranean species. Dry-wood termites are found mainly in Florida, southern California, and the Gulf Coast states. They are more difficult to control, but the damage they do is less serious than that caused by subterranean termites.

Wood has proved itself through the years to be a desirable and satisfactory building material. Damage from decay and termites has been minor in proportion to the total value of wood in residential structures, but it has been a troublesome problem to many homeowners. With changes in building design features and use of new building materials, it is pertinent to restate the basic safeguards to protect buildings against both decay and termites.

Decay

Wood decay is caused by certain fungi that can use wood for food. These fungi, like the higher plants, require air, warmth, food, and moisture for growth. Early stages of decay caused by these fungi may be accompanied by a discoloration of the wood. Paint also may become discolored where the

Figure 182. Northern limits of termite damage in the United States: Line A, by subterranean termites; Line B, by dry-wood or nonsubterranean termites

underlying wood is rotting. Advanced decay is easily recognized, because the wood has undergone definite changes in properties and appearance. In advanced stages of building decay, the affected wood generally is brown and crumbly, but sometimes may be comparatively white and spongy. These changes may not be apparent on the surface, but the loss of sound wood inside is often reflected by sunken areas on the surface or by a "hollow" sound when the wood is tapped with a hammer. Where the atmosphere is very damp, the decay fungus may grow out on the surface, appearing as white or brownish growths in patches or strands or in special cases as vinelike structures.

Fungi grow most rapidly at temperatures of about 70°F to 85°F. High temperatures such as those used in kiln drying of lumber kill fungi, but low temperatures, even far below 0°, merely cause them to remain dormant.

Fungi have definite moisture requirements. Wood-destroying fungi will not become established in dry wood. A moisture content of 20 percent (which can be determined with an electrical moisture meter) is safe. Moisture contents greater than this are practically never reached in wood that is sheltered against rain and protected, if necessary, against wetting from condensation or fog. Decay can be permanently arrested simply by taking measures to dry out the infected wood and keep it dry. Brown, crumbly decay in the dry condition is sometimes called "dry rot," but this is a misnomer. Such wood must necessarily have been damp when the rotting occurred.

The presence of mold or stain fungi should serve as a warning that conditions are or have been suitable for growth of decay fungi. Very moldy or heavily stained lumber, therefore, should be examined for evidence of decay. Such discolored wood may not be entirely satisfactory for exterior millwork because it frequently absorbs more water than does bright wood.

The natural decay resistance of all common native species of wood lies in the heartwood. When untreated, the sapwood of all species has low resistance to decay and usually has short life under decay-producing conditions. Of the species of wood commonly used in house construction, the heartwood of redwood and the cedars is classified as being highest in decay resistance. Quality, all-heartwood lumber is becoming more and more difficult to obtain, however, as increasing amounts of timber are cut from the smaller trees of second-growth stands. In general, when substantial decay resistance is needed in load-bearing members that are difficult and expensive to replace, wood appropriately treated with preservative is recommended.

Subterranean Termites

Subterranean termites are the most destructive of the insects that infest wood in houses. The chance of infestation is great enough to justify preventive measures in the design and construction of buildings in areas where termites are common.

Subterranean termites are common throughout the southern two-thirds of the United States, except in mountainous and extremely dry areas. These termites become most numerous in moist, warm soil containing an abundant supply of food in the form of wood (scraps of lumber, for example) or other cellulosic material. In their search for additional food (wood), they build earthlike shelter tubes over foundation walls or in cracks in the walls, or on pipes or supports leading from the soil to the house. These tubes are from ¼ to ½ inch or more in width and flattened, and protect the termites in their travels between food and shelter.

Since subterranean termites eat the interior of the wood, they may cause a great deal of damage before they are discovered. They honeycomb the wood with tunnels that are separated by thin layers of sound wood. Decay fungi, on the other hand, soften the wood and eventually cause it to shrink, crack, and crumble without producing anything like these continuous tunnels. When both decay fungi and subterranean termites are present in the same wood, even the layers between the termite tunnels will be softened.

Dry-Wood Termites

Dry-wood termites fly directly to and bore into the wood instead of building tunnels from the ground as do the subterranean termites. Dry-wood termites are common in the tropics, and damage has been recorded in the United States in a narrow strip along the Atlantic Coast from Cape Henry, Virginia, to the Florida Keys and westward along the coast of the Gulf of Mexico to the Pacific Coast as far as northern California (Figure 182). Serious damage has been noted in southern California and in areas around Tampa, Miami, and Key West, Florida. Infestations may be found in structural timber and other woodwork in buildings and also in furniture, particularly where the surface is not adequately protected by paint or other finishes.

Dry-wood termites cut across the grain of the wood and excavate broad pockets, or chambers, connected by tunnels about the diameter of the termite's body. They destroy both springwood and the usually harder summerwood, whereas subterranean termites mainly attack springwood. Dry-wood termites remain hidden in the wood and are seldom seen, except when they make dispersal flights.

Safeguards Against Decay

Except for special cases of wetting by condensation or fog, a dry piece of wood, when placed off the ground under a tight roof with wide overhang, will stay dry and never decay. This principle of "umbrella protection," when applied to houses of proper design and construction, is a good precaution. The use of dry lumber in designs that will keep the wood dry is the simplest way to avoid decay in buildings.

Most of the details regarding wood decay have been included in earlier chapters, but they are given here as a reminder of their relationship to protection from decay and termites.

Untreated wood should not come in contact with the soil. The foundation walls should have a clearance of at least 8 inches above the exterior finish grade, and the floor construction should have a clearance 18 inches or more from the bottom of the joists to the ground in spaces without basements. The foundation should be accessible at all points for inspection. Porches that prevent access should be isolated from the soil by concrete or from the building proper by metal flashing or aprons (Figure 183).

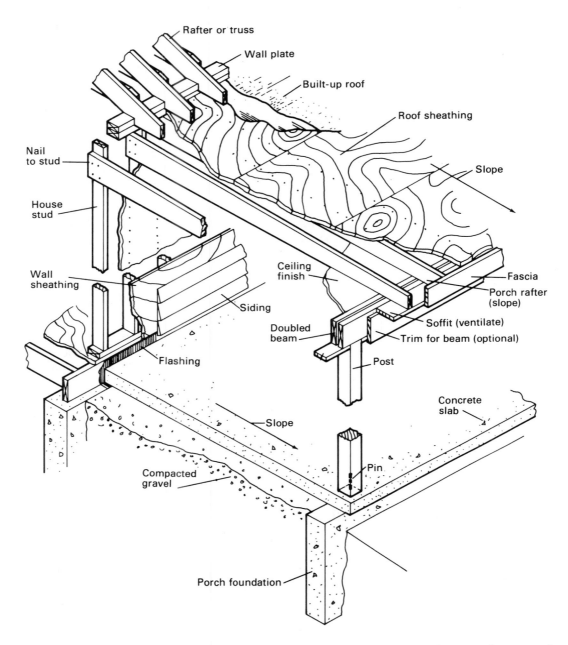

Figure 183. Metal shield used to protect wood at porch slab from decay. This type of construction is not recommended where termites are a serious hazard

Exterior steps and stair carriages, posts, wall-plates, and sills should be isolated from the ground with concrete or masonry. Sill plates and other wood in contact with concrete near the ground should be separated from the concrete by a moistureproof membrane, such as heavy roll roofing or 6-mil polyethylene. Girder and joist openings in masonry walls should be big enough to assure an air space around the ends of these members.

Design Details. Surfaces like steps, porches, door and window frames, roofs, and other projections should be sloped to promote runoff of water. Non-corroding flashing should be used around chimneys, windows, doors, or other places where water might seep in. (Refer to the section on "Flashing and Other Sheet Metal.") Roofs with considerable overhang give added protection to the siding and other parts of the house. Gutters and downspouts should be placed and maintained to divert water away from the buildings. Porch columns and screen rails should be shimmed above the floor to allow quick drying or posts should slightly overhang raised concrete bases.

Exterior steps, rails, and porch floors exposed to rain need protection from decay, particularly in warm, damp parts of the country. Pressure treatment of the wood provides a high degree of protection against decay and termite attack. In regions where the chance of decay is relatively small, on-the-job application of water-repellent preservatives by dipping or soaking has been found to be worthwhile. The wood should be dry, cut to final dimensions, and then dipped or soaked in the preservative solution. Soaking is the best of these nonpressure methods; the ends of the boards should be soaked for a minimum of three minutes. It is important to protect the end grain of wood at joints, for this area absorbs water easily and is the most common point of infection. These treatments work because they provide a treated layer near the wood surface. Any saw-cut after treatment will expose unprotected wood. Let treated wood dry for several days before painting or staining.

Remember that water-repellent treatments are only effective for wood used above ground.

Green or Partially Seasoned Lumber. Construction lumber that is green or partially seasoned may be infected before it comes to the job site with one or more of the staining, molding, or decay fungi and use of this infected wood should be avoided. Such wood may contribute to serious decay in both the structural frame and exterior parts of buildings. If wet lumber must be used, or if wetting occurs during construction, the wood should not be fully enclosed or painted until thoroughly dried.

Water Vapor From the Soil. Crawl spaces of houses built on poorly drained sites may be subjected to high humidity. During the winter when the sills and outer joists are cold, moisture condenses on them and, in time, the wood absorbs so much moisture that it is susceptible to attack by fungi. Unless this moisture dries out before temperatures favorable for fungus growth are reached, considerable decay may result. However, this decay can progress so slowly that no weakening of the wood becomes apparent for a few years. Placing a layer of 45-pound or heavier roll roofing or a 6-mil sheet of polyethylene over the soil to keep the vapor from getting into the crawl space would prevent such decay. This procedure is recommended for all sites where, during the cold months, the soil is wet enough to be compressed in the hand.

If the floor is uninsulated, there is an advantage (because of fuel savings) in closing the foundation vents during the coldest months. However, unless the crawl space is used as a heat plenum chamber, insulation is usually located between floor joists. The vents could then remain open. Crawl-space vents can be very small when soil covers are used; they need have only 10 percent of the area required without covers. (Refer to the section on "Crawl Space Foundations.")

Water Vapor From Household Activities. Water vapor is also given off during cooking, washing, and other household activities. This vapor can pass through walls and ceilings during very cold weather and condense on sheathing, studs, and rafters, causing condensation problems. A vapor retarder of an approved type is needed on the warm side of walls. It is also important that the attic space be ventilated. (Refer to the sections on "Vapor Retarders" and "Ventilation.")

Water Supplied by the Fungus Itself. In the warmer coastal areas, some substructure decay is caused by a fungus that provides its own needed moisture by conducting it through a vinelike structure from moist ground to the wood. The total damage caused by this water-conducting fungus is not great, but in individual cases it can be unusually severe. Preventive and remedial measures depend on getting the soil dry and avoiding untreated wood "bridges" such as posts between ground and sill or beams.

Safeguards Against Termites

The best time to provide protection against termites is during the planning and construction of the building. The first requirement is to remove all wood debris, such as stumps and discarded form boards, from the soil at the building site before and after construction. Steps should also be taken to keep the soil under the house as dry as possible.

Next, the foundation should be made impervious to subterranean termites to prevent them from crawling up through hidden cracks to the wood in the building above. Properly reinforced concrete makes the best foundation, but unit-masonry walls or piers capped with at least 4 inches of reinforced concrete are also satisfactory. *No wood member of the structural part of the house should be in contact with the soil.*

The best protection against subterranean termites is to treat the soil near the foundation or under an entire slab foundation with an approved termiticide. Any wood used in secondary appendages, such as wall extensions, decorative fences, and gates, should be pressure-treated with a good preservative.

In regions that have dry-wood termites, the following measures should be taken to prevent damage:
1. All lumber, particularly secondhand material, should be carefully inspected before use. If infected, discard the piece.
2. All doors, windows (especially attic windows), and other ventilation openings should be screened with metal wire with not less than 20 meshes to the inch.
3. Preservative-treated lumber can be used to prevent attack in construction timber and lumber.
4. Several coats of house paint will provide considerable protection to exterior woodwork in building. All cracks, crevices, and joints between exterior wood members should be filled with a mastic caulking or plastic wood before painting.
5. The heartwood of foundation-grade redwood, particularly when painted, is more resistant to attack than most other native commercial species.

CAUTION: Pesticides can be harmful to humans, domestic animals, desirable plants, and fish or other wildlife if they are not handled or applied properly. Use all pesticides selectively and carefully. Follow recommended practices for the disposal of surplus pesticides and pesticide containers. Although this book reports research involving pesticides, it does not contain recommendations for their use, nor does it imply that the uses discussed here have been registered. All uses of pesticides must be registered by appropriate State and/or Federal agencies before they can be recommended.

Preservative Treatments for Lumber

Pressure treatments force preservative chemicals into wood, providing deep protection against decay and termites. Wood preservatives fit into two general classes: oilborne, such as creosote and petroleum solutions of pentachlorophenol; and waterborne, applied as solutions of inorganic salts.

Creosote and solutions of the heavier, less volatile petroleum oils help protect wood from weathering outdoors but have an odor, lack cleanliness, and are not readily paintable. Volatile oils or solvents with oilborne preservatives, if removed after treatment, leave the wood cleaner than the heavier oils do. Pentachlorophenol may be carried in any of four mixtures: with heavy oil, mineral spirits, methylene chloride, or liquified petroleum gas. Wood treated with pentachlorophenol dissolved in methylene chloride or liquified gas has a dry, paintable, and gluable surface.

Waterborne preservatives provide a clean and paintable wood surface, free from objectionable odor. Because water is added during treatment, the wood must be dried after treatment to the moisture content required for use. Standard wood preservatives used in water solutions include acid copper chromate, ammoniacal copper arsenate, chromated copper arsenate, and chromated zinc chloride.

The color of the wood will not show the quality of treatment. Wood treated with oil-based preservatives, such as pentachlorophenol, is usually light-to-dark brown. Most of the waterborne salt treatments leave a greenish color because they contain copper or chromium salts. Lumber sometimes receives a brightly colored coating that prevents fungus stain during shipment. These coatings are not pressure treatments. They are only surface treatments and give no long-term protection against decay or termites. When buying preservative-treated wood, pay close attention to the stamps, labels, or certifications on them. Treated materials to be used in contact with the ground should be stamped, labeled, or otherwise certified as having received a treatment that is adequate for ground contact.

Treated wood marked "aboveground use" should not be used in the ground. Use these materials only above ground — they contain less preservative than do items treated for ground contact.

Use Pressure-Treated Wood Carefully. The following precautions should be taken when handling wood pressure-treated with creosote, pentachlorophenol, or with preservatives that contain inorganic arsenicals, and in determining where to use and dispose of the treated wood.

Onsite Precautions

1. Wood pressure-treated with waterborne arsenical preservatives may be used inside residences as long as all sawdust and construction debris are cleaned up and disposed of after construction.
2. Logs treated with pentachlorophenol should not be used for log homes.
3. Wood treated with creosote or pentachlorophenol should not be used where it will be in frequent or prolonged contact with bare skin (for example, chairs and other outdoor furniture) unless an effective sealer has been applied.
4. Creosote-treated wood should not be used in residential interiors.
5. Pentachlorophenol-treated wood should not be used in residential, industrial, or commercial interiors except for laminated beams or other building components which have two coats of an appropriate sealer applied. Sealers may be applied at the installation site. Urethane, shellac, latex epoxy enamel, and varnish are acceptable sealers for pentachlorophenol-treated wood.
6. Do not use treated wood in situations where the preservative may become a component of food. Do not use treated wood for cutting boards or countertops.
7. Only treated wood that is visibly clean and free of surface residues should be used for patios, decks, and walkways.

Handling Precautions

1. Dispose of treated wood by ordinary trash collection or by burial. Treated wood should not be burned in open fires or in stoves, fireplaces, or residential boilers because toxic chemicals may be produced as part of the smoke and ashes.
2. Treated wood from commercial or industrial use (for example, construction sites) may be burned only in commercial or industrial incinerators or boilers in accordance with State and Federal regulations.
3. Avoid frequent or prolonged inhalations of sawdust from treated wood. When sawing and machining treated wood, wear a dust mask. Whenever possible, these operations should be performed outdoors to avoid indoor accumulations of airborne sawdust from treated wood. When power-sawing and machining, wear goggles to protect eyes from flying particles.
4. Avoid frequent or prolonged skin contact with creosote-treated wood and with pentachlorophenol-treated wood; when handling the treated wood, wear long-sleeved shirts and long pants and use gloves impervious to the chemicals (for example, vinyl-coated gloves).
5. After working with the wood, and before eating, drinking, and use of tobacco products, wash exposed areas thoroughly.
6. If oily preservatives or sawdust accumulate on clothes, launder before reuse. Wash work clothes separately from other household clothing.

NOISE CONTROL

Little attention has been given to noise control in most single-family homes, but increasing noise pollution indicates a need to consider some control measures. These may include planning to keep out outdoor noise, interior planning to exclude noise from quiet areas, use of sound absorbers in living spaces, and construction that reduces sound transmission. Many of the construction features that enhance energy conservation also control noise.

Exterior Planning

Noise absorption is affected by the shape and orientation of a house. If the narrow dimension faces the exterior noise source, there will be much less sound transmitted to the inside than if the long dimension faces the source. Courtyards facing the noise source not only provide more area for sound transmission, but also provide surfaces that reflect and amplify sound. Landscaping can be used effectively to deflect and absorb sound, but requires more than a hedge or scattered shrubs and trees. A dense forest at least 25 to 50 feet deep or a solid fence can noticeably reduce noise. A more extreme measure, but quite effective, is a berm between the noise source and the house. Provide tightly sealed doors and windows on the side facing the noise source. Double walls, triple glazing, and good weatherstripping are all effective in reducing sound transmission.

Interior Planning

Interior noise control basically involves separating quiet spaces from spaces that have noisy equipment. Spaces with mechanical equipment are best located on an outside wall. Kitchens, bathrooms, and utility rooms can be located on the noisy side of the house or near mechanical equipment. Closets can be effectively used as buffers between bedrooms and noise-producing areas, and they can also be used between bedrooms to provide sound insulation. Back-to-back closets are even better. Doors must be kept closed for closets to be effective. A bookcase or storage wall will also help isolate two adjoining rooms. Doors opening to hallways should be staggered rather than located opposite each other. Special attention should be given to vertical separation; do not locate mechanical equipment in the basement directly under bedrooms.

Sound Absorbers

Some materials absorb sound and change it to heat rather than reflecting it. Sound absorption is often desirable except in the case of music, which often needs reflection to avoid the feeling of a "dead" space. Common absorptive materials in homes are carpet, furniture, drapes, and acoustical ceiling tile. Hard surfaces such as those found in kitchens result in a lot of sound reflection and may not be as conducive to quiet conversation as the living room which has many sound absorbers. Surface-mounted acoustical panels on the walls and ceiling can reduce some of the noise in areas such as kitchens. Absorptive material placed in the heating ducts can reduce sound transmission between connected spaces or from the heating system.

Construction to Reduce Sound Transmission

The effectiveness of wall, floor, and ceiling construction in reducing sound transmission is rated by Sound Transmission Class (STC). The lower the STC, the less effective the construction is in stopping sound transmission. The approximate effectiveness of walls with varying STC numbers is as follows:

STC number	Effectiveness
25	Normal speech can be understood quite easily
35	Loud speech audible but not intelligible
45	Must strain to hear loud speech
48	Some loud speech barely audible
50	Loud speech not audible

Some alternatives in construction include the use of resilient channels, staggered studs, and combinations of sound-deadening board. The addition of insulation to wall cavities also adds to the resistance to sound transmission. Some examples of wall constructions and their range of STC ratings are shown in Figures 184 through 187. Floor-ceiling constructions that provide sound insulation are shown in Figures 188 and 189.

Even though these constructions resist sound transmission, sound may take a route around these barriers. Sound can travel through cracks at the top or bottom of a wall or through electrical outlets or recessed cabinets in opposite faces of the wall placed in the same stud space. Sound may travel around a wall by passing through a floor into a basement or crawl space and back through the floor into an adjoining room. Doors, even tightly sealed, provide a better path for sound than the wall systems designed for sound isolation, and a very small crack under or around a door increases the sound transmission significantly.

Heating and cooling equipment can be a major source of noise. If the furnace is located in a closet in the living area, the walls should be masonry or gypsum drywall should be mounted on resilient channels over wood studs. A solid-core wood or insulated metal door should be used, and it should be tightly weatherstripped. Combustion air should be taken from the attic or crawl space, not through wall or door louvers from the living area. The return air duct and plenum should be lined with acoustic material to absorb the fan noise. Duct openings to different rooms should not be directly opposite each other. Ducts should be sized to avoid air velocities of more than 1000 feet per minute. These velocities create noise in the ducts and at the outlet grilles.

Piping for hydronic heating systems should be wrapped with insulating material to reduce vibra-

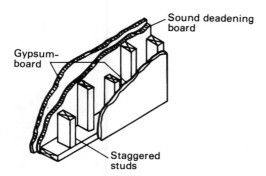

Figure 184. A plain stud wall with gypsumboard on both sides has an STC rating of 32 to 36. Adding a second layer of gypsumboard to each side increases the STC rating to 38 to 41

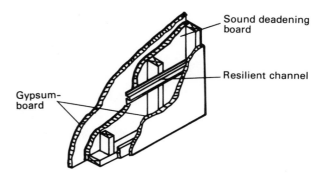

Figure 187. A staggered-stud wall on a single plate with sound-deadening board under gypsumboard on one side has an STC rating of 44 to 46. Adding insulation to the stud cavities increases the STC rating to 46 to 50

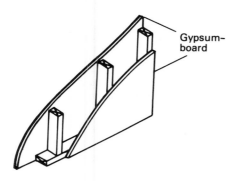

Figure 185. A single-stud wall with gypsumboard on both sides has an STC rating of 32 to 36. Adding a second layer of gypsumboard to each side increases the STC rating to 44 to 47

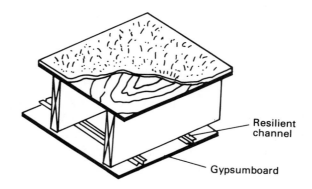

Figure 188. A floor-ceiling structure having carpet, pad, plywood subfloor, and ceiling gypsumboard supported on resilient channels has an STC rating of 46 to 48

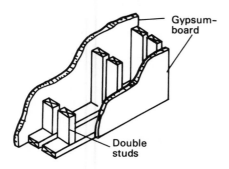

Figure 186. A double-stud wall on separate plates has an STC rating of 42 to 44. If insulation is added to the stud cavities on one side, the STC rating is increased to 50 to 53

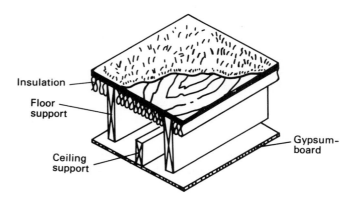

Figure 189. A floor-ceiling structure having carpet, pad, plywood subfloor, and ceiling gypsumboard supported on separate ceiling joists has an STC rating of 51 when 2 to 3 inches of insulation are installed beneath the plywood subfloor

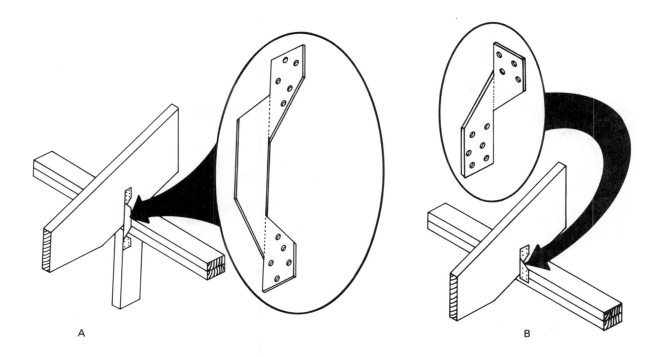

Figure 190. Connectors used to attach trusses or rafters to the wall: (A) connection to stud; (B) connection to top plate

tion. Pipes should be sized to limit the speed of flow, and provisions must be made for venting any air that might get into the system.

WIND, SNOW, AND SEISMIC LOADS

Some geographic areas have loading requirements beyond those expected in conventional construction. These loads are considered in the local building codes and appropriate structural design is required. Wind loads are critical in the coastal areas of the Southeast because of hurricanes. Some parts of the country have heavy snow loads, particularly the high mountain areas. Seismic loads are critical on the West Coast, where earthquakes are a constant threat. This section is not intended to provide engineering design for these extreme loads, but it will present some general considerations for good performance.

Wood construction generally performs well when subjected to natural disasters. Two reasons are that wood members can resist short-term loads considerably above working stresses and that the large number of mechanically fastened joints make the structure ductile.

Wind Load

The primary consideration for good performance under extreme wind load is that all members of the structure be tied together. The roof is most vulnerable and should be well secured to the walls. The walls must also be well secured to the floor and foundation system. A good connection to the foundation is necessary rather than depending on the weight of the house to hold it in place. Wide roof overhangs, carports, and porches need to be well anchored because of the large area for uplift. Connectors should load nails laterally rather than in withdrawal. To do this, sheet metal connectors or straps are often required.

Commercially available connectors can be used for connecting roof trusses or rafters to the wall (Figure 190) rather than toe-nailing to the top plate. Where a rafter and joist system is used, collar beams or gussets are important to hold the roof together at the ridge (Figure 191). Metal straps or plates can be used to tie the wall to the floor and sill plate (Figure

192). This tie can also be accomplished with structural wall sheathing that extends down over the floor framing and is well nailed (Figure 193). Finally, the sill plate must be anchored to the foundation (Figure 194). These connections are further discussed in Chapter 3.

The principle of tying all components of the structure together is often best realized with engineered components such as roof trusses. Connectors are specifically engineered to hold all the parts together. The truss concept is carried a step further in a structure called the truss frame. It combines roof truss, floor truss, and studs into a unified structural component. The studs extend into both the roof and floor trusses, resulting in rigid joints completely tied together with metal plate connectors (Figure 195). The truss frame is designed as an engineered component and fabricated in a truss plant. If the frame is tied to the foundation, it will have great resistance to wind loads. Rigidity perpendicular to the frames is provided by the diaphragm action of roof and wall sheathing and the subfloor. The truss frames are hauled to the building site and placed by a crane in the same manner as roof trusses. The building can be enclosed very quickly using this system; once the

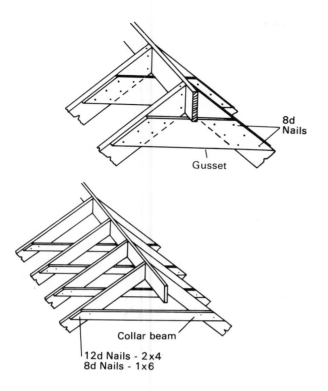

Figure 191. Collar beam or gusset required at ridge in a rafter-framed roof system

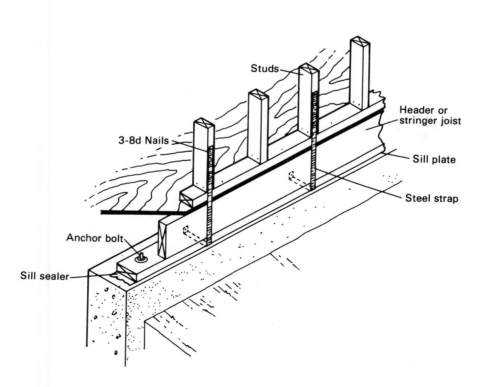

Figure 192. Steel strap for connecting the wall to the sill plate

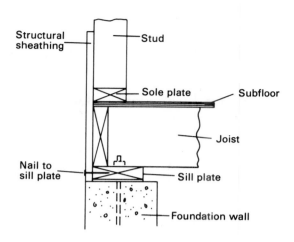

Figure 193. Structural sheathing nailed to sill plate for tying the wall to the foundation wall

frames are set, enclosure with sheathing is all that is required. The truss frame has been accepted by major model building codes and has been successfully used in all parts of the country.

Observation of wind damage has shown that building shape has some influence on overall damage. Hip roofs sustain less shingle damage than gable roofs because of the turbulence around the gable end, which starts removal of the shingles at the edge.

Snow Load

The major consideration for snow load is simply the use of larger structural members. These are usu-

ally specified by the local building code. Rafters and beams in particular are designed for maximum snow-load conditions. Observations have shown little evidence of failures in light-frame houses. Failures reported are generally in commercial buildings with long spans over large, open spaces.

There are some general considerations of shape that may influence snow load. Snow will usually slide off of steep sloping roofs; it will also often blow off of flat roofs where the entire roof is at one elevation. The problem of snow buildup develops on sloped roofs when the wind is perpendicular to the ridge. Turbulence at the ridge causes drifting on the downwind side resulting in an unbalanced loading on the roof structure. Another drift problem develops where two building sections of different heights join. Snow blows off the higher section onto the lower section, resulting in a deep drift. This problem is particularly critical when the lower section is a flat roof.

In a joist-and-rafter roof, it is particularly important that the joists be well nailed to the rafters to prevent rafters from spreading due to outward thrust from the snow load. Bracing the center of the rafters to a center bearing partition may also prevent sag in the rafter caused by a heavy snow load (Figure 196). The best resistance to snow loads is often accomplished with engineered components such as roof trusses.

Seismic Load

The major factors in earthquake resistance are adequate lateral bracing, shear resistance in walls,

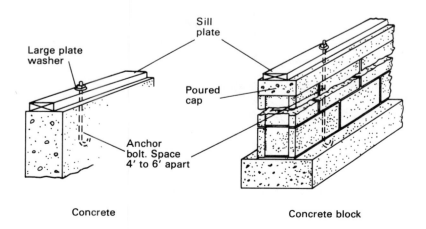

Figure 194. Anchorage of the sill plate to the foundation wall

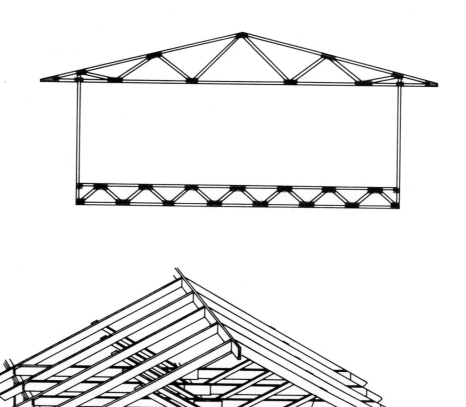

Figure 195. The truss-framed system combines floor, walls, and roof into a unitized frame for structural continuity from the foundation to the ridge

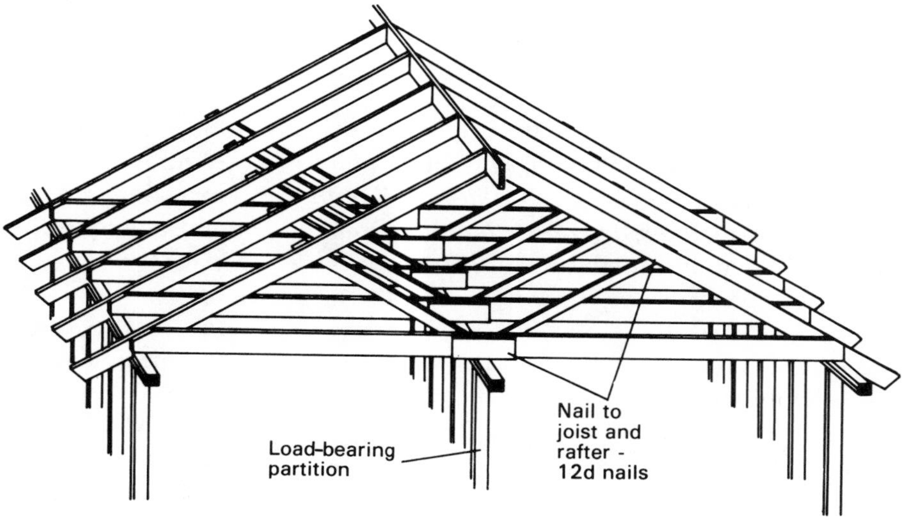

Figure 196. Bracing of rafters to a center-bearing partition to prevent sag from a heavy snow load

Nail to joist and rafter - 12d nails

Load-bearing partition

and good connections between all major components. Buildings that have performed best had simple rectangular configurations, continuous floors, and small window and door openings. These could be described as having a symmetric, "box-like" lateral-resistive system. In addition to the building acting as a unit, anchorage to the foundation is particularly important to avoid having the foundation move out from under the house.

The major cause of failure observed after earthquakes has been inadequate lateral bracing in walls. The best bracing is provided by well-nailed structural wall sheathing. Good diagonal bracing is also acceptable. Where wood diagonals are used, they must be made of high-quality material. Major failures have occurred where wood bracing had large knots. Another problem is racking walls that are not arranged symmetrically. This situation may result in

rotation of the building which can cause collapse.

Another major cause of structural failure in earthquakes has been large openings in walls. These appear to be more critical when they are near a corner. Where large openings such as garage doors have a second story over them, there is particular danger of failure, since the weight of the second story is added to the lack of racking resistance.

The joining of two elements of a building of different heights, as in a split-level house, can also cause problems. The two sections have different frequencies of vibration and may not move together.

Summary

Wood can generally resist short-term loads beyond its working stresses, and the resilience of the structure and redundancy of the large number of connectors add to the ability of the house to support excessive loads. Structural adequacy is improved by good connections between all components and by good lateral bracing. A simple, unified shape is an added plus. Engineered components such as roof trusses or the truss frame perform particularly well when subjected to severe structural loads.

ALL-WEATHER CONSTRUCTION

It is not always possible to avoid construction when the weather conditions are too cold, too wet, or too hot and dry, but there are steps that can be taken to overcome these obstacles. The following paragraphs highlight the major concerns when building in adverse weather. The details of the methods and materials are the subject of other publications cited in the section on *Additional Readings*, such as the *All-Weather Home Building Manual* (NAHB Research Foundation, 1975).

Cold Weather

Builders in cold weather areas plan for winter construction by preparing access roads by late fall. They also excavate for foundations and pour them before heavy frost sets in. The completed foundation is protected by decking the first floor and by covering the bottom of the foundation with straw.

Builders who excavate in winter use a big backhoe with heavy ripper teeth or a big bulldozer with a ripper attachment to break up frozen earth. Scheduling is important when excavating in winter. Builders look for a two- or three-day break in the weather before they schedule a foundation excavation. Excavation is often done and foundation walls poured or laid in three days. The hole for the foundation is ripped and dug the first day, except for the last 12 inches. On the second day, the last 12 inches are excavated and footings are formed and poured. On the third day, the foundation walls are formed and poured or the masonry block is laid.

Concrete for footings and foundation walls comes heated from the supplier after November 15. Canadian and some U.S. builders will pour concrete in temperatures below 0°, but most prefer to pour foundation walls in temperatures not much lower than 10° F. Builders order from 1 to 2 percent calcium chloride in the mix to help the concrete set quickly, and they protect the pour by placing insulation around and on top of the wall forms. Masons use heated mortar with 1 or 2 percent calcium chloride to lay concrete block walls in winter.

Some form of insulation is used around the concrete footings and on the bottom of the foundation to keep frost from getting under the footings and causing them to heave. Builders use straw, hay, or fiberglass-filled, polyethylene-backed blankets. Straw or hay is spread 12 to 24 inches thick over the footings and the bottom of the foundation. The plastic insulating blankets are designed to cover the footing or the entire foundation hole.

Temporary or permanent heat is hooked up as soon as the house is enclosed and is left on until the house is complete. If the hookup is permanent, the furnace is often hung by metal straps from the first floor joists until the basement floor is poured. Temporary heat is usually provided by propane or oil-fired portable heating units called salamanders.

Brick masons in both the United States and Canada use windbreaks or lean-tos to protect themselves from windchill and low temperatures and to keep the mortar from freezing before it sets. Masons will often place one or two portable heaters inside a plastic-enclosed scaffolding to insure that the masonry wall will set and cure properly.

The treated-wood foundation system, discussed in the "Foundations" section of Chapter 2, offers an alternative to concrete or masonry foundations that is less susceptible to damage from cold weather, eliminates the problem of scheduling concrete delivery and the masonry subcontractor, and allows work to proceed on the upper floor and wall framing immediately after the foundation is in place.

Wet Weather

Builders in wet weather areas maintain their production volume despite the rain and the mud. Their primary problems include site drainage, site preparation, material delivery, material storage, excavating, and getting the roof on as quickly as possible to keep the rain out.

The builder's first move in wet weather is to drain the building site and keep it drained of surface water. Careful grading of the lot is the first step in disposing of surface water. To do this, the site is rough graded so that water flows away from the foundation area. Small hand-dug surface drains also remove excess surface water from the foundation area. Slot trenches and drainage pipes work well to drain surface and subsurface water on rolling terrain when the water can be channeled down the hill, but they are less effective in flat, swampy areas where the natural grade is slight.

Preparing the driveway for wet weather construction is the next step. Material deliveries are easier, hand labor is saved, and concrete trucks can get to the foundation area without getting stuck when the driveway has been fully or partially paved. Framing and other heavy materials can be delivered or moved from storage to the working area without bringing in special equipment. Builders in the Northeastern and North Central states use crushed stone or pea gravel on the driveway, along with heavy planks and timbers, to make deliveries easier and to keep concrete trucks from getting stuck. Some builders pour the driveways before foundation work begins, thus providing a solid area for delivery of materials and for working, and a dry area for temporary storage of heavy materials.

Wet weather excavating is most difficult in areas where there are silts and clay soils. Not only does it take longer to excavate muddy clay, but gumbo clays and marine clays will clog trenchers. Rubber-tired equipment is all but impossible to use in mud. Excavators throughout the country use sand and gravel on muddy sites to overcome loss of traction and soil load-bearing problems. Builders in some parts of the South, where gumbo clay is prevalent, spread sand over the entire construction site to provide better soil-working conditions and to aid in landscaping after construction is completed.

Builders in wet weather areas such as the Gulf Coast and Middle Southern states design their schedules around two important elements: site access and "blacking-in" or "closing-in." Framing is often not begun until driveways and sidewalks are poured. Once the slab is poured or the foundation is installed, the important thing is to close in the roof as quickly as possible to keep out the rain. To accomplish this, scheduling the roofing subcontractor to lay the asphalt felt is critical. Many builders in the Gulf Coast states have the framing carpenters do the blacking-in so they will not have to rely on the roofing subcontractor to do that job.

Hot and Dry Weather

Building conditions in the southwestern United States are unlike any other in the country. The climate in parts of southern California, west Texas, New Mexico, Arizona and Nevada is hot and dry. Much of it is desert; temperatures in the summer soar to more than 120°F in some places, while humidity is less than 5 percent. The high temperatures and low humidity, along with wind and dust storms, combine to make difficult building conditions.

Because of the extreme heat, builders start work early in the morning and quit early in the afternoon. Roofers, framers, and masons are often onsite before 5 a.m. and they do not work much after 1 or 2 p.m. Concrete subcontractors usually do not work after 12 noon.

Concrete pouring begins around 5 a.m. and is completed by 9:30 or 10 a.m. Very little concrete is poured after 10 a.m. because the mix gets too hot. The subcontractors use a wet finish and saturate the soil and gravel under the slab with water before they pour. They also spray the finished concrete with a petroleum-base solution or cover the slab with plastic to prevent moisture from evaporating. Special additives are rarely used when pouring concrete in desert areas.

NAILING SCHEDULE

Table 20 contains a list of many of the components that are used in home construction and recommendations as to how these components should be joined. The proper number, size, and method of nailing are essential to ensure the structural integrity of a house. The nail should never be too big, too small, or placed improperly.

Table 20

Nailing Schedule

Materials Being Joined	Nailing Method	Number	Nail Size	Nailing Procedure
Header to joist	End-nail	3	12d	Joist hangers advised
Joist to sill or girder	Toe-nail	2	8d	
Header and stringer, joist to sill	Toe-nail		8d	24-inch on-center
Subfloor, boards:				
1x5 inch and smaller		2	8d	To each joist
1x3 inch		3	8d	To each joist
Subfloor, plywood:				
At edges			8d	6-inch on-center
At intermediate joists			8d	8-inch on-center
Subfloor (2x6 inch, tongue-and-groove) to joist or girder	Blind-nail (casing) and face-nail	2	12d	
Soleplate to stud, horizontal assembly	End-nail	2	12d	At each stud
Top plate to stud	End-nail	2	12d	
Soleplate to joist or blocking	Face-nail		12d	24-inch on-center maximum
Doubled studs	Face-nail		12d	24-inch on-center, staggered
End stud of intersecting wall to exterior wall stud	Face-nail		12d	24-inch on-center
Upper top plate to lower top plate	Face-nail		12d	24-inch on-center
Upper top plate, laps and intersections	Face-nail		12d	
Header, two pieces			12d	12-inch on-center, staggered
Ceiling joist to top wall plates	Toe-nail	2	8d	
Ceiling joist laps at partition	Face-nail	3	12d	
Rafter to top plate	Toe-nail	2	8d	
Rafter to ceiling joist	Face-nail	3	12d	
Rafter to valley or hip rafter	Toe-nail	3	8d	
Ridge board to rafter	End-nail	3	12d	
Rafter to rafter through ridge board	Toe-nail	3	12d	
Collar beam to rafters:				
2-inch member	Face-nail	2	12d	
1-inch member	Face-nail	3	8d	
1-inch diagonal let-in brace to each stud and plate (4 nails at top)		2	8d	
Builtup corner studs:				
Studs at blocking	Face-nail	2	10d/12d	Each side
interacting stud to corner studs	Face-nail	2	12d	24-inch on-center
Builtup girders and beams, three or more members	Face-nail		10d/12d	12-inch on-center
			10d/12d	staggered, each layer
Wall sheathing:				
1x8 inch or less, horizontal	Face-nail	2	8d	At each stud
Wall sheathing, vertically applied plywood:				
3/8 inch and less thick	Face-nail		6d	6-inch on-center at edges
1/2 inch and over thick	Face-nail		8d	12-inch on-center intermediate
Wall sheathing, vertically applied fiberboard:				
1/2 inch thick	Face-nail			1½-inch roofing nail, 3-inch on-center at edges and 6-inch on-center intermediate
Roof sheathing, boards, 4, 6, 8 inches wide	Face-nail	2	8d	At each rafter
Roof sheathing, plywood:				
3/8 inch and less thick	Face-nail		6d	6-inch on-center at edges and 12-inch on-center intermediate
1/2 inch and over thick	Face-nail		8d	

CONCRETE

Concrete consists of a mixture of portland cement, sand, gravel, and various admixtures, combined in various proportions to meet specific conditions or requirements.

The most convenient way to obtain concrete is to order it from a local supplier of ready-mixed concrete. The ingredients for ready-mixed concrete are accurately measured, often in automated plants with computer equipment, and then mixed either at the plant or in a truck mixer, and delivered to the job site. Producers of ready-mixed concrete will generally assist in the selection of appropriate mixes or in developing mixes to fill a builder's specific needs. Local practices in ordering ready-mixed concrete vary, but usually ordering is either by performance or by prescription.

When concrete is ordered by performance, the desired strength is specified by the builder, and the producer is responsible for proportioning and delivering a mixture that will yield the desired strength in a substantial majority of tests. For strength specifications to be meaningful, properly conducted strength tests are required.

When concrete is ordered by prescription, the builder specifies the weight of portland cement per cubic yard, the maximum amount of mixing water, admixtures required, and possibly their dosage rates. In essence, the builder accepts responsibility for the level of quality and performance.

Slump

Slump is a measure of the consistency or stiffness of fresh concrete, expressed in inches. It is influenced by the amount of water — more water means more slump — but water is not the only factor. The type of aggregate, the air content, and the proportions of the ingredients all affect slump.

The slump test is a method of measuring the workability of concrete when wet and also a check of the concrete's consistency from batch to batch. The test consists of filling a cylindrical mold of standard diameter and height with concrete, removing the mold, and measuring the distance the concrete settles after a given period of time. For residential work, slumps range from 4 to 7 inches.

Air Entrainment

Air entrainment is essential for protecting concrete that is exposed to freezing, thawing, and the action of salts used for removing ice.

An air-entraining admixture or air-entraining cement causes microscopic air bubbles to form throughout the concrete. These bubbles act as "relief" valves when the concrete freezes, helping to prevent scaling or spalling of the surface. (Scaling is a general crumbling of the surface cement layer of the concrete. Spalling is a form of chipping in which disc-like pieces loosen and pop out of the surface.) Resistance to deicers, which also cause scaling and spalling, is greater if the air-entrained concrete is dried for about four weeks after curing.

Air-entrained concrete is more watertight, more resistant to sulfate soils, and easier to work, particularly if the mixture is lean or has angular aggregates. Concrete strength is reduced somewhat by air entrainment, but a lower water-cement ratio is possible in an air-entrained mix and this lower ratio makes up for any strength lost because of air entrainment.

Accelerators

Accelerators speed up the setting time and the strength development of concrete and are especially useful in cold weather. They can be combined with water-reducing admixtures. Calcium chloride is the most commonly used accelerator. It is not an antifreeze, but it speeds up the set and makes freezing damage less likely, especially if the concrete is protected from low temperatures while it is curing. Because calcium chloride must be used carefully and may increase drying shrinkage, the following alternative methods should be considered:

- There are five types of portland cement, designated as Types I through V. The types vary in their characteristics, including rate of strength gain. It is conventional practice to use Type I in concrete mixes. If Type II is specified, the resulting mix will gain strength twice as quickly on the first day that the mixture is placed. However, the strengths of mixtures using Type I and Type III are approximately equal after three months.
- Reducing the amount of water relative to the amount of portland cement can accelerate the

rate of strength gain. Too much cement, however, can increase susceptibility to cracking. Altering the water-cement ratio should therefore be done by an experienced professional.

- Higher temperatures during curing speed up strength gain considerably.
- Warming the mix by using heated water can accelerate strength gain.

Retarders

Retarders are chemicals that can be added to the concrete mixture in hot weather, when the concrete may set so quickly that it cannot be finished properly. Retarders are also useful when difficult placements require more time. Some retarders are water reducers or plasticizers. Called water-reducing retarders, they slow down the set while speeding up placement by plasticizing the concrete; however, not all plasticizers retard the set.

In hot weather, concrete sets more slowly when the aggregate or water, or both, are cooled. One effective method is to use chipped ice for part of the mixing water.

Plasticizers

Plasticizers make the concrete more workable with less water. Strength is increased by the low water-cement ratio, and labor costs are reduced since the concrete is more workable. Some water reducers may increase drying shrinkage, and this condition may increase cracking. Other water reducers, however, will reduce shrinkage cracks, according to the manufacturers.

Water reducers may be either accelerators or retarders. The type chosen should fit the circumstances. For example, an accelerating water reducer is suitable for cold weather; a retarding water reducer is suitable for hot weather.

Some water reducers also entrain air. One should allow for the extent of this entrainment when specifying amounts of air-entraining agent. Water reducers are worth investigating if the concrete needs added strength without increasing labor costs.

Superplasticizers

An ordinary water reducer can reduce the amount of water need by 10 to 15 percent while slightly increasing slump. A superplasticizer can increase slump dramatically from an original 3 inches to 7 or 8 inches. Since concrete mixtures with superplasticizers are much easier to place, their use can reduce labor costs.

A superplasticized concrete mix is easier to work because of the almost liquid slump and because of the consistency of the concrete. Cement masons liken it to a temporary lubrication of the mix. It can be chuted more easily at a lower angle and is almost self-leveling.

HEAT FLOW AND INSULATION

There are three primary mechanisms of heat transfer in building systems: conduction, convection, and radiation. In each of these mechanisms, heat flows from a higher to a lower temperature level—from hot to cold.

A common example of conduction is the metal handle on a frying pan. As the pan is heated, the handle becomes hot exclusively by the process of conduction. In general, the more dense the material the higher the rate of heat flow due to conduction. Because metals transfer a great deal of heat this way, they are commonly used in electrical transmission systems. Because they are excellent conductors, energy loss is at a minimum. Conversely, metal elements that extend through building sections are undesirable because of their high level of conduction.

In building materials such as metal windows, the heat flow by conduction can be reduced by use of a "thermal break." A casing of metal encloses a core of material such as wood, which has low thermal conductivity, and the casing itself is not continuous from the inside to the outside. The separation of the casing provides the thermal break.

Heat flow by convection can be observed in a house where second-story rooms are warmer than first-story rooms. This difference in temperature occurs because heated air is less dense than cooler temperature air. The heated air moves up to and across the ceilings of the first-story rooms and up the stairway to the second-story rooms. At the same time, the cooler air, which is more dense, settles to the floors of the upper story rooms and moves across the floors and down the stairway to the first-story rooms.

Warming yourself by sitting in the sun is an example of heat flow by radiation. An old fashioned steam or hot water "radiator" transfers heat by radiation, conduction, and convection simultaneously. The cast-iron structure conducts heat to the outside surface of the radiator. Air flowing between and around the radiator transfers heat by convection. At the same time, the warm surface of the radiator face transfers additional heat to any surface at a lower temperature, such as people, furnishings, and the interior surfaces of the room.

Measuring Heat Flow

Extensive measurements have been made of the heat-flow characteristics of most building materials as well as entire building sections. Rating of heat flow performance involves five forms of measurement: British thermal units (Btus), thermal conductivity (k-value), conductance (C-value), thermal resistance (R-value), and the combined ability of a building section to retard heat flow (U-value).

The *British thermal unit* is defined as the amount of heat required to raise the temperature of 1 pound of water 1° F. A Btu can be visualized as the amount of heat released by the burning of one wooden kitchen match from end to end. As a point of reference, a gallon of water weighs 8.33 pounds. Therefore, it would take about 330 Btu to raise the temperature of water 1° F in a 40-gallon water heater.

Thermal conductivity, referred to as the k-value, introduces elements of size and time and may be applied only to homogeneous materials. The thermal conductivity of a given material is defined as the amount of heat that passes through a 1-inch-thick sample of the material, 1 square foot in area, in 1 hour, with a 1° F difference in temperature between its two surfaces. The lower the k-value, the higher the insulating value. Insulation materials have k-values of 0.5 Btu per-square-foot per-hour per-degree Fahrenheit or less at temperatures normally encountered in building sections. Industrial insulations may have k-values of 1.0 or greater at the higher temperatures for which they are intended and used. The thermal conductivity of a material usually increases with mean temperature.

Conductance, or the C-value, is similar to conductivity but is a more flexible measurement unit. The thickness of the material is not confined to 1 inch. For example, a brick about 4 inches thick or nonhomogeneous materials, such as concrete blocks, can also be measured for C-values.

If the material is homogeneous, it is possible to determine the C-value if the k-value is known, or vice versa, using the relationship: C-value x thickness = k-value. For example, a homogeneous material with a C-value of 0.1 and a thickness of 3 inches has a corresponding k-value of 0.3. The lower the C-value, the higher the insulating value.

Thermal resistance, or R-value, is a measurement of the ability of materials to retard, rather than transmit heat. Mathematically, R is the inverse of C or k. For example, a material with a C-value of 0.2 (1/5) has an R-value of 5.0.

The use of R-values makes it possible to add the thermal values of a whole series of materials. R-values have been measured for solid materials, nonhomogeneous materials, air spaces, and air films on both the inside and outside of building sections. Since R-values indicate the ability to retard heat flow, the higher the R-value, the higher the insulating value. Materials having the same R-value, regardless of thickness, weight, or appearance, are equal in insulating value. One should therefore specify insulation products by R-value rather than simply by thickness.

R-values for some common insulation materials are shown in the following table:

Material	Approximate R-value
Insulation, mineral wool blanket and batt	
Approximately 3 to 3½ inches thick	11.00
Approximately 5¼ to 6½ inches thick	19.00
Approximately 6 to 7 inches thick	22.00
Approximately 8½ to 9 inches thick	30.00
Approximately 12 inches thick	38.00
Insulation, board	
Glass fiber, organic bonded, 1 inch	4.00
Expanded polystyrene, extruded, cut cell, 1 inch	4.00
Expanded polystyrene, extruded, smooth, 1 inch	5.00
Expanded polystyrene, molded beads, 1 inch	3.57
Expanded polyurethane, 1 inch or more	6.25
Polyisocyanurate, 1 inch	7.20
Mineral fiber with resin binder, per inch	3.45
Insulation, blown loose fill	
Cellulosic, per inch	3.13 — 3.70
Perlite expanded, per inch	2.70
Mineral fiber (rock, slag, glass)	
3¾ to 5 inches	11.00
6½ to 8¾ inches	19.00
7½ to 10 inches	22.00
10¼ to 13¾ inches	30.00
13 to 17¼ inches	38.00
Vermiculite exfoliated, per inch	2.13 — 2.27

The *combined ability of a building section to retard heat flow* is called its U-value. The U-value includes air films and air spaces that are adjacent to or a part of the building section. The U-value is mathematically defined as the number of Btus passing through 1 square foot of the combined building section in 1 hour for each degree Fahrenheit of temperature difference. The lower the U-value, the higher the insulating value. An uninsulated frame wall may have a U-value of about 0.25, while a comparable insulated wall will reduce the U-value to about 0.07.

Home Insulating Materials

Home insulating materials retard the flow of heat from the inside to the outside in the winter and from the outside to the inside in the summer.

The most widely used home insulation material is called fiberglass or rock wool. It is composed of fine inorganic fibers made from rock, slag, or sand, with other material added to enhance its service properties. Available forms include flexible batts and blankets, with and without facings; semirigid and rigid boards, with and without facings; and a loose form for blowing or pouring.

Batt and blanket insulation often has a kraft vapor-retarding paper facing with stapling flanges. Sometimes an enclosure of "breather" paper is used on the back side for rock wool materials. Batts and blankets are also available with aluminum-foil facings, including stapling flanges, and in an unfaced form held in place by pressure.

Blown mineral wool must be installed with pneumatic equipment and requires the service of an insulation contractor. Insulation products that may be poured into place can be used by home owners to increase the performance level of attic insulation. As an alternative, many home owners prefer to use faced or unfaced batts or blankets.

Mineral-wool board insulation can be used on the inside face of crawl-space walls and the outside of basement walls. Mineral-wool blankets and boards are available for duct insulation; building blankets should not be used for this purpose. Preformed mineral-wool pipe insulation is also available through industrial insulation contractors for both hot- and cold-water piping.

Other types of insulation used in residential construction include:

- Foamed-plastic insulation boards or sheets, which are used as exterior wall sheathing, foundation insulation, and perimeter-edge insulation for slab-on-grade construction.
- Cellulose fiber insulation, which is primarily used in ceilings and in walls of existing homes. It should be pneumatically installed by an insulation contractor.
- Multiple-layer aluminum-foil insulation, which is sometimes used between furring strips on masonry wall construction. It is fragile and must be installed with great care if it is to be effective.

Combustible vapor-retarding facings on insulation should not be left exposed. They should be covered with finished materials having an acceptable flame spread or fire rating. Breather paper is combustible and, when exposed in accessible space, should be either covered or stripped off after the batts are in place.

LUMBER GRADES

Softwood lumber is divided into three size categories. Finish grades 1 to 2 inches thick are called *boards;* pieces ranging from 2 to 4 inches in nominal thickness are called *dimension lumber;* and lumber 5 inches and thicker is called *timber.* Most framing materials used in light frame construction fall into the dimension lumber category.

Dimension lumber is sold by grade, species, and size. All grades and species suitable for the application should be considered. For economy in construction, it is recommended that the lowest grade suited to a job be used. Douglas fir, hem-fir, or southern pine are good choices for longer spans because they are the stronger species, while a weaker species might be more economical for shorter spans.

Lumber sizes in the United States are given as nominal dimensions in inches. When a piece of lumber is first sawn from a log, it may approach those dimensions. Resawing, surfacing, and seasoning diminish the size considerably, resulting in an actual dimension that is less than nominal.

Dimension lumber is manufactured in lengths of 2-foot increments. The most common lengths are 8, 10, 12, 14, and 16 feet, but most lumber yards stock longer lengths as well. Actual lengths are usually slightly longer than nominal to allow for trimming.

Most framing lumber is surfaced on four sides (S4S) and has eased edges (EE), although some square edge stock is manufactured.

To assign lumber grades, a certified grader evaluates both natural and manufacturing characteristics. Unlike finish carpentry materials, framing lumber is graded primarily for strength rather than appearance. Lumber grading sets quality control standards among lumber mills manufacturing the same or similar products. An official grade stamp on a piece of lumber certifies its assigned grade.

All major building codes require that lumber used structurally be grade-stamped by an agency certified by the Board of Review of the American Lumber Standards Committee. The lumber standard requires that all grade stamps contain five basic elements: the symbol or lumber logo of the quality control agency; the mill number or name; the grade of the material; the species or species combination; and the condition of seasoning at the time of manufacture. (Figure 197).

Figure 197. Sample standard grade stamps for lumber: (A) Southern Pine Inspection Bureau; (B) Western Wood Products Association

Dimension Lumber Grades

Dimension lumber grades are standardized throughout North America, regardless of species or grading agency. Under the National Grade Rule for dimension lumber issued by the American Lumber Standards Committee, there are four basic use categories, with one or more grades in each. The categories are light framing, stud, structural light framing, and structural joists and planks (Table 21).

The grades for *light framing* lumber (2 to 4 inches thick and 2 to 4 inches wide) are construction, standard, and utility. Construction and standard grades, produced primarily by Western and Canadian manufacturers, are commonly combined and sold as "standard and better." They are used for general wall framing, regardless of species. Utility grade, often marketed as "utility and better," can be used for interior framing, plates, blocking, cripples, etc. A fourth grade, economy, is not accepted by building codes and is not recommended for construction.

Studs are marked in an all-purpose grade, called stud grade. This grade designation encompasses lumber 2 to 4 inches thick and 2 to 6 inches wide, with a 10-foot length limit. It is most commonly found in 2x4 and 2x6 sizes, precision-trimmed to specific lengths. When length is not a factor, 2x4

stud grade can be used interchangeably with "standard and better."

The four grades for *structural light framing* lumber (2 to 4 inches thick and 2 to 4 inches wide,) are select structural, No. 1, No. 2, and No. 3. Availability varies in different markets. Most Southern pine is produced in these grades and is not normally available at the retail level in the West. Select structural and No. 1 are commonly used in engineered applications such as roof and floor trusses.

The four grades for *structural joist and plank* lumber (2 to 4 inches thick and 6 inches and wider) are select structural, No. 1, No. 2, and No. 3. The first three, normally sold together as "No. 2 and Better," are used primarily for floor joists, ceiling joists, and roof rafters. Span and load-carrying requirements will dictate the grade, specifics, and size. No. 3 grade is suitable for shorter spans.

Moisture Content

The portion of the grade stamp that designates the condition of seasoning at time of manufacture specifies one of three categories:
- S-GRN — Unseasoned, with more than 19 percent moisture content.
- S-DRY — 19 percent or less moisture content.
- MC-15 — 15 percent or less moisture content.

Table 21

Dimension Lumber Grades and Uses

Use Category	Grades	Description
Light Framing (2x2 through 4x4)	Construction Standard Utility	This category for use where high strength values are not required, such as studs, plates, sills, cripples, blocking, etc.
Studs (2x2 through 4x6) 10 feet and shorter	Stud	An optional all-purpose grade limited to 10 feet and shorter. Characteristics affecting strength and stiffness values limited so that the "Stud" grade is suitable for all stud uses, including load-bearing walls.
Structural Light Framing (2x2 through 4x4)	Select Structural No. 1 No. 2 No. 3	These grades are designed to fit those engineering applications where higher bending strength ratios are needed in light framing sizes. Typical uses would be for trusses, concrete pier wall forms, etc.
Structural- Joists and Planks (Through 4x16)	Select Structural No. 1 No. 2 No. 3	These grades are designed especially to fit in engineering applications for lumber 5 feet and 2x5 wider, such as joists, rafters, and general framing uses.

Southern pine producers who kiln-dry their material may use a KD-19 or KD-15 designation to indicate 19 percent or 15 percent moisture content.

The availability of different levels of seasoning varies in local markets. Dimension lumber up to 2 inches thick is available "green" (unseasoned), "dry" (19 percent maximum), or, in some areas, "MC-15" or "KD-15" (15 percent maximum). But even in a "dry" market, the maximum thickness structural grade available seasoned is 2 inches . Lumber thicker than 2 inches will be shipped "green."

The lumber industry produces two sizes of dimension lumber, depending on moisture content: a "dry" size and a slightly larger "green" size. Once the unseasoned size reaches 19 percent moisture content, it will be the same size as the dry. "Green" and "dry" sizes should not be mixed during construction, even though their structural properties are identical.

PLYWOOD CHARACTERISTICS

APA Markings For Intended Use

Construction and industrial plywood products should be stamped with a marking indicating their intended use. The most widely used markings are those of the American Plywood Association (APA). The markings provide assurance that the product conforms with APA performance standards and/or *U.S. Product Standard PS 1-83* for construction and industrial plywood. Typical APA markings are described in the following paragraphs. The first three markings listed (grade, span ratings, and thickness) will appear on the face of the panel; the last marking listed is an edge stamp (Figure 198.)

Grade. Panel grades are generally identified in terms of the veneer grade used on the face and back of the panel (for example, A-B, B-C), or by a name suggesting the intended end use (APA Rated Sheathing, Underlayment, etc.) of the panel. The highest quality veneer is "A," the lowest "D." The minimum grade of veneer in exterior plywood is "C." "D" veneer is used only in panels intended for interior use or for applications protected from exposure to weather or moisture.

Span Ratings. Some APA trademarked panels, such as APA Rated Sheathing, APA Rated Sturd-I-Floor, and APA 303 Siding, carry numbers in their trademarks called span ratings. These denote the maximum recommended center-to-center spacing, in inches, of supports over which the panel should be placed in construction applications.

APA Rated Sheathing span ratings appear as two numbers separated by a slash, such as 32/16 or 48/24. The left-hand number denotes the maximum recommended spacing of supports when the panel is used for roof sheathing with the long dimension of the panel across three or more supports. The right-hand number indicates the maximum recommended spacing of supports when the panel is used for sub-flooring with the long dimension of the panel across three or more supports. Thus, panel marked 32/16 may be used for roof sheathing over supports 32 inches on center or for subflooring over supports 16 inches on center.

APA Rated Sturd-I-Floor panels are designed for single-floor (combined subfloor-underlayment) applications under carpet and pad. The panels are manufactured with span ratings of 16, 20, 24, and 48 inches. As with APA Rated Sheathing, these are based on application of the panel with the long dimension across three or more supports.

APA 303 Siding is manufactured with span ratings of 16 and 24 inches. It can be applied directly to studs or over nonstructural wall sheathing (Sturd-I-Wall construction), or over nailable panel or lumber sheathing (double-wall construction). Panels with a span rating of 16 inches may be applied vertically direct to studs spaced 16 inches on center. Panels bearing a span rating of 24 inches may be used vertically direct to studs 24 inches on center. All 303 Siding panels may be applied horizontally direct to studs 16 or 24 inches on center, provided that horizontal joints are blocked. When 303 Siding is used over nailable structural panel or lumber sheathing, the span rating refers to the maximum recommended spacing of vertical rows of nails rather than to stud spacing.

Thickness. This number gives the actual panel thickness.

Species group number. Plywood manufactured under *U.S. Product Standard PS 1-83* may be made from over 70 species of wood. These species are divided into five groups according to strength and stiffness properties. Group 1 species are the strongest and stiffest, Group 2 the next strongest and stiffest, and so on.

Exposure Durability

Plywood panels are produced in four exposure durability classifications: Exterior, Exposure 1, Exposure 2, and Interior.

Exterior panels have a fully waterproof bond. They are designed for applications subject to continuous exposure to the weather or to moisture.

Exposure 1 panels are highly moisture resistant. They are designed to resist moisture during long construction delays, or exposure to similarly demanding conditions. However, only Exterior panels should be used for permanent exposure to weather or moisture.

Exposure 2 panels are intended for protected construction applications involving only moderate delays in providing protection from moisture.

Interior panels which lack further glueline information in their markings are manufactured with

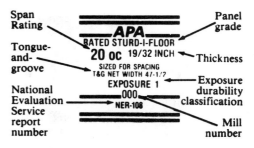

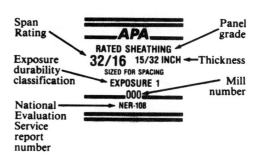

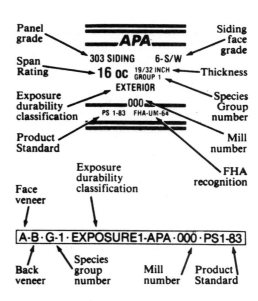

Figure 198. Typical APA registered trademarks

interior glue and are intended for interior applications only.

Mill Number

The mill number is the identification number assigned to the manufacturing facility in which the panel was produced.

Product Standard

U.S. Product Standard PS 1-83 is a voluntary commodity standard developed cooperatively by the U.S. Department of Commerce and the construction and industrial plywood industry. APA performance standards are the result of new manufacturing technology that makes possible the manufacture of structural panel products from wood byproducts and species not provided for in *U.S. Product Standard PS 1-83*. Panels produced under APA performance standards are called APA Performance-Rated Panels. In addition to conventional veneer plywood, APA performance standards encompass such other panel products as composites, waferboard, oriented strand board, and structural particleboard.

PRESSURE-TREATED WOOD

Wood treated with chemicals under pressure to resist decay and insect attack is called pressure-treated wood. This type of wood is classified as a permanent building material by such authorities as the Federal Housing Administration (FHA) and the U.S. Forest Products Laboratory. Properly treated wood members can be expected to last almost indefinitely in most applications.

Pressure-treated wood should conform to the treating standards issued by either the American Wood Preservers Bureau (AWPB), the American Wood Preservers Association (AWPA), or Federal Specification TT-W series. These standards specify chemical quality, quantity retained, and penetration as well as quality control procedures for the treating process.

There are three general classifications of pressure treatments based on the type of preservative: creosote solutions, pentachlorophenol (penta), and waterborne preservatives. Creosote and penta treatments are used widely in farm, ranch, and marina applications. Penta in liquid petroleum gas (LPG) or in light petroleum solvent is also used for fencing and other exterior applications. The waterborne preservatives are widely used to pressure treat lumber and plywood for use in decks, fences, marinas, and all weather wood foundations. The more commonly used waterborne salts for pressure-treating materials to be used for outdoor residential

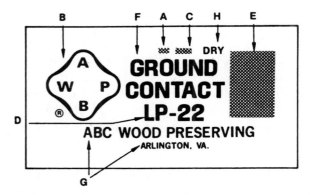

A   Year of treatment
B   American Wood Preservers Bureau trademark
C   The preservative used for treatment
D   The applicable American Wood Preservers Bureau quality standard
E   Trademark of the agency supervising the treating plant
F   Proper exposure conditions
G   Treating company and plant location
H   Dry or KDAT if applicable

Figure 199. Sample AWPB quality mark

purposes are ammoniacal copper arsenate (ACA), chromated copper arsenate (CCA), acid copper chromate (ACC), chromated zinc chloride (CZC), and fluor chrome arsenate phenol (FCAP).

Each piece of pressure-treated wood or plywood should bear a quality mark (Figure 199). Such marks indicate that the technique requirements of a treating standard have been met or exceeded. Codes designating AWPB quality standards that are commonly used in residential construction are listed in Table 22.

Products marked for ground contact are treated to a higher degree of chemical retention than those marked for aboveground applications. In some instances, the aboveground marking may indicate the use of a preservative not permitted for ground or fresh-water contact. In all cases, materials marked for ground contact are suitable for fresh-water installation. Materials marked for ground contact may be used safely aboveground. Materials marked for aboveground use should not be used for ground or water contact.

Pressure-treated wood products can be cut or drilled. However, because the treating chemicals may not penetrate completely through thick materials, the cut ends or holes must be brush treated with a suitable preservative.

Table 22
Codes designating AWPB
quality standards

Preservative	Aboveground Standard	Ground contact Standard
General Purpose Applications:		
Waterborne preservatives	LP-2	LP-22
Light-hydrocarbon solvent/penta	LP-3	LP-33
Volatile-hydrocarbon-solvent (LPG)/penta	LP-4	LP-44
Creosote or creosote/coal-tar solutions	LP-5	LP-55
Heavy-hydrocarbon-solvent/penta	LP-7	LP-77
Special Purpose Applications:		
Waterborne preservatives for use in residential and light commercial foundations	—	FDN
Nonstructural landscape timbers from peeled cores	—	LST
All preservatives for use in marine (saltwater) exposure	—	MLP

The placement of these code designations in the AWPB quality marks is shown in Figure 199.

Wood that is pressure treated with waterborne salts can be stained or painted in the same manner as untreated wood. Wood that is treated with oilborne preservatives can be stained or painted if liquid petroleum gas (LPG), methylene chloride, or other light hydrocarbon solvent has been used as the preservative carrier. It should be specified when ordering that the material be suitable for staining or painting. Wood that is treated with creosote, creosote solutions, or oilborne preservatives in heavy hydrocarbon solvent generally cannot be successfully stained or painted.

NOTE: Prolonged exposure to wood preserving chemicals may present a health hazard. To minimize exposure, one should 1) wear protective gloves and clothing; 2) wear goggles and dust mask when sawing, machining, or sanding for prolonged periods of time; 3) perform all sawing, boring, planing, and sanding outdoors or in well-ventilated areas; 4) wash exposed areas of body with soap and water after handling pressure-treated materials; 5) wash all clothing that was worn while the material was being handled; and 6) avoid use of scraps of pressure-treated lumber in open fires or in a fire-

place, stove, or similar device. The preferred method of disposing of pressure-treated scrap pieces is to bury them.

SQUARE CORNERS

Square corners in house construction ensure that all elements of the house fit together as planned and simplify the installation of such items as sheathing, gypsum wallboard, cabinets, carpeting, countertops, wallpaper, etc. The recommended method of establishing square corners involves the use of a pocket calculator and the Pythagorean Theorem. The Pythagorean Theorem states that, in a right triangle, the length of the hypotenuse (C) is equal to the square root of the sum of the squares of the lengths of the other two sides (A and B).

$$C^2 = A^2 + B^2$$
$$C^2 = (3)^2 + (4)^2$$
$$C^2 = 9 + 16$$
$$C^2 = 25$$
$$C = \sqrt{25}$$
$$C = 5$$

Applying this method to footing layout begins by squaring the lengths of the two sides of the building, adding these two answers together, and taking the square root of the sum to produce the exact length of the diagonal that will produce a perfectly square corner for the footings.

The simplest approach to solving this arithmetic problem is to use a pocket calculator designed to work in feet and inches. If such a calculator is not available, the dimensions will have to be converted to feet and decimal parts of a foot; that is 12 feet 6 inches would have to be converted to 12.5 feet.

Converting dimensions to decimal form: Given a dimension of 25 feet 3⅞ inches, start the conversion by dividing the 7 by 8 to get 0.875 inches. Add this to the 3 inches to get 3.875 inches. Then divide the 3.875 inches by 12 to get 0.32292 feet. Add this result to the 25 to get 25.32292 feet which is the decimal equivalent of 25 feet, 3⅞ inches.

Converting feet in decimal form to feet and inches: Given a dimension of 44.71875 feet, start by setting aside the 44 feet and multiplying the decimal part (0.71875) by 12 to get 8.625 inches. Set aside the 8 inches and multiply the decimal part by 8 to get ⅝ of an inch. The result of the conversion is 44 feet 8⅝ inches which is the feet-and-inches equivalent of 44.71875 feet.

Squaring a foundation layout. A rectangular house is to have a foundation wall with outside dimensions of 52 feet by 32 feet. Squaring these two numbers and adding the squared values gives a value of 3728. The square root of 3728 is 61.05735 feet. Setting aside the 61 feet and multiplying the decimal part (0.05735) by 12 gives 0.68820 inches. This means that the fractional part of a foot is less than 1 inch. Multiplying the 0.68820 by 8 gives 5.5 eighths of an inch or 11/16 of an inch. Therefore, the exact length of the diagonal between the outside corners of the foundation wall should be 61 feet 11/16 inches which is the feet-and-inches equivalent of 61.05735 feet. If the foundation walls are placed so that the length of the diagonal between the outside corners of the wall is 61 feet 11/16 inches, then the foundation will have square corners.

MAINTENANCE AND REPAIR

A well-constructed house will require relatively little maintenance if adequate attention is given to details and to choice of materials, as presented in this book. Many small initial expenses will more than pay for themselves in later maintenance savings. For example, the extra expense of corrosion-resistant nails for siding and trim will save many times that much annually because of the less frequent need for painting. Also, the use of edge-grained rather than flat-grained siding will provide a longer paint life and thus justify the higher cost.

The following paragraphs outline some factors relating to maintenance of the house and how to reduce or eliminate conditions that may be harmful as well as costly. These suggestions can apply to both new and old houses.

Basement

The basement of a poured-concrete or block wall may be damp for some time after a new house has been completed. However, after the heating season begins, most of this dampness from walls and floors will gradually disappear if construction has been done correctly. If dampness or wet walls and floors persist, the owner should check various areas to eliminate any possibilities for water entry.

Possible sources of trouble are as follows:
1. Drainage at the downspouts. The final grade around the house should have a slope away from the building and a splash block or other ways of draining water away from the foundation wall.
2. Soil settling at the foundation wall and resultant pockets in which water may collect. These areas should be filled and tamped so that surface water can drain away.
3. Leaking in a poured-concrete wall at the form tie rods. These leaks usually seal themselves, but larger holes should be filled with a cement mortar or other sealer. Clean and slightly dampen the area first for good adhesion of mortar.
4. Dampness on the interior of concrete-block or other masonry walls exposed above grade after a prolonged rainy spell. A number of waterproofing materials on the market will provide good resistance to moisture penetration when applied to the inner face of the basement wall. If the outside of below-grade basement walls is treated correctly during construction, waterproofing the interior walls is not normally required.
5. There should be at least a 6-inch clearance between the bottom of the siding and the grass. Therefore, at least 8 inches should be allowed above the finish grade before sod is laid or foundation plantings made. This procedure will minimize the chance of moisture being absorbed by siding, sill plates, or other adjacent wood parts. Shrubs and foundation plantings should also be kept away from the wall to improve air circulation and drying. In lawn sprinkling, it is poor practice to allow water to spray against the walls of the house.
6. Check the areas between the foundation wall and the sill plate. Any openings should be filled with a cement mixture or a caulking compound. This filling will decrease heat loss and also prevent insects from entering the basement, as well as reduce air infiltration.
7. Dampness in the basement in the early summer months is often augmented when windows are opened for ventilation during the day,

allowing warm, moisture-laden outside air to enter. The lower temperature of the basement will cool the incoming air, frequently causing condensation to collect and drip from cold water pipes and to collect on colder parts of the masonry walls and floors. To air out the basement, open the windows during the night and close them during the day.

Perhaps the most convenient method of reducing humidity in basement areas is with dehumidifiers. A mechanical dehumidifier is moderate in price and does a satisfactory job of removing moisture from the air during periods of high humidity. Basements containing living quarters and without air conditioners may require more than one dehumidifier unit. When they are in operation, all basement windows should be closed.

Crawl-Space Area

Crawl-space areas should be checked as follows:
1. Inspect the crawl-space area annually for termite activity. Termite tubes on the walls or piers are an indication of this activity. In termite areas, soil in the crawl space or under the concrete slab is normally treated with some type of chemical to prevent termite infestation. Examine the foundation walls for any cracks, since these cracks form good channels for termite entry.
2. While in the crawl space, check exposed wood joists and beams for indications of excessive moisture. In older houses where soil covers have not been used, there may be signs of staining or decay. Use a penknife to test questionable areas. Decayed wood will be soft and provide little resistance to prodding.
3. Soil covers should be used to protect wood members from ground moisture. These may consist of plastic films, roll roofing, or other suitable materials. A small amount of ventilation, as discussed in Chapter 2, is desirable to provide some air movement. If the crawl space does not have a soil cover, install one for greater protection.

Roof and Attic

The roof and the attic area of both new and older houses should be inspected with attention to the following:

1. A dirt streak down the gable end of a house with a close rake section can often be attributed to rain entering and running under the edge of the shingles. This condition results from insufficient shingle overhang or the lack of a metal roof edge. The addition of a flashing strip to form a drip edge will usually minimize this problem.

2. In winters with heavy snows, ice dams may form at the eaves, often resulting in water entering the cornice and walls of the house. The immediate remedy is to remove the snow on the roof for a short distance above the gutters and, if necessary, in the valleys. Additional insulation between heated rooms and the attic space, as well as increased ventilation in the overhanging eaves to lower the general attic temperature, will help to decrease the melting of snow on the roof and thus minimize ice formation. Also, deep snow in the valleys sometimes forms ice dams that cause water to back up under shingles and valley flashing.

3. Roof leaks are often caused by improper flashing at the valley or ridge or around the chimney. Check these areas during a rainy spell to discover the source. Water may travel many feet from the point of entry before it drips off the roof members.

4. Attic ventilators are valuable year round; in summer, to lower the attic temperature and make the rooms below more comfortable; and in winter, to remove water vapor that may work through the ceiling and condense in the attic space and to minimize ice dams. The ventilators should be open in both winter and summer.

To check for sufficient ventilation during cold weather, examine the attic after a prolonged cold period. If nails protruding from the roof into the attic space are heavily coated with frost, ventilation is usually insufficient. Frost may also collect on the roof sheathing, first appearing near the eaves on the north side of the roof. Increasing the size of the ventilators or placing additional ones in the soffit area of the cornice will improve air movement and circulation.

Exterior Walls

One of the maintenance problems that sometimes occurs with a wood-sided house involves the exterior paint finish. Several reasons are known for peeling and poor adherence of paint. One of the major causes may be moisture in its various forms. Paint quality and methods of application are other reasons. Another factor involves the species of wood and the direction of grain. Some species retain paint better than others, and edge grain provides a better surface for paint than flat grain. Chapter 4 covers correct methods of application, types of paint, and other recommendations for a good finish. Other aspects of exterior wall maintenance that homeowners may encounter are as follows:

1. If bright steel nails have been used in applying the siding, rather than galvanized, aluminum, stainless steel, or other noncorrosive nails, rust spots may occur at the nailhead. These spots are quite common where nails are driven flush with the heads exposed. The spotting may be remedied somewhat, in the case of flush nailing, by setting the nailhead below the surface and puttying. The puttying should be preceded by a priming coat.

2. Brick and other types of masonry are not always waterproof and continued rains may result in moisture penetration. Masonry veneer walls over a sheathed wood frame are normally backed with a waterproof sheathing paper to keep moisture out of the wall cavity. When walls do not have such protection and the moisture problem persists, a waterproof coating over the exposed masonry surfaces should be used. Transparent waterproof materials can be obtained for this purpose.

3. Caulking is usually required where a change in materials occurs on a vertical line, such as that of wood siding abutting against brick chimneys or walls. The wood should normally have a prime coating of paint for proper adhesion of the caulking compound. Caulking guns with cartridges are the best means of waterproofing these joints. Many permanent-type caulking materials with a neoprene, elastomer, or other bases are available.

4. Rainwater may work behind wood siding through butt joints and sometimes up under the butt edge by capillary action when joints are not tight. Painting the siding board under the butt edges at the lap adds mechanical resistance to the entry of water. However, moisture changes in the siding cause some swelling and shrinking that may break the paint film. Treating the siding with a water repellent before it was applied would have been effective in reducing capillary action. For houses already built, the water repellent could be applied under the butt edges of bevel siding or along the joints of drop siding and at all vertical joints. Such water repellents are often combined with a preservative and can be purchased at local paint dealers as a water-repellent preservative. In-place application is often done with a plunger-type oil can. Excess repellent on the face of painted surfaces should be wiped off.

Interior

Gypsumboard. The maintenance of gypsumboard interior surfaces is no problem in a properly constructed house. However, damage to the wall surface may sometimes require repairs.

Cracks may develop due to shrinkage of framing or movement of structural members. Structural problems should be solved before proceeding with repairs. Cracks can be filled with joint cement and sanded smooth, as in the original joint-treatment process between sheets.

Accidental damage may result in gouges or holes in the gypsumboard. Gouges or relatively small holes can be filled with joint cement and sanded smooth. Larger holes may require cutting a section from the gypsumboard and replacing it with a new section of board, the same size as the opening. Cut the section to extend between two studs so that the edges of the new section can be supported by the studs. Nail the new section in place and fill the joints around the perimeter with joint cement. Finish the joint by feathering the edges and sanding smooth as in the original joint treatment process between sheets.

Moisture on Windows. Moisture on inside surfaces of windows may often occur during the colder periods of the heating season. The following precautions and corrections should be taken during this time.

During cold weather and in cold climates, condensation or frost may collect on the inner face of single-glazed windows. Water from the condensation or melting frost runs down the glass and soaks into the wood sash to cause stain, decay, and paint failure. The water may rust steel sash. To prevent such condensation, the window should be provided with a storm sash. Double glazing will also minimize condensation. If it still persists on double-glazed windows, this usually indicates that the humidity is too high. If a humidifier is being used, it should be turned off for a while or the setting lowered. If possible, other moisture sources such as houseplants, showers, or cooking should also be reduced enough to remedy the problem. Increasing the inside temperature will also reduce surface condensation. If the problem persists, some type of mechanical ventilation may be necessary.

Occasionally, in very cold weather, frost may form on the inner surfaces of the storm windows. This frost may be caused by 1) a loose-fitting window sash that allows moisture from the house to enter the space between the window and storm sash; 2) high relative humidity in the living quarters; or 3) a combination of both. Generally, condensation on the storm sash does not create a maintenance problem, but it may be a nuisance. Weatherstripping the inner sash offers resistance to moisture flow and may prevent this condensation. Lower relative humidity in the house is also helpful.

Problems With Exterior Doors.
Condensation in the form of water or frost may occur on the glass or even on the interior surface of exterior doors during periods of severe cold. Warping may also result. The addition of a tight-fitting storm or combination door will usually remedy both problems. A solid-core flush door or a panel door with solid stiles and rails is preferred over a hollow-core door to prevent or minimize this warping problem as well as reduce heat loss.

Openings in Flooring.
Finish strip flooring that has been laid at too high a moisture content or with varying moisture contents may be a source of trouble to the homeowner. As the flooring dries out and reaches moisture equilibrium, spaces will form between the boards. These openings are often very difficult to correct. If the floor has a few large cracks, one expedient is to fit matching strips of wood between the flooring strips and glue them in place. In severe cases, it may be necessary to replace sections of the floor or to refloor the entire house.

Another method is to cover the existing floor with a thin flooring, 5/16- or 3/8-inch thick. This method requires removal of the base shoe, fitting the thin flooring around door jambs, and perhaps sawing off the door bottoms. New flooring can best be laid at right angles to original flooring. (For proper methods of laying floors to prevent open joints in new houses, refer to Chapter 6.)

Unheated Rooms.
To lower fuel consumption and for personal reasons, some homeowners close off unused rooms and leave them unheated during the winter months. This low temperature, unfortunately, promotes condensation because surfaces may be below the dewpoint temperature of the air. Certain corrective or protective measures can be taken to prevent damage and subsequent maintenance expense, as follows:

1. Do not operate humidifiers or otherwise intentionally increase humidity in heated parts of the house.
2. Open the windows of unheated rooms for several hours on bright, sunny days for ventilation. This ventilation will help draw moisture out of the rooms.
3. Install storm sashes on all windows, including those in unheated rooms. These sashes will materially reduce heat loss from both heated and unheated rooms and will minimize the condensation on the inner glass surfaces.

Appendix A
Design values for visually graded structural lumber

	For material 2″ to 4″ thick by 2″ to 4″ wide				For material 2″ to 4″ thick by 5″ or more wider			
	Extreme fiber in bending (f)		Modulus of elasticity (E)	Horizontal shear (H)	Extreme fiber in bending (f)		Modulus of elasticity (E)	Horizontal shear (H)
	Single member uses	Repetitive member uses			Single member uses	Repetitive member uses		
Southern pine (Surfaced dry. Used at 19% maximum moisture content.)								
Select structural	2000	2300	1,400,000	90	1700	1950	1,400,000	90
No. 1	1700	1950	1,400,000	90	1450	1650	1,400,000	90
No. 2	1400	1600	1,300,000	90	1200	1350	1,300,000	90
No. 3	775	875	1,100,000	90	700	800	1,100,000	90
Appearance	1700	1950	1,400,000	90	1450	1650	1,400,000	90
Stud	775	875	1,100,000	90	700	800	1,100,000	90
Construction	1000	1150	1,100,000	90	—	—	—	—
Standard	550	650	1,100,000	90	—	—	—	—
Utility	275	300	1,100,000	90	—	—	—	—
Spruce-pine-fir (Surfaced dry or green. Used at 19% maximum moisture content.)								
Select structural	1450	1650	1,500,000	70	1250	1450	1,500,000	70
No. 1	1200	1400	1,500,000	70	1050	1200	1,500,000	70
No. 2	1000	1150	1,300,000	70	875	1000	1,300,000	70
No. 3	550	650	1,200,000	70	500	575	1,200,000	70
Appearance	1200	1400	1,500,000	70	1050	1200	1,500,000	70
Stud	550	650	1,200,000	70	500	575	1,200,000	70
Construction	725	850	1,200,000	70	—	—	—	—
Standard	400	475	1,200,000	70	—	—	—	—
Utility	175	225	1,200,000	70	—	—	—	—
Hem-fir (Surfaced dry or green. Used at 19% maximum moisture content.)								
Select structural	1650	1900	1,500,000	75	1400	1650	1,500,000	75
No. 1	1400	1600	1,500,000	75	1200	1400	1,500,000	75
No. 2	1150	1350	1,400,000	75	1000	1150	1,400,000	75
No. 3	650	725	1,200,000	75	575	675	1,200,000	75
Appearance	1400	1600	1,500,000	75	1200	1400	1,500,000	75
Stud	650	725	1,200,000	75	575	675	1,200,000	75
Construction	825	975	1,200,000	75	—	—	—	—
Standard	475	550	1,200,000	75	—	—	—	—
Utility	225	250	1,200,000	75	—	—	—	—
Douglas fir south (Surfaced dry or green. Used at 19% maximum moisture content.)								
Select structural	2000	2300	1,400,000	90	1700	1950	1,400,000	90
No. 1	1700	1950	1,400,000	90	1450	1650	1,400,000	90
No. 2	1400	1600	1,300,000	90	1200	1350	1,300,000	90
No. 3	775	875	1,100,000	90	700	800	1,100,000	90
Appearance	1700	1950	1,400,000	90	1450	1650	1,400,000	90
Stud	775	875	1,100,000	90	700	800	1,100,000	90
Construction	1000	1150	1,100,000	90	—	—	—	—
Standard	550	650	1,100,000	90	—	—	—	—
Utility	275	300	1,100,000	90	—	—	—	—

Source: National Forest Products Association. *National Design Specification: Wood Construction. Supplement to the 1986 Edition.* Table 4A. The species and grades selected from Table 4A and reproduced here reflect those most commonly used for framing.

Appendix B

Allowable spans for simple floor joists spaced 16 inches on center

Allowable spans for living areas (40 lbs. per sq. ft. live load assumed)

Modulus of elasticity in 1,000,000 psi (E)[1]		1.0	1.1	1.2	1.3	1.4	1.5	1.6	1.7	1.8	1.9	2.0
Minimum required bending stress (f)[2]		920	980	1040	1090	1150	1200	1250	1310	1360	1410	1460
Joist size:	2x6	8'4"	8'7"	8'10"	9'1"	9'4"	9'6"	9'9"	9'11"	10'2"	10'4"	10'6"
	2x8	11'0"	11'4"	11'8"	12'2"	12'3"	12'7"	12'10"	13'1"	13'4"	13'7"	13'10"
	2x10	14'0"	14'6"	14'11"	15'3"	15'8"	16'0"	16'5"	16'9"	17'0"	17'4"	17'8"
	2x12	17'0"	17'7"	18'1"	18'7"	19'1"	19'6"	19'11"	20'4"	20'9"	21'1"	21'6"

Allowable spans for sleeping areas (30 lbs. per sq. ft. live load assumed)

Modulus of elasticity in 1,000,000 psi (E)[1]		1.0	1.1	1.2	1.3	1.4	1.5	1.6	1.7	1.8	1.9	2.0
Minimum required bending stress (f)[2]		890	950	1000	1060	1110	1160	1220	1270	1320	1360	1410
Joist size:	2x6	9'2"	9'6"	9'9"	10'0"	10'3"	10'6"	10'9"	10'11"	11'2"	11'4"	11'7"
	2x8	12'1"	19'6"	12'10"	13'2"	13'6"	13'10"	14'2"	14'5"	14'8"	15'0"	15'3"
	2x10	15'5"	19'11"	16'5"	16'10"	17'3"	17'8"	18'0"	18'5"	18'9"	19'1"	19'5"
	2x12	18'9"	19'4"	19'11"	20'6"	21'0"	21'6"	21'11"	22'5"	23'10"	23'3"	23'7"

Source: National Forest Products Association. *Span Tables for Joists and Rafters,* 1977.

Note: Other tables should be used for other joist spacings.

[1] The modulus of elasticity (E) measures stiffness and varies with the species and grade of lumber, as shown in Appendix A.

[2] The bending stress (f) measures strength and varies with the species and grade of lumber, as shown in Appendix A.

Additional Readings

American Plywood Association. *APA Design/Construction Guide: Residential and Commercial.* Tacoma, Wash.: American Plywood Association, 1979. 55pp., illus.

Designed as a handy reference manual for panel specifiers and users. Contains information on panel grades plus APA specifications for floor, wall, and roof systems.

American Plywood Association. *APA Product Guide: Grades and Specifications.* Tacoma, Wash.: American Plywood Association, 1984. 27pp., illus.

A useful reference for structural wood panel users, specifiers, dealers, and distributions. Illustrates and explains APA trademarks appearing on panel products.

American Plywood Association. *All-Weather Wood Foundation.* Tacoma, Wash.: American Plywood Association, 1978. 37pp., illus.

Describes and illustrates construction of an all-weather wood foundation with either a full basement or crawl space. A list of other information sources is included.

American Wood Preservers Institute. *FHA Pole House Construction, 2nd Edition.* McLean, Va.: American Wood Preservers Institute, 1975. 32pp., illus.

An updated edition of an FHA publication first issued in 1969. Describes a variety of ways to effectively use pole frame designs.

Canadian Wood Council. *Waferboard.* CWC Datafile PB-1. Ottawa, Canada: Canadian Wood Council, 1985. 16pp., illus.

Discusses material quality, specifications, and uses of waferboard.

Humidity, Condensation, and Ventilation in Houses. Proceedings No. 7 of the Building Science Insight Seminar, October-December 1983. NRCC #23293. Ottawa, Canada: Division of Building Research, National Research Council, 1984. 66pp., illus.

Discusses principles and problems of moisture control in houses.

NAHB Research Foundation. *Manual of Lumber- and Plywood-Saving Techniques for Residential Light-Frame Construction.* Rockville, Md.: NAHB Research Foundation, 1971. 88pp., illus.

Most of the information in this manual relates to floor and wall construction and, to a lesser extent, roof construction.

Intended for code officials, building inspectors, builders, subcontractors, and others concerned with cost-effective use of lumber and plywood.

NAHB Research Foundation. *Reducing Home Building Costs with OVE Design and Construction.* Washington, D.C.: National Association of Home Builders, 1977. 135pp., illus.

Describes a practical series of optimum value engineered (OVE) cost-reducing techniques covering each stage of home building.

NAHB Research Foundation. *Insulation Manual: Homes and Apartments.* Rockville, Md.: NAHB Research Foundation, 1979. 149pp., illus.

Provides information on the proper installation, use, economics, and benefits of insulation, and guidance on other energy-conserving techniques for designing and building homes.

NAHB Research Foundation. *Off-Center Spliced Floor Joists.* Washington, D.C. National Association of Home Builders, 1982. Research Reports Volume 4. 58pp., illus.

A manual on the design, fabrication, and installation of off-center spliced floor joists.

NAHB Research Foundation. *Plywood Headers for Residential Construction.* Washington, D.C.: National Association of Home Builders, 1983. Research Reports Volume 5. 48pp., illus.

A manual on the design, fabrication, and installation of plywood box headers.

NAHB Research Foundation. *Residential Concrete.* Washington, D.C.: National Association of Home Builders, 1983. 71pp., illus.

Provides guidelines for ordering ready mixed concrete. Admixtures such as accelerators, retarders, plasticizers, and superplasticizers are discussed. Extensive illustrations are provided on form building, jointing, and basement leakage control.

NAHB Research Foundation. *Truss-Framed Construction.* Rockville, Md.: NAHB Research Foundation, 1984. 48pp., illus.

A manual of design and construction for the truss-frame system that combines roof truss, floor truss, and wall studs into a rigid unit frame.

National Forest Products Association. *All-Weather Wood Foundation System: Design, Fabrication, and Installation Manual.* Washington, D.C.: National Forest Products Association, 1982. 94pp., illus.

Part I of this three-part manual addresses structural design, detailing, and material specifications for architects, engineers, draftsmen, and builders. Part II covers quality fabrication of the foundation. Part III deals with installation methods. Parts II and III are particularly useful to builders and fabricators of treated-wood foundations.

U.S. Department of Agriculture. *Airborne Sound Transmission Loss Characteristics of Wood-Frame Construction* by F. F. Rudder, Jr. Forest Products Laboratory General Technical Report EPL-43. Madison, Wis.: Forest Products Laboratory, 1985. 27pp., illus.

Summarizes available data on the airborne sound transmission loss properties of wood-frame construction and evaluates the methods for predicting the loss.

U.S. Department of Housing and Urban Development and U.S. Department of Labor. *All-Weather Home Building Manual* compiled by NAHB Research Foundation. Guideline 4. Washington, D.C.: Government Printing Office, 1975. 143pp., illus.

Written for the home builder, this manual describes practices that permit construction to continue in cold, wet, or hot and dry weather.

Glossary

Air-dried lumber. Lumber that has been piled in yards or sheds for any length of time. For the United States as a whole, the minimum moisture content of thoroughly air-dried lumber is 12 to 15 percent; the average is somewhat higher.

Anchor bolt. A bolt to secure a wooden sill plate to concrete or masonry floor or foundation wall.

Apron. The flat member of the inside trim of a window placed against the wall immediately beneath the stool.

Asphalt. Most native asphalt is a residue from evaporated petroleum. It is insoluble in water but soluble in gasoline and melts when heated. Used widely as a waterproofing agent in the manufacture of waterproof roof coverings of many types, exterior wall coverings, flooring tile, and the like.

Attic ventilator. A screened opening provided to ventilate an attic space. They are located in the soffit area as inlet ventilators and in the gable end or along the ridge as outlet ventilators. Attic ventilation can also be provided by means of power-driven fans. (See also **Louver**).

Backfill. The replacement of excavated earth into a trench around and against a basement foundation.

Baluster. A vertical member in a railing used on the edge of stairs, balconies, and porches.

Balustrade. A railing made up of balusters, top rail and sometimes bottom rail.

Base or baseboard. A board placed against the wall around a room next to the floor.

Base molding. Molding used to trim the upper edge of baseboard.

Base shoe. Molding used next to the floor on baseboard. Sometimes called a carpet strip.

Batten. A narrow strip of wood used to cover joints or as a decorative vertical member over plywood or wide boards.

Batter board. One of a pair of horizontal boards nailed to posts set at the corners of an excavation, used to indicate the desired level. They are also used as fastenings for stretched strings to indicate outlines of foundation walls.

Bay window. Any window space projecting outward from the walls of a building, either square or polygonal in plan.

Beam. A structural member supporting a load applied transversaly to the member.

Bearing partition. A partition that supports any vertical load in addition to its own weight.

Bearing wall. A wall that supports any vertical load in addition to its own weight.

Berm. A mound of earth.

Blind-nailing. Nailing in such a way that the nailheads are not visible on the face of the work. Blind-nailing is usually done at the tongue of matched boards.

Bolster. A short horizontal wood or steel beam on top of acolumn to support and decrease the span of beams or girders.

Boston ridge. A method of applying shingles at the ridge or hips of a roof as a finish.

Brace. An inclined piece of framing lumber applied to wall or floor to stiffen the structure. Often used temporarily on walls until framing has been completed.

Brick veneer. A facing of brick laid against and fastened to the sheathing of a frame wall or tile wall construction.

Bridging. Small wood or metal members inserted in a diagonal position between the floor joists at midspan to brace the joists.

Built-up roof. A roofing composed of three to five layers of asphalt felt laminated with coal tar, pitch, or asphalt. The top layer is coered with crushed slag or gravel. Generally used on flat or low-pitched roofs.

Butt joint. The junction where the ends of two timbers or other members meet in a square-cut joint.

Cant strip. A triangular-shaped piece of lumber used at the junction of a flat deck and a wall to prevent cracking of the roofing that is applied over it.

Cap. The upper member of a column, pilaster, door cornice, or molding.

Casement frame and sash. A frame of wood or metal enclosing part or all of a sash, which can be opened by means of hinges affixed to the vertical edge.

Casing. Molding of various widths, forms, and thicknesses, used to trim door and window openings at the jambs.

Checking. Fissures that can appear with age in exterior paint coatings. Such fissures, at first superficial, may in time penetrate entirely through the coating.

Checkrails. Also called meeting rails. The upper rail of the lower sash and the lower rail of the upper sash of a double-hung window. Meeting rails are made sufficiently thicker than the rest of the sash frame to close the opening between the two sash. Check rails are usually bevelled to insure a tight fit between the two sash.

Collar beam. A nominal 1- or 2-thick member connecting opposite roof rafters at or near the ridge board. Collar beams serve to stiffen the roof structure.

Column. (a) In architecture: a vertical supporting member, circular or rectangular in section, usually consisting of a base, shaft, and capital; (b) In engineering: a vertical structural compression member that supports loads acting in the direction of its longitudinal axis.

Condensation. Beads or films of water (or frost in cold weather) that accumulate on the inside of the exterior covering of a building when warm, moisture-laden air from the interior reaches a point where the temperature no longer permits the air to sustain, as vapor, the moisture it holds.

Construction, frame. A type of construction in which the structural parts are wood or depend upon a wood frame for support. In codes, if masonry veneer is applied to the exterior walls, the structure is still classified as frame construction.

Coped joint. See Scribing.

Corner board. A board used as trim for the external corner of a house or other frame structure, against which the ends of the siding are butted.

Corner brace. A diagonal brace placed at the corner of a frame structure to stiffen and strengthen the wall.

Cornice. Overhang of a pitched roof at the eave line, usually consisting of a fascia board, a soffit for a closed cornice, and appropriate moldings.

Cornice return. The underside of the cornice at the corner of the roof where the walls meet the gable-end roof line. The cornice return serves as trim rather than as a structural element, providing a transition from the horizontal eave line to the sloped roof line of the gable.

Counterflashing. A flashing usually used on chimneys at the roof line to cover shingle flashing and to prevent moisture entry.

Cove molding. A molding with a concave face used as trim or to finish interior corners.

Crawl space. A shallow space below the living quarters of a basementless house, normally enclosed by the foundation wall.

Cricket. See Saddle.

Crown molding. A molding used on cornice or wherever an interior angle is to be covered. If a molding has a concave face, it is called a cove molding.

Dead load. The weight, expressed in pounds per square foot, of elements that are part of the structure.

Decay. Disintegration of wood or other substance through the action of fungi, as opposed to insect damage.

Deck paint. An enamel with a high degree of resistance to mechanical wear, designed for use on such surfaces as porch floors.

Density. The mass of substance in a unit volume. When expressed in the metric system, it is numerically equal to the specific gravity of the same substance.

Dew point. The temperature at which a vapor begins to deposit as a liquid. Applies especially to water in the atmosphere.

Dimension. See Lumber, dimension.

Door jamb, interior. The surrounding case into which and out of which a door closes and opens. It consists of two upright pieces, called side jambs, and a horizontal head jamb.

Dormer. A roofed projection from a sloping roof, into which a dormer window is set.

Downspout. A pipe, usually of metal, for carrying rainwater from roof gutters.

Dressed and matched. See Tongue and groove.

Drip. (a) A structural member of a cornice or other horizontal exterior-finish course that has a projection beyond the other parts for water runoff. (b) A groove in the underside of a sill or drip cap to cause water to run off on the outer edge.

Drip cap. A molding placed on the exterior top side of a door or window frame to cause water to run off beyond the outside of the frame.

Drywall. Interior covering material which is applied in large sheets or panels. The term has become basically synonymous with gypsum wallboard.

Ducts. Round or rectangular metal pipes for circulating warm air in a forced air heating or air-conditioning system.

Eave. The lower margin of a roof projecting over the wall.

Expansion joint. A bituminous fiber strip used to separate blocks or units of concrete to prevent cracking due to expansion as a result of temperature changes. Also used on concrete slabs.

Face-nailing. Nailing perpendicular to the initial surface being penetrated. Also refered to as "direct nailing."

Fascia. A flat board, band, or face, used by itself or, more often, in combination with moldings, generally located at the outer face of the cornice.

Filler. A heavily pigmented preparation used for filling and leveling off the pores in open-pored woods.

Fire stop. A solid, tight closure of a concealed space, placed to prevent the spread of fire and smoke. In a frame wall, this usually consists of 2x4 cross blocking between studs.

Flagstone (flagging or flags). Flat stones, from 1 to 4 inches thick, used for rustic walks, steps, and floors.

Flashing. Sheet metal or other material used in roof and wall construction to keep water out of adjoining parts of the structure.

Flat paint. An interior paint that contains a high proportion of pigment and dries to a flat or lusterless finish.

Flue. The space or passage in a chimney through which smoke, gas, or fumes ascend. Each such passage is called a flue; the flue together with any others and the surrounding masonry make up the chimney.

Flue lining. Fire clay or terra-cotta pipe, round or square, usually made in all ordinary flue sizes and in 2-foot lengths, used for the inner lining of chimneys with the brick or masonry work around the outside. Flue lining in chimneys runs from about a foot below the flue connection to the top of the chimney.

Fly rafters. End rafters of the roof overhang supported by roof sheathing and lookouts.

Footing. A concrete section in a rectangular form, wider than the bottom of the foundation wall or pier it supports. With a pressure-treated wood foundation, a gravel footing may be used in place of concrete.

Foundation. The supporting portion of a structure below the first-floor construction, or below grade.

Framing, balloon. A system of framing in which all exterior wall studs extend in one piece from the sill plate to the roofplate.

Framing, platform. A system of framing in which floor joists of each story rest on the top plates of the story below or on the foundation sill for the first story, and the bearing walls and partitions rest on the subfloor of each story.

Frieze. A horizontal member connecting the top of the siding with the soffit of the cornice.

Frostline. The depth of frost penetration in soil. This depth varies in different parts of the country.

Fungi, wood. Microscopic plants that live in damp wood and cause mold, stain, and decay.

Fungicide. A chemical that is poisonous to fungi.

Furring. Strips of wood or metal applied to a wall or other surface to even it and to serve as a fastening base for finish material.

Gable. The portion of the roof above the eave line of a double-sloped roof.

Gable end. An end wall having a gable. **Gloss paint; gloss enamel.** A paint or enamel that contains a relatively low proportion of pigment and dries to a sheen or luster.

Girder. A large or principal beam of wood or steel used to support loads at points along its length.

Grain. The direction, size, arrangement, appearance, or quality of the fibers in wood.

Grain, edge (vertical). Edge-grain lumber has been sawed parallel to the pith of the log and approximately at right angles to the growth rings; i.e., the rings form an angle of 45° or more with the wide surface of the piece.

Grain, flat. Flat-grain lumber has been sawed parallel to the pith of the log and approximately tangent to the growth rings, i.e., the rings form an angle of less the 45° with the surface of the piece.

Grout. Mortar that will flow into the joints and cavities of masonry work and fill them solidly.

Gusset. A flat wood, plywood, or similar member used to provide a connection at intersections of wood members. Most commonly used in joints of wood trusses.

Gutter or eave trough. A shallow channel or conduit of metal or vinyl set below and along the eaves of a house to catch and carry off rainwater from the roof.

Header. (a) A beam placed perpendicular to joists, to which joists are nailed in framing for chimneys, stairways, or other openings. (b) A wood lintel.

Hearth. The inner or outer floor of a fireplace, usually made of brick, tile, or stone.

Heartwood. The wood extending from the pith to the sapwood, the cells of which no longer participate in the life process of the tree.

Hip. The external angle formed by the meeting of two sloping sides of a roof.

Hip roof. A roof that rises by inclined planes from all four sides of a building.

Humidifier. A device that increases the humidity within a room or a house by emitting (discharging) water vapor. Humidifiers may consist of individual room-size units or larger units attached to the heating plant to condition the entire house.

I-beam. A steel beam with a cross section resembling the letter I. I-beams are used for long spans as basement beams or over wide wall openings, such as a double garage door, when wall and roof loads are imposed on the opening.

Insulation board, rigid. A structural building board made of coarse wood or cane fiber impregnated with asphalt or given other treatment to provide a water-resistant product. It can be obtained in various size sheets, in various thicknesses, and in various densities.

Insulation, thermal. Any material high in resistance to heat transmission that, when placed in the walls, ceiling, or floors of a structure, will reduce the rate of heat flow.

Jack rafter. A rafter that spans the distance from the wall plate to a hip, or from a valley to a ridge.

Jamb. The side and head lining of a doorway, window, or other opening.

Joint. The space between the adjacent surfaces of two members or components that are held together by nails, glue, cement, mortar, or other means.

Joint cement. A powder that is usually mixed with water and used for joint treatment in gypsum wallboard finish. Joint cement, often called "spackle," can be purchased in a ready-mixed form.

Joist. One of a series of parallel beams, usually 2 inches thick, used to support floor and ceiling loads, and supported in turn by larger beams, girders, or bearing walls.

Kiln-dried lumber. Lumber that has been dried by means of controlled heat and humidity, in ovens or kilns, to specified ranges of moisture content. See also **Air-dried lumber** and

Lumber, moisture content.

Landing. A platform between flights of stairs or at the end of a flight of stairs.

Ledger strip. A strip of lumber nailed along the bottom of the side of a girder, on which joists rest.

Let-in brace. A nominal 1-inch-thick board applied diagonally into notched studs.

Light. Space in a window sash for a single pane of glass. Also, a pane of glass.

Lintel. A horizontal structural member that supports the load over an opening such as a door or window. Also called a "header".

Live load. The load, expressed in pounds per square foot, of people, furniture, snow, etc., that are in addition to the weight of the structure itself.

Lookout. A short wood bracket or cantilever to support an overhang portion of a roof, usually concealed from view by a soffit.

Louver. An opening with a series of horizontal slats arranged as permit ventilation but to exclude rain, sunlight, or vision. See also **Attic ventilator.**

Lumber, boards. Lumber less than 2 inches thick and 2 or more inches wide.

Lumber, dimension. Lumber from 2 inches to, but not including, 5 inches thick and 2 or more inches wide. Includes joists, rafters, studs, plank, and small timbers.

Lumber, dressed size. The dimension of lumber after shrinking from green dimension and after machining to size or pattern.

Lumber, matched. See **Tongue and groove**.

Lumber, moisture content. The weight of water contained in wood, expressed as a percentage of the total weight of the wood. See also **Air-dried lumber** and **Kiln-dried lumber**.

Lumber, pressure-treated. Lumber that has had a preservative chemical forced into the wood under pressure to resist decay and insect attack.

Lumber, shiplap. Lumber that has been milled along the edge to make a close rabbeted or lapped joint.

Lumber, timbers. Lumber 5 or more inches in its smallest dimension. Includes beams, stringers, posts, caps, sills, girders, and purlins.

Mantel. The shelf above a fireplace. Also used in referring to the trim around both the top and sides of a fireplace opening.

Masonry. Stone, brick, concrete, hollow tile, concrete block, gypsum block, or other similar building units or materials or a combination of the same, bonded together with mortar to form a wall, pier, buttress, or similar element.

Mastic. A pasty material used as a cement in such applications as setting tile or as a protective coating for thermal insulation or waterproofing.

Millwork. Building materials made of finished wood and manufactured in millwork plants and planing mills. It includes such items as inside and outside window frames and door frames, blinds, porchwork, mantels, panelwork, stairways, molding, and interior trim. The term does not include flooring or siding.

Miter joint. The joint of two pieces at an angle that is half the joining angle. For example, the miter joint at the side and head casing at a door opening is made at a 45° angle.

Moisture content of wood. See **Lumber, moisture content**.

Molding. A wood strip with a curved or projecting surface used for decorative purposes.

Mortise. A slot cut into a board, plank, or timber, usually edgewise, to receive a tenon of another board, plank, or timber to form a joint.

Mullion. A vertical bar or divider in the frame between windows, doors, or other openings.

Muntin. A small member that divides the glass or openings of sash or doors.

Natural finish. A transparent finish that does not seriously alter the original color or obscure the grain of the natural wood. Natural finishes are usually provided by sealers, oils, varnishes, water-repellent preservatives, and other similar materials.

Newel. A post to which the end of a stair railing or balustrade is fastened. Also, any post to which a railing or balustrade is fastened.

Nonbearing wall. A wall supporting no load other than its own weight.

Nosing. The projecting edge of a molding or drip. Usually applied to the projecting molding on the edge of a stair tread.

Notch. A crosswise rabbet at the end of a board.

On center(O.C.). The measurement of spacing for elements such as studs, rafters, and joists, from the center of one member to the center of the next.

Oriented strand board (OSB). A panel composed of layers, with each layer consisting of compressed strandlike wood particles in one direction, and with layers oriented at right angles to each other. The layers are bonded together with a phenolic resin.

Panel. (a) A thin, flat piece of wood, plywood, or similar material, framed by stiles and rails as in a door or fitted in grooves of thicker material with molded edges for decorative wall treatment; (b) A sheet of plywood, fiberboard, oriented strand board, or similar material.

Paper, building. A general term for papers, felts, and similar sheet materials used in construction.

Particleboard. Panels composed of small wood particles usually arranged in layers without a particular orientation and bonded together with a phenolic resin. Some particleboards are structurally rated. See also **Oriented strand board**.

Partition. A wall that subdivides spaces within any story of a building.

Penny. As applied to nails, it originally indicated the price per hundred. The term serves as a measure of nail length and is signified by the letter "d."

Perm. A measure of water vapor movement through a material (grains per square foot per hour per inch of mercury difference in vapor pressure).

Pier. A column of masonry, usually rectangular in horizontal cross section, used to support other structural members.

Pigment. A powdered solid in suitable degree of subdivision for use in paint or enamel.

Pitch. The measure of the steepness of the slope of a roof, expressed as the ratio of the rise of the slope over a coresponding horizontal distance. Roof slope is expressed in the inches of rise per foot of run, such as 4 in 12.

Pith. The small, soft core at the original center of a tree around which wood formation takes place.

Plate. Sill plate: a horizontal member anchored to a masonry wall. **Sole plate:** bottom horizontal member of a frame wall. **Top plate:** top horizontal member of a frame wall supporting ceiling joists, rafters, or other members.

Plumb. Exactly vertical.

Ply. One thickness of any material used for building up several layers, such as roofing felt, veneer in plywood, or layers in built-up materials.

Plywood. A piece of wood made of three or more layers of veneer joined with glue and usually laid with the grain of adjoining plies at right angles. An odd number of plies is generally used to provide balanced construction.

Primer. The first coat of paint in a paint job that consists of two or more coats; also, the paint used for such a first coat.

Purlin. A horizontal timber supporting the common rafters in roofs.

Quarter round. A small molding that has the cross section of a quarter circle.

Quartersawn. Another term for edge grain

Rabbet. A rectangular longitudinal groove cut in the corner edge of a board or plank.

Rafter. One of a series of structural members of a roof designed to support roof loads. The rafters of a flat roof are sometimes called roof joists.

Rafter, hip. A rafter that forms the intersection of an external roof angle.

Rafter, valley. A rafter that forms the intersection of an internal roof angle. A valley rafter is normally made of double 2-inch-thick members.

Rail. (a) A cross member of a panel door or sash; (b) The upper or lower member of a balustrade or staircase extending from one vertical support, such as a post, to another.

Rake. Trim members that run parallel to the roof slope and form the finish between the wall and a gable roof extension.

Reflective insulation. Sheet material with one or both surfaces of comparatively low heat emissivity, such as aluminum foil. When it is used in building construction, the surfaces face air spaces, reducing the radiation across these spaces.

Reinforcing. Steel rods or metal fabric placed in concrete slabs, beams, or columns to increase their strength.

Relative humidity. The amount of water vapor in the atmosphere, expressed as a percentage of the maximum quantity that the atmosphere could hold at a given temperature. The amount of water vapor that can be held in the atmosphere increases with the temperature.

Resorcinol. An adhesive that is high in both wet and dry strength and resistant to high temperatures. It is used for gluing lumber or assembly joints that must withstand severe conditions.

Ridge. The horizontal line at the junction of the top edges of two sloping roof surfaces.

Ridge board. The board placed on edge at the ridge of the roof, into which the upper ends of the rafters are fastened.

Rise. In stairs, the vertical height of a step or flight of stairs.

Riser. Each of the vertical boards closing the spaces between the treads of stairways.

Roll roofing. Roofing material composed of fiber and saturated with asphalt, supplied in 36-inch-wide rolls with 108 square feet of material. Weights are generally 45 to 90 pounds per roll.

Roof sheathing. The boards or sheet material fastened to the roof rafters, on which shingles or other roof coverings are laid.

Run. In stairs, the net front-to-back width of a step or the horizontal distance covered by a flight of stairs.

Saddle. Two sloping surfaces meeting in a horizontal ridge, used between the back side of a chimney, or other verical surface, and a sloping roof. Saddles are also called crickets.

Sapwood. The outer zone of wood in a tree, next to the bark. In the living tree it contains some living cells (the heartwood contains none) as well as dead and dying cells. In most species, it is lighter in color than the heartwood, but in all species, it lacks resistance to decay.

Sash. A frame containing one or more lights of glass.

Saturated felt. Felt impregnated with tar or asphalt.

Scribing. Fitting woodwork to an irregular surface. With moldings, scribing means cutting the end of one piece to fit the molded face of the other at an interior angle, in place of a miter joint.

Sealer. A finishing material, either clear or pigmented, that is usually applied directly over uncoated wood to seal the surface.

Seasoning. Removing moisture from green wood to improve its serviceability.

Semigloss paint or enamel. A paint or enamel made with a slight insufficiency of nonvolatile vehicle so that its coating, when dry, has some luster but is not very glossy.

Shake. A thick hand-split shingle, resawed to form two shakes; usually edge-grained.

Sheathing. The covering, typically plywood or insulation board, used over studs or rafters of a structure.

Sheathing paper. A building material, generally paper or felt, used in wall and roof construction as a protection against the passage of air and water.

Sheet metal work. The components of a house, such as ducts, flashing, gutters, and downspouts, for which sheet metal is used.

Shellac. A transparent coating made by dissolving lac, a resinous secretion of the lac bug (a scale insect that thrives in tropical countries, especially India) in alcohol.

Shingles. Roof covering of asphalt, fiberglass asbestos, wood, tile, slate, or other material or combinations of materials (such as asphalt and felt), cut to stock lengths, widths, and thicknesses.

Shingles, siding. Various types of shingles used over sheathing for exterior sidewall covering.

Shiplap. See **Lumber, shiplap**.

Shutter. A lightweight louvered, flush wood or nonwood frame in the form of a door, located at each side of a window. Some are made to close over the window for protection; others are fastened to the wall for decorative purposes.

Siding, bevel (lap siding). Wedge-shaped boards used as horizontal siding in a lapped pattern. Bevel siding varies in butt thickness from ½ to ¾ inch and is available in widths up to 12 inches. Normally used over some type of sheathing.

Siding, drop. Siding that is usually ¾ inch thick and 6 or 8 inches wide, with tongue-and-groove or shiplap edges. Often used as siding without sheathing in secondary buildings.

Sill. (a) The lowest member of the frame of a structure, resting on the foundation and supporting the floor joists or the uprights of the wall; (b) The member forming the lower side of an opening such as a doorsill or windowsill.

Sleeper. A wood member embedded in or resting directly on concrete, as in a floor, that serves to support and to fasten subfloor or flooring.

Soffit. The underside of an overhanging cornice.

Soil cover (ground cover). A light covering of plastic film, roll roofing, or similar material, used over the soil in crawl spaces of buildings to minimize the movement of moisture from the soil into the crawl space.

Soil stack. A general term for the vertical main of a system of soil, waste, or vent piping.

Sole or sole plate. See **Plate**.

Spackle. See **Joint cement**.

Span. The distance between structural supports such as walls, columns, piers, beams, girders, and trusses.

Splash block. A small masonry block laid with the top close to the ground surface to receive roof drainage from downspouts and to carry it away from the building.

Square. A unit of measure usually applied to roofing material; it denotes a quantity sufficient to cover 100 square feet of surface.

Stair carriage.   Supporting member for stair treads. Usually a 2-inch plank notched to receive the treads; sometimes called a "rough horse" or "stringer."

Stair landing.   See **Landing.**

Stair rise.   See **Rise.**

STC (Sound Transmission Class).   A numerical measure of the ability of a material or assembly to resist the passage of sound. Materials with higher STC numbers have greater resistance to sound transmission.

Stile.   An upright framing member in a panel door.

Stool.   A flat molding fitted over the windowsill between jambs and contacting the bottom rail of the lower sash.

Strip flooring.   Wood flooring consisting of narrow, matched strips.

String, stringer.   A timber or other support for cross members in floors or ceilings. In stairs, the stringer or stair carriage supports the stair treads.

Stucco.   A plaster for exterior use, made with portland cement as its base.

Stud.   One of a series of slender wood or metal vertical structural members placed as supporting elements in walls and partitions. (Plural: studs or studding.)

Subfloor.   Boards or plywood laid on joists, over which a finish floor is laid.

Tail beam.   A relatively short beam or joist supported by a wall at one end and by a header at the other.

Tenon.   A projection at the end of a board, plank, or timber, for insertion into a mortise.

Termite shield.   A shield, usually of noncorrodible metal, placed in or on a foundation wall or other mass of masonry or around pipes to prevent the passage of termites.

Thimble.   The section of a vitreous clay flue that passes through a wall.

Threshold.   A strip of wood or metal with beveled edges, used over the finish floor and the sill of exterior doors.

Toe-nailing.   Driving a nail at a slant with the initial surface, to permit it to penetrate into a second member.

Tongue and groove.   Boards or planks machined so that there is a groove on one edge and a corresponding projection (tongue) on the other edge, thus allowing a number of such boards or planks can be fitted together. "Dressed and matched" is an alternative term with the same meaning.

Tread.   The horizontal board in a stairway on which the foot is placed.

Trim.   The finish materials in a building, such as molding applied around openings (window trim, door trim) or at the floor and ceiling of rooms (baseboard, cornice, and other moldings).

Trimmer.   A beam or joist to which a header is nailed in framing a chimney, stairway, or other opening.

Truss.   A framed or jointed structure, composed of triangular elements, designed to act as a beam of long span, while each member is usually subjected to longitudinal stress only, either tension or compression.

Truss plate.   A heavy-gage, pronged metal plate that is pressed into the sides of a wood truss at the point where two more members are to be joined together.

Undercoat.   A coating applied before the finishing or top coats of a paint job. It may be the first of two or the second of three coats. When it is the first of two coats, it is synonymous with priming coat.

Underlayment.   A material placed under flexible flooring materials such as carpet, vinyl tile or linoleum, to provide a smooth base over which to lay such materials.

Valley.   The internal angle formed by the junction of two sloping sides of a roof.

Vapor retarder.   Material used to retard the movement of water vapor into walls. Vapor retarders are applied over the warm side of exposed walls or as a part of batt or blanket insulation. They usually have perm value of less than 1.0.

Varnish.   A thickened preparation of drying oil or drying oil and resin, suitable for spreading on surfaces to form continuous, transparent coatings, or for mixing with pigments to make enamels.

Vehicle.   The liquid portion of a finishing material; it consists of the binder (nonvolatile) and volatile thinners.

Veneer.   Thin sheets of wood made by rotary cutting or slicing.

Vent.   A pipe or duct, or a screened or louvered opening, which provides an inlet or outlet for the flow of air. Common types of roof vents include ridge vents, soffit vents, and gable end vents.

Volatile thinner.   A liquid that evaporates readily, that is used to thin or reduce the consistency of finishes without altering the relative volumes of pigments and nonvolatile vehicles.

Waferboard.   A panel material made of compressed, waferlike wood particles or flakes bonded together with a phenolic resin. The flakes may vary in size and thickness and may be either randomly or directionally oriented.

Wane.   Bark, or lack of wood from any cause, on the edge or corner of a piece of wood.

Water-repellent preservative.   A liquid designed to penetrate into wood, to impart water resistance and moderate preservative protection. It is used for millwork such as sash and frames and is usually applied by dipping.

Weatherstripping.   Strips of thin metal or other material, that prevent infiltration of air and moisture around windows and doors. Compression weatherstripping on single- and double-hung windows performs the additional function of holding such windows in place in any position.

Index